P9-CEQ-755

Japan, America, and the Future World Order

Morton A. Kaplan
Kinhide Mushakoji

The Center for Policy Study
The University of Chicago

The Free Press
A Division of Macmillan Publishing Co., Inc.
NEW YORK

Collier Macmillan Publishers
LONDON

The Free Press
A Division of Macmillan Publishing Co. Inc.
866 Third Avenue, New York, N.Y. 10022

Collier Macmillan Canada, Ltd.

Library of Congress Catalog Card Number: 76–2341

Printed in the United States of America

printing number

1 2 3 4 5 6 7 8 9 10

Contents

IV. Technological and Environmental Issues

Introduction

Books on Japan or Japanese-American relations have become a commonplace on the bookshelves of the literate public in both Japan and the United States. In Japan, they are common in both English and Japanese versions. The authors who write these books or the chapters that make up the various symposium volumes include the most distinguished names in journalism and scholarship in both countries.

This book is significantly different from all the others in one important respect. It is the only symposium volume jointly planned and jointly financed by scholarly groups in both Japan and the United States. Unlike the other volumes, where Japanese were invited to write on topics chosen by Americans, the topics treated in the chapters of this book represent the views of both groups of scholars. Even more important, the Japanese chose the Japanese authors while the American selected only the American authors [a new and humbling experience for us. M.A.K.].

There is, as the reader will soon perceive, no uniformity of opinion either within each group of national authors or between them. There are differences between the two groups but they are somewhat like Rorschach ink blot tests. Each reader will perceive them differently. The global culture of professional life is now far too firmly implanted for sharp distinctions to exist between national groups in assumptions or ways of looking at the world. However, to the extent that this matter is susceptible to analysis, we do have papers that deal with how the two nations view each other and the world. Therefore, the editors will let this matter rest with the acknowledgement that, although we did attempt to impose structure on the authors, we deliberately avoided any attempt to arrive at a uniformity of views.

The book is based upon planning over several years and through two conferences, one in Chicago and the other in Tokyo. The host institutions were the Faculty Arms Control and Foreign Policy Seminar of the University of Chicago and the Institute of International Relations of Sophia University, respectively.

This volume does not suffer from bi-ethnocentrism. We are aware that there are important values in the world other than Japanese-American relations. Yet, in a period in which we will be moving either into a world of increasing interdependence and cooperation or retreating into competitive nationalism, relations between Japan and the United States will play a major role in the development of the international system, and, in turn, will respond to these developments.

Because, despite the large literature on the subject, most nations and their relations are perceived in terms of clichés or amorphous generalizations by the public and by much of the media, we believe that this book will be important and useful, not to the fate of the world, but to the understanding of those members of the educated public who read it. If we do not pretend to present a definitive analysis, we believe we avoid many of the clichés and advance, if only slightly, the common understanding of very real problems and prospects that face both nations and the world.

The book is long and speaks for itself. In this brief introduction we note only the general categories into which the chapters fall. The first two chapters, by the editors, attempt to place the problems of Japanese-American relations in a global perspective. Then the paper by Tsou, Najita, and Otake turns to the important problem of Sino-Japanese relations. The chapters by Iriye and Harris on one hand and Watanuki on the other, although different in their methodology, both explore the ways in which each nation looks at the other and at itself. With the chapters by Hosoya, Destler, and Kan Ori, we turn to the internal decision-making processes of both countries and how they affect relationships. Hamada and Kahn and Scalera look at the Japanese role in the world economy. Aliber looks more closely at U.S.-Japanese economic relationships, while the chapters by Ginsburg and Osborn and by Kawata present different perspectives with respect to Japan's economic relations with Southeast Asia. Kawata's chapter also overlaps to some extent with that of Hsiao on the examination of Sino-Japanese economic relationships, while Nakagane examines the Chinese model of economic development and its impact on the world. In the last chapters, Royama and Imai turn to environmental problems, the former with emphasis on Japan and the latter with emphasis on U.S.-Japanese relationships in the global system.

The editors wish to express their appreciation to the Ford Foundation, the Norman Wait Harris Memorial Foundation, the Japan Foundation, the Asia Foundation, the University of Chicago, and Sophia University, without whose generous support and assistance the conferences and this volume would not have been possible. An abbreviated edition of this volume will be published in Japanese.

Morton A. Kaplan
Kinhide Mushakoji

I.
External Policy Issues

Japan
and the International System

Morton A. Kaplan

The Future of Japan

Rising like the Phoenix from the ashes of World War II, Japan has become one of the two or three most important countries in the world in an economic if not yet a political or military sense. Although there was some earlier awareness of the incredible Japanese rate of economic development, no genuine recognition of the major transition that had occurred reached either world or Japanese consciousness until at least the middle, and more likely the late, 1960s.

There is a long history of Western refusal to take the Japanese seriously. The early growth of the Japanese economy from the 1890s until the end of the pre-war period was denigrated by the notion that the Japanese were imitators and produced poor products. Early Japanese victories in the war shocked, but did not illuminate, Western minds; and the ingenuity of the equipment used by the Japanese was given little attention. After all, how could an Oriental people, and especially one so short in stature as the Japanese, compete with the West?

Before the Second World War, Japanese leaders spoke of a co-prosperity sphere in Asia. Today many writers speak of Japanese interests in Southeast Asia and the Indian Ocean. This point of view continues to underestimate the Japanese phenomenon. Japan's high technology society finds its most important trading partner in the

United States and, potentially secondarily, in Western Europe. Its vast capital resources find their greatest opportunities for investment in the United States, Western Europe, Canada, and such rapidly developing nations as Brazil.

Only the imposition of political barriers can forestall a natural development that will make Japan a nation with major worldwide interests. The interests of Japan in the 1980s will be global. Political disturbances almost anywhere in the world will threaten Japanese investments, trade opportunities essential to the stability of her economy, and access to resources. More than any other country, including the United States, Japan will have a stake in the world.

This enormously burgeoning interest, which escapes current attention as much as the Japanese domestic economic miracle escaped attention, is but faintly foreshadowed in Japan's current international political activities and not at all foreshadowed in her current military posture. The Japanese themselves were just beginning to notice it when the current oil crisis diminished their confidence in their future. Before this their attention was diverted by the marginal economic advantages of non-participation in world politics, and by lingering feelings of unworthiness resulting both from their defeat in the Second World War and by a lack of confidence among some intellectuals in Japan's ability to play a major world role without falling back into the militaristic and imperialistic practices of the pre-war period.

For a variety of reasons, these fears are at least partly mistaken. The pre-war activities of the Japanese were in part a counter-reaction to European imperialism. Unless Japan had acted similarly to the major nations and moved into China, she would have been carved up by the Western powers and Russia, as was China, and confronted by them from the Asian mainland.

In addition, the mythology of the period attributed wealth to colonies and conquest. The post-World War II world has demonstrated beyond cavil that wealth is produced by economic investment and that investment opportunities are greatest in developed rather than underdeveloped areas.

The use of military force is an anachronism from the point of view of profit-oriented economies. Military force can serve the purpose only of a state-dominated political system that seeks hegemony for political reasons.

The major danger to Japan, in my opinion, at least in terms of its domestic political values, lies in a potential nationalistic reaction to an inferior international position that fails to match Japan's objective importance in the world. The danger to Japan lies in an unwillingness by other powers to allow her to take her rightful place in the world, or in Japan's own unwillingness constructively to accept those international responsibilities that are an inherent consequence of the transformation of Japanese society and polity.

Continuities in Japanese Politics

In many ways the continuity of postwar political behavior in Japan is a remarkable phenomenon. In the United States, most social scientists are familiar with the generalization that the oddest political movements occur in Southern California and Texas, where the most rapid changes in the economy have produced the greatest personal insecurities in terms of social status. Yet Japan as an entire nation has undergone a development so rapid in its rate of change, at least to the eye of the untrained observer, that it dwarfs that of either Southern California or Texas. The changes in Tokyo are obvious, but the visitor to Sapporo in the north or Fukuoka in the south will also note the extent to which modernity is a feature of the new Japan.

The Japanese countryside was far more traditional than the American farm areas. Yet the rapid transformation of Japan into an urban nation is affecting lifestyles and political activities far more rapidly than anything that happened in the United States. The gerrymandered Japanese countryside is the domain of the Liberal Conservative Party. The Socialist and Communist parties, and even the Komeito, find their recruits primarily in urban areas. Most major Japanese cities are now run by Socialist governments. Only comparatively recently has there been any governmental reaction to the Socialist dominance that the Occupation established in the educational system and the labor unions. Whether this will have any influence upon the contest for the cities is too difficult for an outside observer to guess.

The domestic Japanese economy is a consumer-oriented economy. Young Japanese, with no memories of the hardships of the past, were accustomed until the recent oil crisis to rapidly upward-spiraling standards of living. Yet these expectations are fostered within an economy subject to shock both from the terms of foreign trade and from the standpoint of remittances from abroad. In 1970, for instance, Japan's exports were 10 percent of a gross national product of under $200 billion, whereas American exports were under 6 percent of a gross national product of over $1 trillion. Before the oil crisis it was projected that Japan's gross national product would surpass $900 billion by 1980. Its exports then were projected in the range of over $90 billion, a figure highly subject to political decisions elsewhere. Because Japan remains politically and culturally isolated, her vulnerability to hostile restrictions is greater than that of any other major nation.

There is one striking difference between the Japanese and the American pattern that may account for the tentatively greater stability of the Japanese social structure under the stress of rapid change. Although the traditional Japanese pattern of social organization has been ruptured by urbanization, its industrial pattern of activity, although changing, still mirrors to a considerable extent the older pattern. Although Japan as yet has developed few of the measures of social welfare that characterize Europe and North America, workers who have permanent positions within Japanese industry possess an unparalleled degree of security. Their jobs are secure through retirement, regardless of business conditions; and often after retirement workers can transfer to related industrial or commercial operations. Housing is subsidized and in many cases food is also subsidized. Large bonuses at year's end provide a substantial surplus income for luxury expenditures. Vacation trips are often provided on a group basis at low cost.

Within the operations of an industry or business, a high degree of collegiality and community prevails. Opinions are solicited before decisions are made. The decision process itself is based upon widespread consensus. Although Western experience with committee consensus has usually been quite unfavorable—committees tending to operate below the lowest common denominator of intelligence—the Japanese process apparently is consistent with efficient business decisions. These factors may have contributed to the stability we now see.

Possible Changes in the Japanese Position

However, the current stability may dissipate if the economy is subjected to severe external shock or if changing demographic patterns change the texture of Japanese politics. Even apart from possible instabilities in the Japanese domestic system, shifts in the internal Japanese political process may have far-reaching impact upon Japanese foreign policy. The only major political group in Japan committed to the present Japanese foreign policy orientation toward some form of partnership with the United States is the Liberal Democratic party. This party has borne the brunt of the Nixon shokku.

Former Premier Tanaka stressed a somewhat more independent Japanese foreign policy than did his predecessors. Off in the wings, however, Minister Nakasone, although not opposed to an American connection, stresses a potentially far more indpendent Japanese policy than the current one. Some believe that the current Japanese overtures toward investment in Siberia, given the bad experience with the Russians in the last few years over the questions of costs, represent an attempt even by the present Japanese government to maintain a second string to its bow. Nonetheless, the current ruling majority remains committed to American bases in Japan, reliance on the American nuclear deterrent, and broad cooperation in foreign policy with the United States in matters that do not involve military actions elsewhere in the world.

Neither the Socialist nor the Communist parties—nor Komeito either—accepts the presence of American bases in Japan. Although to date this foreign policy position constitutes one barrier to these parties obtaining a majority in parliament, the increasing urbanization of Japan, despite the present gerrymandering of districts, does not altogether exclude the possibility that one or more of these opposition groups may form the basis of a Japanese government by 1980, with the revolution in Japanese foreign policy that this would entail.

Even apart from their obtaining a majority in an election, the issues that would be raised during their serious bid for majority status might well have a profound impact upon the entire Japanese approach to foreign policy and remilitarization. Current public opinion polls in Japan, and those which have been taken during the past ten years, indicate a substantial majority of the public is opposed to Japanese acquisition of nuclear weapons. However, public opinion polls are often misleading because the questions do not refer to real alternatives. For instance, in the late 1940s Gallup Polls showed that 60 or 70 percent of the American public favored Atlantic union—a position that I do not believe as much as 5 percent of the public would have supported if presented with a concrete program. In this hypothetical form, responses constitute sentiments rather than programmatic intentions.

The Japanese are aware that their prosperity depends upon a favorable context of world politics. They are aware of their relative isolation in political terms. They know that acquisition of nuclear weapons would not likely be well received by Russia, China, or the United States. Moreover, because the present government is disliked by intellectuals, the nuclear issue is a convenient point to put the government on the defensive.

If, however, the American connection were withdrawn, or appeared exceptionally fragile, or if its desirability became a focus of attack by a party or combination of parties with genuine pretensions to victory in the elections, the entire military issue, including the nuclear one, would arise anew. The incumbents would attack the opposition for a foreign policy that threatened to make Japan extremely vulnerable. In this context, the opposition might reconsider its position on nuclear weapons, and its reconsideration might change the entire perspective of the Japanese on the issue, as might a major weakening of the American connection, serious changes in world politics that interfere with détente, or the coming to power of a new generation entirely detached from the memories of Hiroshima.

I am not making a prediction, for the "if" clauses I have included are necessary, though perhaps not sufficient, for a conclusion to be drawn. I am stating that those who firmly predict on the basis of current attitudes what Japan's policy will be in the 1980s may be in for a profound shock, and that this fixation upon current attitudes may misdirect attention from the factors that are more likely to shape future attitudes.

The Impact of Potential Isolation

No individual or nation enjoys insecurity. In a world in which other people do not go berserk, we may not notice the extent to which we are individually vulnerable to attack. In a world of plenty, we may not notice the extent to which we are vulnerable to potential discontinuities in the supplies of food in the stores at which we are able to shop. In the United States, parents give children allowances so that they are not vulnerable to the continual insecurity of begging for funds. In entering into business relationships, we seek to make them contractual so that we are not dependent upon the continual good will of others. Where employment is more short-term, employees often unionize, in which case the contract is held by the union.

It might be that if the NATO forces were disbanded, contrary to the advice of Chou En-lai, the Soviet Union would respond by reducing its military forces. However, an American initiative in this respect would increase the insecurities of the Western European nations. The current self-defense forces of Japan, according to estimates by authoritative Japanese sources, are capable of withstanding an amphibious invasion by a determined aggressor for a period of up to one week. This capability is viewed as providing a residual deterrence, for the invasion would not be costless and it might give the United States time to decide to intervene.

Nonetheless, objectively this is not a very secure situation. To what extent the Japanese public becomes aware of this insecurity depends upon the ambience of world politics and the relationship of Japan with the United States. A crisis in the Far East might vividly bring home to many Japanese the insecurity of their present situation. A serious debate on Japanese foreign policy in the context of a genuinely contested parliamentary election in which the outcome is in serious doubt might focus attention on the potential instabilities in the Japanese situation, and this would be particularly true if some crisis arose in which Japanese interests were involved.

It would be as inappropriate for an American to advise the Japanese on their defense posture as it would be for a Japanese to offer similar advice to an American. For this reason, I wish to remain as abstract as possible in my reasoning, for policy advice is beyond my legitimate purview. But one word of historical experience may be in order. Those policy convulsions or revolutions that are often most profound and far-reaching are those that have not been prepared for in advance and where no concessions have been made. In these cases, when the prior position collapses, it often does so completely.

Several teams in the National Football League have defenses that are known as elastic. They give a little bit but not very much. The object of an elastic defense is to prevent a major breakthrough. It seems to me that the present posture of Japan remains viable as a long-term alternative only if general world prosperity continues, if no important barriers to Japanese trade or investment are thrown up, if the American nuclear umbrella remains credible, if the détentes between the United States and Russia and between the United States and China continue, if relations between Russia and China ameliorate to some extent, if Japan's politics remains democratic, and if a new generation of Japanese does not come to political power with assumptions different in major ways from that of the present ruling Japanese generation. Whether the falsification of only one of these constraints would be sufficient to disrupt the present Japanese posture is problematic. The failure of several of the assumptions, however, would almost surely be sufficient to undermine the basis of the present Japanese foreign and military posture. Therefore, it seems to me that it is important to analyze a number of these potentially upsetting factors to obtain some guidelines as to the real alternatives that confront Japan.

Constraints on Japan's Future

I should like to begin my discussion of these constraints, as they may project into the 1980s, with the United States. Because it is often believed that people project what they prefer, I wish to make very clear that this is not the present case. My own belief is that a very close relationship between Japan and the United States is essential to both countries and to the peace of the world. I believe it would be dishonest, however, to indicate that the United States is likely to act upon the basis of this type of assumption.

The current U.S. administration is obviously far more enthralled with its relations with Russia and China than with Japan. Historically, Europe has been a far stronger interest of the United States than has Asia—I say this despite the fact that the U.S. has had a sentimental interest in China since the days of the clipper ships. Moreover, this preference is not entirely without foundation. Western Europe as a whole is strategically and economically more important to the United States than is Japan by itself. Historical traditions, language, and ethnic similarities create a stronger bond of interest. Yet even in the case of Western Europe, the United States has carried on many of its negotiations with the Soviet Union over the heads of its European allies.

Concessions have been made with respect to armaments and European matters without consultation with our European partners. Although there is much to be said strategically for the "pause" strategy, the Europeans are in part right to suspect that its adoption reflects a reluctance by the United States to use its nuclear weapons in the defense of Europe. We will be far more reluctant to use these weapons in defense of Japan. In either case, during a crisis both Europe and Japan might find themselves under American pressure to make concessions in order to allow America to avoid having to consider employment of its deterrent.

I do not wish to imply that the deterrent has no value, for the United States placed South Korea beyond its defense perimeter and still intervened after the North Koreans attacked. Both the Russians and Chinese are aware of this. Moreover, Japan has an advantage western Europe does not have: that of being a compact series of islands without a land connection to the mainland. It is far less likely to bear the brunt of direct military pressure than is Western Europe and, in this sense, is somewhat more secure. Nonetheless, even if the American deterrent has some value, that value is distinctly limited.

Moreover, as economies are made in the American defense establishment, the capability of the United States to assist the Japanese in a conventional defense will become more limited than it is at present. Even now, it can hardly be regarded as substantial, and the American bases in Japan serve more as a trip-wire in the case of the Japanese and as a rear area for Korean defense than as a front line of defense for Japan in a conventional war sense.

Because the United States is by far Japan's largest trading partner, Japan cannot afford a major rupture in its relations with the United States. On the other hand, it will become significantly more aware as time progresses of increasing limitations in the American commitment to Japan. It is not at all unlikely that the United States will attempt to use this leverage, as well as its defense commitment, to force the Japanese into a posture of global collaboration with American policy. In the oil crisis that followed the Yom Kippur War, the United States, which was almost self-sufficient in oil, put tremendous pressure on its Japanese and European allies to coordinate their policies with those of the United States. Rather than recognizing that the American interest in a strong Japan and a strong Europe required concessions to their immediate energy vulnerabilities, and consequent partial detachment from current American foreign policy, the United States displayed anger and a failure of understanding, particularly with respect to the Japanese. When the United States later suggested a multilateral consumers' meeting on energy, it showed no consistent understanding of the joint American-European-Japanese interest in treating the entire resources problem as a package to avoid future crises. If, instead, it had taken a more enlightened position, it might have sought a policy designed to secure the support of the producer states even though such a modality necessarily would be divorced from the immediate exigencies of American foreign policy.

To the extent that the apparent attitude of the former Nixon Administration continues to dominate American policy, it can be expected that the United States will treat Japan as an appendage of the United States that has no significant alternative to the American connection. The Japanese are likely to find themselves under American pressure on monetary and trade issues, as well as in international confrontations involving the United States where the Japanese posture is of either practical or symbolic value.

The Japanese have one significant advantage over the European nations in this latter respect. They do not have any land frontier with a potential enemy. On the other hand, they are far more vulnerable in terms of their dependence upon trade and access to resources, and more easily isolated inasmuch as they have only a single voice and a single vote in international proceedings.

The current American foreign policy posture seems designed to prevent any substantial development of an independent policy by either Europe or Japan. In this respect, American policy, if I have correctly described it, may have deliberately abrasive aspects that are designed to focus attention on the quarrels between America and some of its allies, thus creating conflicts of interest among them, and to divert attention from longer-term constructive measures that might produce new configurations of interests and new modalities for the conduct of foreign policy.

America's Asian policy bears a relationship toward its Japanese policy, but not a direct one. The United States seeks to insure that Asia is not dominated by any single hegemonic power that is antagonistic to the security interests of the United States or to its long-term interests in a pluralistic world in which democratic values both in the United States and abroad are safeguarded. In this respect, although the United States has no current intention of becoming involved in another Vietnam, with its incapacitating domestic and external political and military consequences, it does desire to maintain a capacity to assist Asian nations in maintaining their own independence, and to retain a limited military presence in Asia that deters at least some aggressions and that permits at least some rapid limited interventions, if only in the form of military supplies and advice. In this respect, it desires to be able to "show the flag" when required.

Although I believe that the American bases in Japan, however essential to the defense of South Korea, impose a higher political cost than the likelihood of their use or deterrent value warrants, there is little doubt that the American military, and the State Department, regard the bases as important, and perhaps essential, to the general Pacific policy I have outlined. This policy requires mid-Pacific basing at Midway and farther basing at alternative points such as Taiwan, Australia, and the Philippines. The Indian and the current Australian governments are attacking the American build-up at Diego Garcia on the ground that it will produce a Soviet-American naval race in the Pacific Ocean area. However, it is designed to maintain an American presence in the general Pacific area. Although the bases in Japan, Taiwan, the Philippines, and Australia are partially substitutable for one another, Diego Garcia is fundamental to the American South Pacific posture. There is little doubt that this posture will become increasingly low-key in the future, with a consequent reduction of the American presence in Thailand and elsewhere. Even so, Diego Garcia constitutes a minimal presence for the entire South Pacific area and a key link to the American posture with respect to the Eastern portions of the Middle East oil fields and the route to Africa. In this sense, it permits a global military strategy and avoids an increasingly fragmented one.

The current American posture in the Pacific, thus, may be viewed as having two aspects: the resurrection of the global posture via the link at Diego Garcia and the increasingly low-key posture of the United States in Southeast Asia. In this respect, American policy can either stay where it presently is or move in either of two directions. The movement into Diego Garcia can be viewed as part of a longer term return to a global policy from which the United States has been in at least partial retreat since the low-point of the Vietnam war. On the other hand, if the increasingly low-key character of the American involvement is part of a "slippery slope" policy, we may see the retreat of the United States from influence in South and Southeast Asia. Which route the United States pursues is of essential importance to Japan, for it will influence Japanese access to resources in Southeast Asia and its use of the sea lanes, particularly those involving routes through or around the Indonesian islands.

A second area of concern for Japan involves Russian policy. Let me make it clear that I believe that the present Russian policies of détente and of improving the Russian standard of living, with which General Secretary Brezhnev is associated, are serious policies that are being pursued with genuine vigor. Although there is some internal opposition to these policies, the reasons for them are evident. The Soviet Union is concerned about its long frontier with Communist China. The relative backwardness of the Soviet economy is forcing Russia into hard choices that confront it with substantial political problems as a consequence of the fact that the Russian populace is becoming consumer-oriented. Despite, or perhaps even because of, the Czechoslovak affair of 1968, the Soviet Union is finding it imperative to resolve its relationships with its Eastern European partners in a more flexible manner. There is also a growing problem of legitimacy with respect to the Soviet regime that can be resolved only by success on the diplomatic front and economic improvement at home.

Essentially the one-party regime in the Soviet Union bases its legitimacy upon its "scientific" interpretation of Marxist doctrine. Only in this sense can it be said to represent the masses. The existence of a competing Maoist regime in China and the history of the Soviet party after the demise of Stalin have created a serious crisis with respect to this source of legitimacy. Beyond this, Soviet experience with post-modern administrative state techniques have done much to undermine the belief that "contradictions" are produced only by the class distinctions proclaimed in Marxist theory. As a consequence, much of Marxist political theory is becoming irrelevant in the Soviet Union.

On the other hand, the current Soviet regime shows no desire to wither away. It is led by tough men, practiced in the arts of power, who seem determined to maintain control. Confronted by a vigorous Europe, a powerful United States, a determined China, and a prosperous Japan, the middle group of the Soviet leadership can find success only by détente abroad, economic success at home, and continued, or even increased, internal repression of political dissent.

This is a potentially unstable combination, for the required economic successes will produce tendencies toward relaxation internally that will need to be combatted even more vigorously. Meanwhile, successful détente abroad will undermine the perception of potential foreign threats as a requirement for tight control at home. A reduction of forces in Europe, moreover, will make the Eastern European partners of the Soviet Union far more restive, thus producing foreign policy initiatives on their part that increasingly will become a threat to the repressive Soviet Apparatus.

For these reasons, the present, and thoroughly justifiable, policies of détente being pursued by the United States are producing the seeds from which may sprout a terrible reversal of Soviet policy. If the American presence in Western Europe is significantly reduced over a period of years, and if during this period the Soviet economy is partially modernized by assistance from Western Europe, the United States, and Japan, a new generation of Soviet leadership, not identified with current policies, may seek to solve its internal and alliance difficulties by a reversal of policies. These could include the Finlandization of Western Europe, the reimposition of tight control on the Eastern European states, and the exertion of strong political, and perhaps military pressures, on the competing Communist regime in China. Again, I wish to make clear that I am not predicting this. There are ways of avoiding this, and they can be pursued by resourceful noncommunist regimes.

It is obvious that if the scenario I have sketched comes to pass, Japan will be in the center of the vortex. It will not be the immediate focus of Russian pressure, for China will bear that onus. However, Russia will expect Japan to play a central role in pressures upon China. In this world, Japan will be confronted by a Soviet version of the carrot and stick. China, in self defense, will be forced to employ similar pressures against Japan. A relatively unarmed Japan in this situation will find itself attempting to buy off both sources of pressure and, as with respect to all cases of blackmail, the bill will constantly increase. Worst of all, these pressures will be reflected in the competing parties that participate in the internal Japanese political process. This will weaken the Japanese political system, increase the potentiality of a successful coup by one party or the other, and diminish the resistance of the Japanese to external pressures as a consequence of internal lack of cohesion.

The Nuclear Issue

From a Japanese point of view, consideration of the acquisition of a nuclear weapons system is premature, quite apart from any other objections the Japanese might have. One major argument against a Japanese system—the compact quality of the Japanese geopolitical position—is, however, oversimplified. It is true that the total destruction of Japan—and of England, France, and West Germany, for instance—is a simpler matter than destruction of the Soviet Union, the United States, or China. However, although current assertions of "overkill" are grossly exaggerated, the essential fact is that either the Soviet Union or the United States could do so much damage to the other in a first strike that physical "survival" would be a very attenuated phenomenon. Such an attack, of course, would be irrational, for, by removing all hostages, the disincentives to launch a second strike are also removed. In short, a Japan in possession of a secure second-strike force—perhaps one located in the Pacific Ocean—would not be significantly worse off than Russia or the United States. Indeed, the compact nature of the Japanese land mass might discourage limited nuclear attacks in a way that would not be true with respect to Russia or the United States because of the difficulty of limiting collateral damage in Japan and, therefore, of avoiding a major reduction in the disincentive to launch a massive counterattack.

From a Japanese point of view, the strategic difficulties of acquiring a nuclear force now include the fact that a Japanese force stationed in the Pacific would not be capable of reaching major Russian European cities; it would be insufficient, given present Japanese capabilities, for threatening the up to 500 dispersed targets that would constitute a major deterrent to China; and it would be of major significance only against the United States. For this reason, a Japanese government would be unwise to run the international and domestic political difficulties of acquiring a nuclear force.

The strategic disincentives for acquiring such a force will not apply by the early 1980s. The political disincentives also will likely change in a significant way by then, but projecting these changes is obviously moot and subject to specific scenarios.

Whether or not the Japanese should acquire such a force is, as we have mentioned, a matter for Japanese decision. It is inappropriate for the United States to pressure the Japanese in either direction, although I believe we should facilitate with American assistance any decision the Japanese make.

One argument made by Americans against Japanese acquisition of nuclear weapons is based upon poorly examined dogma. It is asserted that Japanese possession of a nuclear force will decrease world stability by increasing the likelihood of an accidental war or an attack by an irrational state.

This attitude has dominated American policy since the early days of nuclear power. It underlay our lack of cooperation with the British, despite the wartime agreements with them, and our obnoxious behavior toward the French. As a consequence, although we failed to prevent the French from acquiring a nuclear force, our actions insured that the force would be unstable.

Beyond this, American policy demonstrated to the world that acquisition of nuclear weapons against the opposition of the United States was an easy task and that this could be accomplished "on the cheap." If the French had acquired their force with American cooperation, that force would have been a stable one and the lesson would have been reinforced that only rich countries can afford nuclear forces and that even these rich countries require cooperation from a major nuclear power.

The American posture overlooked the extent to which the spread of nuclear weapons to moderately rich states would dampen the incentives for a nuclear arms race. In what remains essentially a two-power world from the standpoint of major nuclear systems, both the United States and the Soviet Union fear a technological breakthrough by the other that would make either vulnerable to the other's first strike. Because of the long lead times in weapons development, this stimulates the qualitative arms race.

Although this incentive would not entirely be eliminated in a multi-nuclear world, it would be seriously dampened for the following reason. The likelihood that any single nation could achieve a breakthrough sufficiently great to make all other nuclear powers vulnerable obviously would be very small in a multi-nuclear world. Thus the incentive to spend large sums in a qualitative race would be dampened.

The incentive to strike at only one of the possible opponents would be negligibly small in a multi-nuclear world. That very action would demonstrate the irresponsibility of the state that so acted, its dangerous character, and the need to contain it. Thus, at the worst it would touch off a counterattack by the remaining nuclear powers, and at the best it would touch off a spiraling arms race which it could not win.

For much the same reasons, a multi-nuclear world would be far less vulnerable to an accidental war. In a two-power nuclear world, an accidental explosion is not very likely to touch off a war if the forces are reasonably protected in terms of a second-strike capability. Nonetheless, the incentives to strike back are greater than in a multi-nuclear world. In the first place, it is clearer, although not entirely so, where the weapon was launched. Second, the possibility of gaining a decisive advantage by striking first cannot be excluded. Third, the nation that launches the accidental attack may be so fearful of a counter-response by the attacked state that it follows the accidental launch with a full-scale attack. Recursively, the recipient of the attack, fearing precisely this, launches its own full-scale attack. The existence of other major nuclear powers reduces this cycle of fear substantially for the very same reasons given with respect to the launching of a first-strike in the absence of an accidental attack.

On the other hand, an American policy that ensures the spread of nuclear weapons will occur in the face of American opposition also ensures that these systems will be unstable, that they will not reduce the incentives for a first-strike or an accidental war, and that the wrong lesson will be learned by extremely small countries that under foreseeable circumstances could not afford stable nuclear systems and the political structures which are far more given to irrational decisions than those of the major nations. It ill behooves the United States and the Soviet Union—two nations that, however interested in arms control, are almost completely uninterested in arms reduction—to pressure other countries not to go nuclear.

Japanese Vital Interests

Apart from the earlier scenario that indicates potential threats to Japanese national security, what are the vital interests the Japanese need to protect? They require a relatively open world scientific community as a framework for the continued development of their technological society. This entails developments in computer technology and nuclear and solar energy processing. They require access to external sources of energy supply on a reasonably competitive basis. They require access to a wide variety of raw materials, particularly given the poverty of the Japanese islands in this respect. They require sufficient export access at least to pay for their required imports. They have a definite interest in preventing a Sino-Soviet combine that would confront them with a unified hostile Asian mainland. In particular, for obvious geopolitical reasons, the continued independence of at least South Korea is of great importance to Japanese security. They require relative freedom of the seas for their commerce. And they require adequate deterrence of attack, whether this deterrence be purchased by alliance systems, increases in their conventional armed forces, the development of tactical nuclear weapons to be used against amphibious attacks, new laser-controlled ballistic missile defense systems, nuclear retaliatory systems, or some combination of these conditions.

The urbanization of Japan resulting from increased industrialization makes Japan peculiarly vulnerable to all the potential disruptions attending post-modern societies. However desperate the situation of the Japanese may have been during the last period of blockade at the end of the Second World War, the present-day Japanese social and political systems are far more vulnerable to disruptions stopping short of the employment of military force against Japan proper.

In the final analysis, Japan cannot purchase its own national security in purely independent terms, for, even if it developed a nuclear system, this system could not effectively be used to prevent disruption of the commercial activities of Japanese ships at sea, trade barriers, or exchange controls that threatened its access to food, energy, and raw materials. For instance, by the 1980s, when Japan will be dependent upon both Siberian and Middle Eastern energy resources, if either area cut off access to the Japanese, Japan would be confronted with a problem that it could not solve by itself. Although I do not believe that even as rich and continental a nation as the United States can maintain its national security independently, Japanese vulnerability is qualitatively far greater.

Thus we seem to be confronted by a contradiction. I am projecting that Japan will be one of the two or three most powerful nations in the world and one of the weakest. Yet both statements are correct, for the potential Japanese influence and impact on the world are as great as I state; and, at the same time, the Japanese vulnerability to external manipulation is potentially at least equally great. Which of these characteristics becomes more significant depends upon the context of the international environment that enfolds Japan in the 1980s.

Much, but far from all of this, will depend upon actions taken by Japan. The American role is also central, and this must be a disheartening fact to Japanese who observe current American policies that are so neglectful of them. In part, these policies rest upon the beliefs that were held by the former Nixon administration that the Japanese have nowhere else to turn. Yet, surely a legitimately prideful and powerful people will view the current American relationship as at best a mixed blessing. Perhaps the United States overlooks the fact that nowhere in the Pacific area can the United States find a more natural friend than Japan, provided that the Japanese are treated with the sincerity that their sagacity and industriousness have earned.

Prospects for the Future

We have already indicated to a considerable extent the prospects for Japanese-American relations that are dependent upon the future major strategic decisions that both nations might take. At one extreme we have a reasonably well-armed United States leading a firm alliance in Europe, extending a credible nuclear umbrella over Japan, and pursuing détente with the Soviet Union and China. In this case, the prospects for the continued peaceful and prosperous development of Japan and continued good relations between the two nations are very strong.

At the other extreme, the United States reduces its military commitments to other countries, its alliance connections with Europe become attenuated, and the umbrella over the Japanese is either withdrawn or becomes very leaky. This case frees Russia to sharpen its conflicts with China. In such a world Japan may be impelled to search for security either through rearmament or through reassurance from one of the Communist countries. In this future, relations between Japan and the United States likely will become very weak and perhaps even bitter.

Projections along the military-strategic axis probe only one dimension of the important world continuum. The recent oil crisis calls to the fore another dimension of the problem that is fully as important as the former. The monetary and energy crises of the past few years signal the breakdown of the economic arrangements that until then had endured through the entire postwar period and that had permitted genuine stability in the international system.

During the next few years we will be making the decisions that will cast the future of the international system along this dimension for the next generation. One end of this continuum is that of intense economic competition among the nations of the world. In this extreme case, we will find no alternative to floating parities for currencies. Therefore, those nations that wish to avoid those domestic consequences of trade deficits that are normally induced by free market mechanisms will resort to quotas, other restrictions, and blocked accounts. In the absence of organizations designed to insure the free flow of resources from one nation to another, monopolistic groupings will form, the purposes of which will be to secure unilateral advantages. This will be a world of diminishing economic growth, slowing international growth in trade, and cutthroat competition. Japan especially will be vulnerable. Its access to markets in Europe will be gravely threatened. And a United States competing with Japan for markets in Latin America will punish Japan within its international markets. In such a world friendship between the two nations, let alone a security treaty, will not survive. Japan, being particularly vulnerable to resource cut-offs, will be driven to desperate measures to compensate, although it will be difficult to predict what these measures might be in the absence of a concrete scenario.

There is an intermediate posture that ought to be considered: consumer cartels organized to match producer cartels. The Japanese obviously cannot join the latter and they will surely be invited to join the former. However, there will be sharp competition and reprisals between the cartels. The consumers will direct these reprisals against the most vulnerable members of the producers' cartel. Conversely, however, the producers' cartel will direct its pressures against the most vulnerable members of the consumers' cartel. Japan clearly will be among the most vulnerable of the consumers, given its complete dependence upon external sources of supply and the extent of its trade rivalry with the other consumers. Moreover, because its policies will appear hostile to developing nations, a consumers' cartel will meet domestic political opposition in some of the nations that otherwise would be natural members of it. Such opposition will make it difficult to maintain the solidity of the cartel and to assure divisions of supplies within it. In this respect, for instance, it might be difficult to sell a consumers' cartel within a Japan in which the opposition vote rises significantly. And the vulnerability of such Western nations as Belgium and France to secession from the cartel would only emphasize the pressures that would be placed upon Japan. In such a world there would be some remnants of the Japanese-American relationship, but they would be subjected to those intense pressures rebounding from the economic pressures upon Japanese internal politics. Again, the Japanese would be forced to consider radical alternatives.

A third mode of international economic organization would be one in which producers and consumers jointly agreed to maintain commodity banks designed to prevent interim shortages of resources or rapid changes in price levels. In such a world, producers would be provided with investment opportunities to compensate for the eventual loss of income from the depleted resources, while the consumer nations would refrain from investing in alternate energy and resource sources for agreed periods of time. Such a world would be one in which there would be a strongly developing form of international organization for the handling of economic problems the scope of which is beyond individual states or small groups of states. Because these problems are functionally distinguished, there might well be no overall organization, but instead a series of parallel functional groupings. In this world, the interdependencies among nations would be emphasized. As a consequence, it would be a world with a lowered threat structure and one in which the continued existence of good relations between Japan and the United States could be projected with some degree of assurance.

In such a world, one other institution might be adopted; one that I believe would further strengthen the future of Japanese-American relations. This organization should not be founded by the primary activity of any single nation. Indeed, the dominance that the United States has within NATO would be inconsistent with the objectives of such an organization.

What I am proposing is an organization of the democratic nations of the world; one designed to foster democratic values. This organization should be unrelated to current alliance or economic systems. If a member of the Warsaw Pact introduces political democracy, it should be permitted to join without leaving the Warsaw Pact. Brazil and Greece, however valuable they may be to the United States in other respects, should not become members of this organization.

The organization should be sharply separated from the current controversies that divide the democratic nations. If it is used to attempt to solve current exchange problems, or to agree upon a distribution of energy resources, it will be eviscerated at the very outset, for it will become the focus of conflicting rather than unifying interests.

It would be a mistake to attempt to outline the organization of this new grouping precisely. However, it should contain an international court of human rights before which cases could be submitted either by member states or by citizens of member states without veto and the decisions of which would not be subject to veto. It would hear cases concerned with denials of the right of emigration, the right to education, the right to organize opposition parties that accept the basic democratic framework of government, the right to publicize one's view, the right to fair trial, the right to humane treatment, and the right to non-discrimination on the basis of race, color, creed, or sex. This is suggested as an indicative list, not an exhaustive one.

The court would also hear cases concerning the independent agencies to be established by the joint parliament of the new organization. The joint parliament would establish, for instance, a Manhattan project on energy that would be funded by all the member states and with participation of scientists from all the member states. It would fund another project on ecology. These projects, at least initially, would all be knowledge-oriented. They would provide the foundation for the solution of problems but would not commit the organization in areas of sharply conflicting interests. Hopefully this would change as the organization gained experience and as common interests developed.

I have said that this organization might have members from competing alliance systems and with different types of economic organizations. Yet it should become evident that the things we have most in common with other nations in the long run, if not in the short run, respond to our views of man and of the appropriate role of political organization. Therefore, I seriously doubt that any member of this organization, after it becomes firmly established, could fail to receive support from other members if it became subject to military threat, political pressure, or economic discrimination.

Moreover, as the international Manhattan projects produce striking results, as I have no doubt they would, this organization will become the focus of progressive world attention. It will become the symbol of technological progress, of intelligence, and of humanity. The citizens of the member nations will have a clearer view of the purposes of their national foreign policies; and the discrepancies that real world exigencies entail will not be as psychologically disturbing. For the same reasons, the national leaderships that respond to these exigencies will have a firmer method for relating them to the overall goals of their foreign policies.

Membership in the organization will become an attraction. Those who are not members—and membership is voluntary depending only upon adherence to the political requirements of human freedom—will begin to see themselves as being in the backwash of world civilization. Authoritarian states will no longer be able to argue that their dictatorship protects national security, for that same protection could be gained by becoming a member of this organization, without any restriction on the right to economic experimentation. On the contrary, such economic experimentation would be reinforced by other advantages naturally flowing from membership, including increased economic cooperation of a voluntary nature.

Although the organization would not interfere militarily in any of the nations that refused to accept court decrees, punishing only by suspension or expulsion, the existence of the organization would provide an external standard that would reinforce the continuity of democratic practices within member states. Yet these pressures would be brought not by any particular external national state—a form of pressure that would be obnoxious to national sentiment—but by an independent judiciary representing all member states.

I do not wish to overstate the case for this organization. It might never be established. If it is established, it might not work. Yet the case for it is strong; it makes sense. And it may make sense in a way that might mobilize the energy of the best among us—something that cannot be said for current policies. We have not yet been able to articulate the democratic values for which we stand internationally and to relate those values at the same time to a course of foreign policy that implements them in an understandable way. This organization would close that gap. In a democratic age, that is essential.

East Asia, the United States, and Japan: Four Proto-Scenarios

Kinhide Mushakoji

The Problems: To Predict the Unpredictable

We are facing a period of great uncertainty. In the 1950s and 1960s, bipolarity in the international system had divided the East Asian regional system in such a way that it was easy to label each actor as either a "free world" (capitalist), a "communist" (socialist), or a "neutralist" (unaligned) country. Each category, then, could be associated with a certain style of international behavior, and the developments in regional politics could be predicted provided that the initiatives of the two extra-regional superpowers were known. Regional happenings unplanned or unforeseen by them were negligible factors which could not change the great lines of the political developments in the region, and hence could be considered as "noise." Although some uncertainties had been introduced in the course of the 1960s by the growing Sino-Soviet conflict, it was only when the end of the Vietnam War approached and such unexpected moves as the visit of President Nixon to Peking finalized the process of multipolarization that uncertainty became a predominant characteristic of the East Asian regional dynamics.

Since then various events broke the certainty of the Cold War patterns. The events included the attempts by a growing number of East

Asian governments, so far known as "anti-communist," to follow suit with Nixon in establishing lines of communication with the socialist countries. This put an end to the certainty of the system that previously had been polarized into communist versus anti-communist countries (with perhaps the exception of Indonesia).

These governments remain anti-Communist as ever, and often they accompanied this move of international détente with domestic measures heightening internal tensions.[1]

In addition, the positions of the regional and extra-regional countries were now increasingly unpredictable. The Nixon Doctrine, unlike previous U.S. declarations of foreign policy positions such as the Truman Doctrine, lent itself to different interpretations. The position of China was also unclear. The Russians were proposing a scheme of regional security which was difficult to fit into the previous pattern. The visit of Premier Tanaka had caused people to think that Japan was embarking on a new and more articulate line in her Asian policy, but the impression was not corroborated by later developments.

In this state of uncertainty, where no precedent seems to be of any use in predicting the future, what can we say about the interrelation between East Asia and the U.S.–Japanese dyad? Can we design scenarios with some predictive power about such an ambivalent future? More generally, is it not impossible to predict what will happen after a system change on the basis of information obtained about the state of affairs before the transition? All of these are questions we answer negatively.

Under such conditions, we will attempt to approach the problem from an unconventional angle. Rather than search for an estimation of a "surprise-free future," we will try to look for a body of information which can be of some use even in a highly uncertain setting. We will not try to propose long-range scenarios which are supposed to resemble reality. Rather, we will analyze the past to find the basic factors which are likely to play a role in shaping the future.

This approach tries to provide the information needed to give shape to different kinds of scenarios and, therefore, will be called "proto-scenario building." We propose four proto-scenarios on the trilateral interaction between the United States, Japan and the East Asian countries. Others may attempt to construct variant scenarios responsive to the factors we specify.

1. The Philippines and the Republic of Korea are two examples of this trend.

Four Levels and Five Features

At least four levels of analysis must be distinguished in the study of relationships between the United States and Japan in East Asia. The first level is the dyadic relation between the two countries. On this level, East Asia is nothing but the *environment* where two countries interact. Here, the focus of attention is either how the environmental factors taken as independent variables determine the state of the bilateral system, or how the U.S.-Japanese dyadic relations play the role of an independent variable that determines the state of the East Asian regional system.[2]

The second level of analysis is the tripolar system among the United States, the Soviet Union, and the People's Republic of China. Here, the East Asian region is considered not just as an environment, but as an arena of inter-polar competition and cooperation.[3]

A third level of analysis is the East Asian regional system to which Japan belongs and within which the United States plays the role of a deeply involved extra-regional actor. This level of analysis emphasizes the dynamics of intra- and extra-regional transactions, and various patterns of sub-regional coalitions and integrations, with which the United States and Japan interact.[4]

The fourth level of analysis goes to the grassroot level of the domestic political systems of all the regional actors, and looks for the linkage-political phenomena characterizing the East Asian region.

The actors are not only the sovereign states and their governments. They are the various geographic, ethnic and occupational interests, the political movements and parties, the elites and counter-elites, and the

2. Cf. Kinhide Mushakoji, "Atarashii Nichi-Bei Kankei o saguru" (In Search of a New U.S.-Japanese Relations), *Komei*, No. 123 (January 1973), pp. 29–36.

3. For an application of a tripolar model to Asia, see Zbigniew Brzezinski, "The Global Triangle" (paper prepared for the Europe-American Conference, Amsterdam, March 1973).

As to a game-theoretical treatment of a tripolar system with the addition of Japan, and using a four-person and two discriminated actors paradigm, see: Mitsuo Suzuki, ed. *Kyoso Shakai no Game no Riron* (Game Theory for a Competitive Society), Tokyo, 1970.

4. There are two paradigms used in this connection. One is the transaction-flow analysis approach with a field theory model as one sub-unit, the other is the international organization membership study approach which can be applied both to the IGOs and the NGOs. On the former approach, see: Tong-Whan Park, "Peaceful Interactions in Asia," *Comparative Political Studies*, January 1973, pp. 419–442. On the latter: Michael Haas, *The Asia Way: An Operational Code of a Diplomatic Style and Its Political Achievements* (paper presented to the Annual Convention of the International Studies Association, New York, March 1973). See also: Goh Cheng-Teik, *South-East Asia: Peace through Neutralization* (paper presented to the Japanese Peace Study Association Meeting, September 1973).

transnational and multi-national non-governmental organizations. All the linkage interactions and structures in East Asia with special emphasis on the Japanese and American ones belong to this level.[5]

The scenarios derived from each of the four levels of analysis differ not only in terms of the actors under consideration, they differ also in the structural and functional features they use as their basis of prediction. We can at least distinguish the following two structural and three functional features which determine the difference among the four levels.

First, any model should identify the characteristics of interactions and transactions among the actors. On the first level, we must focus our attention on the U.S.-Japanese economic and political interactions and transactions. On the second, the tripolar interactions on nuclear arms control deserves more attention. On the third, regional interactions and transactions among the East Asian countries are of central importance. On the fourth, the inter- and intra-national, as well as the transnational, flows of information, goods and services have to be studied. In this way, each model emphasizes a different kind of interaction and transaction; and it is hard to judge which one is most important for our scenario.

The second structural feature which deserves special attention is the character of the structures which emerge from the above-mentioned interactions. What are the mutual role expectations among the actors? What kinds of horizontal or vertical relations of interdependence or dependence exist among the actors? Do their interactions occur in a structural framework which is formal or informal, rigid or flexible, simple or complex? These and other questions need to be answered before any scenario building can take place.

The structures which have to be studied differ again according to the levels. On the first, it is the bilateral structures which are of great importance, such as the ones giving certain regularities to U.S.-Japanese security and diplomatic and economic relations. On the second, it is the tripolar structures, or the asymmetry caused by the lack of stable structures involving the People's Republic of China (PRC) as compared to the various structures developed around the U.S.-Soviet relations which should be investigated. On the third, we have to address ourselves to the regional and sub-regional patterns of organization and integration or the lack of them. On the fourth, we have to

5. A linkage political study of the following type should be made about the East Asian region: Douglas A. Chalmers, "Developing on the Periphery: External Factors in Latin American Politics," James Rosenau, ed., *Linkage Politics*, New York, 1969.

study, among other things, the new transnational structures and the linkage structures related to economic, and sometimes the security, relations of the regional and extra-regional states.

Moving to the functional side, we have first to deal with the various factors which determine the degree of stability of the system. On the first level, the factors which stabilize or destabilize U.S.-Japanese relations must be identified. On the second, the same should be done for the tripolar balance of power. On the third, it is the stability of the East-Asian regional system which is in question. On the fourth, the factors determining the stability of the linkage system are the focus of our attention.

A second functional feature is related to the degree of uncertainty of the system on the five levels. Diplomatic, economic, and other factors which build into U.S.-Japanese relations are certainly important on the first level. On the second, we are interested in tripolar uncertainty, especially as it involves Sino-Soviet relations. On the third, it is useful to look into the uncertain future of the regional and sub-regional patterns of interactions and integration. On the fourth, the uncertain linkage between international developments and domestic political trends is especially important.

The third and last functional feature is the pattern of novelties and innovations which exists or is lacking in the system. If some unexpected new developments or unprecedented initiatives are to transform U.S.-Japanese relations, the tripolar balance, regional integration, and the linkages between regional and domestic politics, we must try our best to foresee where such developments are likely to take place and from whom such initiatives can be expected to come. On the first level, we may examine the innovative influence of new technological breakthroughs that can influence the energy problem, security relations, or the state of both countries' economy. On the second, new arms control developments are of great importance. On the third, regional leadership leading to new patterns of integration cannot be overlooked. On the fourth, social change affecting local, national, international, and transnational relations can bring about an entirely new state of affairs.

We have already referred to our belief that it is not advisable to build long-term scenarios in this highly unpredictable setting of East Asia. We can, however, propose proto-scenarios that indicate the original conditions, the original directions of future developments, and some points of reference for future revisions of the scenarios. We will try to discuss briefly four such proto-scenarios that are derivable from the above-mentioned matrix.

Four Proto-Scenarios

A U.S.-Japanese Proto-Scenario. U.S.-Japanese relations in the context of East Asia have so far been characterized by a disparity in the level of actions and initiatives between the two actors. During the 1950s and 1960s, the major political, military and economic decisions which shaped the state of affairs in East Asia were made by the United States, which requested Japan's cooperation when necessary. The latter's response to these demands was generally conditional acquiescence, with domestic factors setting the limits of Japanese cooperation. This pattern of interaction was institutionalized as the U.S.-Japanese Mutual Security Treaty.

Several factors altered this situation since the late sixties; one of them was related to bilateral relations between the two countries and two others to the changing nature of their response to environmental stimuli.[6]

First, the rapid economic growth of Japan created a state of rivalry between herself and the United States.[7] The U.S. expects now that Japan, who has acquired a sufficient economic capability, would be more willing to assume responsibilities in the area of security matters, while Japan expects that her new economic power will allow her to free herself from her over-compliance on the U.S. policy line in East Asia. It is true that the so-called "oil shock" following the fourth Middle East crisis changed the picture at least in the mind of the Japanese. The self-esteem and pride concerning Japanese economic power was found to be illusory when this country's dependence on the Third World —especially on the Arab countries—was proven so overwhelming that her economic prosperity would not continue unless the suppliers of energy and other resources were cooperative. Japanese pessimism, however, was not necessarily shared by the Americans, who feel that despite her vulnerability, Japan's economy has succeeded in surmounting the impact of the oil shock rather well compared to the other consuming countries. Thus, the gap between the self-image of the Japanese and the American image of Japan may become in the future the cause of an overexpectation by the U.S., or of underperformance by Japan.

Second, the reduction of the American politico-military presence in East Asia, proposed in the Nixon Doctrine, materialized in the course of the U.S. efforts to disengage itself from the Vietnam War, and

6. About the U.S.-Japanese communication gap resulting from these developments, see: Kinhide Mushakoji, "The American-Japanese Image Gap," Henry Rosovsky, ed., *Discord in the Pacific*, New York, 1972.

7. Cf. Henry Owen, ed., *The Next Phase in Foreign Policy*, Washington, 1973, pp. 25–27.

exemplified by Nixon's visit to Peking, changed the strategic and political as well as the economic conditions of East Asia. This major change in the American grand strategy creates a state of uncertainty as to the U.S. role in the region. More recent events following the victory of North Vietnam and of Provisional Revolutionary Government seem to indicate the intentions of the United States to reduce its operations in Southeast Asia and to put an increasing emphasis on the security of Northeast Asia, and especially on South Korea and Japan. It is clear that the statements made by various U.S. government officials as to the American commitment to protect the Republic of Korea or Japan, which refer to the possible use of nuclear weapons, were designed to reduce uncertainty over the American commitment. However, they have polarized domestic opinions in Japan and thus act as a destabilizing factor. The future dyadic relations between Japan and the U.S. will certainly have to cope with this dilemma: to reduce uncertainty the American side will tend to destabilize Japanese opinion; and, in an effort to stabilize Japanese opinion, Japan will increase uncertainty over the two countries' relations.

Third, as a consequence of Japanese economic growth, her share in the Southeast Asian market has become so predominant that it causes distress among the regional countries. Many think that Japan is going to fill the power vacuum left by the United States, triggering criticism in many Southeast Asian countries about a rising Japanese militarism. In Northeast Asia, Japan's economic role in South Korea is already predominant. The strong insistence by the United States about the indivisibility of Korean and Japanese security is going to increase the dependence of the former on the latter country in a manner that is destabilizing because of the strong anti-Japanese feeling in Korea and the division in the Japanese public about Japanese-Korean relations.

Fourth, it is also important to notice the fact that Japan and the United States now have to face the impact of the Third World offensive; and there is reason to suppose that the difference of the two countries' interests—the former is a resource-poor country and the latter is one of the most resource-rich industrial countries—is bound to create conflicts and contention. Japan, being dependent on the oil producers as well as on other resource-rich developing countries, cannot take the risk of adopting the hard line often proposed by her ally. The American promise to supply her with sufficient resources in case a conflict with the Third World cuts off Japan from the supply she normally gets from that part of the world is not entirely convincing. To reduce dependence on the Third World, should Japan increase her already considerable dependence on the United States? Did not the "soybean shock" indicate what would be the consequence if Japan were to rely too heavily on one ally, however trustworthy it may seem to be? As a consequence of this problem the divergence in the two partners' approach to the Third World is bound to increase future uncertainty as to both countries' policy vis-à-vis the other Asian countries, who all belong to the Third World.

In view of the above four remarks, we must liberate ourselves from two stereotyped scenarios: one predicting that Japan is going to increase its share of the burden, in economic, political, and military terms, so far carried by the United States in Asia; the other predicting the deterioration of U.S.-Japanese relations and the rise of a Japanese Gaullism with, possibly, a Japanese *force de frappe*. We must take into account many factors which are bound to influence the future relations of the two countries and their impact on the region.

It seems clear that the U.S.-Japanese relations are heading into a difficult future. Destabilizing factors and uncertainties will tend to increase. We must, however, keep in mind the fact that both Japan and the United States have learned from their recent past experiences, and that they are intensifying exchanges of information and mutual consultation. This is a factor which should be taken into consideration when we build our scenarios on the future of U.S.-Japanese relations. The two countries' dyadic relations will be determined by the capability of the parties to the dyad to adjust their policies in order to cope with destabilizing factors in a situation where uncertainty dominates.

On the structural level, it is necessary to assess the role the U.S.-Japanese Mutual Security Treaty is likely to play in the future. Two possibilities exist: one is that in connection with the American efforts to reduce uncertainty as to her commitments in East Asia, the role of this treaty is played up; the second is that the treaty's visibility is reduced and it becomes a symbol of the U.S.-Japanese partnership, as it has tended to be since the so-called Sino-American détente. In the former case, the Treaty will play a destabilizing role that polarizes Japanese public opinion; and, if no innovative efforts are made, it will contribute to the materialization of the second scenario mentioned above. If the second possibility comes about, a more stable but probably more uncertain situation will prevail, where the dyadic powers will have to readjust their policies time and again according to changing environmental conditions.

As novelty factors which cannot be lightly treated, we must take into account the possibility that a new administration in Washington or a new majority party (or coalition) in Tokyo may change the dyadic relationship. On the former side, the negative effects of a new isolationism or the positive effects of an innovative global policy that brings about an authentic détente should not be excluded from our scenarios. On the latter, the danger of an irrational explosion of nationalistic feelings and the hope that a new leadership, conscious of Japan's responsibilities concerning peace and development in the region, must be considered side by side.

The dyadic scenarios we can derive from the above considerations cannot be complete if we do not take into account the others: tripolar relations, the regional setting, and especially the linkage between international politics and domestic conditions in Japan and in the United States.

However, the dyad's capability to tolerate uncertainty, its flexibility in coping with destabilizing factors both domestic and international, and its capacity to encourage innovation in both parties' policy, will all have a considerable impact on the other scenarios, and this is probably the crux of the U.S.-Japanese proto-scenario.

A Tripolar Proto-Scenario. The second level proto-scenario concentrates on the power balance among the three poles; the United States, the Soviet Union, and China. East Asia appears as an arena for their power competition, and what matters most is the shift in the power balance of the superpowers in the region. Thus, three major developments are cited. One, as in the first scenario, is the reduced U.S. presence in Asia. A second factor is the increasingly active posture of the Soviet Union in the area, including the activities of the Russian fleet in the Indian and Pacific Oceans, the expansion of economic relations with regional countries, and the Soviet proposal for a regional security arrangement. A third factor involves the growing activity of China and mutual efforts to open relations between China and different East Asian countries through unofficial or official channels.

This scenario considers regional political dynamics within the framework of this tripolar context. The rapprochement of some of the countries in the Association of Southeast Asians Nations (ASEAN) with China is an example of the various adaptive measures taken by the regional countries, which see their traditional policy of reliance on the United States no longer valid in the new context. Japan, also, is expected to develop a new policy line. It will try to become less dependent on the United States and to seek to improve its relations with both China and the Soviet Union. Japan's "equidistance" policy is not an easy approach for other nations to accept. U.S. high officials have asserted that it was inappropriate for Japan to keep an equal distance from the United States, an ally, and China or the Soviet Union, both adversaries. On their side, each of these two countries has put pressure on the Japanese government to stop her from becoming too friendly with the other. It is well known that the Chinese suggestion that a statement of joint opposition to the hegemony of the two big powers should be inserted in the Peace and Friendship Treaty between Japan and China was strongly criticized by the Soviet Union. It is foreseeable that such tripolar stresses on Japan's foreign policy will increase; and, given the adaptive approach of Japanese foreign policy, the more pressure there is, the more uncertain Japanese foreign policy will become.

According to this proto-scenario, the greatest factor of instability is the Sino-Soviet conflict.[8] The nuclear power balance between the Soviet Union and the United States is seen as a stabilizing factor, especially now that a Sino-American communication channel has been opened. Uncertainty is built into the system by the fact that China will have no part of arms control agreements among the nuclear powers. The future policy of Japan, especially in connection with her nuclear option, is also a factor for uncertainty, as the insurmountable Diet opposition to the Miki government's attempt to ratify the nuclear non-Proliferation Treaty (NPT) during the spring of 1975 indicated.

Novelty and innovation in the tripolar relations possibly will occur when tripolar agreements on nuclear matters becomes possible. Another concrete setting in which innovative action may be possible is the Korean peninsula, where a tripolar guarantee may contribute to the process of peaceful reunion of the divided country. Given Japan's geographic location, it is not excluded that she will play an innovative role in this connection.

It must be noted, however, that such innovative moves may require an improvement in the patterns of communication among the three major actors. Although a reappearance of a monolithic Sino-Soviet bloc is highly unlikely, if it does occur, it may become a destabilizing factor, especially on the Korean peninsula, where the South would fear an attack from the North, that is now improbable because of lack of joint support by the two socialist powers. Nevertheless, the achievement of a modus vivendi, or the mutual recognition of the principles of peaceful coexistence by them, seems necessary before any constructive joint moves can be made by the three poles to establish a peace structure in the region. For the time being, the Soviet proposal for a regional collective security arrangement cannot be accepted by those countries who fear that it may endanger their relations with the PRC. It is, thus, more

8. About the Sino-Soviet Conflict and Asia with special reference to China, see: Tatsumi Okabe, *Gendai Chugoku no Taigai-Seisaku* (The Foreign Policy of Contemporary China), Tokyo, 1971.

realistic to seek increased contacts and communications, accompanied by tacit bargaining on disarmament and arms control measures, than to hope that a new regional structure may be built by the three contending powers.

At this point, the predictions of this proto-scenario can be based only on decision-making variables related to the intentions and decisions of the three powers, the technological variables related to their nuclear capability and the possibilities of finding acceptable arms control measures. Geopolitical variables must be taken into account, also, in order to assess the possibilities of various courses of action of the Big Powers in the region.

As to the decision-making variables, one crucial aspect of the tripolar relations is determined by the policy orientation of the American leadership, which can be either isolationistic, power-politics oriented, or internationalistic.

The policy orientation of the Soviet and Chinese leaderships can be either inward-looking, ideological, or national-interest oriented. The emergence of isolationism in America, as well as a resurgence of ideologically oriented trends in the latter two countries, may have a destabilizing effect on tripolar relations, while the maintenance of an American power-political tendency and of the national-interest orientation in the Soviet Union and in China will tend to maintain the status quo and to hamper the emergence of innovative trends. In case isolationism and inward-looking policies prevail, one of the consequences would be increased uncertainty as to tripolar relations.

Taking these factors into consideration, we may distinguish two tripolar scenarios: one assumes high tension and the other low tension in tripolar relations. According to the first one, Russia and China are assumed to compete in the region. The consequence of the reduction of the American presence forces regional countries, notably Japan, to shoulder part of the American burden. The consequence of the Sino-Soviet conflict is first reflected in an increased Russian presence in the ocean areas of the region and then gradually in different countries of the region, whence Russia would hope to build a power position to contain China.

The high-tension scenario may materialize if the consequence of the victory of the socialist forces in Indochina tends to intensify Sino-Soviet rivalry in the region. In terms of domestic factors, if an ideological emphasis prevails in both China and Russia, this scenario will have a greater probability. In terms of interaction and structural features, if no efforts are made to facilitate communication between China and Russia, and if the international system does not provide a meeting ground for the two countries, there is a high-tension condition which cannot be avoided so easily.

Another aspect of the high-tension scenario is related to the fear often expressed in the United States about a *domino* effect created by the socialist superiority in Vietnam, Cambodia, and Laos. This effect, however, is not so easily realized unless the domestic conditions of the countries in the region call for a social change which cannot be carried out by any of the political leaders of the region except the socialists. If the regional countries produce alternatives to a socialist political-system change, there will be no room for a high-tension scenario to materialize.

The low-tension scenario is based on the assumption that the tripolar balance leads to multipolarization and release of tension among those poles. This means that East Asia can hope for a period of relative quietness. The divided countries start to search for a path to unification. The regional countries seek to maximize their chance of survival by establishing good relations with as many of the superpowers as possible. They obtain by the very nature of multipolarization a much greater degree of freedom. The relative importance of factors not directly related to high politics among the big powers becomes more important. One can argue that the big powers, i.e., not only the United States but also the Soviet Union and China, must have learned the lesson of the Vietnam War, which indicates clearly the limits of the influence exercised by the superpowers. If this is the case, there will be a much larger part played by the third and the fourth scenarios.

It is thus possible to say that the tripolar scenario is going to become a better basis for prediction if the high-tension scenario materializes, and that if the low-tension scenario proves to be true, factors not directly related to the three superpowers will play a more important role.

A Regional Proto-Scenario. The previous two models focus on the policies and actions of the extra-regional or regional powers. However, one can build predictions on the future state of affairs in East Asia on the basis of the patterns of interaction and organization in the region.

As we saw before, during the cold-war period, the bipolar system imposed on the regional countries a choice between the two power blocs; and this determined the patterns of alliance—or of nonalignment—in the region. On the economic level, there has been a more geographically determined pattern of cooperation that is centered in the Economic Commission of Asia and the Far East. Attempts for subregional integration were made in the core area of Southeast Asia with the idea of Maphilindo (Malaysia, Philippines, Indonesia), and the development of the Association for Southeast Asia (ASA) into ASEAN.[9]

With the decreasing importance of the bipolarity-determined patterns of organization, which had led to such regional organizations as SEATO and ASPAC, it can be foreseen that both economically determined patterns of organization and sub-regional attempts for integration will play a more important role in the future.

It is especially important to take into consideration the trends of realignment following the victory of socialism in the Indochinese peninsula. The effort of the ASEAN countries to adapt themselves to the new state of affairs in the region takes two forms: one an attempt to open ASEAN to the socialist Southeast Asian countries so as to make it a forum where a modus vivendi can be found, the other a defensive reaction seeking a balance among the big powers.

The reorganization of this regional alignment is not inconsistent with the policies of the United States on the one hand and of Japan on the other. In the past, some American specialists expressed expectations about ASEAN's role in serving sub-regional security requirements. It seems, however, that this organization is headed toward neutralism. Japan, on her side, is interested in the economic aspect of the regional dynamics of organization building. She has already developed a group of organizations in which she plays an important role.[10]

It is, however, indispensable to recognize the structural limitations of regional integration because of the low degree of interdependence and complementarity among the Southeast Asian States. The historical rivalries among the regional actors also obstruct the possibilities of regional integration. The widening economic gap between Japan and the Southeast Asian countries cannot be but a major factor of instability. To this is added a new gap between the more advanced and the less advanced of the developing countries, such as between Singapore and Malaysia.

One of the major characteristics of the patterns of organization in Southeast Asia among the different countries is the redundancy of the various regional and sub-regional organizations which, unlike the case of Europe and other continents, overlap with slightly different members. This seemingly uneconomic pattern contributes to the

9. About the patterns of organization in Southeast Asia particularly, see: Michael Haas, *op. cit.*, and Somsakdi Xuto, *Regional Cooperation in Southeast Asia*, Bangkok, 1973.

10. About regional organizations and the role of Japan in them, see: Kinhide Mushakoji, "Asia no Kincho-Kanwa no Kozo (The Structure of Tension-Reduction in Asia)," *Asia Quarterly*, July, 1973, pp. 2–31.

stabilization of the region since the failure of one of the organizations is covered by the emergence of a new one. It can be hoped that this flexibility will permit the creation of a loose organization which enables the region or the sub-regions to settle their differences peacefully.[11] It must be recognized, however, that this redundancy and flexibility of the regional structures and organizations do not help in reducing uncertainty.

Uncertainty, in this context, comes not only from the regional countries but also from the big powers. It is unclear for the regional countries whether their regional scheme will survive the rivalry and competition of the power blocs. The ASEAN idea to set up a neutral zone in Southeast Asia is motivated by the concern of its members to reduce this kind of uncertainty. In addition to the politico-military hazards generated by tripolar competition, another factor of uncertainty lies in Japan's lack of expressed goals or principles regulating her economic activities.

Despite the many factors of instability and uncertainty, an innovative initiative supported by a strong leadership may promote a new pattern of regional integration. Such leadership may be exercised by a regional country or by an extra-regional one, in which case a new problem for the region would be to internalize this exogenous influence.[12]

This regional scenario emphasizes the consequences of the new patterns of regional alignments appearing in East Asia as the polarizing influence of the cold war recedes. There are two such developments which compete with each other. One is the pattern of sub-regional alignments, which seem to grow, such as that of ASEAN. If such attempts to organize a group of developing regional actors succeed in creating a dynamics of integration, this can give the region an internal momentum which may eventually grow into a countervailing power that reduces the influence of the regional and extra-regional great powers. The other development is the increasing influence of Japan on the economic-transaction patterns and the governmental and non-governmental patterns of economic organization in the region. If this tendency overrides the one mentioned above, this will result in a more or less apparent Japanese economic domination of the region. Thus, this regional proto-scenario allows us to generate two different versions: one oriented toward a sub-regional integration, the other toward a Japan-centered regional system.

More specifically, it is important to bear in mind the fact that in any event the difference between the American and Japanese "images" of

11. Cf. Estrella D. Solidum and Roman Dufsky, "A Divisible and Graduated Peace," *Asian Studies*, Vol. XI, No. 3 (December 1973), pp. 13–36.

12. Cf. Amitai Etzioni, *Political Unification*, New York, 1965, pp. 47–50.

Southeast Asia will not disappear. We suggest the following differences in the images: the predominantly economic concern of the Japanese versus the more political and military concerns of the United States; the latter's tendency to view the future "regional order" in Southeast Asia as a more decentralized but basically unchanged regional security system for the anti- or non-communist states of the region versus the Japanese tendency to consider this system as unworkable after the Vietnam War experience.

It is also necessary to define the diverging interests in the two countries that affect their policies on Southeast Asia. We do not have enough evidence about how much influence the American industries (and the multi-national corporations having their headquarters in this country) have on the policy-making process of the U.S. government. On the Japanese side, although difficult to substantiate, it is commonly said that Japanese economic circles (the Zaikai) are active in determining Japan's economic policy vis-à-vis the Southeast Asian countries. Through the Ministry of International Trade and Industry (MITI), there is an effort to control the so far disorderly behavior of the Japanese business firms in the region. This may have some linkages with the Zaikai and the MITI-level economic negotiations with the U.S. Japanese economic interests may be protected, either by an alliance (for the progress of Southeast Asia) with the United States, by competing with American economic influence in the region, or by taking a go-between position between North and South. Although the U.S. would prefer the first alternative, it is most likely that Japan would choose the third one. This is probably the crux of U.S.-Japan relations in Southeast Asia in this scenario.

A Linkage-Political Proto-Scenario. The linkage-political scenario is the most complex of the four proto-scenarios. It has to integrate in a coherent system the diverse variables of the transnational, international, national, and local levels. In addition, a long-range perspective on political and social development must be linked with the short-term socio-political dynamics.

The present state of linkage-political developments in the various parts of East Asia is characterized by various trends that amplify or cancel each other according to the particular situations. Starting from the shortest term situations, we may mention the influence of post–cold war leadership patterns in the region.[13] As various leadership styles developed to face the bipolar competition of the big powers, with dif-

13. Elite studies such as those developed in the following book should be expanded to cover the post-bipolar period: Werner Levi, *The Challenge of World Politics in South and Southeast Asia*, Englewood Cliffs, N.J., 1968, pp. 5–48.

ferent degrees of personalism, elitism, and nationalism, there are now new types of leaderships, dictatorial or consensus-oriented, that try to cope with the new situation. Each of the different styles needs to monopolize linkage group control. Some leaders do it by establishing a restriction on communication and try to become the sole link between the others, often to the point of imposing a dictatorial form of government. Others try to represent in domestic and international politics the interests and aspirations of the modernizing elite that monopolizes the role of linkage group in their country.

The leadership style that prefers to reduce communication among the masses and the outside world tends to be reinforced by the requirement, at least on the governmental level, of engaging in relations with the East Asian socialist countries: China, the Democratic People's Republic of Korea, and the socialist states in the Indochinese peninsula. The fear that open contact with these countries may stimulate public dissidence makes the leaders of many of the Asian countries extremely reluctant to permit free contacts on a people-to-people level. This tendency exists both in the anti-communist as well as in the socialist countries. It is doubtful, however, that such a policy can be perpetuated in face of an increasingly politicized public that demands freedom of speech and participation in the affairs of the state, including foreign relations. This is why we can derive the two additional scenarios from this one. Before referring to these scenarios, we must consider the longer term trends.

A longer term trend of great importance involves the increasingly influential transnational linkages produced by multi-national corporations.[14] These firms—attracted by resources, markets, cheaper labor, and lack of anti-pollution regulations—have a complex impact on the economic and political systems of the East Asian countries. They are agents of economic development and urbanization, as well as causes of an increased economic inequality; and they trigger in many places new economic nationalism and anti-foreign dependence campaigns. This complex phenomenon involves multi-national corporations of American and Japanese origin, which together represent 60 percent of such firms in East Asia.

We must not forget that this trend is related to an even longer range one: the modernization of the region. The various destabilizing effects of the various tension factors that accompany any process of moderni-

14. About the role of the multi-national corporations in Asia, see, for example: Ashok Kapour, *The Multinational Enterprise and the National State in Asia* (a paper presented at the Research Conference on the Multi-national Corporation in the Global Political System, University of Pennsylvania, April 1971).

zation tend to be reinforced by political and economic inputs from the international system.[15] The governments in the region try to impose stability by force or by delaying the introduction of drastic but indispensable social reforms such as land reform. The economic gap generates political opposition among different ethnic, linguistic, or religious groups. These, and many other factors of instability, combine to produce a highly uncertain state of affairs that is amplified by uncertainty at the international level. External support to the ruling elite or to counter-elites intensifies this tendency.

Novelties and innovative initiatives may, however, come from the modernizing as well as the counter-modernizing elites, if their creativity is not hampered by dependence on foreign initiatives in economic and technical aid or in political matters. Experience has shown that the assumption that economic aid would create more stable regimes in East Asia was wrong. The consequences of aid depend on how the big powers cooperate with the domestic efforts of the regional countries to find their own way of development.

It is important to take note of the growing nationalism that prevails in all the Asian countries. The nationalism takes different forms, sometimes autocratic and sometimes popular, sometimes reactionary and sometimes radical. But one common feature is the refusal to be subjugated to big powers either politically or economically. In general, we have seen economic nationalism grow during the course of the 1960s. This economic nationalism replaced the politicized nationalism of the Afro-Asian solidarity period. Now, the end of the Vietnam War will probably encourage the growth of a more politically aware nationalism.

This consideration leads to different lines of prediction. One possibility is a gradualistic political-development process under an enlightened national leadership and with a gradual reduction of the degree of penetration by big-power influence. The other possibility is an internal polarization of many of the regional countries between elites in power who stifle social reforms and counter-elites supported by dissatisfied sectors of the society. Such polarization would produce regional tension in proportion to the penetration of these nations by multi-national corporations or big-power influence. Depending on the reactions of such external actors, endemic instability would prevail in the linkage

15. As to the need to overcome the effect of the Vietnam War on the study of politics in Southeast Asia which oriented scholarship toward shortsighted analyses of the present state of affairs, and on the role to be attributed to the studies of political development in the region, see: Tooru Yano, "Tonan-Asia Seiji Kenkyu wo meguru Sho-Mondai (The Problems Related to the Study of Politics in Southeast Asia)," *Asia Quarterly*, July 1973.

system. And this would have an impact on Japan and the United States in their relations with neighboring big powers.

The linkage which exists between a mounting opposition to Japanese economic expansion and criticism of governments—based on a growing aspiration for political participation among students and other social strata that are insufficiently integrated in the political system—was demonstrated by the student-centered demonstrations in Thailand and especially Indonesia during the visit of Premier Tanaka to these countries in January 1974. The present reaction pattern of Japanese society is clearly adaptive in that it emphasizes the need for Japanese business enterprises to adjust their behavior, and for Japanese in general to make themselves "better understood." Yet, we must carefully study the factors that may lead Japan to change its approach under domestic or external stress. Although the fear of a Japanese "gunboat policy" expressed by many Southeast Asian observers is perceived by the majority of Japanese as unlikely, we must take into account the fact that the root of Japanese militarism was not purely related to a thirst for power, but rather to a sense of economic inferiority.

On the American side, the Nixon Doctrine seems to indicate a determination to avoid being pulled into a position of protecting governments who face domestic problems. Does this mean that in the future Japan will become more adventurous and the United States will become less so? This is a matter that deserves empirical study.

Principles of Scenario Building

It might be argued that the four proto-scenarios should be combined into one all-inclusive scheme. However, they are based on contradictory assumptions. The tripolar model assumes that the government leaders of the East Asian countries make their decisions in order to adapt to the new tripolar system, while the linkage model assumes that they are predominantly interested in maintaining their power in face of destabilizing domestic political dynamics. If one wants to combine the two models, it is necessary to define how much of the decisions can be accounted for by each of the factors. Otherwise, a combination of the two scenarios would create only confusion.

From a different point of view, it seems that certain scenario mixes provide better answers to certain questions. For example, it is easier to use the linkage model to predict the viability of a given economic cooperation policy of Japan vis-à-vis an East Asian country than to use a tripolar model. But it is better to use the latter to determine the probability of a rapprochement between an East Asian country and China.

The problem of finding the best combination of the scenarios can be solved only by approximation. It may be possible to propose a few hypotheses about the relative predictive value of the four proto-scenarios.

The bipolar international system dominated international events in the relevant period: U.S.-Japanese relations, the East Asian regional system, and the domestic situations in the East Asian countries. Although the tripolar system is definitely exerting a considerable influence over the other three levels, it does not dominate them. U.S.-Japanese economic relations, for instance, are increasingly independent of it. Although ASEAN is influenced by the Vietnam situation, it has an internal dynamics of its own quite different from that of SEATO or ASPAC. As to the internal conditions of the regional countries, domestic factors shape the state of affairs more than foreign ideological influences, although there is still a strong system-dominant tendency as indicated by the fact that big power "détente" creates more internal tension.

Second, long-range future developments in East Asia can be hypothesized to depend more on the regional and the linkage factors than on the two others. The influence of the big powers may add uncertainty or retard the process of national and regional integration in East Asia, but it is unlikely to alter its course.

Factors obstructing both development and integration are predominant in the region. But, this is another reason for expecting the emergence of novelties and innovative actions that will give to the regional and linkage models a special importance. It is hard to believe, in the long run, that the East Asian people would continue to accept the present state of penetration and dependence given the various symptoms of nationalism and the demand for social change in the region.

A third hypothesis relates to the increasing degree of freedom of the actors. Unlike the situation of the bipolar period, the developing multipolar setting permits the actors to choose the level on which they want to operate. Regional structures in East Asia can become more and more viable and effective in counteracting tripolar rival influences or Japanese economic predominance. This depends on regional initiatives and on the American and Japanese East Asian policies, which are not determined by the logic of the cold war any more. All countries can design their activities in a much freer way than they could during the sixties. In this connection, it is important to consider the scenarios not as deterministic of the future, but as models of alternative futures in which freedom of decision by the various actors is relatively great.

These hypotheses have to be tested before they can be definitely accepted. However, we may adopt them as working hypotheses for the moment.

We terminate this very preliminary discussion by a call for innovative scholarship. A desirable future will not be achieved if our actions are based on the obsolete beliefs of the bipolar period.

There is a fundamental problem we must not overlook in our study of U.S.-Japanese relations in Southeast Asia. This kind of study should not be made only by researchers of the two industrialized countries. This objection is based both on a nationalistic normative judgment and on a more scientific cognitive basis. A joint study excluding the Southeast Asians themselves may be used against their interests, and it will distort the facts because of a biased cognitive map based on U.S.-Japanese experience heterogeneous to the Southeast Asian reality.

The latter criticism is especially valid in terms of our "regional proto-scenario" where the leading actors belong to the region. As to the first motive, we must be careful not to make our study policy-oriented without a Southeast Asian input. This reflection may be biased by the very nature of Japan as a go-between/in-between country caught in the dilemma of dealing with both the United States and the Southeast Asian nations; but we submit the point for discussion.

Sino–Japanese Relations in the 1970s

Tang Tsou
Tetsuo Najita
and Hideo Otake

I.

The years of 1971–73 will go down in history as a watershed in the development of East Asian politics, if not world politics as a whole. The China and Japan which have emerged in this new power structure stand in sharp contrast in their internal and external orientations. In domestic affairs, the common themes in the history of the two societies have not prevented China and Japan from becoming two important models of national transformation. In foreign affairs, the asymmetry of national powers and international positions is accompanied by a sharp divergence in attitudes and approaches. A fledgling nuclear power with a backward and developing economy confronts the second most economically powerful nation in the non-Communist world whose defense power still remains quite modest in spite of her rapidly increasing defense budget. The relative invulnerability of China with 800 million people in a basically agricultural country of 3.6 million square miles throws into sharp relief the extreme vulnerability of Japan with

Tetsuo Najita and Tang Tsou wish to acknowledge the research support given by the Center for Far Eastern Studies of The University of Chicago. Tang Tsou expresses his appreciation for a research grant from the Joint Committee on Contemporary China of the American Council of Learned Societies and the Social Science Research Council which enabled him to do his part in revising this paper in the Summer of 1975.

her dense concentration of population and industry. Yet prior to the energy crisis, the general view of the specialists was that the economic gap between China and Japan was likely to widen rather than narrow during the rest of the decade. But the energy crisis has forcefully underscored the economic vulnerability of Japan. At the same time, the revised estimates of oil deposits in China have reopened the question of her economic potentials. But the answer must be sought by taking into account future agricultural development, importation of grains, and defense expenditures, as well as the probability of an increased rate of industrial growth following the stepped up importation of modern machinery and plants for use in heavy and chemical industries.

The subjective orientations and objective position of China and Japan in international affairs also stand in sharp contrast. Since the establishment of the People's Republic in October 1949, China has been confronted with a series of crises. Some of these crises have posed a real threat to her national security and others have prevented her from eliminating a rival regime and unifying the country. Yet brought up in adversity, accustomed to failures, inured to dangers, and experienced in achieving political gains with initially meager means in a protracted struggle, the Chinese revolutionary leaders have overcome some of these crises and have succeeded at the very least in maintaining the posture of a confident nation in the ascendancy, in accepting setbacks with equanimity, in making the best of extremely unfavorable international situations, and in adjusting their operational policies to their present capabilities and current reality without forsaking China's national purpose. They take a long view of history in which the ebb and flow of immediate events are passing phenomena. They have formulated a series of positive and negative principles for major areas of foreign policy.[1]

1. These principles are: opposition to hegemony of great powers, condemnation of spheres of interest, denial of any ambition to be a superpower, affirmation of her status as an economically backward country in the Third World, proclamation of support for "all oppressed people and nations" in their opposition to foreign aggression, interference, control, and subversion, the advocacy of the doctrine of self-reliance, the five principles of peaceful coexistence, the eight principles governing foreign aid, the renunciation of the first use of nuclear weapons coupled with the demand for their complete elimination, and the support for a nuclear free zone in Latin America. Flexible in their character and subtle in their implications, they are generally consistent with each other and serve the present interests of the nation without foreclosing future possibilities. They are used to stake out a claim for leadership of the Third World, establish a moral and political position for dealing with the other major powers on a basis of equality, and project an ideal future world order. The development of China's political influence in the Third World would compensate somewhat for her military and economic weakness relative to other great powers.

Defeated in World War II, occupied by the United States and subsequently obliged to enter the cold war on the American side, Japan had practically no alternative other than to support the American position. However, the Japanese government has seldom been an enthusiastic partner in this crusade. This was partly due to its careful cost-benefit calculations, but mainly due to two ideological elements: the strong pacifist-isolationist sentiment among the leaders as well as the masses of the population; and skepticism about the American interpretation of aggressive intentions and military capacity of Asian, and particularly Chinese, communism. Therefore, Japan has refused, as she did during the Vietnam War, to provide direct military aid to Asian governments in their wars against indigenous Communist movements. She also resisted the repeated demands of anti-Communist countries in Asia for international organizations such as the ASPAC or bilateral committees such as the Japan-Taiwan Cooperation Committee to take a more clear-cut position against communism. Furthermore, Japan has kept her military defense capability to a minimum and has resisted the requests by the United States for further rearmament. In other words, Japan has developed her self-defense forces at a minimal level, calculated to maintain American military guarantee and friendship.

Relying on the alliance with the United States, Japan gave first priority to industrial recovery and growth. Thus, Japan actively pursued an "economic diplomacy" in which foreign policies, including political matters, were evaluated in terms of economic advantage. Her leaders have sought to conduct this economic diplomacy within a stable international framework. Therefore, her foreign policy appeared purely pragmatic and often shortsighted, although this policy has actually been closely intertwined with a long-term vision of national economic well-being. As a practical matter, Japanese foreign policy has been one of constant adjustment to the forces of the international economy, as in the quest of raw materials and export markets, which gradually resulted in Japan's economic expansion in various areas of the world, especially in Asia and the United States. In sum, Japan's long-term foreign policy is best not to be seen in political terms—as is the case with China, the United States, or the Soviet Union—but primarily in the light of immediate and future economic needs. If Great Britain acquired her empire in a fit of absent-mindedness, it can be said that Japan became the world's second richest capitalist country and a world power in a period of "benign neglect" of *Realpolitik* and low posture in international affairs.

Despite the recent success in opening a dialogue with the United

States and in establishing formal diplomatic relations with Japan, China still occupies the least favorable position in the maneuverings among the four major powers in the Far East. The Soviet military threat remains. In spite of the Shanghai Communique, the Chou-Tanaka Communique, and Foreign Minister Ohira's statement to the press in Peking, no substantive progress has been made toward the solution of the problem of Taiwan. Indeed, the appointment of Leonard Unger as the new ambassador to Taipei, the American agreement to the establishment of two Chinese Nationalist consulates in Kansas City and Portland, the continued economic vitality of Taiwan, and President Ford's reaffirmation of the American commitment to Taiwan after the collapse of the Thieu regime in South Vietnam have been developments contrary to Peking's expectations.

Japan's national fortune has followed a course totally unforeseeable thirty years ago. As Japan now enters the new era of equal partnership with the United States, however, the past neglect has left a lingering impression to many foreign observers of a Japan without political direction and in search of a role in international affairs which is still to be defined. Japan's strategic insecurity and her dependence on natural resources and markets outside her borders have made her vulnerable to drastic changes in international politics and economic policies whose effect would be immediately felt, as the Yom Kippur War in the Middle East and the Arab oil embargo vividly showed. In comparison with China, the twofold problems confronting Japan are complex in a different way. One problem is to maintain a delicate balance between herself and both China and the Soviet Union, the Arab nations and the United States, and Communist and non-Communist nations in Asia, especially North and South Korea. To achieve an amicable balance, Japan must avoid unilateral provocation and maintain a rational and deliberate posture (sometimes to a fault leading to excessive delays), so as not to jeopardize the fruits of the past and the advantageous position of the present. The other problem is to compete with the large, basically self-sufficient powers, the United States, China, and the Soviet Union. Moreover, Japan's decision-making process is also relatively cumbersome for it involves intense competition among bureaucratic, factional, and partisan groups. Thus, Japan has to learn how to evolve long-range policies in a new era in which her political influence is bound to increase.

The question before us is: given the sharp contrasts in internal and external orientations and the asymmetry in national power and international position, how will Sino-Japanese relations evolve in the remaining years of the 1970s? Would a fledgling nuclear power in pursuit of her national and revolutionary interests blackmail an affluent nation? Or alternatively, would military power always follow economic power? Would political domination inevitably come with economic penetration? Would a fully armed and nuclear Japan achieve hegemony in Asia and threaten the national security of China? In other words, would the present asymmetry in the types of national power be transformed into the hegemony of the one or the other in East Asia? Or would it lead to a shifting and complex equilibrium with the great capability in one sphere canceling out that in another realm and thus facilitating "peaceful coexistence" and further improvement in Sino-Japanese relations? Or would Japan become a neutral nation, forsaking the security treaty with the U.S. and foregoing the American nuclear umbrella? Or would the Sino-Japanese rapprochement soon lead to a tacit alliance or co-hegemony over East and Southeast Asia in opposition to the Soviet Union and in competititon with the U.S.?

II.

In attempting to answer these questions, we shall not follow the usual format of examining scenarios in which certain possibilities may become actualities, and then estimating the likelihood that these conditions will indeed come into existence. Instead, we shall examine only the possibility of intense Sino-Japanese struggle for leadership or hegemony in East Asia. In the context of this examination, our assessment of the other possibilities will become quite obvious. There are three reasons for this heuristic decision. First, Sino-Japanese rivalry for regional leadership is explicitly or implicitly considered by many scholars and influential men of affairs as the crux of the problem. As former Foreign Minister Etsusaburo Shiina, a pro-Taiwan leader of a minor faction in the Liberal-Democratic Party (LDP), noted, "competition (with China) for Asia has already begun."[2]

Second, if this concept is accepted without qualifications, it may become a self-fulfilling prophecy in a relatively short period of time. An unqualified acceptance would lead the political actors to overlook other factors precluding or restraining such a rivalry and to adopt policies which contribute to its rapid intensification. If, however, statesmen self-consciously resist and oppose what may be thought to be one of the many possibilities, or even a highly-probable development, and if scholars carefully and assiduously analyze and direct our attention to the full complexity of the situation, they could, by their

2. Cited in *Japan and East Asia* by Donald Hellman (New York: Praeger, 1972). Hellman's book is built around this notion.

combined efforts, at least delay the actualization of that undesirable tendency and perhaps even prevent it altogether.

Any complex situation contains within itself conflicting tendencies and many possibilities. The highest form of statesmanship consists not of passive acceptance of the undesirable dominant tendency as a historical inevitability, but of creative development of new policies which will strengthen those tendencies leading to a desirable outcome and conducive to the realization of noble visions. In this respect, the task of scholars in the social sciences is not to describe a deterministic universe or to stress the inevitability of a particular outcome, but to facilitate and encourage creative statesmanship. Both statesmen and scholars may fail in the end but they will fail with good conscience.

Finally, the methodological choice of focusing on one major possibility has the advantage of avoiding repetition and redundancy in the discussion of the various aspects of the complex situation and issues which would be unavoidable in a systematic examination of all the possibilities.[3]

Our method of exposition is to begin with the notion of Sino-Japanese rivalry and then to take into account other factors step by step

3. In our analysis, we shall not take into account certain extreme contingencies such as a possible but not highly probable all-out Sino-Soviet war, an unlikely total collapse of the Japanese economy, and the unthinkable consequences of a total change in China's political system. We cannot rule out entirely the possibility of the loss of power by the LDP to a coalition of "progressive" forces which would be preceded by many international and internal upheavals such as a world-wide uncontrollable inflation or depression, a precipitous decline in American influence, a corresponding rise in Soviet and Chinese power, irreconcilable conflict between Japan and the U.S. in the economic sphere, an irreversible process of economic deterioration in Japan, a sharp reduction in the standard of living of the majority of the people, the disintegration of the LDP following unbridgeable factional conflicts, and finally, a resolution of the sharp differences in the orientations of the opposition forces. There will be enough time for us to reassess our perspective should these presently unexpected developments become realistic possibilities.

In the near future, China will be confronted with the problem of political succession. If a collective leadership under Premier Chou En-lai emerges, it will probably press forward the present policies in the direction of rapid increase in Sino-Japanese cooperation in exchange for a common posture toward the Soviet Union, for a loosening of the Taipei-Tokyo ties or for the purpose of accelerating China's industrial economic development. If political leadership passes to the hands of Chiang Ching, Wang Hung-wen, Chang Chun-Chiao, and Yao Wen-yuan, China will probably adopt an even more reserved attitude toward the West, a more revolutionary rhetoric in her announcements, and a more positive policy toward the Third World. But any new leadership must still take into account the constraints imposed by the international power configuration. Given the ignorance of the outside world about China, and the uncertainties confronting the Chinese themselves, it is our view that speculations on the identity of the successors to Chairman Mao or their future policies are less meaningful than an assessment of the broad alternatives available to them, and the impact of the policies of the other powers on the likelihood that one or the other of these options will be chosen.

so as to come to grips with the full complexity of the present situation and puzzling uncertainties. The notion of Sino-Japanese rivalry for leadership or hegemony in East Asia rests on a set of assumptions, leads to a set of policies, and contains a set of implications. It begins with the idea that East Asia forms a regional sub-system with China and Japan as the principal actors. One can follow Donald Hellman and others to use the term "East Asia" to include China, Japan, Korea, Taiwan, and Southeast Asia. As such, this idea is purely descriptive and acceptable. Since China and Japan are neighbors "separated only by a strip of water," they naturally have profound concern with the political posture and military capability of each other. Since they are the two major powers whose territories lie exclusively in East Asia, they are sensitive to the foreign policy orientations and internal political developments in nations in that region, particularly in the buffer zone in the Korean peninsula. A certain amount of conflict and competition is therefore quite natural.

But when the regional approach to Sino-Japanese relations is combined with the old fashioned view of geopolitics and *Realpolitik*, the notion of Sino-Japanese struggle for leadership or hegemony in East Asia emerges. This notion assumes that because of geographic proximity, both China and Japan place the political, military, and economic relations between themselves and with nations in East Asia above those of nations outside the region, and that the importance of their ties with the latter lies primarily in the effects which these have on the developments inside the region.[4] To this assumption is sometimes added two other premises which start from different points of departure, but ultimately reinforce the initial assumption.

For Japan, it is assumed that the promotion of economic interests and relations entails, in the first instance, political influence and ultimately the use of military power to reinforce political influence and economic relations, and that even in the latter part of the twentieth century military power can effectively promote economic interests. For China, it is supposed that the export of revolution can always produce political control over a country which in turn can be used as an instrument to dominate that country's economy and to jeopardize Japan's economic interests. The corollary of these premises is that Japan will adopt a program of massive rearmament sufficient to protect her economic and political interests and to back up its conventional military power with

4. For a perceptive analysis of the relative importance of geographical proximity and other factors such as technology and economic structure, see Charles Wolf, Jr., "International Transactions and Regionalism: Distinguishing 'Insiders' from 'Outsiders' " (Santa Monica, Calif.: Rand Corporation, 1973), p-4922/1.

nuclear weapons. China will push forward her revolutionary program in East Asia and use her political and military power to compensate for her economic weakness while seeking to develop her economy rapidly with the primary purpose of competing with Japan.

III.

While the possibility of Sino-Japanese rivalry for leadership or hegemony in East Asia cannot be ruled out entirely, particularly in the long run, there are several factors which militate against this possibility and which call into question the validity of some of its assumptions. First and most obviously, this analysis does not take sufficiently into account the presence of the United States and the Soviet Union in East Asia and the effects of their presence on Sino-Japanese relations. Despite the total elimination of her influence in Vietnam and Cambodia after the collapse of the Thieu and Lon Nol regimes, the United States remains a Pacific Power—in Korea, in the Philippines and on aircraft carriers on the high seas. Moreover, it is not likely that in the 1970s the Japan–United States Security Treaty will become inoperative or that the United States will abandon her bases in Japan and Okinawa. As of this writing in mid-1975, it looks certain that the U.S. will maintain her commitments to Taiwan during the Ford administration, including formal diplomatic relations and the defense treaty between Washington and Taipei. Unless there is a drastic change in the international configuration of power or in American internal politics, it will be difficult for any government in the remaining years of the 1970s to renounce these American commitments.

Conceivably, the United States can maneuver Japan into a rival position with China, making Sino-Japanese rivalry the main feature in East Asian politics. Indeed, American policies in the past had such an implication. After Dulles became Secretary of State, the United States strongly urged Japan to rearm on a large scale and to participate militarily in regional defense, and demanded the establishment of diplomatic relations between Tokyo and Taipei as a precondition for a mutual security pact. More recently during Nixon's first administration, Secretary of Defense Laird repeatedly urged Japan to step up her effort in rearmament and to play a greater role in East Asia.

Particularly intriguing is the inclusion in the Nixon-Sato Communique of November 1969 of the statement that "the maintenance of peace and security in the Taiwan area is also a most important factor for the security of Japan." It seems that this so-called "Taiwan clause" was proposed by Japan as a concession to the United States in order to facilitate the return of Okinawa to Japanese control. Legally it served the purpose of linking Taiwan to Article VI of the U.S.-Japan Security Treaty. It thus strengthened the legal foundation for the use by American forces of Japanese bases to protect Taiwan in case of a Chinese Communist military attack on that island. But, in retrospect, this statement on Taiwan may have had more profound implications than it appeared on the surface. We now know that within a few weeks after its inauguration, the Nixon administration formulated a new China policy. Kissinger told *Newsweek* recently that "the Chinese knew what we wanted as early as June, 1969."[5] But, at the time, no one could confidently predict the Chinese response to America's initiative.

In this situation, the Taiwan statement had two implications. If a dialogue could not be established and a détente could not be achieved, the Taiwan clause would involve Japan more deeply in the defense of Taiwan. More importantly, it suggested to Peking that the alternative to a détente with the United States would eventually be a Taiwan under the joint guarantee and influence of both Japan and the United States. The latent political influence of Japan among Taiwanese based on past personal, political, educational, and cultural ties and on the present economic interests would be openly, forcefully, and effectively asserted. The geographical propinquity of Taiwan to Japan, some Japanese leaders' fond memory of a Japanese-ruled Taiwan, and the existence of a fairly strong pro-Taiwan group in the LDP would make Japanese influence the predominant one replacing the more remote, less intimate, and less passionate concern of the United States. Once established, the Japanese political influence and military involvement in the defense of Taiwan would become intense, undermining Peking's aim of regaining Taiwan. Peking would therefore view Japan's involvement in the defense of that island as part of a rapid program of large-scale rearmament in Japan. Furthermore, with the Taiwan clause, Japan seemed ready to take a first step from self-defense to regional defense advocated by Dulles many years ago. The prospect before Peking would be rivalry throughout East Asia with a rearmed Japan perhaps with nuclear weapons at a time when she was threatened by the Soviet Union along her northern border and opposed by the U.S. elsewhere.

If this was indeed Peking's perception, it is not unreasonable to believe that the Taiwan clause in the Nixon-Sato Communique gave Peking additional incentive to make the subsequent decision to open a dialogue with the United States. If some sort of understanding with the United States could be reached over the issue of Taiwan, and if a

5. *Newsweek*, July 30, 1973.

détente with the United States could be achieved, the American effort to involve Japan more deeply in the defense of Taiwan would decrease or at least lose its justification in the eyes of the Japanese. Alternatively, Japan would be put in the unenviable position of antagonizing China on the most sensitive issue of Taiwan and acting as a general rival of China while the United States would be backing away from her uncompromising posture.

When the Chinese leaders studied the documents and books published in the United States, they must have come across a signal and an implied threat. In the policy memorandum written by Richard Moorstein and Morton Abramowitz, which proved to be the general blueprint for the Nixon-Kissinger policy toward China, they wrote:

> Time may not be on China's side. Peking's leaders may feel the United States must eventually withdraw and leave Taiwan to its fate, but they also must have deep doubts about a resurgent Japan's growing interest in Taiwan. They have expressed fears that Taiwan would again enter a "Japanese sphere of influence" and about a resurgent Japan's growing interest in Taiwan. Concerned with reducing the likelihood of these eventualities, Peking might respond to partial solutions "in principle" that fell well short of actual reversion of Taiwan to the mainland at an early date or even any fixed date at all.[6]

It is not inconceivable that such a signal and an implied threat were conveyed to the Chinese through the third parties or during Kissinger's secret trip to Peking in July 1971.

Confronted by the prospect created by the Nixon-Sato Communique and subsequently elaborated in American published documents or communications, Peking launched a multi-faceted policy. Premier Chou En-lai's trip to Pyongyang solidified the alliance with North Korea in the face of the common danger presented by the Nixon-Sato Communique. The overthrow of Prince Sihanouk's government in March 1970 enabled Peking to play an active role in bringing about the Summit Conference of the Indochinese Peoples and thus sharply increase her prestige and influence in Indochina. Within Japan, Peking gave verbal support even more unequivocally than before to the opposition parties and the dissident factions within the LDP. She launched an intensive propaganda campaign against the revival of Japanese militarism, which was said to be inevitably linked with the Sato government's intrusion into Taiwan, its commitment to South Korea, and its general ambition in East Asia. It is quite clear to outside observ-

6. *Remaking China Policy*. Cambridge, Mass.: Harvard University Press, 1971, pp. 4–5.

ers that in Peking's propaganda potentiality was described as actuality. But the Chinese themselves were clearly aware of this fact. As Premier Chou En-lai told James Reston in August 1971:

> When you oppose a danger, you should oppose it when it is only budding: Only then can you arouse public attention. Otherwise, if you are to wait until it has already developed into a power, it will be too strenuous.[7]

When stripped of its propagandistic elements, the series of articles and speeches contained an analysis of Japan's foreign policy in the future which was not basically different from the views of a few pro-Taiwan members of the LDP or from some of the scholarly American analyses prior to the Shanghai Communique which saw the inevitability of Japan's rearmament and nuclearization for the purpose of protecting Japan's economic interests and supporting Japan's new role in East Asia.

One other aspect of Peking's policy was to continue to probe America's intention in contacts through third parties leading to Kissinger's secret trip. In this process, Peking's penchant for secrecy served her well. Secrecy prevented the opponents of Sino-American détente from voicing their opposition and organizing themselves into a powerful political force. It also became one of the main elements of Nixon shock. The shock was all the more severe for Japan because it was Washington which had kept Japan from a rapprochement with China and because it was Japan's concession to the United States in the Taiwan clause which triggered Peking's escalated attack on the Sato government and opened up for Japan the prospect of becoming Peking's principal non-Communist enemy.

After Kissinger's visit, it was Japan rather than the United States which bore the brunt of Peking wrath, in so far as the issue of Taiwan and the question of the two Chinas were concerned. Despite the principal role played by the Nixon administration in working out the new two-Chinas formula in the United Nations announced by Secretary of State William Rogers in August 1972, Premier Chou told Reston that "This statement issued by the United States Secretary of State was a self-contradictory formula worked out under the pressure of the talks between the Japanese Government and the Chiang Kai-shek representative in Tokyo." He noted that Japan "has started to harbor ambitions" over Taiwan.[8] Reston was surprised by the "vehemence" of Chinese feeling and impressed by their real worry about Japan.

7. *The New York Times, Report from Red China* (N.Y.: Avon Books, 1971), p. 95.
8. *Ibid.*, pp. 82, 86, 95. A few weeks later, Chou told a group of Chinese visitors that if

Confronted with this severe verbal attack against "Japanese militarism," Japan's leaders denounced it as a misunderstanding of Japan's position in international politics or as a mere propagandist campaign lacking substance. Japanese leaders also regarded this attack as unjustified because it was China, not Japan, which had developed nuclear weapons and maintained massive military forces. The Japanese leaders viewed the Taiwan clause not as evidence of rising Japanese militarism, but as a concession to American pressure. They did not feel Japan had the capacity or intention to defend Taiwan militarily in place of the United States. The memory of World War II and lessons of the Vietnam War confirmed them in their view about the undesirability of direct military involvement in defense of Taiwan.

Thus, after an initial confusion, Japan's leaders accepted the new arrangements worked out by Nixon and Chou and sought to adjust Japan's political and economic policies to the emergent situation. They began to exploit the new opportunities by establishing closer economic relations with non-Communist countries. Prime Minister Sato tried to contact Peking along this policy line, although perhaps not wholeheartedly, but was rebuffed. It appeared that in Peking's judgment Sato would soon resign and it would be more advantageous to wait for the next Prime Minister.

Prime Minister Tanaka's visit to China and Premier Chou En-lai's conciliatory policy succeeded in averting the potential if not the actual danger that Sino-Japanese confrontation over Taiwan and general rivalry in Asia would become the main axis of East Asian politics—a rivalry which would seriously jeopardize the internal development and foreign relations of both nations. They gave China and Japan a period of time to work out a relationship on a different basis. The summit meeting solemnized a genuine compromise and mutual concession which produced no victory or defeat for either party. The establishment of a new relationship defused the issues of the revival of Japanese militarism and the U.S.-Japan security treaty.[9]

---

the U.S. withdraws from Taiwan and Japan steps in, China would be ready to go to war with Japan.

9. According to Takeo Kimura, Premier Chou told him that "Japan forms a country, armaments for self-defense are necessary . . . this is a matter to be decided by the Japanese people and is not a matter in which another country should interfere." *Asahi*, 27 January 1973. See also *Nihon Keizai*, 26 January 1973. *Asahi*, 18 January 1973.

Liao Cheng-chih, the principal executor of China's policy toward Japan, said: "I cannot support the U.S.-Japan Security Treaty structure but its functions directed toward China have already lost substance, and we will not take particular issue with it at this late date. As a practical question, Japan will probably have to rely on America's nuclear umbrella for some time to come. . . ." *Yomiuri*, 12 March 1973.

After his trip to China, Prime Minister Tanaka found it possible to push forward the

At the present moment, a complex triangular relationship rather than Sino-Japanese rivalry is the principal fact insofar as the United States, China, and Japan are concerned. This pattern will most likely persist in the rest of the decade. By this brilliant diplomacy from November 1969 to September 1972, Premier Chou succeeded in averting the most threatening prospect of a confrontation with a rearmed Japan entrenched in Taiwan and backed by the United States equally committed to the defense of Taiwan and to limiting China's influence in East Asia. But in the new triangular relationship which now exists, China remains in an uncomfortable position. While China's relations with both have been put on an entirely different basis from that existing before 1972, she is still confronted with two allies who are learning to work closely together and enjoy intimate political, cultural, and economic relationships. The crucial issue of Taiwan which we shall discuss in greater detail in a different context has proved to be difficult to resolve. Peking is likely to pursue a policy of alternately improving her relationship with one of the two allies as a lever or inducement to move the other in the same direction. The contrast between Japan's willingness to reaffirm the principle of one China in signing the Sino-Japanese agreement on aviation in April 1974 and America's moves in bolstering the diplomatic and consular ties with Taiwan has been followed by a marked increase in the warmth of Sino-Japanese relations coupled with a visible cooling off in the Chinese attitude toward the U.S. This change in attitude may have reflected a decision to place Sino-Japanese cooperation ahead of further rapprochement with the U.S. in Peking's scheme of priorities. President Ford's reaffirmation of American commitment to Taiwan on 6 May 1975 could only reinforce this decision.

In the long run, Japan occupies the most favorable position in this triangular relationship on the condition that she takes a position on Taiwan more favorable to Peking than the United States now takes. Maintaining such a position would alleviate the fears of those Japanese leaders that the American nuclear umbrella as a protection against China might become unreliable in the distant future, or that the United States would use it as a bargaining counter in negotiations over serious economic issues which could not be settled in purely economic terms on their merits. It would be a less costly alternative to large-scale rearmament and nuclearization which could not be undertaken without precipitating serious political conflicts in Japan and unpredictable reper-

---

Fourth Defense Plan. Ambassador Ingersoll was reported to have said on 5 January 1973 that "the United States is not urging Japan to play a military role beyond the defense of its own country with conventional weapons." This statement was very different in spirit from the Nixon-Sato Communique of November 1969.

cussions elsewhere. Positively, it would give Japan room to maneuver in her relations with China during a period when Japan is redefining her role in Asia and in the world.

IV.

Sino-Japanese relations form one side of the triangular relationship not only among the United States, China, and Japan but also among the Soviet Union, China, and Japan. In both triangular relationships, China's ultimate fears and hopes are presently riveted on her relations with the other powers rather than on her relations with Japan. From China's point of view, it is her relations with the Soviet Union and the United States which constitute the most significant factors shaping her foreign policies, while her relations with Japan are viewed in terms of their effects on her relations with the two superpowers. For Japan, there is scarcely any doubt that American-Japanese relations are accorded the highest priority in her foreign policy, while her relations with China and the Soviet Union are in a state of flux. To a very large extent, Sino-American and Sino-Soviet relations will in the near future shape Sino-Japanese relations rather than the other way around, although China presumably hopes that in the long run greatly improved Sino-Japanese relations amounting to a tacit alliance will reinforce the rapidly developing national power of China to bring about progressive shifts in the relative power balance between China and the two superpowers. The neglect of the role of the Soviet Union in East Asia is another omission which vitiates the analysis and projection based on Sino-Japanese rivalry as the main feature in East Asia.

From China's point of view, the primary fact in East Asian politics and even world politics is the military threat from the Soviet Union and Soviet attempts to contain China. It is this perception which persuaded Peking to change her policy toward Washington and which was partly responsible for her conciliatory policy toward Japan. Chairman Mao Tse-tung's New Year's instruction in 1973: "dig tunnels deep, store grains everywhere and never seek hegemony" was obviously issued with the Soviet military threat in mind. Premier Chou En-lai in his political report to the Tenth Party Congress in August 1973 told the Chinese to be fully prepared "particularly against surprise attack on our country by Soviet revisionist social-imperialism."

Given the military capability of the Soviet Union in both conventional and nuclear weapons, her readiness to use military power in Czechoslovakia in 1968, and her theory of "limited sovereignty," the Chinese fear of the Soviet Union appears to be well-grounded in reality.

But even if a Soviet attack does not come, the disposition of Soviet forces along the Chinese border and the rumors and veiled threats of a Soviet attack serve many purposes. It has been our judgment since 1966 that one of the immediate and primary purposes of Soviet troop disposition and military threats has been to influence the struggle for power in China and thus her long-term political development and foreign policy orientations. The military disposition along the Chinese border also reduces Peking's political influence and international prestige. The re-entry of the Soviet Union under Khrushchev's successors into the Vietnam tangle was merely the beginning of the intensification of Soviet efforts to contain China. The North Vietnamese-Vietcong offensive in early 1972 was made possible by the Soviet supply of sophisticated weapons rather than by China's encouragement or perhaps even in spite of Peking's advice. The Soviet-Indian treaty of 1971 was a decisive stroke of Soviet diplomacy which turned the balance of power in South Asia sharply in favor of the Soviet Union and drastically against the Chinese. Brezhnev's proposal for an Asian collective security system is recognized by Peking as a move to check Chinese influence. The victory of the Vietcong and the North Vietnamese has been followed by rumors of an intensified Sino-Soviet maneuver for influence in South Vietnam. In the rest of the decade, Peking must continue to give first priority to this military-political threat. She is also likely to view Sino-Japanese and Japanese-Soviet relations in terms of their impact on the Sino-Soviet conflict.

For the Soviet Union, it is to her advantage to enlist Japan as her junior partner in her conflict with China, to make Japan the primary target of Chinese hostility, and to dissipate Japan's political energy and resource in an artificially-created conflict with China—a role for Japan analogous to that envisaged by Dulles in the context of Sino-American conflict in the 1950s. In addition to its economic motive, the Soviet invitation to Japan for joint development of oil and other resources in Siberia was a political move to use economic inducements to complicate Sino-Japanese economic and political relations. According to Kunio Muraoka, the supply from Tyumen would at most be only about eight percent of the Japanese oil import in 1980.[10] But the strategic significance of a pipeline along the Chinese border or a new trans-Siberia railroad some distance to the north of the existing one was not lost on China.[11] Even if Japan's dependence on Soviet oil and gas sup-

10. *Japanese Security and the United States* (Adelphi Paper, no. 95), p. 13.

11. Liao Cheng-chih frankly told his Japanese audience that "if thought is given to the fact that oil pipeline from Tyumen Oil Fields will mean the supplying of fuel to the Soviet Forces aircraft and tanks to invade China, considerable measures to counter this

ply is small, the Soviet Union would use whatever leverage she gains in her dealing with Japan. The rapid development of economic relations between Japan and the Soviet Union would disrupt Japan's policy of maintaining "equal distance" between the Soviet Union and China.[12]

The political implication of this joint enterprise would not be dissimilar to the Nixon-Sato Communique of 1969. If China should react in the same fashion toward Japan as it did from November 1969 to early 1972, serious misunderstanding would develop between the two nations. Only this time it would be much more difficult to remove this misunderstanding by another summit conference. If this misunderstanding continued to develop and deepen, the Soviet Union would succeed in her first step in promoting Sino-Japanese rivalry, turning Japan into a junior partner in the Sino-Japanese conflict. Moreover, a cooperative Japanese-Soviet economic relationship, when combined with Sino-Japanese misunderstanding, would hinder any further development in the Sino-American détente. The astute Soviet experts on the United States who showed their astounding shrewdness in engineering the profitable grain deals are certainly not unaware of the fact that a large body of American experts and officials firmly believed that the United States should not move ahead of Japan in cultivating good relations with China. Thus, Japan is the key to the Soviet policy of isolating China in East Asia. If this diplomatic maneuver were to be successfully accomplished, the Soviet Union would have solved her "China problem" and could turn her attention and shift her resources to other parts of the world. When confronted with the prospect of Soviet-Japanese-American "collusion" against China, Peking might find it necessary to make the best possible deal with the Soviet Union and the Soviet Union would again move to the middle position where it could exploit the Sino-American impasse over the Taiwan issue and China's traditional fear of Japan.[13] The Japanese government is quite conscious of the political and military implications of the joint development of Siberia for China and the United States. Japanese leaders also fear "possible arbitrary actions by the Russians such as violating contracts, not paying agreed prices, and excluding the Japanese from

---

must be taken, and Japan must keep clearly in mind that we will harbor 'bitter feeling' toward Japan too." *Yomiuri*, 12 March 1973.

12. This point was brilliantly argued by Professor Kinhide Mushakoji in his article in *Asahi Journal*, 20 April 1973.

13. Senator Barry Goldwater declared on the Senate floor on 3 June 1975: "Communist China has done something that Europe has failed to do: namely, obtained the military respect if not fear on the part of the U.S.S.R. It is in our national interest in the foreseeable future that China remain a counterbalancing force." He expressed his concern that after

sufficient inspecting facilities on joint projects."[14] Japan feels particularly vulnerable to these violations because she has few countermeasures to take. Thus, Japan wants the United States to join some of the more important projects in part to mitigate Chinese protest and also to avoid the danger of being maneuvered by the Soviet Union in its conflict with China. Furthermore, since Japan does not wish to be overly dependent on the Soviet Union for raw materials, she is trying to diversify her suppliers of raw materials by embarking in joint ventures in South America, Canada, the Near East, Africa, Australia, Southeast Asia, and China. The Sino-Soviet conflict, however, has placed Japan in a strategically favorable position. Given the Sino-Soviet rivalry, Japan does not fear the excessive pressure of either China or the Soviet Union or both powers in an anti-Japanese alliance. Thus, just as China seeks benefits from both Japan and the United States to counterbalance Soviet moves, Japan pursues a policy of deriving advantages from both China and the Soviet Union, establishing closer relations to both without antagonizing either.

In any event, a protocol was signed on 22 April 1974 governing the conditions of a loan of $1 billion from the Export-Import Bank of Japan to the Soviet Union to finance three projects involving the development of coal, gas, and forestry resources in Siberia. While a subsequent general agreement on the coal project was signed in accordance with the protocol, the gas project has not made much progress because it is conditioned on American participation which is not forthcoming. The joint project to develop oil fields in Tyumen encountered even more serious obstacles. It is subsequently known that in April 1973 China contracted with Japan's International Oil Trading Company to deliver one million tons of high grade, low sulphur crude oil through December 31, 1973, at the low price of about $3.75 a barrel and without any other conditions.[15] In July, the Chinese government was reported to have promised to export to Japan 10 percent of the total oil produced in China. In 1974, 4 million tons were exported to Japan. In 1974, crude oil production in China was estimated at 65.3 million tons, an increase of 20 percent in one year. In October 1974 a tentative agreement was made for the export of a minimum of 8 million for 1975.[16] By one

---

Mao's death a pro-Soviet faction could take power in China and that if the Sino-Soviet alliance should be revived, "this would represent the first—I repeat, the first—unbeatable alliance yet seen on this planet." *Congressional Record*, 94th Congress, 1st session, Vol. 121, no. 85, (3 June 1975), p. 2.

14. F. C. Langdon, *Japan's Foreign Policy*, p. 178.

15. *The New York Times*, May 12, 1975. Recently the Japanese complain of the high wax content of the Chinese crude oil

16. Joint Economic Committee, *China: A Reassessment of the Economy*, 94th Congress, 1st Session (10 July 1975), pp. 5, 240.

Japanese estimate which is probably too high, China will produce 400 million tons of oil by 1980 and can be expected to export at least 40 million tons to Japan. According to a most recent American estimate, China total oil production by 1980 will be more than 200 million tons a year of which approximately 50 million tons may be exported. By making slight adjustments in consumption or output growth the Chinese could raise the surplus to 65 million tons.[17] By comparison, the expected amount of crude oil import from the Soviet Union to Japan will, at best, be 25 to 40 million tons a year in 1980. But the availability of oil from the Soviet Union would be conditioned on a huge loan from Japan to finance the Siberian oil project which would also have serious military and diplomatic implications. As of this writing, Japan has decided to hold off on the Siberian project partly and perhaps largely because of the prospect of buying China's oil without the diplomatic and financial risks inherent in the Siberian venture.

While she was fending off the Soviet maneuver to bind Japan hand and foot with economic ties, Peking was planning a diplomatic countermeasure of her own to frustrate the Soviet policy of establishing an "Asian Collective Security System" to contain China. From the very beginning, when it made its first formal appearance in the Shanghai Communique issued by the Chinese and American governments on February 27, 1975, the principle of opposition to efforts by any country or group of countries to establish "hegemony in the Asian-Pacific region" was unmistakably aimed by the Chinese at the Soviet Union.[18] Identical wordings were included in Point 7 of the Joint Statement signed by Chou En-lai and Kakuei Tanaka in Peking on September 29, 1972,[19] although the implicit meaning attributed to it by the Chinese was partially balanced by the sentence preceding it to the effect that "the normalization of relations between China and Japan is not directed against third countries." In the negotiations on a treaty of peace and friendship which was envisaged in Point 8 of the joint statement, Peking has insisted on a clause opposing "hegemony" by any power in Asia, arguing that the two nations must further develop their relations on the basis of the joint statement rather than retreat from it. The Miki government has so far refused to include such a clause. As of this writing, no progress has been made on this issue. Hence, Sino-Soviet relations have continued to influence the development of Sino-Japanese relations for better or for worse as our analysis suggests.

17. *Ibid.*, pp. 5, 247. In late summer and early autumn of 1975, there were reports that the Chinese were planning to slow down the growth rate of oil production.

18. *Peking Review*, 3 March 1972, p. 5.

19. The sentence reads: "Neither of the two countries should seek hegemony in the Asian-Pacific region and each country is opposed to efforts by any country or countries to establish such hegemony." *Peking Review*, 6 October 1972, p. 13.

V.

Up to this point, we have suggested that the presence of the United States and the Soviet Union in East Asia has resulted in two triangular relationships, and that Sino-Japanese relations constitute a subordinate rather than the dominant side of these triangles and can be understood only in these contexts. These two triangular relationships with Sino-Japanese relations as a common base add up to a quadrilateral relationship in which the four sides are considered to be more important than the common base and have greater actual or potential influence in shaping the common base than the other way around. But the controlling relationship in this quadrille remains that between the two superpowers, who alone possess the full panoply of military, economic, and political powers. Thus, militarily and in terms of its dominant political relationship, the world is still basically bipolar although other relationships are assuming greater importance as time moves on. The impact of this global system on the regional system has been obvious although the regional system also reacts on the global system. The American endeavor to open a dialogue with China has been interpreted as an attempt to bring China into the scale in order to redress the political balance which was in danger of shifting more and more in favor of the Soviet Union. It has also been interpreted as a move which was designed to make the Soviet Union more amenable to the U.S. overture to negotiate various issues. Whether or not these interpretations are correct, it is clear that America's new China policy was directed not to China alone but represented a move on the chessboard of the global game of power politics. In order to preserve America's favorable position in this quadrilateral relation, any move toward a greater understanding with the Soviet Union must be accompanied and reinsured by some movement in improving Sino-American relations.

The global system will also influence the development of the regional system in another way. It tends to dilute the intra-regional relationships. As neither Japan nor China is purely a regional power but becomes increasingly involved in global affairs, extra-regional relationships will be more important than Sino-Japanese rivalry in East Asia. This is particularly the case with Japan whose economic interests are primarily global rather than regional. What happens in the United States, the Middle East, and Western Europe more directly concerns Japan than economic and political development in East Asia. In this regard, China's increasing interest in the Third World with which she identifies herself will also not jeoparadize the improvement of Sino-Japanese relations. For example, China's activities in Tanzania and Zambia have absorbed a proportionately large share of China's attention and foreign aid and have had no obvious adverse effects on Japan's position.

Given the Soviet military-political threat, China has a common interest with the U.S. in opposing the expansion of Soviet influence in every part of the world. But unless the U.S. could agree to a resolution of the Taiwan issue satisfactory to Peking, there is a limit to Sino-American rapprochement and cooperation. Hence, Peking's policies toward the U.S. have been extremely ambivalent and have moved on several levels. On the one hand, Peking welcomes the maintenance of American military strength in Western Europe and explicitly acquiesces in the U.S.-Japan Security Threaty. On the other hand, she vehemently attacks both the superpowers while endeavoring to bolster the position and influence of the Third World of developing countries and the Second World of developed nations. Peking envisages a global configuration of power in which the Third and Second Worlds would take advantage of the American-Soviet contradictions and stalemate to effectively restrain the two superpowers. This global vision implies that China will attribute greater value to Sino-Japanese than to Sino-American cooperation and trade—so long as the U.S. maintains her commitment to defend Taiwan. She hopes that Sino-Japanese cooperation will become the main feature in East Asian politics, and one of the main factors leading to a change in American policy toward Taiwan.

VI.

So far we have outlined the existing and potential structure of relations in East Asia and the world at large which may affect the development of Sino-Japanese relations. We have concluded that intensive Sino-Japanese rivalry is not likely to be the main feature of East Asian regional politics. But there are several issues between China and Japan which must also be briefly examined. One is the generalized fear that the two contrastive political systems may not find it easy to coexist peacefully. This generalized fear finds expression first in the specific complaints and anxiety on the part of Japan that China has in the past tried to interfere in Japan's internal politics and to influence Japan's foreign policy by supporting the position of the opposition parties. Some Japanese leaders share a vague fear of a communist revolution in Japan supported by foreign communist regimes. The possibility that China would support a revolution led by JCP seems quite remote to most observers, particularly in view of the strained relationship between the CCP and the JCP. But the growing strength of the JCP in the general elections and the unpredictability of actions of either party remind conservative Japanese leaders of the possibility of this so-called "indirect invasion." On her part, China considered the peace treaty and the establishment of diplomatic relations between Japan and Taiwan as a case of even more flagrant interference in the internal affairs of China.

As an understanding was being reached over the question of Taiwan at the summit meeting, the Chinese gave verbal assurances not to interfere in Japan's internal affairs. According to Prime Minister Tanaka, the following exchange took place: "We said (to the Chinese side): 'we ask you not to interfere in our internal affairs. We ask you not to join hands with the JCP.' In response to this the Chinese side said: 'We will not interfere in the internal affairs of Japan. We will not export revolution, and even if we tried to, it cannot be exported.' "[20] But this affirmation of non-interference does not include the cessation of criticism of the JCP. Liao Cheng-chih told the Yomiuri Newspaper Reporters Mission that "our dear Mr. Kenji Miyamoto says that China's criticizing the Japanese Communist Party is interference in internal affairs, but we will do this to the last. . . ."[21]

After Prime Minister Tanaka's visit to China, the Chinese became quite circumspect even in their private remarks. According to Takeo Kimura, Premier Chou used such careful expression regarding Japan's domestic questions as "I hope that you will listen to my statements as a mere reference, as they may become intervention in domestic affairs."[22]

In the future, China may well continue to attempt to cultivate Japanese opinions in all circles in order to influence Japan's foreign policy. Indeed, this is one of Peking's most effective measures which she can use to compensate for her lack of economic power and generally unfavorable position in the quadrilateral relations. Shortly after the Chou-Tanaka meeting, *Jen-min jih-pao* published a summary account of the past efforts of Japanese leaders to achieve normalization of Sino-Japanese relations. It concluded with the following words: "The Chinese people will never forget the numerous Japanese friends who have paved the way for Sino-Japanese friendship and the restoration of diplomatic relations between China and Japan. . . . Of course difficulties of one kind or another will arise in future contacts after the restoration of diplomatic relations, but we are convinced that through the common efforts of the Chinese and Japanese peoples, all difficulties will surely be surmounted and new progress made."[23] Thus, the issue

20. *Asahi*, 1 October 1972.
21. *Yomiuri*, 12 March 1973.
22. *Asahi*, (Evening ed.) 18 January 1973.
23. *Jen-min jih-pao*, 6 October 1972, p. 4, translated in *Peking Review*, 13 October 1972, p. 18.

of interference on each other's internal affairs has been defused although it may well be revived if the question of Taiwan remains insoluble and comes to a head again. As for Chinese intervention in the internal power structures in Japan, namely Chinese support for a Japanese revolutionary movement, the possibility seems negligible due to the relative internal stability of Japan, the strained relationship between the JCP and CCP, and the Chinese principle of "self-reliance" on the part of revolutionary forces.

The other issue which can cause complications in Sino-Japanese relations is competition in Southeast Asia and in the Third World as a whole for economic and political influence—a point which is frequently stressed by the forecasters of intense Sino-Japanese rivalry in East Asia. Insofar as Southeast Asia is concerned, Indonesia, which is an important source of supply of oil for Japan, falls into a separate category. At the moment, Peking's political and economic influence there is almost nil. Without a navy of surface ships and transports, China poses no threat and can exert no military pressure. Insofar as China's military threat and pressure are concerned, the situation regarding the Philippines is not too different. This will remain so for many years to come. As for economic competition elsewhere in East Asia and the underdeveloped world, certain ground rules or understandings seem to have been reached as a result of the summit meeting. As Nakasone said after his meeting with Chou En-lai, China would give economic aid to underdeveloped countries but stress would be laid on agriculture and light industries while Japanese aid would be centered on heavy industrial materials. The conclusion is that "Japan and China will not come into conflict."[24] But China also recognized that China and Japan follow two different methods of managing two different social systems. In addition, one rests on vastly superior economic power and technology while the other on political skills and experience. Each has its own strengths and weaknesses. Chou told Kimura, "if Japan is to pursue profits too intensively, this will lead to 'exploitation' and cause revulsion among peoples in these areas . . . (while laughing). If this is to happen, this will be what China is waiting for."[25] Kimura reported that "Chou even went so far as to give me advice, saying . . . . that it may be good for Japan also, if Japan carries out its economic policy, based on reciprocity and equality."[26] Many Japanese scholars came to similar conclusions some time ago.[27]

24. *Yomiuri*, 19 January 1973.
25. *Asahi*, 18 January 1973.
26. *Toyo Keizai*, 17 February 1973.
27. For example, Professor Shinkichi Eto suggested that "we should radically restudy

To Kimura, Chou described China's aid policy in the following terms: "China first makes what the other side needs, also China educates local persons; and when they master the professions they are engaging in, China leaves them in their countries for the benefit of their countries." Like many other domestic and foreign policies of China, this idealistic policy rests squarely on realistic economic and political calculations. Given her low level of economic and technological development, China cannot compete successfully with Japan or other economically advanced nations on purely economic and technical terms for markets, resources, and political influence in underdeveloped areas. By setting up a few demonstration aid projects in selected areas with unusually favorable terms, Peking established a standard of comparison which puts economic activities and aid of other nations in unfavorable lights. These examples would be welcomed by the developing countries as a leverage for gaining better terms from developed countries, if not for their intrinsic economic importance. They will bolster Peking's political influence and claim for leadership in the Third World. They can be used to induce a sense of dissatisfaction against the economic activities and aid programs of the advanced nations.

If the people in a developing country should desire to assert their economic independence and to use their political power against the established economic interests of foreign powers in their country, the traditional methods of "gunboat diplomacy" or even large-scale military action no longer seem to be an adequate remedy in an age of rising nationalism and guerrilla warfare, if there is a strong and farsighted political leadership supported by a fully mobilized and organized population. The same conclusion regarding the impotence of military power also applies to indigenous revolution with a popular base. The only alternative is for the advanced nations to pursue a policy of economic strangulation and a political policy of manipulating the demands and preferences of specific political and social groups. Thus, the competition between China and Japan in East Asia and the Third World in general will not take on a military dimension but will be conducted in primarily economic and political terms—which may not be entirely unhealthy for these two competitors or for the underdeveloped nations concerned.

---

and reform our economic and cultural cooperation policies." *Jiyu*, May 1972. Kunio Maraoka wrote that "aid to Southeast Asia must be carried out so that the advancement of Japanese commercial interest is kept to the minimum" and expressed the hope that "economic cooperation would become an inherent component of Japan's security policy." *Japanese Security and the U.S.* (Adelphi Papers, no. 95) p. 32.

Korea is another potential area of conflict between China and Japan. But as a buffer zone between the two countries, China and Japan's assessment of the importance of Korea and their policies are also affected by their overall diplomatic postures toward each other. This point is brought out clearly by the events since the Nixon-Sato Communique. From the Korean War to 1969, Peking looked at the Korean peninsula largely from the viewpoint of political and military confrontation with the United States. As a result of the Sino-Soviet conflict and the ambiguous position taken by North Korea in this dispute, Peking-Pyongyang relations were for a number of years less than intimate. The Nixon-Sato Communique which opened up the prospect of a Japanese-dominated Taiwan and South Korea brought about a dramatic closing of ranks between Peking and Pyongyang against Japan as well as against the United States. The immediate endorsement by Peking in the editorial of *Jen-min jih-pao* on 15 April 1971 of DPRK's policy of "independent unification of the Fatherland" suggested the close coordination between the two nations.[28] In retrospect, one can even see certain parallels between the aims, strategies, and tactics of Peking's policy toward Taiwan on the one hand and those of Pyongyang's policy toward South Korea on the other. Both called for "peaceful unification," contacts, and negotiation between the parties of a divided nation, and withdrawal of American forces from the territories concerned. Ultimately, both wanted the United States to terminate the defense commitments. Both attacked Japanese imperialism and militarism. Peking demanded the abolition of the Tokyo-Taipei peace treaty; and Pyongyang, the Japan-ROK treaty.

A more interesting but more speculative point emerges if one ponders upon these parallelisms in the light of the history of the Korean War. The most intriguing fact about the Korean War is the timing of the invasion of South Korea—the fact that it was launched before Peking could complete the elimination of the Chiang regime on Taiwan. This crucial decision, which in the opinion of many scholars was made by Stalin, led through a chain of events to the *de facto* separation of Taiwan from China which threatened to become a permanent situation. Even if one accepts the view of other scholars that Pyongyang jumped the gun and advanced the date of invasion without Stalin's consent or even knowledge,[29] the Soviet Union must, from Peking's viewpoint, be held responsible for all the adverse consequences because of the com-

28. See the translation "Korean People's Struggle for Unification of Fatherland Will Win," *Peking Review*, 23 April 1971, pp. 11–12.

29. This interpretation is effectively developed by Robert R. Simmons in his excellent book, *The Strained Alliance*, New York: The Free Press, 1975.

manding role of the Soviet Union in planning the Korean War, her control over supplies, and her lack of vigilance in keeping a watch on the Korean armed forces.

In any event, the tremendous sacrifice and risks incurred by Peking in the Korean War helped save North Korea but jeopardized China's most important interest. While North Korea became a drain on Peking's resources, she could not be considered a loyal friend of China in the Sino-Soviet dispute. The Chinese have constantly endeavored to learn from past experience and seldom made the same mistake twice. Now with full control over her own policies, Peking is not likely to schedule any move on the unification of Korea ahead of the unification of China, or to place some broadly defined and long-term Chinese interests in a unified Korea ahead of her determination to unify her own country so long as this latter objective is not utterly impossible to achieve. Peking's endorsement of Pyongyang's policy of peaceful unification and the parallelisms in the two nations' policies toward unification constitute an indication of the sense of priority in Peking, although they are also rooted in other obvious military and political considerations. For Peking, they rule out the use of force in the Korean peninsula at least for an undefined period of time. Peking is certainly not unaware of the fact that peaceful unification between the two relatively equal parties is much more difficult to achieve than between China and Taiwan, not to mention the strong American military presence and Japan's greater concern over South Korea. So long as China's peaceful unification has not been achieved it is improbable that Peking would make any move to support North Korea in achieving unification which will again jeopardize the return to Taiwan. The only proviso to this guess is that neither the North nor the South Korean regime would collapse and no viable successor regime could be established to maintain the present stability in the Korean peninsula. This line of analysis developed by us in the summer of 1973 has been confirmed by the events after the collapse of the Thieu regime. In the joint communique issued on 26 April 1975 at the end of Kim I Sung's visit to Peking, the Chinese government "reaffirms its resolute support to the Korean people in their just struggle for the independent and *peaceful* unification of their fatherland."[30] By implication, Peking again ruled out the use of force to unify Korea, at least for the time being.

In contrast to the relationship between China and North Korea, Japanese-South Korean relations since 1965 have been largely

30. *Peking Review*, 2 May 1975, p. 9. Italics added. See also Vice Premier Teng Hsiao-ping's speech, *ibid.*, p. 12. For the analysis of Chinese policy by the American Government, see *The New York Times*, 29 April, 29 May, and 15 June 1975.

economic. At least, most Japanese leaders have defined them as such. The policy orientation which we previously identified in the general discussion of Japanese foreign policy governs Japanese policy in South Korea. That is, Japan depends on the American guarantee for Korean security, which most Japanese leaders agree is essential to Japanese security. Despite repeated demands by the United States, Japan has been hesitant to commit herself to military cooperation with South Korean armies. However, Japan accepted the burden of helping to modernize South Korean military forces by supplying plants of heavy industries as aid, partly because it would provide Japan with the opportunity to increase her economic interest in the long run. At the same time, Japan sought to balance this industrial aid to South Korea by establishing an unofficial trade agreement with North Korea in early 1972. Again, we encounter a basic trend of thought in Japanese leaders, namely, the best strategy toward the Communist regime is to increase trade with them, because Asian communism derives much of its appeal and strength from nationalistic aspiration to be powerful and prosperous. Helping them in their nation-building through trade, it is believed, would decrease their belligerent posture toward Japan. At the present time, many Japanese leaders seem to feel that although the communization of South Korea might threaten Japan's security, Japan should not go beyond allowing American forces the use of their base in Japan in accordance with the Mutual Security Treaty. Other Japanese leaders would support the following analysis by Kunio Maraoka which would put an even narrower limit to Japan's action.

"At the moment any prospect of direct military participation by Japan in the peninsula is counter-productive; in Japan there will be no political consensus for it, and in Korea it will be unacceptable because of the past memory of Japanese rule. Moreover, a force hostile to South Korea is not necessarily hostile to Japan. Therefore, allowing the United States to use Japanese bases in such contigency (which the government would be inclined to do) would not meet the full support of the nation. Hence, any military cooperation with Korea would be deeply divisive in Japan, and would never become a possibility."[31] Whether this relaxed attitude toward South Korea can survive the reexamination of foreign and military policies in Japan after the fall of South Vietnam remains to be seen.

VII.

With the possible exception of some Japanese-Soviet deals which would weaken China's defensive position, Taiwan is potentially the

31. Kunio Maraoka, *op. cit.*, p. 22.

single most important issue which can disrupt the ongoing Sino-Japanese rapprochement and turn it into Sino-Japanese antagonism and rivalry in East Asia. It is recognized by many observers that China showed intense interest in effecting a rapprochement with Japan as soon as possible once the Tanaka cabinet was formed. Peking apparently expected that Japan would adopt a public position on Taiwan which would go far beyond the Shanghai Communique and thus lead eventually to further changes in America's commitment to that island.[32] Peking also hoped no doubt that as a consequence of this public position Japan would follow a set of policies which would further weaken her various ties to Taiwan and facilitate the process of peaceful unification. For these reasons, China made significant concessions to Japan. She voluntarily renounced her demand for indemnities, although her bargaining position on this point was weakened by Taipei's waiver of similar claims in the Tokyo-Taipei peace treaty. She tacitly recognized the continuance of trade and economic relations between Japan and Taiwan. She gave assurance over non-interference in Japan's internal politics. She showed understanding of Japan's annoyance over Chinese analyses of Japanese militarism. She did not take serious issue with Japan's self-defense power and the U.S.-Japan security treaty. Chairman Mao personally accepted Prime Minister Tanaka's explanation of his phrase "cause trouble" in the latter's statement of apology for the damage done to China in all the years of Japanese aggression and war.[33] The Chinese negotiators came up with a formula to resolve a terminological impasse by a decision to express "politically" the termination of the state of war in the Preamble and to use the expression "the abnormal state of affairs" in Paragraph One.[34] The only major point on which she insisted was the clause regarding the status of Taiwan in the Joint Communique and the sentence concerning the termination of the Tokyo-Taipei peace treaty in Foreign Minister Ohira's statement in his press conference in Peking.

But the agreement on the Taiwan issue is so vague and general that divergent interpretations of the understanding are bound to arise. The only unambiguous result was the establishment of diplomatic relationship between Peking and Tokyo and the termination of diplomatic relations and the peace treaty between Tokyo and Taipei. Even Paragraph Three in the Joint Communique on the issue of Taiwan[35] can be

32. For example, Mr. Saeki in *Toki No Ugoki*, 1 November 1972.

33. Prime Minister Tanaka's report to the LDP General Assembly of members of both houses, *Asahi*, 1 October 1972.

34. Foreign Minister Ohira's remark, as reported in *Tokyo Shimbun*, 1 October 1972. He commented that "the other side was taking a more forward-looking position than I had imagined."

35. This paragraph reads: "The Government of the People's Republic of China

given an interpretation which minimizes its significance. For example, Foreign Minister Ohira stated: "Japan actually has not said that Taiwan is a territory of the People's Republic of China. We are only saying that it is a territory which ought to belong to China. There is no difference at all from the past, and it is nothing more than shifting diplomatic relations to Peking."[36] He affirmed that "we will not assist the independence movement in Taiwan or have ambitions toward Taiwan." This was a significant concession to Peking but there is nothing to prevent various private groups from supporting the independence movement just as they did in the past.

One of the questions which will assume crucial importance as time goes on is the applicability of Article Six of the U.S.-Japan Security Treaty (the "Far Eastern Clause") to Taiwan and the status of the "Taiwan clause" of the Nixon-Sato Joint Communique of November 1969. Immediately after his return from Peking, Foreign Minister Ohira was asked: "Would it be all right to leave the Taiwan clause of the Nixon-Sato Joint Communique of 1969 as it is now?" Ohira's answer was: "It is quite all right. Relations between Japan and China were normalized with the U.S.-Japan Security Treaty structure as it is. If it had not been all right (for the Chinese side), the Joint Communique could not have been drawn up."[37] He was also reported as having said: "We attended the negotiations with the standpoint of not impairing U.S.-Japan relations."[38] On the same subject, Prime Minister Tanaka stated: "The U.S. stands on the premise that China will not resort to armed force against Taiwan. . . . Such a situation (as the involving of the U.S.-Japan treaty) can be avoided; there is no possibility of such a situation arising."[39]

In November, the Tanaka government announced its "unified view" in the following terms: "The Taiwan clause set forth the recognition of the top leaders of Japan and United States at the time in 1969. Since then, the situation surrounding Taiwan has changed, the possibility of armed conflicts arising has disappeared. In the light of this background, the recognition has also changed. Regarding the point as to whether it will not be interference in internal affairs, Taiwan is an inseparable part of the People's Republic of China and, basically, it is

---

reaffirms that Taiwan is an inalienable part of the territory of the People's Republic of China. The Government of Japan fully understands and respects this stand of the Government of China and adheres to its stand of complying with Article 8 of the Potsdam Proclamation."

36. *Bungei Shunju*, December 1972.
37. *Asahi*, 1 October 1972.
38. *Asahi*, October 1972.
39. *Asahi*, 1 October 1972.

China's internal question. We hope that it will be settled peacefully between the parties directly concerned. Standing in this judgment, careful consideration will be given to the operation of the U.S.-Japan Security Treaty."[40] In explaining this unified view, Foreign Minister Ohira expressed the government's belief that it was not desirable to argue a hypothetical situation. He asked for the opposition parties' understanding and assured them that "careful consideration will be given, keeping in mind friendly relations between Japan and China in the future." Regarding the Far Eastern clause, Mr. Kenzo Yoshida, the Director General of the Asian Affairs Bureau of the Foreign Minister, gave a similar answer to an interviewer.[41] It is obvious that Peking was far from totally satisfied with these interpretations. After an interview with Premier Chou En-lai, Takeo Kimura reported the following remark by Chou: "Concerning the fact that the Chinese side did not touch on the Security Treaty when Tanaka visited China, he stated that this is because Foreign Minister Ohira stated that the Security Treaty will not apply to Taiwan."[42] Obviously, Chou must have also assumed that Japan took a similar position on the Taiwan clause.

Hence, despite surface cordiality and warmth, the Sino-Japanese maneuvering over the question of Taiwan goes on under different ground rules. As to be expected, Peking continues to try to weaken the various ties between Tokyo and Taipei, sometimes using economic inducements as a lever. Tokyo attempts to develop trade with Peking while keeping her economic advantages in Taiwan. In this respect, the delay in concluding an aviation agreement between Japan and China is illuminating. Liao Cheng-chih argued China's case in political terms as follows: "It will be a problem if the line is extended as it is and planes were to fly from Haneda, Taipei, and Shanghai to Peking. That would mean two Chinas, and we cannot accept that in any way."[43] Liao's interpretation of the Sino-Japanese understanding on the issue of Taiwan is as follows: "At the time of the restoration of the Sino-Japanese diplomatic relations last year, Foreign Minister Ohira asked us to 'understand the questions of Japan's investments in Taiwan and its air route.' Toward this, the responsible persons of the Chinese side said that 'China cannot accept these questions legally, but it can understand that such questions actually exist.' "[44] In other words, for Peking, these questions are not excluded from future discussions and negotiations.

40. *Asahi*, 8 November 1972.
41. *Toki No Ugoki*, 1 November 1972.
42. *Nihon Keizai*, 26 January 1973.
43. *The Daily Yomiuri*, 21 April 1974.
44. See also, Minoru Shimuzu, "LDP in Turmoil," *Japan Times*, 25 April 1974.

Accordingly, Peking at first demanded that the Tokyo-Taipei air route be cut, pointing to the precedent that China had been prevented from sending even a special flight to Japan prior to the restoration of Peking-Tokyo relations. After this demand was rejected firmly by Japan, Peking asked that changes be made on the flag and the name of the company painted on the Chinese Nationalist planes. In response, Tokyo replied in effect that she was not in a position to impose a change. The two sides finally reached a compromise under which Foreign Minister Ohira issued a statement declaring that "the Japanese government does not recognize the insignia on the Taiwan aircraft as a national flag nor does it recognize China Airline (Taiwan) as an airline representing a state."[45] Immediately after China's announcement, Taiwan herself took steps to cut the Tokyo-Taipei air route, with the hope that such a move would prevent the Diet from ratifying the agreement or it at least would strengthen the hand of the pro-Taiwan group (the Seirankai), and create serious difficulties for the Tanaka Cabinet. This episode suggests that Peking would try to obtain the most favorable interpretation possible of the Sino-Japanese understanding on the question of one China so as to deal a blow to Taiwan's international prestige and to isolate Taiwan. But it would accept a compromise which does not run counter to the phraseology of the Joint Communique and the Ohira statement of September 1972. It achieved a diplomatic victory which was magnified by Taiwan's overestimation of the political power of the Seirankai, her willingness to be used by the Seirankai as an instrument in the intra-party struggle within the LDP, and her self-inflicted damage in terminating the Tokyo-Taipei air route.[46] The China-Japan air route has little economic significance in the short run. But both sides sought the agreement mainly for political reasons. To Peking, it meant a step, however small, toward the achievement of a one-China situation and toward the improvement of Sino-Japanese relations which is one of the indispensable elements in the ultimate solution of the Taiwan issue. To Japan, it is a highly desirable move to induce the Soviet Union to compete for her favors, and to maintain her "equal-distance" diplomacy. It may also have been seen in the context of negotiations over China's export of oil to Japan. Hence, both sides reached a satisfactory compromise after a prolonged negotiation of nineteen months, with China giving up her earlier demands and Japan assuming the risk of temporarily losing the lucrative Taipei-Tokyo air route. The Tokyo-Taipei air route was reestablished in late summer, 1975.

45. *The Daily Yomiuri*, 21 April 1974.
46. See also, Minoru Shimuzu, "LDP in Turmoil," *Japan Times*, 25 April 1974.

Future negotiations and relations between China and Japan will continue to reflect the contrasts in the approaches and bargaining powers of the two nations. The newly acquired ability to export oil has given China a bargaining counter in the economic sphere. But she still needs imports from Japan more than Japan needs Chinese imports. To make up for her weak economic bargaining position, she must continue to appeal to Japanese opinions on the basis of the mutually agreed upon principle of one China, the guilt feeling and good will of the Japanese, and a generalized anxiety over possible conflict with China. The internal divisions in Japan over China policy can also be exploited. Official and semi-official contacts on all levels have become an important instrument of diplomacy. Thus, it came as no surprise that Peking sought to bring pressure on the Miki government over the issue of inclusion in the peace treaty of a clause opposing "hegemony" by any power in Asia by successfully persuading a Japanese Socialist delegation to accept the Chinese position.[47] On her part, Japan relies on her present economic strength in her dealing with Peking. As cultivating opinions takes a long time to produce results and even longer to translate them into changes in public policies, Peking must proceed slowly and tentatively in order to obtain acceptable terms, or at least wait until the results of her efforts are known one way or other. Since economic strength can produce immediate, advantageous bargains, Japan desires quick agreements covering a longer period of time. But the Chinese desire to compete with the Soviet Union and to prevent the rapid development of Soviet-Japanese economic relations has had the opposite effect of forcing the Chinese not to delay an agreement with Japan for too long a period.

In the long run, however, there is another factor at work. While the balance of economic strength is temporarily on the side of Japan, the balance of vital interests in Taiwan is on the side of China. The Chou-Tanaka summit meeting already reflected this balance of vital interests. Although the relative importance of Taiwan to the economy of Japan has never been doubted by Japanese leaders, the strategic importance of Taiwan to the security of Japan is being re-evaluated by some Japanese observers. At the same time, China's export of oil to Japan and import of heavy machinery in the next few years may make China a more important trade partner than Taiwan. The unification of Taiwan will remain a foremost Chinese objective while the relative importance of Taiwan to Japan may further decline. Peking is apparently counting on the possibility that in the long run this balance of vital interests will enable her to achieve her objective.

47. *Peking Review*, 14 May 1975, p. 6.

What is the future of Taiwan? Our speculations on this subject are probably no better than oracle bone divination. But certain things can be said for the purpose of eliciting discussion. Peking's present policy of peaceful unification rests squarely on military realities in the Taiwan Straits, the continuing American commitment to defend Taiwan, and the general international environment. This situation will remain unchanged for some time to come. Peking is counting on the possibility of isolating Taipei diplomatically first. As of the early autumn of 1975, Peking's position in its negotiations with the United States was that the latter should first withdraw American troops from Taiwan, then terminate the defense treaty, and finally sever diplomatic relations with Taiwan. It does not expect all these three steps to be taken immediately but gradually over a period of time. Peking may also be hoping that with the development of great economic strength in the next few years, she can use her increasing economic power as leverage to isolate Taipei economically by making economic relations with Peking more profitable than that with Taipei. It is hoped that diplomatic and economic isolation, together with the concomitant decline in morale and economic strength, would make the political inducements offered by Peking to achieve unification more attractive than they are now.

But Peking is also very realistic about the prospect of peaceful unification. She is apparently aware of the fact that the death of Chiang Kai-shek has increased rather than decreased the chances of the emergence of an independent Taiwan. Many American observers asserted explicitly or said by implication that Peking had renounced the use of force over the issue of Taiwan or had reached an understanding with the American government to that effect. We have found no evidence that Peking has made such a commitment. Peking's policy at the present time is to achieve unification by peaceful means. She has never ruled out the resort to force, the threat of force, or such forcible measures as a naval blockade in the future.[48] Her refusal to renounce the use of force is a necessary element in her endeavor to persuade Taipei to negotiate a settlement. Moreover, the term "peaceful unification" has very special meaning when used by the Chinese Communists. It includes achievement of unification through negotiation against the background of overwhelming military superiority on the Chinese

48. On the occasion of commemorating the twenty-seventh anniversary of the 27 February Uprising in Taiwan against the Nationalist government, Fu Tso-yi, the ranking former Nationalist general on the mainland, issued a written statement warning his former Nationalist colleagues in Taiwan that "the Taiwan Straits are today no longer an obstacle to the liberation of Taiwan." This statement was given wide publicity by Peking and caught the attention of Western observers. For the statement, see *Peking Review* 8 March 1974, p. 20.

Communist side. If the policy of peaceful unification cannot be successfully implemented, a shift to the use of force or the threat of force is possible. Such a shift is congruent with the Chinese Communist pattern of integrating "peaceful political struggle" and "armed struggle" and alternately using one of these as the principal form of struggle. The question is whether the military balance warrants such a shift.[49]

The long period of time in which a change in military balance will warrant a shift to the use of force to recover Taiwan will also witness many unforeseeable political developments and changes within China, Taiwan, and the world as a whole. If China succeeds in making a real breakthrough in her economic development, cultural renaissance, and scientific progress, while Taiwan suffers an economic decline, the attraction of China for Taiwan will increase and the prospect of Taiwan's return will improve. Otherwise, a serious political constraint will be imposed on any attempt to regain Taiwan even if Peking acquires the necessary military capabilities. The sentiments of the Chinese mainlanders and Taiwanese on Taiwan will be another weighty political factor.

The potential capability of the Nationalist government to make atomic weapons introduces an additional complication. No matter what sort of plan Peking has drawn up—peaceful unification or the resort to force some time in the future—one of the most immediate and urgent tasks is to cultivate the favorable sentiment of the Taiwanese and Chinese mainlanders in the larger context of creating an overwhelming climate of world opinion that China is one and indivisible. Hence, the tremendous efforts made by Peking in this direction and the political position taken by Peking in the negotiation over air routes. The general and vague principles embodied in the Chou-Tanaka Joint Communique and the Ohira statement of September 1972 can be given concrete meaning only when they are applied to specific issues. A series of solutions to concrete problems will determine the meaning of these general principles and the direction in which the ultimate fate of Taiwan will be decided. Until China and Japan could reach substantial agreement on the many specific issues over Taiwan, a Sino-Japanese non-aggression pact would be out of the question. Conversely, it is not inconceivable that Peking would be willing to offer political and economic inducements in the form of intimate cooperation throughout East Asia or some sort of informal alliance or co-hegemony, which are so attractive that Japan's economic stakes in Taiwan would become insignificant by comparison. But Peking would not be in a position to

49. For a recent report on the views of Chinese leaders which support our analysis, see *Chün Pao*, 23 June 1975. *Chün Pao* is a pro-Peking bi-weekly published in New York.

offer such political and economic inducements until her political and economic capabilities to act in the international sphere have increased dramatically and the power of the Soviet Union and the United States has suffered a corresponding decline. This is a possible development in the long run and should be watched carefully; but it will take time to materialize. When it should come to pass, the quadrilateral relations among the four powers in East Asia would undergo a drastic change and the Sino-Japanese relations would become the dominant factor in East Asia. With this change, the global configuration of power will also take on a different shape, with China, Japan, and some countries in the Third World forming a center of power to balance the influence of the U.S., the Soviet Union, and perhaps Western Europe.

VIII.

The projection of Sino-Japanese rivalry in East Asia does not only rest on various assumptions regarding the structure of power relationships in East Asia or on certain judgments and policy recommendations on specific issues over which China and Japan might come into conflict. It also has definite implications for Japan's defense program and political development. For the projection assumes that China and Japan will come into serious conflict over a variety of issues throughout East Asia on which the interests of Japan and the United States might diverge and Japan might not receive U.S. military support. The logical inference is that Japan must acquire the necessary conventional military power to defend these interests. Since a rapid program of rearmament will likely give Japan superiority in conventional military capability, China would be tempted to resort to the use of her nuclear weapons or to nuclear blackmail in order to redress the balance and to uphold her interests. The inevitable result would be the acquisition of nuclear weapons by Japan.

In contrast, we have argued that given the present structure of political relationships in East Asia, it is unlikely that Sino-Japanese rivalry would develop to such an extent that massive conventional and nuclear rearmament would become a vital necessity for Japan as a measure to defend her interests against China. We have also suggested that military power has serious limitations when it is used to protect economic interests or to deal with the unstable internal situation and possible revolutionary changes in East Asia. In this section, we have no intention of dealing with the technical problems of conventional and nuclear weapons. We shall only make several brief observations on the question of military power insofar as it bears on Sino-Japanese relations.

At the present moment, China does not have the necessary conventional military power to pose any threat of an invasion of Japan. This situation will probably remain unchanged in the rest of the decade. In many discussions of the possibility of Japan's acquisition of nuclear weapons, the nuclear threat from China rather than from the Soviet Union has usually been cited as Japan's most likely incentive. This focus on China's nuclear threat probably stems from a feeling that the Soviet nuclear threat is of such a dimension that it looks like a "natural disaster" while the Chinese threat can be countered. It is also probably the outcome of a tendency to compare the United States with the Soviet Union and Japan with China, and the Japanese sense of equality with the Chinese in the structure of international power. In addition, it is a legacy of the Sino-American confrontation in which Japan associated herself closely with her American ally on all political issues and which intensified Sino-Japanese antagonism and obscured the chances of possible compromise. It is a response to the Chinese propaganda attacks on Japanese militarism in the past which offended Japan's image of herself as a pacific nation. But this focus on the Chinese nuclear threat will probably be blurred as a result of the long-term effects of the Sino-Japanese rapprochement in which the two nations seek to resolve the differences over various concrete issues through compromise or mutual concessions.

There is another point which deserves to be mentioned. China's decision to acquire and develop nuclear weapons was a response to the nuclear threat first from the United States and then from the Soviet Union. Any nuclear weapons systems which would be sufficient to deter a nuclear attack from the Soviet Union and the United States would also be sufficient to cover Japan and other Asian nations. They do not represent any independent cost to China in economic terms. Obviously, China's acquisition of nuclear weapons has had visible political repercussions on her Asian neighbors. But these repercussions have been largely contained as a result of the general recognition of the serious threat under which China must formulate her military policies. In contrast, a decision for Japan to go nuclear would be taken as a move with China as her primary target. If Kunio Maraoka is correct, "the level of force required to deter China would probably be substantially larger than that needed to deter the Soviet Union."[50] As a

50. *Op. cit.*, p. 24.

result of past history, the political impact of such a decision on other Asian nations would be profound and not so easily contained. Moreover, China's future nuclear weapons program would be limited by her economic and industrial capabilities and her level of scientific and technological development, whereas Japan is not under similar constraints once Japanese scientists abandon their refusal to work on nuclear weapons. Even the nuclear superpowers would have to ask the question whether Japan would be content with being a second-rate nuclear power once she embarks on a program of nuclearization. If indeed Japan should go all the way, the international system would undergo another major change. We do not have the competence to discuss the questions of "defensive" nuclear weapons, keeping the nuclear option open, technical feasibility, economic cost, and incipient vulnerability. But it takes only a layman's knowledge to assert that profound political changes would take place in Japan if and when Japan should decide to go nuclear.

The explosion of an atomic device in India in July 1974 has brought to the surface the submerged trend toward proliferation of nuclear weapons. It has led to the postponement of Japan's plan to ratify the non-proliferation treaty. If India and other nations become nuclear powers, the pressure on Japan to acquire nuclear weapons will increase. But given Japan's internal political situation, her high level of economic and technological achievements, the absence of an implacable enemy, and the overwhelming public opposition to nuclear weapons, it is highly doubtful that Japan will embark on a policy of nuclearization. It is more likely that in line with political advantage and opportunity costs she will simply keep her nuclear option open as she has tended to do so far.

Maintaining the policy of non-nuclearization but keeping the nuclear option open implies that Japan would continue to rely on America's nuclear umbrella for protection against the Soviet and Chinese nuclear threat, to depend on the United States Navy to protect the sea lanes, and to use Japan's overwhelming economic power to protect her own economic interests in underdeveloped countries. The reliability of America's nuclear protection has often been discussed. So has the desirability of establishing good relations with other nations in order to decrease the reliance on the United States and reinsure Japan's security. Insofar as Sino-Japanese relations are concerned, the only issue which could have led to a military confrontation was Taiwan. If a Sino-American military confrontation over Taiwan should occur and threaten to involve Japan as a result of the invocation of the Far Eastern clause of the U.S.-Japan treaty, the question of the reliability of the

American nuclear umbrella would not arise. The problem would be whether Japan will be willing to allow the United States to use her bases for such purpose under the present formula of "giving careful consideration." As our previous analysis suggests, if a nuclear war threatens to develop over Taiwan, it would be the United States—not Japan—who must first answer the fateful question of how much sacrifice she is willing to make to defend Taiwan.

For China, developing nuclear and conventional military capabilities is a matter of survival and a necessary means to achieve the unification of the nation. But the tremendous actual and opportunity costs in terms of its financial and manpower resources are obvious to the Chinese leaders.[51] Vis-à-vis the United States, the level of force to be achieved would depend on both the prospect of recovering Taiwan and what would be required for that purpose. Nuclear force at this level will also present an objective threat to Japan. But the Chinese leaders are not likely to be foolish enough to use nuclear blackmail against Japan or escalate their conflicts with the Japanese government to such a level as to trigger a Japanese decision to acquire nuclear weapons.

IX.

In sum, we have argued in this paper that it is improbable that East Asian politics will turn on Sino-Japanese rivalry as its main axis. Instead, Sino-Japanese relations form the common base of two triangular relationships—one governing the relations among China, Japan, and the United States, and the other governing the relations among China, Japan, and Soviet Union. In either of these triangles, Japan occupies a more favorable position than China. It is quite true that as the power occupying the middle position, Japan is sometimes the object of pressure from the other two powers. There is also the danger that Japan will be maneuvered into becoming the main antagonist of China in either one or both of these triangular relationships. But given Japan's favorable position and her skill at negotiation, she will be able to absorb such pressures and perhaps even counter them. In both triangular relationships, Sino-Japanese relations are much less intense than Sino-Soviet, Sino-American, and American-Japanese ones either in terms of enmity or in terms of the long-term consequences of the interchanges. Sino-Soviet conflict and hostility are now the primary source of tension

51. There are indications that there was a debate among top leaders from 1969 to 1971 over the extent to which defense industries should be rapidly pushed forward on a large scale at the expense of manufacturing machinery for agriculture and other industrial development.

in East Asia. Japan's policy of maintaining equal distance between the rivals has a great deal of merit, but it is not exactly easy to implement. Given the fact that since the Chou-Tanaka meeting Japan has adopted a position less favorable to Taiwan than that of the United States, the latter is now viewed by Peking as the main obstacle in its maneuvers against Taiwan. These two triangles with a common base form themselves into a quadrilateral relationship. But the actions and policies of the two superpowers still dominate the relations among the four powers.

Within the above context, the Sino-Soviet rapprochement since the Chou-Tanaka meeting has yielded initial common understanding regarding the questions of interference in each other's internal politics, the defense power of Japan, the United States-Japan Security Pact and China and Japan's respective roles in developing countries. China is now unlikely to place the unification of Korea ahead of the unification of her own country. Therefore, the problem of Korea is not likely to be the cause of serious Sino-Japanese conflict. The only bilateral issue which can cause serious trouble between China and Japan is Taiwan. Another unresolved issue is the question of inclusion in the peace treaty of a clause opposing hegemony by any power (meaning the Soviet Union) in Asia. Unless satisfactory solutions can be found for the many concrete problems that remain regarding Taiwan and the Soviet Union, Sino-Japanese rapprochement will not advance at a rapid pace in the foreseeable future, as for example towards the much discussed goal of concluding a Sino-Japanese non-aggression pact.

But none of the unresolved issues is likely to lead to military conflict. In the unfavorable position which China finds herself in the quadrilateral relations, China's best hopes lie in maintaining tolerable relations with Japan and the United States so as to fend off Soviet military pressure and counter Soviet efforts to contain China. The remaining years of the 1970s will witness neither an intense Sino-Japanese rivalry nor a sudden blooming of Sino-Japanese friendship. But the probability of a gradual increase in Sino-Japanese cooperation in East Asia is higher than the intensification of Sino-Japanese conflict. Thus, the 1970s will be a decade of complex interactions among the four powers in which Japan will embark on her new, historic role as a pacific world power, maintaining an ambivalent and non-committal stance toward both nuclear weapons and a large-scale conventional force; and China will continue to seek to demonstrate her ability to turn the much improved but still adverse circumstances into new opportunities for creative development.

In our view, Sino-Japanese relations in the 1970s will not be comparable to the 1930s. Power politics as they impinge on the East Asian region is much more closely integrated with the larger international system. This basic fact calls into question the validity of the regional approach which focuses its attention almost exclusively on Sino-Japanese relations, a view that derives its inspiration from the analogy with Far Eastern diplomacy in the 1930s. We do not believe history will repeat itself.

II. Internal Processes and Images

United States Policy toward Japan: Problems of Understanding

Akira Iriye and Neil Harris

"Let us continue to seek understanding with each other and among all peoples," President Gerald Ford told the Japanese Emperor on 19 November 1974, at the banquet the latter held in honor of the first American President ever to visit Japan while in office. "Let us work together," Ford continued, "to solve common problems, recognizing the interdependence of the modern world in which we all live."

Understanding of each other and of their common problems was a key theme not only at the banquet but also at the various meetings Ford and Secretary of State Henry Kissinger had with Japanese officials. Moreover, the theme was equally stressed by reporters who covered the historic visit. "Language, cultural traditions and different business practices create barriers and continue to make real understanding difficult," wrote Norman Pearlstine in the *Wall Street Journal.* Besides the differences in their negotiating techniques and rituals, the writer noted, even those Americans and Japanese "who have tried to develop close personal ties have often failed through lack of understanding." Richard Halloran of *The New York Times* agreed. "On a personal basis," he wrote, "there are few peoples in the world more different than Japanese and Americans in their behavior and attitudes." And yet, according to Pearlstine, these difficulties and differences have "been overridden by more important common or complementary goals."

Why? Both Halloran and Pearlstine would argue that the basic factor is pragmatism. Japanese and Americans find their close strategic, political, and economic ties advantageous and in their respective interests. Despite lack of real understanding, self-interest keeps the two together.

Such a formulation, which seems to have been accepted by most commentators in the United States, raises some interesting and fundamental questions. Are pragmatic considerations without an underpinning of cultural understanding a stable guide to policy? Are official negotiations and policies without a sense of personal ties sufficient in ensuring a friendly relationship? As the world moves to the second half of the 1970s and enters what appears to be an age of scarcity, can American-Japanese relations continue as they have on the basis of practical national interests?

It may, of course, be open to question whether there really is as little understanding between the two peoples as many think. Certainly, as Halloran wrote, "poll after poll and the personal experiences of Americans here [in Tokyo] show that Japanese get along well with Americans despite the formidable obstacles." Japanese writers have produced voluminous quantities of literature dealing with the United States, and virtually all of them assume that culturally the two peoples share certain outlooks, problems, and even dilemmas. Expressions such as "America's problems are our problems," or "America's dilemmas will some day be ours"—not only social but cultural problems are implied—are found in Japanese writings on America. The key thesis in the three-volume *Japan and America* (1973), a collection of essays by Japan's leading Americanists, is that in Japan there has persisted a sense of affinity with the United States over the years which has grown even stronger as the latter grapples with problems of cultural identity or mass society. Such a feeling of kinship and intimacy is absent in most circles in the United States. With a few notable exceptions such as the essays in James W. Morley, *Prologue to the Future* (1974), Americans seem to assume that there are insurmountable obstacles to psychological and intellectual rapport across the Pacific. Hence the almost ritualistic incantation of the need for "understanding" whenever officials and writers talk about American-Japanese relations.

Any discussion of understanding or lack thereof must start with specific groups and individuals who do the "understanding." The fact that the Japanese tend to believe they "understand" the Americans better than vice versa is due to the existence in Japan of numerous circles of people who are in daily contact with American culture. It is necessary to ask, therefore, which groups in the United States constitute the "foreign policy publics" specifically dealing with Japan. This paper gives an outline of these publics and then tries to characterize their perceptions of Japan in order to clarify problems inherent in intercultural relations. Since the Second World War was a watershed in American-Japanese relations, some reference will be made to contrasting patterns and characteristics between the period before and after the war.

First of all, there are economically-oriented groups which have established a much wider network of foreign policy publics than before the Pacific War. While earlier the United States was usually Japan's best customer, the bulk of Japanese exports to America consisted of silk goods, only tangentially affecting the lives of the mass of people. Japan in turn purchased cotton, wheat, flour, and some machine goods from the United States, but these were noncompetitive items and generated no serious political issue until the 1930s. Since the 1950s, however, the pattern of Japanese-American trade has become diversified, and more commercial and industrial establishments in America have been involved in Japanese economic life. Most important has been the changing quantity and content of Japanese exports into the United States. These items have necessitated the setting up of sales offices and marketing agencies throughout America, the most important of which is JETRO, the Japan External Trade Organization, which is designed to keep American manufacturers and exporters aware of what is happening in Japanese industry and trade. Thus, Japanese goods are much more visible in the United States, and American goods much more visible in Japan, than before 1941. Obviously, various groups in the United State are directly involved, and they tend to interpret American-Japanese relations from their respective perspectives. In the export field, managers of consumer goods companies, automobile manufacturers, agricultural producers, and the like have sometimes been adamant against Japan's tariff policy, quota system, and marketing mechanism where many middlemen take their profits before the consumer even sees the merchandise. Since over 80 percent of Japanese imports have been raw materials and food, exporters of major capital goods and manufactured consumer items have been particularly insistent that Japan open its doors more widely to foreign trade. They work through formal and ad hoc associations, through lobbying groups in Washington which work on Congress as well as the Executive branch, and through their influence on media writers. Their views are echoed frequently on the business and consumer pages of daily newspapers, and sometimes even on the editorial page. In big commercial centers such as New York and Chicago, economic interest groups have ready access, through their leaders, to editorial writers whose opinions often reflect their own.

Exporters, however, may encounter a pressure generated from within the United States to curtail their business with Japan. This happened during 1972–73, when the dollar devaluation, combined with a Japanese economic boom, created a tremendous demand on certain American commodities, in particular large appliances, logs, hogs, beef, and soybeans. The excessive exportation of these items, now that they were much cheaper relative to the yen, created an acute shortage and a consequent price increase in the United States. As the average American home became more expensive to build, and the average citizen found the price of pork and beef prohibitive due in part to the increasing price of soybeans to feed livestock, pressures were generated by consumer groups to do something about the situation.

Parallel to these export problems is the fact that Japanese imports into the United States for years produced a reaction in those segments of the country where the imports seemed to compete best against domestic products. First the cotton textile mills in the South during the 1950s, and then retailers and manufacturers of cars and small electric appliances in the rest of the country began voicing their resentment of cheaper Japanese imports. Here again, they normally worked through their Congressional representatives and through a media campaign. Local politicians took up the issue to express their understanding of the plight of their clients. They all became ad hoc foreign policy publics when they joined together to insist upon a specific policy decision. They engaged in a fierce propaganda campaign with supporters of liberal importation—those who were engaged in the trade themselves through sales offices and marketing agencies.

The trade picture has become increasingly complex because Japanese companies have begun to invest in the United States to manufacture goods for sale in America and other countries. The U.S. Sony Corporation has set up a plant in San Diego, the Kikkoman Shoyu (soy sauce) Company in Wisconsin, and the automobile manufacturers Nissan and Toyota on the West Coast. In 1973 the assets of the eight biggest Japanese banks in the United States amounted to $9 billion. Such investments have been generally welcomed by various American communities which stand to benefit from the infusion of outside capital that would create jobs. Although goods produced in these factories compete with domestic American products, there seems to have been much less resentment of this than of regular Japanese imports. As substantial Japanese capital begins to be invested in agricultural and mineral resources, however, a reaction may set in. Given the ecological consciousness of the public, the investment by Japanese in copper mines, forestry, or land may evoke local fears.

Labor unions are another economic group playing a key role in

Japanese-American relations. Traditionally supporters of liberal trade policies, labor has become increasingly protectionist. Their basic fear is of cheap foreign labor producing goods that will compete with American products. Foreign laborers, especially Asian ones earning low wages, are pictured as working willingly for American capitalists abroad who pay slightly better than average wages; while the former learn otherwise inaccessible technology and produce sophisticated goods that compete with domestic American goods, even allowing for shipping charges and import duties. Thus, the AFL-CIO has been demanding some sort of restraint or curtailment of American capital outflows which to them mean job outflows on the order of 500,000 per year, and import inflows which destroy any attempt at trade balancing. It has also been pressing for international fair-labor standards to equalize wage differentials among various countries, and for the curbing of the export of technology. Here labor is diametrically opposed to business corporations, and both sides have tried to influence Congress and public opinion through active lobbying and propaganda efforts. In terms of Japanese-American relations, labor would not be particularly concerned with removing Japan's restrictions on American investments in Japan. If anything, labor would welcome such restrictions. But they would still be adamant against a large inflow of goods that were wholly or partially manufactured in Japan. It should be noted, however, that Japan is not singled out for attack as often as other countries, since Japanese wages are now fast catching up with American levels and are expected to surpass them in the 1980s according to JETRO. When labor attacks a flood of cheap foreign textiles, the criticism applies to Korea, Taiwan, Hongkong, and other countries as well as to Japan. Purely in economic terms, then, American labor may not constitute as crucial a foreign policy public with respect to Japan per se.

Before the war, United States-Japanese economic competition in third countries was a key theme. There has been much less of it since the end of the war. China, where the two countries were constantly pictured as being economically antagonistic toward one another, has only recently become a sizable market for Japan or the United States, and elsewhere in the world they have not engaged in fierce competition to such an extent that it becomes part of public perceptions of each other. But the situation may change again, especially after the Nixon and oil "shocks." As Japan begins to diversify its trade pattern and to intensify its effort to increase sales to and purchases from Southeast Asia, Latin America, and the Middle East, American commercial interests may become hurt, and this may produce noticeable domestic repercussions. Before the war the Japanese were accused of unfair business practices abroad to undersell foreign competitors. Today, although there are still charges of "dumping," pressures may be more indirect. For instance, devaluation of the dollar, or revaluation of the yen, would restore competitive advantages for American commodities, and industrial and banking groups in the United States have taken active positions on the issue. Another more subtle campaign is to spread sinister images of Japan such as "Japan, Inc." or "ugly Japanese" (although the latter, like "economic animal," is essentially a Japanese expression). Most effective would be the image of Japan as so mercantilistically export-minded and economically oriented that its corporations have neglected important aspects of life such as social welfare, medicine, housing, sewerage, and preservation.

These images have penetrated public consciousness in the United States through the mass media. It would be interesting to investigate whether there has been a change in the relationship between the mass media's images of Japan and those of special interest groups such as business and labor. Both before and after the war, economic issues comprised a significant segment of newspaper reports on Japan, although it would seem that the ratio has been higher after the war because of the absence of any military crisis. It also seems true, however, that there has not been much improvement in U.S. newspaper coverage of Japan. Even today very few daily newspapers station a permanent correspondent in Japan, and there has been little change in the attitude of editors that a correspondent should not become too specialized, lest he become useless for anything else. Few, if any, correspondents stationed in Tokyo can read and speak the language; they have their headquarters in the Foreign Press Club and have little contact with Japanese journalists. Their Japanese contacts are usually men who speak English and can communicate with Americans—which means a dozen or so Japanese academics. Under the circumstances, it is not very easy to do extensive or balanced reports on what is happening in Japan. Newspaper items about Japan tend to deal with American foreign policy matters, economic problems, or glimpses of traditional, quaint customs.

In looking at the cultural aspect of Japanese-American relations, one development stands out as a striking feature of the postwar period. Today there are many more American scholars specializing in Japanese history, literature, and similar subjects. Before the war, whenever there was a crisis in the two countries' relations, the public usually had to turn to a former missionary or a generalist for comments on Japan. Now there are several hundred academic specialists throughout America who have studied the language and make Japanese studies their lifelong preoccupation.

In 1910, when George Blakeslee of Clark University organized a conference to discuss the United States-Japan crisis—probably the first such conference—he had to turn to missionaries, businessmen, geographers, and others with no profound expertise on Japanes matters to write papers. Even during the 1920s and the 1930s, when the Institute of Pacific Relations held various conferences to debate Pacific questions, most of the American participants were generalists and journalists, Today it would not be at all difficult to find several Japan specialists in any part of the United States. During 1971–72, when there was much animosity after the "Nixon shocks," the Japan specialists in the United States were extremely alert and efficient in organizing various ad hoc meetings and conferences to discuss ways to alleviate the tension. Virtually all Japanologists shared the concern of Edwin O. Reischauer for maintaining a sane relationship between the two countries on the basis of a mutual understanding that goes deeper than political expediencies or economic compatibility. Their continued presence now makes an enormous difference in generating pressure for better relations across the Pacific. Even though they are not always heard by the unconverted, and while their views are not always solicited or, if solicited, accepted by the mass media, their ability to gather together with alacrity and speak with one voice implies the existence of a special foreign-policy public as far as Japan is concerned.

As before the war, there is also an intermediate layer of subspecialists: those who are well-educated in other areas and treat Japan as a peripheral topic to their specialty. These men—David Riesman, Herman Kahn, Zbigniew Brzezinski, among others—may sometimes be more influential in molding American opinion than the experts because they have a wider perspective, a larger public audience, and more connections with policy-makers. They do not attend Japan specialists' meetings, but they write frequently for mass-circulating newspapers and magazines. Then there are those who are less articulate and hardly recognized widely, but who have an interest in Japanese culture or its people. Some may have travelled to Japan; others may have taken a college course or two in Japanese history; still others may be lovers of Japanese movies, devotees of judo and martial arts fads, or connoisseurs of Japanese prints and paintings. Although college course offerings are only a rough index, the phenomenal expansion in the number of Japan-related courses and enrollments in them after the war would seem to indicate that there now is a far larger number of people who comprise a potentially Japan-oriented public.

Undoubtedly the trend has been assisted by the spread of television, which has acquainted the mass of people for the first time with glimpses of life in Japan, no matter how distorted the impression.

Whether the trend has peaked is a matter that is seriously being debated by concerned specialists. The recent cutbacks in federal support for area studies, and the decisions by the Ford Foundation and other organizations, hitherto the main private benefactors of Japanese and Asian studies in the United States, to discontinue academic institutional grants, have seriously undermined the effort by the specialists to train their successors and to recruit promising young students into the field. Major universities are frantically looking for funds, and it may well be that their success will depend on the size of the foreign policy public in the United States who have a special interest in Japan.

What happened to the two groups which played unique roles in Japanese-American relations before the war: West Coast exclusionists and professional Sinophiles? The exclusionists achieved their goal shortly after Pearl Harbor when Japanese residents were removed from the West Coast, many of them never to return. However, the movement lost its raison d'être with the end of the war, and conditions in postwar California and other western states were such that a crudely anti-Oriental exclusionist sentiment subsided, if it did not disappear entirely. Japanese-Americans have entered the professions and now occupy some prominent positions in local politics and businesses, helped especially by the statehood of Hawaii in 1960. Although older Californians who remember the prewar days (a distinct minority) apparently are still convinced of the righteousness of their earlier cause, there is little overt animosity today, and certainly no organized movement comparable to the prewar exclusionist campaign. The 1965 immigration act, doing away with the quota system, has made any such movement meaningless, at least as a political protest. To the extent that one talks of a special foreign policy public, one should note the emergence of Japanese-Americans, rather than their detractors, as a political force. They are well organized, with a lobbying body in Washington, and their local chapters and associations are extremely sensitive to any signs of alleged discrimination and unfair practices. They have close ties with Japanese businessmen from Japan and with the local consulate. They provide a dependable market for Japanese goods, as well as a pool of human resources for Japanese corporations establishing their branch offices and factories in the United States. Perhaps their most important role as a public would be through their living and working in the United States; Americans often come to know Japan through Japanese-Americans.

As for pro-Chinese groups and individuals, they have gone through a turbulent epoch in their relations with the government, with the public, and with one another, to an extent never duplicated in the case of Japan-oriented groups and individuals. Sinophiles continued to influence policy and the way the public viewed Japan after 1945, but their voice became fractured by internal dissension and their status in society became suspect because of the Chinese civil war. Many of those who had been outspoken friends of China and critics of Japan saw themselves subjected to often ferocious attacks during the early cold war years. To be pro-Chinese was no longer an unambiguous proposition since China was splintered into factions. By coincidence, men like Owen Lattimore and Edgar Snow, who, because of their knowledge of and sympathy for the Chinese Communists, were assailed during the McCarthy era, had advocated a relentlessly harsh policy toward Japan. Now that Japan was to be America's ward, then ally, the trend had turned to give pro-Japanese, anti-Communist writers like Joseph Ballantine, Joseph Grew, and Charles Tansill a wider hearing. In the meantime, China specialists, who had demonstrated their support for the Chinese cause against Japan during the 1930s, were no longer free to return to China for a postwar visit, and they soon lost touch with individual Chinese on the mainland. Some of these specialists, like John K. Fairbank and Harold Isaacs, went to Japan more regularly, and it was no longer plausible to label them Sinophiles in the traditional sense. They became as friendly toward Japan as they had been toward China.

In the meantime, as the Communists defeated the Nationalists and went through their turbulent period of political consolidation, agricultural experimentation, and cultural upheaval in the 1960s, America's China experts became more than ever divided. The Committee of Concerned Asian Scholars, while created in response to the war in Vietnam, had a sizable contingent of China scholars. Some of them made it their cardinal task to attack the older generation of specialists for their alleged failure to comprehend the realities of the Chinese Revolution. Little of this sort, it may be noted, has happened among Japan specialists. Although there are substantial mutual criticisms and generational differences of outlook, Japanese scholarship in the United States has not suffered from the fratricidal disputes that have rent apart the Sinologists. Under the circumstances, there are many kinds of Sinophiles, and they have not been as effective as before the war in matters relating to Japan.

Nevertheless, the thaw in Sino-American relations during 1971–1972 encouraged the reappearance of erstwhile Sinophiles like Barbara Tuchman and Joseph Alsop. The Nixon trip to China was preceded by extensive commentary by these writers, as well showings of old newsreels depicting the Japanese invasion of China. It seemed a nostalgic rediscovery of the 1930s, when one could be proud to be a friend of China and condemn Japanese aggression. Because of the new situation in which both China and Japan are emerging as strong actors in Asian politics—where Japanese friendship or Chinese hostility is no longer taken for granted—the reappearance of professional Sinophiles may be of some importance. It should be noted, however, that there are generational and other gaps among China experts and sub-experts to a larger extent than among their Japan equivalents. Before the war, Pearl Buck could probably speak for those Americans who loved China and hated Japanese militarism. Today it would be difficult to find a similar figure.

Finally, the list of foreign policy publics concerned with Japan would be incomplete without the inclusion of some ad hoc groups such as those interested in the preservation of whales, the energy crisis, or the prevention of cruelty to animals. From time to time there appear small groups of men trying to turn public attention to subjects that are relevant to Japanese-American relations. Japan has been condemned for the killing of whales in the ocean, for its lax enforcement of pollution laws, and for its people's alleged mistreatment of domestic pets. Occasionally, these protests become news items and serve to spread an image of Japan. Somewhat different in category would be politically oriented organizations that try to influence Japanese-American affairs from a particular viewpoint. For instance, Jewish groups in the United States follow the course of Japanese policy in the Middle East very closely. Any move on the part of Japan that gives the appearance of siding with either Israel or the Arab countries is likely to evoke an immediate response. Similarly, Korean, Taiwanese, and other nationality groups in the United States periodically write to newspapers and engage in propaganda work in connection with Japanese policy toward or behavior in their home countries. For instance, during the dispute over the future of the Sengaku islands, Chinese groups and individuals throughout the United States rose en masse to protest Japanese claims and the apparent American support for them. They placed full-page advertisements in newspapers and conducted demonstrations. Whether because of this movement or not, the State Department backed down from its earlier position that the status of the islands was unequivocally clear.

Whether American views of and attitudes toward Japan at the mass level are more informed today than before 1941 is difficult to determine. The fact that there seems to be more publics interested in

Japanese affairs may indicate that the masses are now caught in more complicated crosscurrents of opinions and advice concerning Japan. Middle America's perception of Japan, if such exists, may not be very different from what it was earlier: a combination of casual knowledge, generalized clichés, and curiosity. Here the determining factor would not be one's education, occupation, or special interests, but rather one's degree of nationalism. Japan would be viewed favorably insofar as it seems to behave in a way that does not damage American power, interests, or prestige. The nationalistic response would be reinforced by memories of the war, which in turn would be transmitted to the younger generation through textbooks and teachers, both stressing patriotism and an ethnocentric view of history. It remains to be seen in what ways, if at all, Vietnam, Watergate, the Sino-American détente, the oil crisis, and other recent phenomena will affect Middle America's perception of itself and of American relations with the rest of the world. To the extent that the White House in 1973–74 acknowledged the end of the cold war and the era of American omnipotence, and has been found to have been engaged in clandestine bombings abroad and break-ins at home, a super-patriotic image of America may give way to a more balanced self-perception. The "rabid American citizen," whom Rudyard Kipling called "a very difficult class to deal with," may come to take a more charitable view of other countries and peoples. If so, a psychological climate might be created in which Japanese-American relations could be discussed in a more open-minded fashion.

Those on the fringe of Middle America, as well as those outside, undoubtedly have their own perceptions of American relations with the rest of the world. Although it is difficult to document this, it can be easily inferred that for those who reject contemporary American values for one reason or another, Japan is no real alternative. It appears to be simply another materialistic, work-oriented country with problems of pollution and waste vastly magnified, where people pursue earthly rewards and export vulgar tastes. China is the true alternative to those Americans who do not like what they see in advanced capitalist countries, including Japan. They are impressed with the discipline and dedication of the Chinese people, or with the intelligence and sharpness of Chinese leaders. If an average American were asked which country he would like to visit first, China or Japan, he would most certainly choose the former, believing Japan to be more of the same, whereas China would be a totally novel experience.

This sketch has tried to pinpoint some of the groups in the United States that have played various roles, some more potential than actual, in the evolution of American-Japanese relations. At any given moment and on any given issue, some of these publics are mobilized; the number of publics actually involved as well as the membership in each public will vary from issue to issue, as will the degree of public interest. United States relations with Japan are a sum total of all these phenomena, and it seems clear that there is no fixed context in which these relations operate at all times. Rather, there are numerous contexts and various ingredients in each context which create a milieu for policy-making. Problems of "understanding" are extremely complicated since all these groups and individuals do their part in contributing to understanding or misunderstanding.

Nevertheless, it seems possible to delineate certain themes in U.S. relations with Japan by examining the types of "understanding" or "misunderstanding" which Americans show toward Japan. For instance, for some groups and individuals understanding is a matter of world politics and strategic realities. Their perceptions range from belief in inevitable conflict between the two powers to advocacy of a more or less permanent alliance. In either case, the two countries' relationship is considered a function of power realities. Understanding at this level is related to one's perception of the international system. More specifically, it entails a view of the whole structure of the "Pacific Quadrilateral." American observers of Japanese affairs have asserted that Japan should be playing a more active role in the quadrilateral relationship, and that this should be welcomed by the United States. As James Reston wrote in December 1971: "Now the problem is to get a successful and competitive Japan to share the common burdens of maintaining peace in the Pacific basin, without reviving her militaristic traditions, without destroying her economic progress, and without destroying her ambitions to be on good terms not only with the United States, but with the other two major powers in the Pacific, China and the Soviet Union."

One possibly fundamental point that is likely to be subjected to growing debate is Reston's contention that Japan and the United States should share the common burdens in the Pacific. Opposition could arise to such a proposition, not necessarily with respect to Japan's growing power, but to the maintenance of American power in the Pacific. The future of United States-Japanese relations depends to a large extent on the willingness of the United States to remain a key power in the Pacific. In the aftermath of the Indochina War, however, the American public may find distasteful President Nixon's assertion (March 1971) that "after all, we are a Pacific power." Earl Ravenal and other advocates of retrenchment have called for curtailment of commitments in the Pacific and Asia, leaving the area to other countries to manage in any way they like. They have been very vague as to where to draw the line—Hawaii, Guam, the Marshalls?—but to the extent that there is a reaction against Asian involvement, this will prove to be a crucial factor in determining the shape of Asian-Pacific politics and the geopolitical aspect of American-Japanese relations.

Reston described Japan as "competitive." The adjective became almost synonymous with Japan in American perception during the late 1960s and the early 1970s. It defined the economic aspect of Japanese-American relations, another level in the American "understanding" of Japan. As President Nixon said in a news conference in September 1971, "the United States and Japan inevitably are going to be competitors because we are both strong economies." The theme of economic competition goes back to earlier decades, but it gained much wider circulation during the early 1970s as Japan emerged as the number two industrial power in the capitalist world. More recently, Japanese have become competitors not only in export trade but also in purchases, as they import large quantities of lumber, foodstuffs, and especially oil. Since the oil crisis of 1973, "competition" has entailed attempts by various countries, including Japan and the United States, to ensure an adequate supply of raw materials, indicating a trend toward "resources diplomacy."

In the economic context, American understanding of Japan reflects fairly specific concerns. Some special-interest groups—retail merchants of domestic products, labor unions whose members comprise textile mills, housing contractors hit by increasing prices of lumber, and the like—advocate stern measures to cope with the competition. They often appeal to nationalism, like the Chevrolet dealer in Arizona who placed an advertisement in a local newspaper exhorting readers to remember Pearl Harbor and not buy a Japanese car. Such an outburst is understandable but also detrimental to understanding, and calmer voices have stressed the need for moderation and the spirit of cooperation, not competition. Criticizing the administration's "distinct tone of nationalism, which has characterized American economic policy abroad especially since August 1971," a *New York Times* editorial of September 19, 1972, argued that such a policy "confuses competition among businessmen, which requires intergovernmental cooperation in setting rules of fair play, with intergovernmental rivalry, which is the route to economic warfare." In another editorial, appropriately entitled "Cooperative Competition," the *Times* insisted that commercial competition among nations should take place within a cooperative framework, not in an atmosphere of fierce rivalry. We must recognize, the editors pointed out, "that each nation has a basic and long-term interest in the prosperity of others as well as itself. What the nations of the world need to create is a cooperative environment in which their individual businesses and industries can trade and compete." As these ideas gain in influence, the nationalism and ethnocentricity of the climate in which Americans view Japanese competition will lessen, and the relationships between the two countries will become saner. But the matter is related to an overall perception of Japanese-American economic relations, where their respective interests and needs must be taken into consideration. Here again, their competition or cooperation is part of the international economic picture, and ultimately their economic partnership will depend on their ability jointly to formulate an approach to such pressing problems of the day as food and fuel shortage, exchange instability, pollution control, and technological innovations.

The mention of these problems leads to probably the most important dimension in Japanese-American relations. The two countries can be seen as sharing many fundamental problems as well as aspirations of modern society. The United States and Japan are not simply military allies and economic rivals; they are also two highly developed, industrial mass societies. As such they can either cooperate to face and deal with their common concerns, or each can go its own way. There seems to have been growing awareness of this community of concerns. When Henry Kissinger included Japan in his new Atlantic Charter proposal (23 April 1973), observers felt it was a proper thing to do. His view that "Japan must be a principal partner in our common enterprise" sounded plausible on an economic level, although the idea of Japan as an Atlantic nation was incongruous on the level of mutual security or military strategy of the Atlantic Charter. As Kissinger said, "We must identify interests and positive values beyond security in order to engage once again the commitment of peoples and parliaments. We need a shared vision of the world we seek to build." During their visit to Tokyo in November 1974, President Ford and Secretary Kissinger continually stressed the need for cooperation, not competition, between the two countries in solving the problems of food and energy shortages.

At least some Americans seem to have accepted the view that the urgency of solving these problems transcends any inherent cultural differences or psychological distances that might exist between Japan and the United States. What Kissinger termed "positive values beyond security" are seen as no longer confined to exclusive Western civilization, but as applicable on a worldwide scale. The awareness of common destiny can be helpful in creating an intellectual readiness to discuss U.S.-Japanese relations in a broad framework so that the two peoples may be viewed as sharing not only common needs but also common values.

For over a century after the opening of Japan by Perry, American needs and American values predominated in providing a vocabulary for dealing with U.S.-Japanese relations. That was perhaps why most Americans felt so little need to "understand" Japan. For over two decades after the Second World War, Japanese reconstruction and development took place within the framework defined by the United States. Japan, as a State Department memorandum of January 1945 put it, was to be integrated into "the family of economically interdependent and peace-loving nations." The assumption, as old as American history, was that each country's peaceful economic development was conducive to the creation of a more peaceful world. The crushing economic difficulties of the 1970s have sharply challenged that assumption, and the advanced industrial societies, as well as the oil-rich countries and the less developed nations, are faced with the serious question of defining their national objectives. If these difficulties should impel the American and Japanese peoples to broaden their horizon and picture themselves as real partners in preserving world civilization, the 1970s could yet prove to have been a decade of significant achievement in American-Japanese understanding.

Self-Images of Japan and the United States in a Changing World

Joji Watanuki

Self-Images

A self-image is the definition of the self vis-à-vis others. It contains both emotional and cognitive components, as when we speak of self-feeling or self-perception. Moreover, "self" often means the organizing principle of the individual; therefore, if one fails to define oneself, one will be unable to act consistently. Thus, the understanding of someone's "self-image" is important for understanding or predicting his behavior in relation to others.

However, can we talk about the "self-image" of Japan or the United States? How useful would such a concept be? In the first place, we might talk about the state as an actor, and look for some mysterious, collective self-definitions or esprit d'etat which can explain the state's behavior. However, empirical sociologists are tempted to break down such gross concepts into more demonstrable slices. The images of the foreign policy decision-makers and opinion leaders concerning the definition of the state's "self," that is, its mission, role, and future perspective vis-à-vis other states, deserve initial attention. We can learn of the self-images of Japan and the United States, in the post-World War II period, through studies of memoirs and other records of U.S. Presidents and Secretaries of State on one hand, and those of Japanese Prime Ministers and Foreign Ministers on the other. We then can examine these self-images of the U.S. and Japan and their vicissitudes over time. Also, analyses of the attentive public, that is, of the leading opinion makers—both individual writers and mass media—can assist in determining the self-images of Japan and the United States.

However, in this paper I shall focus on mass mood, that is, the images of the mass public concerning the role, position, and task of each country as an international actor. The prime reason for doing this is as follows. Although the mass public has only a vague image concerning such remote problems as the role of their nation in the world, and although their vague images are little more than a mood that is susceptible to manipulation and changes in circumstances, still, in such open and democratic societies as the U.S. and the post-World War II Japan, these moods and images function as constraints on the decision-makers. The decision-makers, who are politicians, tend to cater to the mass mood. If the decision-makers want to change national policy by attempting to persuade the mass public, they have to be careful to select a familiar rhetoric to which the public is responsive. As a step to such further analysis, we shall consider the characteristics of the mass mood of Japan and the U.S. concerning their roles in the world.

Continuity and Discontinuity

Needless to say, we cannot ignore historical factors in dealing with a social phenomenon. Self-images of a nation—whether held by decision-makers, opinion leaders, opinion-submitters, or attentive or mass publics—are historically bound. One is often tempted to point out recurrent patterns that are idiosyncratic to a nation. In the case of the U.S. recurrent fluctuations of mood from introversion to extroversion in American foreign policy have been observed.[1]

In a different context, some observers note a possible recurrent pattern in Japan's self-image: the fluctuation between Asian and away-from-Asia orientations. An extreme case of the Asian orientation was the notorious idea of the "Greater Asian Co-prosperity Sphere" during World War II. Examples of the latter include the strong attempts to imitate, admire, and catch up with Western Europe and/or the United States.

However, comparing the U.S. and Japan, and especially thinking of mass opinion, I would like to argue that we perceive post-war Japan as a case of strong discontinuity from pre-war Japan. In contrast with the mood favoring territorial expansionism by military means that charac-

1. Frank L. Klineberg, "The Historical Alteration of Moods in American Foreign Policy," *World Politics*, January 1952.

terized Japan in pre-war days, in post-war Japan a mood favoring pacifism, or at least non-territorial expansion and non-reliance on military means, has firmly established itself.

Present State of Self-Images in the U.S. and Japan

United States. There are signs of change both in policy choices and in mass opinion to lessened extroversion. According to a survey of Americans, "complete internationalism" has decreased from 30 percent in 1964 to 18 percent in 1972, although moderate internationalism has increased from 27 percent to 35 percent.[2] The character of "national fears" mentioned by the respondents has changed remarkably during this period. Fear of "war" has declined from 64 percent in 1959 to 35 percent in 1972; and fear of "communism" has dropped from 12 percent in 1959 and 29 percent in 1964 to 8 percent in 1972. On the other hand, fear of "lack of law and order" has increased from less than 5 percent in 1959 and 5 percent in 1964 to 11 percent in 1971 and 16 percent in 1972, and the fear of a "drug problem" has risen from less than 5 percent in 1959 and 1964 to 7 percent in 1971 and 9 percent in 1972.

Table 1 shows the change of American moods concerning the country's mission in the world. However, in spite of the decline in internationalism, 39 percent of Americans are still prepared to go to the very brink of war, and a plurality believes in the mission of preventing the spread of communism. This presents a remarkable contrast to the mood of the Japanese public.

Beside the fluctuation between extroversion and introversion, or between internationalism and isolationism, Gabriel Almond set forth five other characteristics of the mood of the American people on international affairs:[3] changes "from unstructured moods in periods of equilibrium to simplification in periods of crisis"; shifts in mood from euphoric to dysphoric, from optimistic to pessimistic; oscillation and ambivalence between tolerance to difference or even encouragement of new things, on one hand, and intolerance to difference on the other, which takes the form of ideological imperialism; ambivalence toward, and fluctuation between idealism which prizes generosity, good will, and Christian ethical ideals, on one hand, and, on the other, cynicism, which regards self interest as the basic motive of all behavior; superior-

2. William Watts and Lloyd A. Free (eds.), *State of the Nation* (N.Y.: Potomac Associate, 1973), p. 203. The 1972 survey was done in June 1972 on 1,806 national samples.
3. Gabriel A. Almond, *The American People and Foreign Policy* (N.Y.: Harcourt, Brace & Co., 1950), pp. 54–65.

Table 1

The United States should maintain its dominant position as the world's most powerful nation at all costs, even going to the very brink of war if necessary.

	1964	1968	1972
% Agree	56	50	39
% Disagree	31	40	50
% Don't know	13	10	11

The United States should take all necessary steps, including the use of armed force, to prevent the spread of communism to any other parts of the free world.

	1968	1972
% Agree	57	46
% Disagree	29	43
% Don't know	14	11

ity and inferiority. Concerning the last point, Almond argues that since Americans are similar to parvenus, they tend to have an inferiority complex toward the Old World, and at the same time, they "tend to judge other nations and other cultures according to a strictly American scoreboard, on the basis of which America is bound to win."[4]

If Almond's explanation is correct, what characterizes the American attitude toward international affairs is its characteristic change from one extreme to another according to the felt threat from the international environment. However, changeability is not peculiar to the American people. The question is whether the range and speed of fluctuation is greater and more rapid in America than elsewhere. In order to answer this question, two factors should be explored. One is the role and function of the mass media in causing fluctuation in the mass mood. Another is the nature of the issues or events that touch upon the sensitivity of the American public.

In this connection, and concerning the Japan-U.S. relationship, the last point which Almond mentioned—superiority-inferiority complex—seems to deserve special attention. The superiority-

4. *Ibid.*, p. 63.

inferiority complex is not peculiar to the American people; it is as universal as ethnocentrism. The Japanese especially tend to think in superiority-inferiority terms both in their personal and international relations. However, one peculiar element concerning the position of Japan in the mind of the American public is that of racism, i.e., prejudice against non-white peoples and nations. Needless to say, the most notorious cases were the anti-Japanese-immigrant movement in California in the 1920s and the relocation of all Japanese and Japanese-Americans from the West Coast during World War II. Of course, the present-day U.S. is not what it was in the 1920s and the 1940s in this regard. Because of the awakening of minority groups in the U.S., the U.S. is turning into a multi-ethnic nation. However, can we really say that racism has died completely in the U.S.?

Japan. it is important to ask whether the pre-war way of thinking in Japan has been transformed. The self-image of the Japanese in the pre-war and wartime periods had been characterized by such attributes as justification of expansion by military means, strong craving for the position of world power, sense of mission as a savior of Asia, and an inferiority-superiority complex. Of course, these were the result of indoctrination from above, and the mass public had only a diluted replica of this image.

Defeat in the war and the subsequent occupation smashed this kind of self-image. In the early period of occupation, as the demilitarization of Japan was an aim of the occupation, pacifism was encouraged. This culminated in the famous Article 9 of the Japanese Constitution, which forbade reconstruction of the armed forces. Japan was strictly secluded from the rest of the world, and the Japanese were conditioned to think in quite isolationist ways, except for their ties with the U.S. The U.S. had acquired an overwhelming position in the self-image of the Japanese. For instance, according to a survey conducted in 1949, the U.S. virtually monopolized the choice in terms of "liked country." (See Table 2.)

After more than twenty years since the end of the occupation, and with the huge economic power of Japan, how are the Japanese people thinking about their nation in the world? Is the pre-war type of thinking reviving?

According to various surveys, including ours,[5] there is no sign of a

5. IIR, Sophia survey on international perception of the Japanese people, which was conducted in June 1972. Preliminary report of that survey is available as *Contemporary Japanese Perceptions of International Society*, IIR, Sophia University, Research Papers Series A-13, 1973.

Table 2

Most Liked Country
(in percentages)

	National Institutions	National Character	Country would most like to visit
United States	45.8	42.8	44.5
Great Britain	8.6	6.0	2.1
France	0.7	1.3	3.2
Switzerland	2.2	0.6	3.0
USSR	1.0	0.8	. . .
Others	41.6	48.5	47.2

Published in the *Yomiuri Shimbun*, August 15, 1949. The survey was conducted in August 1949 on national samples.

revival of the pre-war type of thinking. On the contrary, the pattern of thought that originated in the period immediately after the war strongly persists. On the other hand, Japan's recently increased economic power, and concomitant international pressures, have been producing certain changes in the minds of the Japanese concerning Japan's international role.

Let me explain. First, as for the persistence of post-war thinking, the prevalence of pacifism and to some degree of neutralism in the minds of the Japanese should be mentioned. Support for Article 9 persists among the public. Younger and better educated people support Article 9 and the constitution as a whole. The special feeling of the Japanese against nuclear weapons—the origin of which can be traced to Hiroshima and Nagasaki—continues to persist both among the mass public and the opinion leaders. And there is no sign of decline of such feelings, in spite of the tremendous growth in Japan's economic power and foreign arguments that Japan's nuclear armament is unavoidable.

Neutralism, unlike nuclear pacifism, does not have the support of the majority of the mass public or the Japanese government. On the other hand, it has been the stand adopted by the largest opposition party —the Japan Socialist Party—and also has caught the minds of roughly one-third of the Japanese mass public.[6] The rightist minority in Japan has been charging that the Japanese people have not yet recovered from the servile mentality enforced under the occupation.

Several kinds of criticism have been coming from abroad. There has been criticism of Japan's "free ride" on the U.S. defense budget. More recently, with the increase in Japan's economic power, others have criticized Japan's isolationism and have urged Japan to take a more positive international role—not necessarily a military role, but an economic or political role.

In this respect, we notice several signs of change in the mood of the Japanese public in the direction from isolation to internationalism, although they are not inconsistent with pacifism and neutralism. Ironically, from the perspective of American critics of Japan's isolationism, the immediate phenomenon is a declining U.S. image in the mind of the Japanese. The U.S. has ceased to monopolize the attention and feeling of the Japanese people. (See Table 3.) In a sense, it is a normal process of diversification and amplification of international images. Younger and better educated poeple show more diversified attention and feelings toward a variety of nations. They like Western Europe more, and, in terms of attention and the necessity for the improvement of relationships, China and the Soviet Union attract their attention more. They tend to approve the idea of more increased and tolerant aid to developing Asian countries.

However, there is no sign of either the revival of the pre-war sense of mission or the emergence of a new-type sense of mission. According to surveys, the Japanese people tend to shun the idea of Japan as a world power, and they prefer a self-definition such as "middle power" (*chukyu-kokka*).

Another characteristic of the new image is that partisanship or self-definition as conservative or progressive (*kakushin*) divide Japanese opinion very sharply, especially in evaluations of the relationship between Japan and the U.S. Socialists, Communists, or progressives are more critical of the U.S. and more inclined to closer relationships with China and the Soviets. Also, progressives have more understanding and sympathy toward developing Asian nations than do the conservatives. On the other hand, in terms of "liked nations," they

6. Cf. Douglas H. Mendel, Jr., "Japanese View of the American Alliance in the Seventies," *Public Opinion Quarterly*, Vol. XXXV, No. 4 (Winter, 1971–1972), p. 525. Preference for alignment with "free nations," "Communist bloc," or neutralism has been stabilized throughout the 1960s: about 40 percent prefer "free nations"; 30 percent prefer neutralism; and only one or two percent of the respondents choose "Communist bloc."

Table 3

Longitudinal Change of the Most Liked Country
(in percentages)

	1950[1] August	1957[2] November	1965[3] September	1972[4] July
United States	65.7	27	31	12.6
West European Countries	X[5]	X	X	25.8
Great Britain	2.1	3	X	X
France	1.3	4	X	X
West Germany	0.5	2	X	X
Switzerland	3.9	X	X	X
U.S.S.R.	1.6	1	1	0.7
China	0.5	2	3	4.4
Taiwan	X	X	1	0.3
Korea	X	X	0.4	5.0
Other Asian Countries	X	X	1.1	1.8
India	X	6	2	X
Others	1.5	8		1.2
Non-aligned	22.9		60.5	25.8
None, All	X	47		36.5

1. *The Yomiuri Shimbun*, August 15, 1950. Over 20-years-old living in six large cities, n = 4,142.
2. *Americana*, March 1961, p. 46. National sample, over 20-years-old. Survey conducted by Chuo Chosasha.
3. *The Yomiuri Shimbun*, October 17, 1965. National sample, over 20-years-old, n = 3,000.
4. IIR, Sophia survey.
5. Since the list of the names of countries in each survey was different from each other, X indicates "not applicable" category in that survey. Moreover, 1965 *Yomiuri* survey used the question asking the most liked country from the neighboring countries of Japan, thus omitting West European countries.

1, 2, and 3 are cited from Akira Kurihara, "Nihonjin no ajia zo," in Yasaka Takagi (ed.), *Nichibei kankei no kenkyu* (Tokyo: Tokyo Daigaku Shuppankai, 1970), Vol. 11, p. 51.

tend to choose Western European countries more than the conservatives. Thus, in the case of progressives, their international images are more complicated than those of the conservatives. They are less pro-U.S.; they feel a necessity to establish closer relationships with China and the Soviets; and they have understanding and sympathy for other developing Asian countries; but emotionally they are attracted by Western Europe.

Contrast of Self-Images Between Japan and the U.S.

In spite of the tendency of the U.S. to turn to introversion, the American public is more extroverted than the post-war Japanese public; moreover, the U.S. has a far stronger sense of mission than Japan. The pacifism and neutralism of the Japanese is not necessarily isolationist, as we saw in the case of Japanese progressives. However, even the internationalists among the Japanese tend not to support positive policies or positive actions by Japan in the international arena. Their mood is to "do no harm." In my opinion, the Japanese need more positive ideas concerning Japan's role in the world—ideas that are compatible with the post-war pacifism and neutralism.

On the U.S. side, the question is whether the still strong sense of mission of the U.S. is appropriate in a changing world. As measured by opinion polls, the extrovertive moods of the U.S. public are still excessively colored by what Professor Brzezinski calls "power realism." On the other hand, Brzezinski pointed out the emergence of a new type of internationalism in the U.S., what he calls "planetary humanism."[7] If so, can we foresee the growth of "planetary humanism" in the minds of the American public?

7. Zbigniew Brzezinski, "U.S. Foreign Policy: the Search for Focus," *Foreign Affairs*, July 1973, pp. 712–714.

Japan's Decision-Making System as a Determining Factor in Japan–United States Relations

Chihiro Hosoya

Recent years have witnessed a new turn of events in Japan-U.S. relations. It appears to have taken place not in the direction of cementing their existing close ties, but rather of loosening them, as symbolized by President Nixon's sudden announcement of his trip to China, and by a series of wrangles over such economic issues as textiles, monetary policy, American investment in Japan, and Japan's purchase of American products. Although the two countries still maintain the alliance relationship, with an increasing amount of bilateral trade valued at more than $15 billion, it is noticeable that a political cleavage has developed, however small, between them.

The change of bilateral relations between Japan and the U.S. is certainly related to the changing pattern of the global and regional international system. The emergence of Japan as an economic power on the international scene is also an important factor in the deterioration of the Japan-U.S. relations. Japan's rapidly growing economic activities have produced a search for markets and natural resources all over the world, often causing friction and competition with American economic interests. Further, the setback the U.S. suffered in Vietnam has spread a mood of frustration and irritation among various circles in the U.S., which has caused the American government to advocate a less tolerant policy toward Japan.

Obviously, the plane of common interests is still much wider than that of potential conflicts for both countries. It is, however, hard to say whether they will continue to drift apart or whether this trend will reverse. It will depend in part upon the development of the general international system, and in part upon the future configuration of the domestic political and economic environment of each country.

The purpose of this paper is to explore some features of Japan's foreign policy decision-making system as one of the domestic factors restraining its future course of action, and to project Japan's policy on Japan-U.S. relations in the context of its decision-making system.

An additional purpose of this paper is to clarify the similarities and differences in the patterns of the foreign policy decision-making systems of the two countries, for each nation has a "perception gap" regarding the working of the decision-making system of the other country. And this "perception gap" often causes an avoidable conflict for both governments, as in the case of the dispute over the textile issue.

Truncated Pyramid Pattern

The political system of prewar Japan lacked strong, unitary leadership. Under the Meiji Consitution, in principle the supreme authority for the conduct of foreign affairs was under the Emperor's control. The Emperor, who theoretically was in a position to bring about the ultimate integration of policy within the decision-making system, in actuality did not directly intervene in the decision-making process, although he made efforts at times to express his views on external matters in a circumlocutory way. Except for the case of Japan's ending the Pacific War, the Emperor had restrained himself from exercising his theoretical supreme power to direct Japan's foreign policy.

The Prime Minister in prewar Japan was nothing more than *primus inter pares* in the cabinet; he could not even dismiss a dissident minister of his cabinet. Furthermore, the integrative power of the Prime Minister in the government was considerably mutilated by the doctrine of the independence of the supreme command, which placed matters pertaining to military command outside of the competence of the cabinet. It was a system in which the governmental leaders at the top found it difficult to exert as much control as required by their positions over the making of important decisions; and it could be properly termed a "truncated pyramid" system.

With the Emperor playing only a symbolic role in postwar Japan, the Prime Minister now stands at the top of the decision-making structure.

The Japanese Prime Minister, who is empowered under the postwar constitution to appoint and dismiss cabinet members at will, and is not hampered by the doctrine of the independence of the supreme command, holds stronger control over the foreign policy decision-making process than did his prewar predecessors.

In this context, several cases can be mentioned in which the Japanese Prime Minister in the postwar period, when confronted with crucial foreign policy issues, took the leadership in steering the nation: Premier Hatoyama Ichiro, in the case of Japan's normalization of its relations with the Soviet Union; Premier Sato Eisaku, in the case of reversion of Okinawa; and Premier Tanaka Kakuei, in the case of Japan's normalization of its relations with China.

Nevertheless, the Japanese Prime Minister continues to hold less power in the formation of foreign policy than his American counterpart, and the pattern of a truncated pyramid system still persists in some respects. President Nixon is often likened to an American emperor; and there is a lament that goes, "No one knows what Nixon's next move may be. There is no way to stop his actions, as he acts as if he were guided by the Divine Providence." The Japanese Prime Minister's power looks dwarfed when one considers President Nixon's dramatic mining of Haiphong Harbor, a performance that brings home strongly to the American people the "explosive expansion" of the options that he had gathered into his own hands.

The difference of the decision-making power held by the highest ranking decision-maker in Japan and the United States is undoubtedly due to the difference in their parliamentary and presidential political systems. In addition, the Japanese Prime Minister must necessarily rely upon political support from the leaders of the various factions of his own political party, as well as on the financial support of the business community, in order to attain and hold his position. Thus, unlike the American President, the Japanese Prime Minister, who does not have a fixed term of office, must resign if he loses the support of the leaders of his party and the major business circles.

Fear of losing party or business community support is less restrictive on an American President in making bold foreign policy decisions. President Nixon, for example, could announce his forthcoming visit to Peking, which obviously marked an abrupt change in policy, without lengthy prior consultations with political leaders and the rest of the government bureaucracy. A move of this sort is simply beyond the competence of a Japanese Prime Minister, who before reaching a final decision on any substantial change in Japan's foreign policy must make an exhaustive effort to consult a wide spectrum of the Japanese leadership in politics, business, and the bureaucracy in order to obtain the fullest range of support for any eventual decision.

Mikoshi Politics

One of the dominant features that makes the postwar decision-making system in Japan distinct from the prewar one lies on the relevance of the intra-party politics of the Liberal-Democratic Party to the governmental decision-making process, and the much elevated role played by the leaders of the factions of the Party. Although it is an exaggeration, it might be said that the LDP has taken the place of the military of prewar Japan in terms of affecting the process of making decisions on crucial external affairs. There are few major decisions Japan has made in the postwar period in which factional politics of the LDP has not been involved.

The Prime Minister, who can hold his position because of his leadership of a "mainstream" factional coalition of the LDP, must be closely watchful of the debate among factions over major foreign policy issues, and of the effect of governmental decisions on the dynamism of factional politics. It is in this context that the leaders of major factions, as well as key personnel responsible for party organs, enter the stage of the decision process. Thus, largely circumscribed by the intra-party politics of the LDP, the decisional latitude of the Japanese Prime Minister in major foreign policy issues becomes much more limited than that of the American President.

Bureaucratic politics is also related to the process of making foreign policy decisions. The high officials of governmental agencies, such as the Ministry of Foreign Affairs, the Ministry of International Trade and Industry (MITI), and the Ministry of Finance join the decision game as players according to the significance and the nature of the issues. Generally speaking, the bureaucratic circles hold advantageous positions due to their competence in gathering information on the external setting and supplying it to governmental leaders. The image held by the governmental leaders of their nation's external environment is based on the information these bureaucratic circles supply, and they are often bound by the image created within the bureaucratic apparatus. Also, in choosing the actions to be taken toward other nations, the governmental leaders have to rely upon the expert knowledge of bureaucratic circles concerning military, diplomatic, and economic affairs, and upon their technical skill and facilities. In this way, the scope of options for the decision-makers can be circumscribed by bureaucratic circles, and even their evaluation and ranking of priorities may be prescribed by them.

The "bureaucratization" of the policy-making process is a phenomenon that is generally observed in modern states. President Nixon, fearing bureaucratic disruption of his policies, immediately upon his assumption of office carried out a drastic reformation of the bureaucratic structure by revitalizing the National Security Council. His object was to center control over foreign policy in the President's hands and to get rid of the malady of the "bureaucratization" of the policy-making process.

In Japan, where the bureaucratic power traditionally has been influential on the governmental decision-making process, no drastic measures designed to overcome the disease of the "bureaucratization" have been taken. No organ comparable to the National Security Council exists, and certainly no Henry Kissinger is present in Japan. Although the American President commands various channels of information —including the CIA, the military, and the Department of State—the Japanese Prime Minister mainly relies upon information provided by the Ministry of Foreign Affairs. Even the LDP organs charged with external affairs, such as the Foreign Affairs Research Committee and the Policy Affairs Research Council, are often said to perform merely the function of working on the documents prepared by government officials and to approve them without much change.

The leaders of business circles seem to increase in importance in postwar Japan with respect to foreign policy issues. Unquestionably, they are more involved in the process of formulating foreign policy of an economic character; yet, their involvement is not limited to economic issues. While exerting influence indirectly through MITI or the faction leaders of the LDP, they get involved at times in the decision process in a more direct way. One cannot gain insight into Japan's policy-making process toward the U.S., the Soviet Union, and China, or its economic aid policy, without understanding the influence of its business leaders.

With the Prime Minister as the central player, there are a number of players, regular and ad hoc, who vary in their degree of influence upon Japan's foreign policy. Once the Far Eastern Department of the British Foreign Office made an interesting and penetrating observation concerning the decision-making system of prewar Japan. It likened the system to the Japanese custom of carrying Mikoshi—a light, portable wooden shrine—and said: "The general direction is not in doubt, but the speed and manner of progressing is the resultant of thrusts from one side and counter-thrusts and restraints from the other. The shrine sways widely from one side of the road to the other—backs and fills—sometimes it stays poised and stationary, sometimes it lands the entire party in a ditch. But the bearers all know where they are going and sooner or later that is where they take the shrine."

With the military departing from the position of the central bearer of the Mikoshi parade, the pattern of the decision-making process of postwar Japan has undergone a change; yet it seems that no basic change has occured concerning the Mikoshi-style of decision-making. The bearers all know that they are going in the direction of pursuing economic interests and expanding the economic power of the nation and compete with one another for various alternatives. Competition is going on among various circles and groups: the "mainstream" versus "anti-mainstream" or "hawks" versus "doves" within the LDP; the Ministry of Foreign Affairs versus the Ministry of International Trade and Industry over international economic policy; big business versus medium-size business, and so on. At times they form a group coalition.

Thus, a decisional outcome is to be "the resultant of thrusts from one side and counter-thrusts and restraints from the other." With the Prime Minister lacking strong traction power, the Mikoshi parade moves slowly, taking a zigzag course.

Consensus Decision

Emphasis on consensus in reaching decisions must be noted here as another trait of the Japanese decision-making system. It is a traditionally accepted notion that great efforts must be made to gain consensus among the components of the decision-making system, rather than to take a majority vote in making a major decision. A good historical example can be drawn from the case of the heated debate over the conclusion of the military alliance with Nazi Germany in 1939. In spite of more than seventy meetings of the Five-Minister Conference between January and August 1939, the Hiranuma cabinet could find no way to accommodate the views of the Army on one hand, and of the Navy and Foreign Office on the other; thus, it simply stayed in a state of indecision. Japan's Pearl Harbor decision represents another case. It was not until a consensus was finally reached among all of the members of the Liaison Conference and the Cabinet in response to receiving the Hull Note of 26 November 1941, that Japan made an ultimate decision on opening hostilities with the U.S.

Consensus is sought of course, in the process of making foreign policy decisions in the U.S., too; but relative emphasis placed on consensus-building is different in the two countries. It appears that the U.S. system does not allow the governmental leaders to pay the price of consuming a great deal of time and of losing necessary timing by requiring the building of consensus among the consituents of the decision-making system.

Perhaps more remarks may be needed to account for the Japanese emphasis on a consensus decision process. It is essential in Japanese society for the leaders of organizations to make a maximum effort to obtain the views of their constituents, even if only for appearance's sake, to save face and to maintain harmonious relationships. Japanese society may be characterized as one where a system of mutual reliance is dominant. The higher echelon people lean on their subordinates and vice versa; the business circles lean on the bureaucratic circles and vice versa. It is a system of mutual reliance which places emphasis on interrelationships and on the maintenance of organizations. Consensus-building tends to be more important in the decision-making of this kind of society.

Japan's Foreign Policy Options

The decision-making system of Japan's foreign policy, which I have described, imposes restraint on the government and inhibits bold action in foreign affairs. It is a formidable task for them to create a consensus on the issues of foreign policy that involve a confrontation of views among various groups and circles. Further, it means a great political risk for them to pull the "Mikoshi" rashly, with much strength, in a certain direction. A cautious approach is needed to balance the "Mikoshi"; and sometimes political maneuvering must be prudentially conducted even at the cost of much time. It is a system that makes it difficult for the decision-makers to introduce an innovative policy in foreign affairs, and that induces them to make incremental decisions which do not deviate too greatly from the line of extension of the hitherto followed course. Thus, a strong impetus that presses the governmental leaders to examine a new course seriously must come from outside the system.

A historical look at Japanese foreign policy demonstrates many cases in which external pressure has been the most dominant factor accounting for a change in Japan's course of action. By "external pressure" I imply not only an action by a foreign country directly affecting Japan, but also a significant change in Japan's external environment. A recent case is offered by the Japanese policy of normalizing relations with

China. Without the "Nixon Shock" it must have been much more difficult and taken much more time for the Japanese government to take steps toward establishing normal relations with Communist China.

There are diverse domestic pressures exerted on the political leaders to bring about a change in Japanese foreign policy. For instance, the rise of nationalistic sentiment among the general public and the rank and file of the LDP, and mounting social unrest resulting from the failure of governmental policy in dealing with land distribution and environmental destruction. Of course, the departure of the LDP from governmental power will have a determining effect on Japan's course of action. These problems, however, lie beyond the task of this paper.

Country Expertise and United States Foreign Policymaking: The Case of Japan

I. M. Destler

If the U.S.-Japanese alliance is to be renewed and strengthened, concludes one recent analysis, "The U. S. government should become attuned to the fine detail of internal politics in Japan and act with sensitivity to these factors."[1] Another similarly stresses that "the fine details of governmental structure and process, of lines of influence and channels of communication, of political stakes, of the interplay of issues, of the 'state of play' in another capital must be clearly and widely understood."[2]

Such an aim can be pursued by a variety of means. Broad studies can be undertaken to analyze the policymaking systems of the two countries, like the current Brookings Institution project in which the author is engaged. Regular Japanese-American dialogues can be organized between groups from the respective official, academic, business, and other professional communities. Reform of the media and of educational processes can be attempted, with the hope that the literate population of each country will develop a deeper, more sophisticated understanding of the other. But even granted substantial success along all

1. Graham T. Allison, "American Foreign Policy and Japan," in Henry Rosovsky, ed., *Discord in the Pacific*, Columbia Books (for the American Assembly), 1972, p. 45.
2. Michael H. Armacost, "U.S.-Japan Relations: Problems and Modalities of Communication," *Department of State Bulletin*, 15 January 1973, p. 64.

of these lines, the number of people in each country with a considerable interest and understanding about the other will remain quite limited. If such interest and understanding are to be reflected in national policies, then, two further questions must be asked. How likely are such people to be able to exercise substantial influence on these policies? And what can be done to affect the prospects of their doing so?

This chapter represents a tentative effort to analyze the influence of U.S. "Japan experts" on American foreign policy toward that country. For purposes here, "Japan expert" will be defined to include: (a) those with a major professional identification as Japan specialists; (b) those with specific official responsibility (especially in the State Department) for U.S.-Japan relations; and (c) those with considerable knowledge and interest about Japan, enough to make them sensitive to the particular features of Japanese politics and underlying cultural traditions.[3] It thus includes what Akira Iriye and Neil Harris characterize as the "intermediate layer of sub-specialists" in another chapter of this book.[4] And one further qualification will be added—"Japan experts" will be limited to those who are significantly concerned about the overall Japanese-American relationship per se, rather than being interested in Japan just because it is important to other policy objectives (like a textile agreement or military base rights). The Japan experts whose influence is considered here will usually be those within the U.S. government, whether on a temporary or career basis. But the analysis is intended to apply to outside experts as well. Moreover, partly because the "insiders" are the most likely channel by which the views of outside experts can be brought to bear on government decisions, the rise and fall of inside experts' influence is probably rather closely linked to that of the influence of the broader "expert" community.

3. This definition is designedly a broad one. It encompasses a far larger group than the few hundred Americans who would merit the label of "Japanologist": a person deeply versed in Japanese language and culture whose primary professional identification is as an expert in the country and/or its politics, history, culture, literature, etc. This runs the risk of misleading some readers. But this broader definition of "Japan expert" is appropriate to the purposes of this chapter. A phrase conveying the meaning with greater precision—*e.g.*, "Americans sensitive to Japan and giving high priority to the U.S.-Japan relationship"—would be too cumbersome. And expertise is relative. Few are the Reischauers who serve in official positions. In comparison to most U.S. officials who affect policy toward Japan, those fitting under our definition *are* experts. They are also the only dependable links between these other officials, on the one hand, and the "true" Japanologists on the other. And finally, generalizations about the limited influence of "Japan experts" in the sense used here will apply even more to the smaller group whose expertise meets more demanding specifications.

4. See A. Iriye and N. Harris, "United States Policy toward Japan: Problems of Understanding," p. 91.

Expert Influence: How Much Is Enough?

The case for a greater policy contribution from Japan specialists is a familiar one. Partly it is based on apparent Administration insensitivity to the impact on Japan of policy steps taken for other purposes—the "Nixon Doctrine" declarations of 1969 and 1970, the soybean fiasco of 1973, and above all the opening toward China. Partly it is based on deficiencies in the way direct issues with Japan have been handled, above all the textile negotiations. And finally, it reflects a concern with what seemed to be the Nixon-Kissinger approach to Japan more generally. This includes a pattern of wanting to deal seriously only at the summit or the Kissinger level, and of then feeling frustrated or betrayed once such dealings do not end up resolving major issues as expected. It also includes a tendency either to take Japan for granted or (according to some critics) to assume that Japanese movement to a more independent policy stance is inevitable (and perhaps even desirable for the U.S.). This Nixon-Kissinger approach is related to the so-called "five-power world" that that Administration apparently wanted to build internationally. This was seen as requiring direct "diplomacy at the top" with strong executive counterparts in other major power centers with whom binding deals could be cut.[5]

U.S. -Japan experts (and Americans interested in Japan more generally) tend to voice many of these criticisms and concerns. So calls for enhancement of their influence are, of course, de facto pleas for changes in the U.S. policy approach. They were doubtless so regarded by Mr. Kissinger when he was urged to put more Japan experts on his National Security Council staff. And regardless of one's position in the debates between Kissinger and his critics, one should not assume that U.S. policy toward Japan—or toward any country—will automatically be "better" policy the greater the degree of "country expert" influence and control. Obviously there will be times when broader U.S. interests, international or domestic, need to be pursued at some cost to the U.S.-Japan relationship. And Japan experts, being usually "advocates" of "their" country, will often oppose such action. Moreover, country experts can have other recurrent weaknesses—a tendency to exaggerate the long-term costs of being politically and personally unaccommodating to Japanese leaders on short-term issues; a bias toward conservatism; an assumption that the people and the views of the Liberal

5. For a more extended analysis of this pattern in Nixon-Kissinger foreign policymaking generally, see pp. 295–319 in my *Presidents, Bureaucrats and Foreign Policy*, Princeton University Press, 1974 edition. This chapter was also published separately as "The Nixon System: A Further Look," *Foreign Service Journal*, February 1974, pp. 9–14 and 28–29.

Democratic Party and the Gaimusho will dominate Japanese policy in the future.

It becomes necessary, then, to distinguish *analysis* from *prescription*, to separate (insofar as is possible) the question of *what determines the extent of expert influence* from the distinct (though related) question of *how much such influence is desirable*. On the latter question, the author's present position is that greater "country expert" influence on U.S. policy toward Japan would have been desirable during the past few years, and that in the immediate future the impact of these experts on America's Japan policy is likely to be too weak rather than too strong. This latter conclusion, in turn, flows from the analysis of the determinants of expert influence with which this chapter is mainly concerned. For the trends are not in the experts' favor.

To telegraph its punches, this chapter will argue that the recent decline in the influence of Japan experts stems in part from a basic conflict between two goals that Americans concerned about Japan tend to espouse—(1) greater public and official *attention to Japan;* and, (2) greater *receptiveness to Japan expertise.* When attention to Japan increases, it is usually because influential Americans find Japanese behavior to be importantly related to their essentially non-Japanese concerns, ranging from specific domestic and international product markets to the world monetary or political order. They involve themselves in U.S.-Japanese relations to achieve policy objectives that are frequently uncongenial to those whose interest and priority is to the relationship itself. Their involvement, in turn, puts major U.S.-Japan issues into political arenas and policy frameworks where the Japan experts' expertise is seen as of limited relevance and (in part) suspect.

Before developing this argument, however, we will first consider the general policymaking process which U.S. Japan experts must seek to influence. Next we will look briefly at recent history to describe and illustrate the decline in their impact. Then we will move to a more general analysis of the reasons for this decline.

U.S. Foreign Policymaking—A Bureaucratic and Domestic Political Process

United States policy toward Japan emerges from the large and complex process which generates overall American foreign policy. Officials from a wide range of "line" departments and agencies—State, Defense, CIA, Treasury, Agriculture, Commerce, etc.—deal with many Japan-related issues in their day-to-day work, seeking to make official decisions and actions as consistent as possible with their agencies' policy objectives and interests. Involved also are "staffs" such as those of the National Security Council, the Council on International Economic Policy, and the Office of the Special Trade Representative. The interdepartmental nature of major issues requires these officials and agencies to cooperate and to compete: Okinawa is inevitably a question of defense *and* diplomacy; trade policy requires a blending of a range of foreign policy and domestic policy considerations.

Decisions and actions emerge from all levels of this governmental system, through a continuing process of bargaining labeled "bureaucratic politics." Major issues are seldom decided all at once, nor does "policy" usually emerge from a calculated process of centralized advance planning. Rather, the U.S. policy course is typically determined day by day, piece by piece. To influence these daily U.S. decisions and actions, officials need leverage, which is drawn from "bargaining advantages." The most important "bargaining advantages" for American foreign policy officials include: formal authority or responsibility on an issue; the backing of constitutents outside the executive branch; recognized expertise; involvement in regular "action processes" (such as budget review or cable clearance); access to or control over information; the ability to produce good, relevant staff work; and the personal confidence of the President and of other influential officials. The distribution of influence varies with the substance of an issue, and with the form in which the issue arises. It varies also over time, as some men and institutions rise while others fall.[6]

Such "bargaining" among officials (and between them and influential people and interests outside government) is not, of course, a uniquely American phenomenon. Though the U.S. foreign policy bureaucracy is unusally large and organizationally complex, "bureaucratic politics" is present, presumably, in all national governments. Indeed, such dispersal of power is often cited as particularly characteristic of the *Japanese* foreign policymaking system—with its strong career bureaucracies, and with its Prime Minister constrained by the need to maintain his support coalition in order to remain in office.[7] When Prime Minister Sato proved unable to "deliver" on his apparent

6. For more extended treatment of the organization and politics of United States foreign policymaking, see my *Presidents, Bureaucrats and Foreign Policy*, Princeton University Press, 1972 (expanded edition, 1974); and Morton H. Halperin, *Bureaucratic Politics and Foreign Policy*, Brookings Institution, 1974. For more on "bargaining advantages," see Graham Allison, *Essence of Decision: Explaining the Cuban Missile Crisis*, Little, Brown and Company, 1971, pp. 168–69; Roger Hilsman, *To Move a Nation*, Doubleday, 1967, pp. 559–61; and Halperin, *Bureaucratic Politics*, Chapter 12.

7. See Chihiro Hosoya, "Japan's Decision-Making System as a Determining Factor in Japan–United States Relations," on pp. 117.

summit conference promise to President Nixon to resolve the U.S.-Japan textile dispute, this was cited as evidence of the contrast between the two systems. Nixon had the power to cut such deals and make them stick, it was argued, whereas Sato did not. Indeed, some critics of the "bureaucratic politics" approach as applied to American foreign policy have been heard to suggest that the government for which it may really be apt is the one whose seat is Tokyo.

There is much in the President-Prime Minister contrast. This chapter hopefully illustrates that attention to bureaucratic and broader domestic politics can be useful in explaining *American* foreign policy decisions and actions. But it is important to acknowledge right away that the U.S. system *does* differ from that of Japan (and other major democratic countries) in the relative strength of the chief of government, the President, and in his separation from the legislative branch.[8] The President is elected as an individual for a fixed four-year term. His principal Cabinet advisers are not usually "colleagues" and potential rivals, as in Japan or other parliamentary systems, but rather individuals brought to prominence by him. Lacking political bases of their own, they are generally dependent upon his confidence if they wish to have policy influence. White House aides are even more dependent. Nor is the President answerable to the Congress in the sense that a Prime Minister is to the legislature from which he comes, though the other side of this particular coin is that the U.S. Congress is far less responsive to Presidential leadership than is, for example, the Japanese Diet to the Premier.

Still, it is not necessary to jump from these recognized differences in political structure to a conclusion that the nature of policymaking is fundamentally different in the two countries. For the second paragraph of this section can serve as a characterization of *Japanese* policymaking if one substitutes "Japan" for "U.S.," "Japanese" for "American," and "Prime Minister" for "President." The distribution of "bargaining advantages" differs as between the systems, but "bargaining" pervades them both. Even certain widely-cited cultural characteristics of Japanese policymaking can be incorporated into such a political

8. Bureaucratic politics analysts have generally stressed the limitations and constraints to which Presidential power is subject, taking their cues in part from Richard E. Neustadt's classic book, *Presidential Power*, Signet, 1960. They (we) have been right in doing so, since such constraints have been (and still are) widely ignored. However, a comparative government focus underscores the President's relatively greater autonomy, and his domination of the process compared to what prevails in other countries. In recognition of this power, Halperin devotes a separate chapter to "Presidential interests," emphasizing that his influence and role in the process differs in kind, not just in degree, from the Cabinet officials and lesser bureaucrats below. (See his *Bureaucratic Politics and Foreign Policy*, Chapter 4. See also my *Presidents, Bureaucrats and Foreign Policy*, Chapters 4 and 5, and "Epilogue.")

framework. Considerable "consensus" and widespread consultation is important in both political systems—witness, for example, the joy and relief in Washington during the first month of President Gerald Ford. Insofar as more consensus is expected in Japanese political culture, however, this serves to enhance the influence of lower-level officials on their seniors, and of minority groups affected by particular governmental actions on the substance of these actions. *Amae* psychology has a related and similar effect. If "dependence" gives subordinates and weaker parties the right to expect their interests will be protected by their superiors, this likewise tends to equalize bargaining power. But decisionmaking remains a political process as earlier characterized.

Nor does the Nixon-Sato textile example prove any fundamental system difference. By their agreement, the President was meeting the demands of the American textile industry, the dominant U.S. interest group on the issue. What Premier Sato had to do was far more difficult—to deliver on terms strongly *opposed* by the government agency (MITI) and the domestic textile industry which together would have to implement them. And insofar as Nixon's agreement to Okinawa reversion was in some way related, this was founded—as will be later noted—on a careful bureaucratic consensus-building effort of several years duration. By contrast, Nixon and Kissinger seem to have hoped that, on textiles, Sato's agreement could substitute for the existence of such a consensus in the country making the concession.

Still, the President's particular strengths in the foreign policy sphere are important to an understanding of the American system. It is he, under the Constitution, who has the power to appoint and instruct diplomatic representatives, to negotiate treaties, and to command the armed forces. And the postwar world has, of course, provided unparalleled occasions for the use of these powers. Presidents with such strength and independence have been increasingly unwilling to depend mainly on the State Department (or other "line" foreign policy agencies) for advice and action on international matters to which these Presidents give high priority. Nor are they required to do so by either custom or statute—in fact, the Secretary of State's basic congressional grant of authority is to "perform and execute such duties as from time to time be enjoined or entrusted to him by the President of the United States."[9] Instead, seeing the bureaucracy as "unresponsive" to their interests and priorities, Presidents have gone "over the heads" of the ongoing foreign policy government in two related ways. The first is by creating staffs based in the White House to watch, prod, coordinate,

9. Don K. Price, ed., *The Secretary of State*, Prentice-Hall (for the American Assembly), 1960, p. 2.

and at times substitute for these line bureaucracies. The second is by the separating of certain key decisions from these bureaucracies *and* from most members of these White House-based staffs—with a President taking them instead upon the advice of a small, closed circle of aides in whom he has confidence. This circle is likely to include some but not all of his senior foreign policy advisers such as the Secretary of State, the Secretary of Defense, and the Presidential Assistant for National Security Affairs.

If through such means a President could, in fact, control and direct all the major actions of the U.S. government in the international arena, this would lead to a coherent and purposive overall foreign policy, at least insofar as the President's own intentions added up to one. But two "facts of life" make this impossible. The first is that on the issues he personally addresses, the President remains constrained in typical political ways—by his need to support those officials whose continued effectiveness he most values; by his dependence on instruments operationally controlled by permanent bureaucracies; by the capacity of Congress to undercut many of his policy initiatives unless Congressional concerns are taken into account. The second is that neither the President nor his top advisers can determine all U.S. policy actions themselves. For these actions are too many in number—and too diverse in substance—to be controlled by the decisions of a small circle who designedly limit their communications of their purposes with bureaucrats below them, or by staff officials whose credibility as Presidential agents is, more often than not, difficult to maintain. The usual result is that much of U.S. foreign policy is not very coherent or consistent, specifically including overall Nixon Administration dealings with Japan. The State Department, which has the organizational depth and breadth to bring coherence to a wide range of U.S. foreign policy provided it has Presidential support, is weakened because Presidents don't feel the Department is their own and tend to work above or around it. This was particularly the case—in differing ways—during the Kennedy regime and the first Nixon Administration. Or a situation may arise like the present one (or like that of Dulles under Eisenhower). In this case the Secretary of State is indisputably the preeminent foreign policy official, but can only handle a few issues effectively himself and won't delegate the others to either subordinate "political" appointees or senior Foreign Service Officials.

When, then, does U.S. foreign policy show reasonable purpose and coherence? The most obvious situation is when the President and one or a few top aides seize upon a few issues they consider of overriding importance. Thus Nixon and Kissinger stressed relations with Russia and China and the Vietnam war, and directed their power, skill, and attention to dominating them week by week. The second, less-noted situation conducive by policy coherence arises when a group of officials somewhere below Cabinet level, drawn from one or several departments, succeeds in controlling and giving direction to an area of U.S. foreign policy which is, for the top leaders, a second-order affair. Such a group requires, it must be emphasized, the general sympathy of their supervisors, for top leadership can at any time take action which will reverse or stall the efforts of those below, or preempt the issue area entirely. Moreover, Presidents and Cabinet officials will almost inevitably be involved personally to some degree in summit conferences and Cabinet-level discussions, or on those many other occasions when a high-level signature is necessary to move a matter forward within the U.S. government. Unless what they say and do on such occasions is consistent with the aims and advice of the group of subordinates, the latter lose their ability to control or "manage" U.S. policy. And in the process of coordinating the two levels, an important facilitating and "circuit-connecting" role is usually played by sympathetic White House aides, at least one of whom is frequently an important member of the sub-Cabinet "group."

Within this general system, how have specific issues vis-à-vis Japan been handled in recent years? It is time to turn now to a brief treatment of the Kennedy, Johnson, and Nixon years.

1961–72: The Decline of "Country Expert" Influence

The Kennedy and Johnson Administrations evidenced only limited top-level U.S. government interest in Japan. After his much-lauded appointment of Edwin Reischauer as Ambassador, Kennedy paid so little attention to the country that Japan is not even listed in the index to Schlesinger's foreign policy-dominated, 1,031-page memoir-history, though Reischauer is mentioned twice. Lyndon Johnson's *The Vantage Point* reflects a similar non-interest, as do the memoirs of his national security adviser, Walt W. Rostow.[10] However, these Presidents and their top subordinates were generally aware of the importance of the

10. Arthur M. Schlesinger, Jr., *A Thousand Days: John F. Kennedy in the White House*, Houghton Mifflin, 1965; Lyndon Baines Johnson, *The Vantage Point: Perspectives on the Presidency, 1965–1969*, Holt, Rinehart and Winston, 1971; W. W. Rostow, *The Diffusion of Power 1957–1972*, The Macmillan Company, 1972. Theodore Sorensen's memoir, *Kennedy*, Harper and Row, 1965, includes two Japan references in its index, both to pre-1961 events.

Nor did the Eisenhower Administration pay Japan any more high-level heed. In Townsend Hoopes' books, *The Devil and John Foster Dulles*, Atlantic-Little, Brown, 1973, no Japan issue or episode between the 1951 peace treaty and the abortive Eisenhower trip of 1960 received as much as a page of attention in the over 400 pages devoted to the Dulles Secretaryship.

relationship, and sympathetic to initiatives to strengthen it. Thus, the U.S.-Japan Joint Ministerial Conferences were inaugurated in 1961. Thus, American diplomats pressed sometimes incredulous Europeans to get Japan admitted to the OECD. It was, as Clapp and Halperin note, "a period in the U.S.-Japanese relationship when policy was left pretty much in the hands of the experts," and specifically to the "middle-level bureaucrats in both the State department and Defense Department, most particularly those who had a continuing interest in U.S.-Japanese relations."[11] But it was of critical importance that these bureaucrats were working with explicitly or tacitly delegated authority from inattentive, but generally sympathetic, top officials.

It was during this period that the bureaucratic groundwork was laid for the 1969 Nixon decision to return Okinawa to Japan. In some respects this is quite surprising. One generally expects policymaking dominated by middle-level officials to be cautious and status-quo oriented, particularly if a prominent role is played by the State Department country desk which normally tends to emphasize short-run maintenance of good relations with its "client" country. The creative, pro-reversion efforts are even more surprising in that they required getting the U.S. military to make a major apparent sacrifice of its interests. But in the Okinawa case, the "experts" performed brilliantly. Their sensitivity to Japan made them recognize the political impossibility of keeping U.S. administrative jurisdiction indefinitely, and started them moving on the problem early enough so that governmental decision-making could be undertaken piece-by-piece in a non-crisis atmosphere. Their sensitivity to bureaucratic politics was reflected in their careful cultivation of the U.S. military, in their insistence that representatives of the Joint Chiefs be brought in on each step and that they be encouraged to plan militarily for the post-reversion situation. Both the avoidance of crisis and the cultivation of the military had the effect of minimizing the danger of formation of a strong military-conservative-congressional opposition to reversion on strategic and (U.S.) nationalist grounds. Finally, the "experts" had the good fortune of possessing a case for reversion that was easy to understand and that most recent U.S. Presidents would have found weighty. For as noted earlier, these Presidents recognized the general importance of good U.S.-Japanese relations even if day-to-day pressures directed their attention elsewhere. If action could be taken to secure this objective with minimal bureaucratic or broader political costs to the President, and

11. Priscilla A. Clapp and Morton H. Halperin, "U.S. Elite Images of Japan: The Postwar Period," in Akira Iriye (ed.), *Mutual Images: Essays in American-Japanese Relations*, Harvard University Press, 1975. See also Morton H. Halperin, "U.S.-Japanese Relations: The Changing Context," *Pacific Community*, October 1973.

with no serious damage to other policy objectives, the President's answer was likely to be "yes."[12]

Two of the key bureaucratic "movers" for reversion (Richard Sneider and Morton Halperin) joined the Kissinger staff at the time of Nixon's inauguration, and the U.S. ambassador in Tokyo—U. Alexis Johnson—became Under Secretary of State. By May 1969 Nixon appears to have accepted the basic argument for Okinawa reversion, though negotiations on the terms continued until the summit that November, and the detailed arrangements were not fully worked out until mid-1971. But this decisive "expert" role was not to be duplicated on other major Nixon Administration Japan issues. By fall 1969, both Halperin and Sneider had left Kissinger's staff. By late 1972, Henry Rosovsky could note that U.S. paper-writers for the Shimoda American Assembly conference were "almost without exception—extremely critical of our own current policies."[13] And in July 1973, the most distinguished of America's Japan experts denounced Nixon Administration treatment of Japan as "absolute folly." This sorry record, said Edwin Reischauer, was "due to the fact that no one at the White House knows anything about Japan."[14]

The textile issue was the most dramatic case of an issue being handled by "non-experts." Leaving aside the question of whether the United States was to seek restraints on Japanese synthetic textile exports—a matter essentially settled by President Nixon's campaign commitment in 1968—there were certainly "experts" within the bureaucracy with both the textile and Japan expertise required to handle it, most notably Assistant Secretary of State for Economic Affairs Philip Trezise. But such persons had neither the Presidential mandate nor the industry confidence which were politically necessary to play this role. Commerce Secretary Maurice Stans did, and if his early handling of the issue was counter-productive for U.S.-Japanese relations, it was reasonably successful in assuring the U.S. industry (and the President) that the negotiating initiative was a serious one, and that State Department efforts to "water down" the President's commitment would be effectively resisted. Much later, after numerous failures and fiascoes, a quite different approach was tried—the missions of Ambassador-at-large David Kennedy which shut out the State Department Japan experts even more effectively.[15]

Ironically, by U.S. postwar standards, the Nixon Administration

12. These reflections have been stimulated by reading draft chapters of the current Brookings Okinawa case study by Priscilla Clapp and Haruhiro Fukui.

13. Rosovsky, ed., *Discord in the Pacific*, p. 3.

14. Quoted in *New York Times*, 15 July 1973, p. 3.

15. Those observations are based on the Brookings case study by Haruhiro Fukui, Hideo Sato, and this writer.

comes out quite well in terms of attention paid to Japan. Richard Nixon came to office knowing Kishi and Sato personally, and with an interest in Japan probably greater than that of any of his recent predecessors. In his first year, Nixon gave high priority to mending America's alliance relationships, and for Japan he saw Okinawa reversion as an indispensable step toward this goal. And even after 1969, as the U.S.-Japanese relationship grew more and more frayed, he continued to give Japanese matters much greater personal attention than any other U.S. President since Truman. As for Henry Kissinger, it wouldn't be an outlandish estimate to suggest that he has spent, perhaps, ten times as great a proportion of his time on Japan as did the previous Presidential National Security Assistants, McGeorge Bundy and Walt Rostow.

Aside from the early attention to strengthening the alliance, however, this Nixon-Kissinger attention to Japan was not primarily the product of a larger policy design. Unlike the calculated cultivation of China, the time they spent coping with Japan was largely extracted from them by the pressure of events. This has meant, in terms of our earlier analysis, that policy coherence built around strong, middle-level bureaucratic leadership has not been replaced by coherence imposed from the top, but rather by a pattern of inconsistent, semi-coordinated U.S. actions toward Japan taken with other U.S. objectives uppermost in mind. But recent developments reflect *more* than the idiosyncrasies of Nixon-Kissinger style. Some of the events which have shaped recent U.S. policy toward Japan have been idiosyncratic, like the early Nixon Administration's obsession with the textile quota issue. More enduring, however, is the fact that Japan's economic rise has made impossible the top-level neglect of Japan of the early and mid-sixties, especially during the recent crisis of America's world economic position. And this rise has, in turn, focused greater attention on Japan's present and potential role on the world diplomatic-political scene.

The U.S.-Japan relationship remains an "unbalanced" one. But while the oft-cited "attention gap" continues, it is equally true that general U.S. "attention" paid to Japan has been rapidly increasing since the mid-sixties. This has been especially true among U.S. interests potentially affected both by Japanese economic activity and by U.S. policy actions influencing this activity. For them, as for the President and his major policy officials, Japan issues have become too important to be left to the Japan specialists.

The Limits of Expert Influence—A General Analysis

In some respects, of course, increased attention to Japan sharply heightens the demand for Japan experts' services. Japan studies programs multiply. Japanologists are invited to more conferences, asked to give more lectures, offered more jobs, and probably sell more copies of their books. In the government, too, the increased importance of Japan means there are many more bureaucrats who need to know *something* about Japan. They need to, most obviously, because their objectives require negotiating something with Japanese bureaucrats, or at least will be affected in some way by official Japanese action. They also need some Japan knowledge for their bureaucratic credibility. In order to establish their right to be taken seriously on a Japan-related issue, they need to be able to speak knowingly (if not always knowledgeably) about MITI and the Gaimusho, about the latest trade or military budget figures, about Japanese government leaders and bureaucrats and their operating styles.

Yet this sort of knowledge can often be very superficial. And at the same time as Treasury, Commerce, and White House aides (for example) are seeking it, they are also competing for influence with the "Japan experts," those in the State Department as well as elsewhere. This limits their willingness to defer to expertise greater than theirs, or to imply in any way that it entitles its holders to special influence. Rather, those newly concerned with Japan will tend to fill in the blanks of their knowledge by applying American models to Japanese institutions which have similar labels and similar apparent forms. Japan is, after all, a major world power, with a democratic political system, a modern capitalist economy, and a large, functionally differentiated bureaucracy.

And when seemingly persistent Japanese phenomena cannot be encompassed within this conceptual framework, there is a tendency to jump to the other extreme by adopting ideas (like "Japan, Inc.") which suggest something totally alien to Western experience. The Japan experts are appalled, but their frequent parallel role of Japan *advocates* (particularly as seen by bureaucratic adversaries) makes their protests easy to discount and their expertise easy to dismiss.

At the same time, issues affecting U.S.-Japan relations become less and less "Japan issues," and more and more issues of "great power relations," "world monetary reform," "agricultural commodity policy," or a "President's political commitment." The expertise in these matters is usually held by others.

Japan in U.S. Domestic Politics. As Japan becomes more important (as measured, for example, in relative GNP, exports, etc.), more United States political interests and actors are likely to perceive stakes in what Japan does or what the U.S. government does in its Japanese relations. How to deal with Japan becomes an important issue for debate as the

Congress considers general trade legislation, as in 1970 and 1973. More U.S. businessmen feel a need to influence their government's dealings with Japan, whether they seek access to the Japanese market for export or investment purposes, or protection in our own market. More politicians see potential gains in scapegoating, denouncing the Japanese government for "arrogance" or "unfair" business practices. A smaller number seeks the role of statesman-intermediary, as did Senator Jacob Javits during the textile dispute.

Japan experts find it difficult to operate effectively in this wider political forum. To them standard political statements about Japan are often so erroneous or misleading as to defy being taken seriously. Yet to rebut them is to sound like an advocate for the Japanese case. Moreover, the real concerns of U.S. political actors usually involve not what is happening in Japan, but the impact of Japanese actions—public or private—on *American* society. On this the experts may have no special claim to knowledge— though many have taken it upon themselves to acquire such knowledge.

The prominence of Japan-related issues in U.S. politics is not, of course, a simple linear function of Japan's share of the world economy or U.S. import markets. Southern state legislatures were pushing boycotts of Japanese textile products as early as 1956, and California was passing anti-Japanese legislation during Theodore Roosevelt's Presidency. Nonetheless, Japan's rise on the world scene does seem to be the fundamental underlying reason for increased attention to Japan by Americans.

Japan Issues as Functional Issues (Particularly Economic). Once the postwar GATT-Bretton Woods system was in place, U.S. economic policy toward Japan could emphasize two major strands—securing her a viable, somewhat sheltered place in that system, and making side deals on textiles, etc., to protect politically sensitive United States industries. Both were easily accommodated within the bilateral U.S.-Japan relations framework, and the first did much to strengthen it. This approach could be taken because Japanese economic policies in the early postwar years had relatively little impact on the overall operations of the world economic system. Today, this is no longer the case. Undervaluation of the yen in 1969–73 was a world economic problem, and even before that there was a growing belief (shared by some Americans essentially sympathetic to Japan) that Japan was clinging to economic advantages that were no longer justifiable, and doing real damage to larger world economic and monetary relationships in the process. Today, monetary and trade reform efforts depend significantly on

Japanese involvement and cooperation, in sharp contrast to the forties and fifties when decisions about the basic structure of the world trade and payments systems could be made without serious Japanese participation. Japan is indisputably one of the three great capitalist economic power centers. Economic specialists concerned with global problems have to concern themselves very seriously with what sorts of economic policies Japan is likely to adopt, and should adopt.

But if what the U.S. government wants Japan to do is directed at these purposes, it is the trade and monetary officials who are likely to dominate the decision process, not those with specific responsibility for Japan. It was, after all, Paul Volcker, Under Secretary of the Treasury for Monetary Affairs, who secretly visited Tokyo in Feburary 1973 to prepare the way for the second dollar devaluation.

Another sort of problem arises from the interdependence of domestic and international economic policy, underscored by the 1973 soybean export control fiasco. Even if one believes that some sort of export limitations was very likely in summer 1973, the handling of the issue was abominable, vis-à-vis both Japan and Europe. Since the way was not prepared diplomatically, it came across as an erratic, arbitrary action taken without any apparent regard for the interests of countries the United States had been cultivating for years as export markets. Yet the most important actors in such a decision were, almost inevitably, the chief economic policy officials and the Secretary of Agriculture. "Diplomatic" handling of the issue, then, was likely to depend upon the disposition and ability of top Administration foreign policy officials to weigh in for the protection of diplomatic and trade relationships. Japan experts were not well enough placed to know when and whom to warn; they didn't know that any such decision was pending.

This leads to the third way that increased U.S. attention to Japan tends to cause Japan experts to lose influence—preemption by top-level officials.

Top-Level Preemption of Japan-Related Decisions. In his classic article, "How Could Vietnam Happen?" James C. Thomson, Jr. refers to the "banishment of real [Vietnam] expertise brought on by the 'closed politics' of policymaking as issues became hot: the more sensitive the issue, and the higher it rises in the bureaucracy, the more completely the experts are excluded while the harassed senior generalists take over (that is, the Secretaries, Under Secretaries, and Presidential Assistants)."[16]

16. *Atlantic*, April 1968, p. 49.

Japan has little in common with Vietnam, and the Nixon Administration was very different from its Johnson predecessor. But Nixon and Kissinger certainly practiced "closed policymaking" to an unparalleled degree, designedly and purposively. And it was practiced by others in that Administration on Japan-related issues—when David Kennedy and Peter Peterson took over the textile negotiations in the spring of 1971, when John Connally dominated the international monetary scene in the aftermath of August 15 that same year and apparently in the "crisis decision" to impose soybean export controls in 1973.

While that Administration has been accused (with some justice) of neglecting Japan, what is notable, as mentioned earlier, is the number of major Japan-related decisions and actions that were taken in the White House. For the same factors associated with increased attention to Japan that have made issues "political" and "functional" have also pushed them to the White House, and encouraged their resolution on criteria other than how they will affect Japanese politics and U.S.-Japan relations. But at the White House another element enters, important in any administration but particularly in the Nixon regime. For Presidents *are* concerned with bilateral relationships, with the sum of U.S. dealings with particular countries and national leaders. President Nixon was especially concerned—in fact, he seemed to be building his much-stressed "structure of peace" around the personal relationships that he and his chief aide developed with other national leaders, especially Brezhnev in Russia and Chou in China. And he and Kissinger stressed time after time that specific bilateral issues with a particular country should not be separated but "linked," as part of the overall U.S. bargaining relationship with the country concerned.

Why then didn't Nixon and Kissinger draw heavily on that Japan expertise which would seem essential to building such a relationship? Basically, the reason seems to be that they felt they didn't have to. Earlier reference was made to the Nixon-Kissinger need for counterpart leaders at the top of governments abroad with whom to cut "deals." Specifically, it was derived from the institutional requirements of their closed foreign policymaking system domestically and the sought-after "balance of power" system internationally. More generally, however, it is anything but exceptional for national leaders to thirst for conceptual frameworks which give order to the welter of world political systems and events. Johnson was receptive to Walt Rostow's particular world vision, just as Nixon welcomed the major intellectual service Kissinger performed for him by incorporating the foreign policy ideas and inclinations of Nixon (and of Kissinger) into a broader, relatively coherent doctrine and basis for action. And their particular approach gave Nixon and Kissinger a normative basis for prodding the Japanese Prime Minister to behave like a world statesman. Far from seeing a need to understand peculiarly Japanese institutions and adapt accordingly, they saw a need to get the Japanese to behave like Nixon and Kissinger. So when Premier Sato made a textile promise and then didn't keep it, they did not ask whether, given the nature of Japanese politics, it was fruitful to seek one's objectives by squeezing promises out of a Japanese Prime Minister who didn't seem to have the power at home to deliver. Rather, one must educate the Japanese about the world system, or at least make it clear that there are costs to their unwillingness or inability to play the game by our rules. And since they saw a more independent Japanese posture as both inevitable and quite acceptable for U.S. interests, and unlikely to be carried too far, Nixon and Kissinger saw little cost (and perhaps even some gain) in the periods of strained relations which such an approach inevitably entails. Had Japan been an object of assiduous diplomatic cultivation, like China, there would have been a greater Nixon-Kissinger interest in things Japanese. But, of course, this is not the case.

Also limiting top-level receptiveness to Japan expertise is the widely-shared doubt that a sophisticated, nuance-sensitive diplomatic approach to the Japanese government would yield significant short-term results. Like most country specialists (Sovietologists excepted), Japan experts tend to be advocates of Japan's interests, or at least of U.S. sensitivity to these interests. But the Japanese government is slow-moving, and to those Americans interested in specific quick policy results, deference to Japanese political processes and sensitivities seems a prescription for accomplishing very little. But if the Japanese system seems poor at responding positively to sensitive, careful outside diplomatic approaches, it seems extraordinarily good at adapting to *faits accomplis.* Indeed, Commodore Perry's "black ship" has become a symbol of the role that the unwanted but irresistible, externally imposed change in Japan's international environment can play in spurring Japanese internal policy movement. To many in the U.S. government, the "Nixon shocks" have worked. Unilateral U.S. actions and threats forced exchange rate adjustment and a textile agreement after diplomatic approaches had failed. By this not-uncommon view, "the Japanese" will do something only when forced to do it, but then they will accommodate quite adroitly and will not retaliate. The long-range dangers of this approach are repeatedly cited by Japan experts—above all, the resultant fueling of anti-American sentiment which could contribute, over time, to political changes in Japan that bring a swing in Japan's international position far greater than is dreamt of in the Nixon-Kissinger philosophy. But politicians and statesmen live in the short run. And isn't the Japanese Prime Minister still placing great political stock in the U.S. relationship, even looking to summit conferences and prospective state visits (à la Nixon) as means of shoring up a weak position at home?

A Final Factor: Japan as Incipient Adversary

Finally, there is another factor limiting expert influence on Japan policy which is related to increased U.S. attentiveness. This is the view of Japan as incipient adversary. Japan experts talk in terms of "partnership." So did the Nixon Administration. But it seemed to view Japan in considerable degree as an *economic* adversary, and the balance of power approach, at minimum, diluted the alliance character of the relationship. And some officials were less ambiguous. The widely held "Japan, Inc." conception of a unique, alien economic threat predisposes its adherents to see Japan as more adversary than ally. Thus a "member of the Nixon Cabinet" widely believed to be Maurice Stans could tell a *Time* magazine reporter in the spring of 1971: "The Japanese are still fighting the war, only now instead of a shooting war it is an economic war. Their immediate intention is to try to dominate the Pacific and then perhaps the world."[17] The spread of this conception is directly related, of course, to the thawing of the cold war. For Americans, the diminished perception of a "Communist threat" emanating from Russia and China has inevitably weakened the force of the argument that Japan is essential as an ally to contain that threat.

The influence of any individual or group on a particular government policy area depends considerably on how much their conception of the problem is shared by those in power, how much they and the "decisionmakers" have reasonably consistent objectives. If Japan experts tend to be sympathetic with the position and interest of "their" country, their ability to affect national policy will inevitably rise and fall according to whether or not this sympathy is shared.

Conclusions

It seems clear, then, that the influence of Japan experts on U.S. foreign policymaking has declined in recent years. In part this has been the product of the idiosyncrasies of the current Administration, and of the issues which happen to have come to the fore. But this reduced

17. *Time*, 10 May 1971, p. 85.

influence also is a product of longer term phenomena. Japan is increasingly important in U.S. domestic politics. Japan issues tend to become multilateral, functional economic issues as that country's economic importance increases. Top-level preemption of Japan issues is triggered by Japan's increased importance in American politics and economics, and facilitated by the strength and autonomy of the American Presidency in foreign policymaking. This top-level takeover has assumed particular features because of the Nixon-Kissinger approach and style. But the analysis here suggests that such preemption would likely have increased anyway during this period, and is likely to remain a strong factor in U.S.-Japanese relations in the future.

One must recognize that much of this is entirely legitimate and reasonable. Japan issues *are* too important, with too many implications for other U.S. policy objectives and interests, to be left to the Japan specialists. But that is not the present danger. Rather, it is the opposite, that Japan experts will not have sufficient influence, that U.S. policy decisions will not be made with sufficient understanding and calculation of their likely impact on that country, and that they will not be pursued with an approach and style which maximizes the chance for a tolerable, mutually beneficial, long-term relationship.

If one decides, then, that Japan experts need to increase their influence, how can one advise them to go about doing so? Much, obviously, is out of their hands. They cannot determine the identity, personal styles, and broad policy approaches of the President and his chief aides. They cannot control the wide range of political and economic forces, domestic and international, which push certain issues to the forefront at certain times. But precisely because Japan experts cannot control these matters, they must learn to understand them better, to adapt to them, and to use them to advance rather than retard their own policy aims. They need to be able to argue their cases in terms of widely shared U.S. policy values other than America's stake in U.S.-Japan relations, however important this stake may be. They need to be sensitive to, and operate effectively within, the bureaucratic and broader domestic political arenas in the United States. They need to be experts—as some are—in some policy area other than Japan—trade is the most obvious example. They need to think about mobilizing de facto "alliances" within the bureaucracy on particular Japan-related issues with officials representing American interests who care little about Japan, but whose objectives happen to coincide with the "experts' " own. (And they can be considerably aided by more skilled efforts by *Japanese* actors to influence the U.S. decisionmaking process, especially by acting so as to support these American "experts.")

None of this has never been done before. The Okinawa reversion decision was cited earlier as one where the "experts" were in control, and where a notably statesmanlike decision was reached for reasons of overall U.S.-Japanese relations. Yet these "experts" were able, at least tactically, to accomplish this *not* because of their sensitivity to Japan, but because of their sensitivity to the interests of *American* bureaucrats and institutions, their ability to accommodate military policy needs, their ability to maneuver within the *U.S.* system. It is unreasonable to expect that future issues of comparable importance can remain essentially "inside," middle-level issues as Okinawa did. But the lesson is still highly relevant.

For U.S. policy on politically and economically volatile issues will never be the product of country experts calculating and controlling every move and placing the interest of the relationship above the political and economic concerns of other Americans—in and out of government—who have stakes in the outcome. For them even to try this is a sure recipe for their exclusion from real policymaking on the most important matters. Rather, over the longer term, the most effective, reasonable U.S. policy toward Japan will arise if there are strong foreign policy officials who see their role as *mediating* between the needs of the relationship (and of the Japanese), on the one hand, and the pressures of domestic politics and the demands of other U.S. policy objectives, on the other. Such policy leaders might or might not be "Japan experts" as defined in this paper. But they would, at a minimum, be open to what the Japan experts had to say, and view it as an important, valid input into the policies which emerge.

Political Factors in Postwar Japan's Foreign Policy Decisions

Kan Ori

I.

Scholars who are concerned with domestic determinants of foreign policy can be broadly categorized into three groups. Their foci of study vary in scope and in relevant "time-span," and these can be arranged in three concentric circles.[1] The first group, which constitutes the innermost concentric circle, consists of those scholars who are interested in what might be called "decisional" variables, variables related to specific foreign policy decisions. Their attention is on those actors who affect individual decisions or on specific situations that lead to particular foreign policy decisions. The analyses are concentrated on various components of formal government institutions concerned with foreign policy such as members of the National Security Council, State De-

I wish to thank conference participants, both in Chicago and Tokyo (April 1974), for their valuable comments on my conference paper. My special gratitude is due to Professors Chihiro Hosoya (Hitotsubashi), Morton Kaplan (Chicago), James Morley (Columbia), Kinhide Mushakoji (Sophia), Sadako Ogata (I.C.U.), Michio Royama (Sophia) and Hiroharu Seki (Tokyo), many of whose ideas are incorporated in this revised version of my Conference paper. I also wish to thank Dr. Lee Kam Hing, Lecturer at the Department of History, University of Malaya, for his assistance on the paper.

1. Cf. Patrick J. McGowan and Howard B. Shapiro, *The Comparative Study of Foreign Policy: A Survey of Scientific Findings* (Beverly Hills: Sage Publications, 1973), pp. 35–51, particularly Figure 6, "Maximum Rates of Change in Variable Categories," p. 46.

partment officials, and Presidential "foreign policy" advisors in the case of the United States or the "middle echelon" bureaucrats in the case of prewar Japan. They direct their study to the interplay of these major players, their roles in foreign policy, their style of decision-making, and the immediate situational variables leading to certain major and often critical foreign policy decisions. In Japan, we have a considerable body of scholarly works in this area, and such an approach is well represented in a chapter here by Professor Chihiro Hosoya, who is one of the pioneers of foreign policy decision studies in Japan.

The second group of scholars deals broadly with domestic political actors involved in the decision-making processes of foreign policy. These scholars consider not only the bureaucratic components but also other "political" variables pertinent to the study of foreign policy behavior. Their concern extends to the role of political parties, the activities of "foreign policy" interest groups, the nature of the political party system, the degree of political competition and conflict, the level of political institutionalization,[2] and so forth. In other words, the emphasis of these scholars is on the political factors related to foreign policy decisions rather than on the specific foreign policy decisions themselves. They would assess various domestic political actors, whether or not they are formal government components of foreign policy decision-making, to the extent that they influence foreign policy behavior. These "political structure" variables encompass a broader scope and require a longer time-span than the elements studied by the first group of scholars. Such an approach is basically the preserve of comparativists, but so far there are very few studies in this field in Japan.

The third group of researchers examines the impact of the general public on foreign policy behavior. They are concerned with such mass

2. "Institution," in general terms, refers to "especially well-delimited, stable and enduring patterns of behavior (infused with values [norms] which order patterned behavior)." Roger W. Benjamin and Kan Ori, "Nihon ni okeru seito no seidoka," Japanese Political Science Association (ed.), *Gendai nihon ni okeru seijitaido no keisei to kozo* [*Nenpo Seijigaku*, 1970] (Tokyo: Iwanami Shoten, 1971), p. 72; Roger W. Benjamin and Kan Ori, "Process Analysis and Change and Stability in Japanese Electoral Politics," a paper presented to the International Sociological Association Meetings, Toronto, Canada, August 19–24, 1974 (p. 9); Carl J. Friedrich, *Man and His Government: An Empirical Theory of Politics* (New York: McGraw-Hill, 1963), p. 70; Samuel P. Huntington, *Political Order in Changing Societies* (New Haven, Conn.: Yale University Press, 1968), chapter 1; Adam Przeworski and John Sprague, "Concepts in Search of Explicit Formulation: A Study in Measurement", *Midwest Journal of Political Science*, Vol. XV, No. 2 (May 1971), pp. 183–218; Richard Sisson, "Comparative Legislative Institutionalization: a Theoretical Exploration," in Allan Kornberg (ed.), *Legislatures in Comparative Perspective* (New York: David McKay Co., Inc., 1973), p. 19.

factors as public opinion and political culture that have relevance to foreign policy issues. These "cultural" variables, which constitute the third concentric circle in the scheme, are wider in scope and are of a longer time-span than the other two categories. The study of foreign policy from this perspective is provided in a chapter of this book by Professor Joji Watanuki, one of the foremost empirically oriented sociologists in Japan.

My concern here is with "political" variables in the second concentric circle of the scheme. They are among the least studied by foreign policy specialists; yet, "political" variables seem to be very important when we attempt any study of major foreign policy decisions of postwar Japan. This is primarily because postwar foreign policy, which has been intimately connected with major domestic issues throughout the entire period, basically has been determined by domestic politics in Japan.[3] As an example, many of Japan's controversies on national security and defense, which have involved its relations with the United States, have been important in the domestic Japanese political process. And positions on these controversial issues have been determined by such domestic considerations. Not only did Japan's normalization of relations with the People's Republic of China involve leading domestic political actors such as the Japan Socialist Party and Komeito, but the manner in which this was accomplished was reflective of the factional nature of Japanese politics. Despite the fact that the linkages between domestic political factors and external affairs were much in evidence in postwar Japan, no systematic study of the relationship between Japan's political structure and its foreign policy has been made beyond the level of case studies.[4]

While the purpose of this chapter is not to provide such a systematic study, it is hoped that descriptive accounts of postwar Japan's foreign policy determinants referred to here will stimulate research along such lines. After identifying major political determinants of Japan's postwar foreign policy, their salient aspects are explained and their possible consequences on future U.S.-Japan relations are discussed. Some frag-

3. For a critical review of the linkage politics model and related empirical studies, see my chapter on "Kokusaiseiji to Kokunaiseiji no renkei," in Kinhide Mushakoji and Michio Royama (eds.), *Kokusaigaku no riron* (Tokyo: University of Tokyo Press, 1975) pp. 143–190. On the importance of domestic political restraints on Japanese and American foreign policy decisions in particular, see Professor Hiroharu Seki's research proposal to the Peace and Communication in the Pacific Conference, August 1973, East-West Center, University of Hawaii.

4. As to the extreme scarcity of literature relating the domestic political structure to foreign policy behavior, despite the realization by scholars of international relations of its importance, see McGowan and Shapiro, *op.cit.*, pp. 75–91.

mentary ideas for future research are also suggested in the accompanying footnotes.

II.

As to political determinants affecting postwar Japan's foreign policy, four major components can be tentatively identified. They are: (1) the ruling Liberal Democratic Party (conservatives) and the factions within it; (2) the Japanese political party system as a whole; (3) big business and other "foreign policy"-related interests; and (4) government agencies involved in foreign policy. These four determinants are basically isolated and derived from several case studies of postwar Japan's major foreign policy, and are drawn in part from my general understanding of Japanese domestic politics.[5]

The Liberal Democratic Party and Its Factions. The close involvement of the ruling political party in foreign policy is one of the most noteworthy aspects of postwar Japan. In a case study of the Russo-Japanese Peace Agreement of 1956, Professor Donald Hellmann observed that the "most striking feature of the Soviet negotiations is the extent to which control of policy was concentrated within the Liberal Democratic Party," and that "other components of Japanese politics were able to affect the formulation of policy only insofar as they were able to reach conservative [*i.e.*, the Liberal Democratic Party] decision-making."[6] I do not believe that this pattern of party domi-

5. Case studies of postwar Japan's three major external relations with the United States, China and the USSR used here were: Donald C. Hellmann, *Japanese Domestic Politics and Foreign Policy: The Peace Agreement with the Soviet Union* (Berkeley and Los Angeles: University of California Press, 1969), Akio Watanabe, *Sengo nihon no seiji to gaiko: Okinawa mondai o meguru seijikatei* (Tokyo: Fukumura Shuppan, 1970); Haruhiro Fukui, *Party in Power: The Japanese Liberal-Democrats and Policy-making* (Berkeley and Los Angeles: University of California Press, 1970), "Relations with the People's Republic of China," pp. 227–262; Johannes A. Binnendijk, "The Dynamics of Okinawa Reversion, 1949–1969" in Gregory Henderson (ed.), *Public Diplomacy and Political Change* (New York: Praeger, Publishers, 1973), pp. 1–169; George P. Jan, "Party Politics and Japan's Policy toward Communist China," *Orbis* (Winter, 1971); J. Stephen Hoadley and Sukehiro Hasegawa, "Sino-Japanese Relations, 1950–1970: An Application of the Linkage Model of International Politics," *International Studies Quarterly* (1971), pp. 131–157; Frank C. Langdon, "Japanese Liberal Democratic Factional Discord on China Policy," *Pacific Affairs* (Fall, 1968); and *Kokusai bunkakaikan* (ed.), *Nichibeikankei no kenkyu* (Tokyo: University of Tokyo Press, 1970). Cf. also Kan Ori, "Japanese Public Opinion and Sino-Japanese relations, 1969–1972," in Shunichi Takayanagi and Kimitada Miwa (eds.), *Postwar Trends in Japan* (Tokyo: University of Tokyo Press, 1975), and George P. Jan, "Public Opinion's Growing Influence on Japan's China Policy," *Journalism Quarterly* (Spring, 1971).

6. Hellmann, *op.cit.*, p. 149.

nance in foreign affairs was an aberration of the immediate post-Occupation era. It has been regularized throughout the postwar period, and continues to this day. At least all the case studies I have examined point to the pivotal importance of the "party" variable in postwar Japan's foreign policy. To be sure, the role of the ruling party in Japan is not as prominent as that of the Communist Party in the U.S.S.R., but the party's role is far more significant than in the American situation.[7]

The primacy of the Liberal Democratic Party (LDP) in the making of foreign policy is determined by various factors. In the context of this chapter the most important of the factors is the pattern of electoral support.[8] I am not arguing however that the Japanese electorate necessarily supported the conservatives' foreign policy since issues of foreign policy *per se* seldom figure in the elections. Issue preferences of the parties or the electorate have not been that crucial in any election outcome in Japan.[9] Rather, my point is simply that the Japanese electorate voted the Liberal Democrats into power (for whatever reasons they may have had), thereby enabling the LDP to form the government alone. Furthermore, by providing the party with an absolute majority in the Diet, the electorate virtually gave LDP leaders a free hand in foreign policy which is unconstrained by the various oppositions. As indicated by the general pattern of party support in Table 1, the salient fact to note is the continued dominance of the conservatives in the government except for a brief period during 1947–48 when a Socialist-led coalition ruled Japan. The present conservative party, the Liberal Democratic Party, has held the reins of government without interrup-

7. As to the five prototypes of political structure related to the degree of involvement of political parties in foreign policy decisions, see my piece in Mitsura Uchida *et al.* (eds.), *Gendai seijigaku no kisochishiki* (Tokyo: Yihikaku, 1975).

8. For one, external restraints (e.g., the military) on governmental decisions were removed after the war. For another, a more positive role was assigned to the ruling party in the formation of public policy in postwar Japan since the Diet became "the highest organ of the State" under the 1947 Constitution.

9. For example, Professor Michio Royama, one of the leading social critics of Japanese foreign policy contends that "one of the most important facts to be taken into account when assessing the future orientation of Japanese foreign policy is the low correlation between the preferences of individual voters vis-a-vis foreign and defense policies, and the declared policies of the respective political parties to which they give their support" (Michio Royama, "The Domestic Factors Affecting Japanese Foreign Policy: Problems of the Year 1970," in Chihiro Hosoya and Kan Ori (eds.), *Annual Review* (Tokyo: Japan Institute of International Affairs, 1965–68), p. 6) See also Roger W. Benjamin and Kan Ori, "Parties, Factions, and *Koenkai* in Japanese Electoral Politics," a paper presented to the Conference on Political Party Organization and Development, East Lansing, Michigan, March 1973, and Kan Ori, "Some Empirical Notes on the Japanese Legislative-Politicians," a paper presented to the Conference on the Parliamentary Politician in Asia, organized by the Research Committee on Legislative Development, International Political Science Association, Penang, Malaysia, March 14–17, 1975.

Table 1

Results of Postwar General Elections for the House of Representatives, 1947–1972

Percentage of the House Seats

Elections	LDP[1]	JSP[2]	DSP	JCP	Komei	Minor Parties	Independents
1947[3]	60.3	30.7	—	0.8	—	5.4	2.8
1949	74.5	10.3	—	7.5	—	5.1	2.6
1952	69.6	23.8	—	—	—	2.4	4.1
1953	66.5	29.6	—	0.2	—	1.3	2.4
1955	63.6	33.4	—	0.4	—	1.3	1.3
1958	61.5	35.5	—	0.2	—	0.2	2.6
1960	63.3	31.0	3.6	0.6	—	0.2	1.2
1963	60.6	30.8	4.9	1.0	—	—	2.7
1967	57.0	28.8	6.2	1.0	5.1	—	1.9
1969	59.3	18.5	6.4	2.9	9.7	—	3.2
1972	55.2	24.0	3.9	7.7	5.9	0.4	2.9

Percentage of Popular Votes

Elections	LDP[1]	JSP[2]	DSP	JCP	Komei	Minor Parties	Independents
1947[3]	58.9	26.2	—	3.7	—	5.4	5.8
1949	63.0	13.5	—	9.7	—	7.2	6.6
1952	66.1	21.2	—	2.6	—	3.4	6.7
1953	65.7	26.6	—	1.9	—	1.4	4.4
1955	63.2	29.2	—	2.0	—	2.3	3.3
1958	57.87	32.9	—	2.6	—	0.7	6.0
1960	57.5	27.5	8.7	2.9	—	0.3	2.8
1963	54.7	29.0	7.3	4.0	—	0.1	4.8
1967	48.8	27.9	7.4	4.8	5.4	0.4	5.4
1969	47.6	21.5	7.7	6.8	10.9	0.2	5.3
1972	46.8	21.9	7.0	10.5	8.5	0.3	5.0

1. The first postwar election of 1946 is excluded from this table.
2. From 1947 to 1955 inclusive, LDP. stands for all the major conservative parties. Since the 1958 election, it means the Liberal Democratic Party.
3. From 1947 to 1955 inclusive, JSP. stands for all the Socialist parties. Since the 1958 election, it means the Japan Socialist Party.

Adapted from Jichisho Senkyobu (ed), *Shugiingiin Sosenkyo Kekkashirabe, 1973.*

tion since its formation in 1955, although its position has been perceptibly weakened since the 1967 general elections for the House of Representatives. At the same time, the Japan Socialist Party, the second major party, has never controlled more than 36 percent of the House, and thus has constituted no more than a third of the opposition throughout the postwar period. Furthermore, other minor parties in the period from the end of the Occupation in 1952 to 1967 have been insignificant. (Changes since the 1967 elections will be noted later.)

As long as the Liberal Democratic Party enjoys a comfortable majority in the House of Representatives, it can form the government by itself. Despite the factionalized nature of politics within the LDP, its members loyally vote *en bloc* in the Diet because the party maintains fairly strict discipline in the legislature. The president of the Liberal Democratic Party automatically becomes the prime minister, and he, in consultation with factional leaders of his party, organizes the cabinet. This then allows the party leaders to dominate the government's foreign policy. And since the Japanese Diet members, unlike their counterparts in the American Congress, do not cross-vote; and the Japanese parliamentary standing committee leadership, again unlike the American practice of seniority rule, is party-controlled, all the measures sponsored by the party and government, including those of foreign policy, are supported by the Liberal Democratic Party majority in the House of Representatives.

Moreover, the Liberal Democratic Party is well equipped with its own policy-making organs. This contrasts sharply with the case of the Republican or the Democratic party in the United States. All the government measures, regardless of their origin of inspiration or initial formulation, are channeled through the formal policy organs of the party: the Policy Affairs Research Council and the Executive Council. Although both party organs are controlled by the leadership it is significant to note that every public issue, be it domestic or foreign, has the potentiality of being politicized within the ruling Liberal Democratic Party. In the words of Professor Frank Langdon, the policy deliberative bodies of the Liberal Democratic Party function "virtually as a part of the governmental process".[10]

The factions within the Liberal Democratic Party make up another crucial determinant of Japan's foreign policy. For example, factional struggle was a most critical factor that affected the outcome of Japan's negotiations with the Soviet Union in 1955–1956. In this case, accord-

10. Frank C. Langdon, "Japan's Foreign Policy-Making Process," in Y. C. Kim (ed.), *Japan in World Politics* (Washington: Institute for Asian Studies, 1972), p. 8.

ing to Professor Hellmann, Prime Minister Ichiro Hatoyama and Ichiro Kono, who was then the Minister of Agriculture and Fishery and also a leader of a powerful faction, motivated primarily by factional considerations, worked at cross purposes with the Foreign Office headed by Mamoru Shigemitsu of another rival faction.[11] More recently, the 1972 normalization of Sino-Japanese relations had a definite factional character. Kakuei Tanaka effectively used the issue of normalizing relations with Communist China to obtain the support of the Ohira, Nakasone, and Miki factions (among other factors), and there is no doubt that the establishment of this pro-Peking Tanaka coalition expedited the restoration of diplomatic relations with mainland China (even though international-system factors like the Chinese overture in this case were as important as factional elements). I might add that since the normalization, the factional relations within the LDP have become so complex that the conservatives are finding it increasingly difficult to arrive at a consensus on Sino-Japanese relations. Likewise, the involvement of factional infighting in foreign policy controversies contributed directly to the fall of two prime ministers. One was Ichiro Hatoyama, referred to above, and the other was Shinsuke Kishi whose downfall was caused by the anti-Security Treaty controversy of 1960. More recently, as one astute student of Japan's foreign policy noted, various economic interests related to foreign policy tend to be articulated more frequently along factional lines, as evidenced in both the textile dispute between the United States and Japan and the Sino-Japanese aviation agreement.[12] Furthermore, we are beginning to see the phenomenon of what might be called "foreign-related factionalism" in Japan.[13] Two recent examples show, firstly, that there is a tendency for Tanaka to be supported by the People's Republic of China while Takeo Fukuda is backed by the U.S.S.R., and secondly, that the intraparty factional split is beginning to be manifested in the Sino-

11. Hellmann, *op. cit.*

12. Comments by Royama in the Tokyo Conference on the U.S.-Japan Relations, (April 1974).

13. The concept of "foreign-linked factionalism" was suggested and utilized by Professor Alan Dowty (Hebrew University) in his "Foreign-Linked Factionalism as a Historical Pattern," *Journal of Conflict Resolution*, Vol. XV, No. 4 (1971). For his definition of the term, see *Ibid.*, p. 431. I deliberately changed the term to "foreign-related" in order to connote much broader, looser, and more indirect linkages with a foreign polity (as appeared, for instance, in the Sino-Japanese normalization process) than Dowty's "foreign-linked factionalism." In the language of James Rosenau, mine would include "reactive" as well as "emulative" processes. Also, my usage here does not limit to the seizure or wielding of "power by non-legitimate means," nor specific to seeking or accepting "aid from other states." (*Ibid*). In fact, I have in mind the more or less legitimate, society-approved kind of linkages.

Japanese aviation negotiations. Originally in the foreign policy field, the linkages were between foreign powers and various opposition parties (say, the People's Republic of China and the Japan Socialist Party), but now this confrontation between the conservative LDP and the leftist parties on foreign policy issues is shifting to intra-LDP factional fights, thus internationalizing the factional disputes.[14]

It is also well to remember that these factional considerations on foreign-policy behavior are compounded by the factional nature of Japanese politics in general, which is well institutionalized in the postwar era, and which undoubtedly affects the quality of political leadership in foreign affairs as well. It is to be noted, first of all, that all Japanese political parties, with the exception of the Komeito, have factional divisions. The LDP, for instance, is a coalition of about ten factions (it fluctuated between seven to thirteen factions), while the Japan Socialist Party itself is made up of several factions with varying shades of socialist orientation. LDP candidates for the House of Representatives are primarily recruited through the factions, and thus electoral campaigns of the conservatives are conducted along these factional lines. Furthermore, the factional leaders are prominent in securing party nominations for their followers, providing them with much of the needed campaign and other funds, and giving various kinds of organizational assistance. We have very few systematic studies on this subject,[15] but one empirical study shows the extent of the intraparty struggle in Japan's two major parties. It was found, for example, that 44.5 percent of the Liberal Democrats, and about one-third of the Japan Socialist candidates viewed members of their own party as primary rivals in the 1967 elections for the House of Representatives, while only 10.9 percent of the LDP candidates and 27.9 percent of the Socialists regarded the candidates of other parties as their main opponents.[16]

Once these conservative candidates are elected to the Diet, their career advancement in the government and in the party is determined on the basis of their factional affiliation, since cabinet posts are awarded principally to maintain a judicious balance of the various factions within the LDP. This is also true in the appointment of party posts, committee chairmanships in the Diet, and political viceministerships in the government. Thus, factional affiliation is essential

14. Royama, the Tokyo Conference comments.

15. For a critical review of the literature of intraparty factions with a suggestion of a theoretical framework for the future study, see Roger W. Benjamin and Kan Ori, "Factionalism in Japanese Politics," *Annual Review* (1970), pp. 76–93.

16. Hajime Shinohara and Yoshinori Ide, "Images of Election held by the Successful Candidates: the Case of Japan in 1967," a paper presented to the International Political Science Association convention, 1967.

for both electoral and patronage purposes for the rank and file members of the LDP in the Diet.[17]

Conversely, the factional arrangement is important for the factional leaders of the LDP. The leaders compete among themselves for the post of party president (which *ipso facto* means prime minister) when the party election takes place every three years (which used to be every two years). To win the party presidency, the successful factional leader must obtain a majority in the party convention which is overwhelmingly dominated by the LDP Diet members. So, an aspiring faction leader must have a winning coalition to capture the party presidency, the result of which is usually the formation of a "main current" majority and "anti-main current" minority. An astute observer of Japanese diplomacy noted that in this kind of situation, "almost any major policy problem is a potential issue that might be used to undermine the dominant faction head as the minority factions struggle to replace him with one of their own chiefs."[18] Foreign policy, of course, is no exception. In fact, the involvement of intraparty factions in external affairs ensures that every major foreign policy issue will be considered as a domestic problem.

I have reasons to believe that the involvement of party factionalism in Japan's foreign policy decisions (especially of the governing LDP) will be continued in the 1970s and 1980s, primarily because the factional system, as I have already pointed out, is highly institutionalized in Japan. Consequently, the LDP intraparty factions will continue to have both a direct and an indirect impact on Japan's foreign policy in the years to come. However, it must be stressed that factions in the LDP are basically "patronage" factions, not "policy" factions. Thus, whenever factions are related to foreign policy issues, they are usually channelled through the faction leaders. There exist, however, rather broad policy-oriented opinion groups within the LDP which are transfactional. The Afro-Asian group and the Asian group are examples of these. The former, for instance, strongly favored the normalization of diplomatic relations with Peking, while the latter took a pro-Taiwan stand on the China issue before the normalization.

The factional nature of politics as operative in the LDP recruitment and leadership selection system has considerable bearing indirectly on Japan's foreign policy. This indirect impact has perhaps more impor-

17. For a functional approach to this question, see George O. Totten and Tamio Kawakami, "The Functions of Factionalism in Japanese Politics," *Pacific Affairs*, Vol. XXXIX, No. 2 (Summer 1965). As for criticisms of the functional approach in general and on the article in particular, refer to Benjamin and Ori, *op. cit.* (1970), pp. 79–80.

18. Langdon, *op. cit.*, p. 10.

tant long-run consequences for Japanese foreign policy behavior. For one thing, the factional character of the LDP will render it very difficult for a Japanese prime minister to vigorously exercise his leadership in external affairs. In sharp contrast to the American president whose control over foreign affairs is pretty well complete, despite the "bureaucratic" constraints and recent indications of Congressional "interference," a Japanese prime minister is clearly circumscribed by the factional political framework. Even though he formally enjoys a three-year term as party president, the power and even the incumbency of a Japanese prime minister in fact rest largely on the factional power-configuration within his party. I believe that this is a serious political constraint on Japanese foreign policy options. For example, during his incumbency between 1972 and 1974, Premier Tanaka faced not only a formidable factional opposition headed by Takeo Fukuda, his rival for the party presidency in the previous convention, but also from the three faction leaders who had helped to bring about the Tanaka cabinet, each of whom now aspires to become prime minister. (This in fact turned out to be the case in late 1974). Under these circumstances, Tanaka was constrained from making major policy decisions that could antagonize other faction leaders. Instead, he had to make every effort to establish a consensus among the various factions, and this forced him to take the course of least resistance.[19]

Accustomed to this kind of consensus-based group decision-making, Japanese political leaders are more "situational" in international behavior than American leaders. And this will have a considerable bearing on future U.S.-Japan relations as it certainly has had in the past. Moreover, this situation is likely to give rise to a time-lag problem in responding to foreign demands, for it usually takes time to arrive at intraparty consensus, particularly on controversial foreign policy issues. Both of these points are stressed by simulation specialists such as Professor Kinhide Mushakoji.[20]

19. Shuzo Kimura, Staff Researcher, Foreign Affairs Committee, Japanese House of Councillors, suggested at the Tokyo conference on the U.S.-Japan relations (April 1974), that the diplomatic weakness created by intra-LDP factions may paradoxically be a strength in that Japan in its foreign policy behavior can always have on hand an excuse. This may be the case, but that I would say depends on the parties concerned. On this point, see James B. Kessler and Kan Ori, *Anti-Japanese Land Law Controversy in California* (Tokyo: Institute of International Relations, Sophia University, 1971). I also feel that this is a matter of empirical question even though impressionistically speaking what Kimura said did occur in the normalization of Sino-Japan relations and the Okinawa reversion negotiations.

20. For example, see Kinhide Mushakoji, "Cross-cultural Comparison of Tension-coping Communication—A Discussion on Experimental Design," a paper presented to the IXth World Congress of the International Political Science Association in Montreal, Canada, 19–25 August 1973.

Throughout the entire post-Occupation era, the United States has been so accustomed to equate Japanese foreign policy with that of the governing conservative parties (the LDP since 1955) whose primary concern was the maintenance of close U.S.-Japan relations, that it has paid little or no attention to the foreign policy of other Japanese political parties. However, the political configuration in which only one party had a dominant control of the government and the country's foreign policy is being altered to an extent such that both American and Japanese leaders must adjust to the foreign policy demands of other parties as well as take serious note of intra-LDP factions and the involvement of big business (all of which will be discussed in detail later in this chapter).

Hitherto, various factions within the LDP have not been particularly critical for U.S.-Japan relations because there is a basic consensus among the LDP factional leaders on the nature of U.S.-Japan relations, especially on the security question. This may no longer by the case in the future, particularly as the conflict of economic interests between the United States and Japan is likely to come up at the factional level. U.S.-Japan relations will be further complicated by the emergence of multiple "foreign-related" factions even within the Liberal Democratic Party.[21]

The Political Party System. None of the case studies I have referred to point to the importance of the "party system" variables. This is understandable because the postwar Japanese party system has been dominated up to the present by the conservative LDP, and thus decisions on foreign policy have by the large been made by its leaders. However, the "party system" variables will become increasingly important in the future because they are likely to constrain Japan's foreign policy deci-

21. As to the future research task, the role of the governing party (at present, the Liberal Democratic Party) in Japan's foreign policy decisions should be studied in two directions: inward and outward. The first is the relationship between the party and its factions in foreign policy decision-making with special reference to the degree of party cohesion on foreign policy issues. The other is the relationship of the LDP with external forces such as other political parties, the military, and the bureaucracy. For example, one of the most important research areas is to ascertain systematically the extent to which the LDP has, in fact, dominated Japan's foreign policy decisions since 1955. This pattern of postwar party-dominance in external affairs must be compared with the prewar pattern of foreign policy decision-making, as it is suggested that in the pre-1945 era government agencies and other political forces such as the military played a more decisive role. As to the available literature in English on the LDP and its factions, consult Fuki, *op. cit.*, and Nathaniel B. Thayer, *How the Conservatives Rule Japan* (Princeton, New Jersey: Princeton University Press, 1969). On the LDP factions, refer to the footnotes of Benjamin and Ori, *op. cit.* (1970).

sions as time passes. This will be so particularly in the case of future U.S.-Japan relations.

What then will be the Japanese electoral alignment of the seventies and eighties? It is difficult to predict accurately the future electoral pattern of party support, but one thing is very clear. The secure electoral dominance of the Liberal Democratic Party is now in some danger of being threatened. The new trend has been characterized by Japanese analysts as the TAKOKA (multi-partization) phenomenon. This basically describes a situation which with the steady decline of popular support for the conservative LDP, it is not the Japan Socialist Party —traditionally the major and only significant opposition party—which makes gains proportionately to the Liberal Democratic Party's losses, but the minor opposition parties such as the Japan Communist Party and the Komeito which will make gains.

Thus, the former political configuration where only one opposition party, the Japan Socialist Party, had sufficient political strength to significantly challenge the governing party is changing. Even though the TATOKA phenomenon has been evident for some time in the local elections of urban areas, this became obvious only in 1967 as far as the House of Representatives elections were concerned. On that occasion, the LDP lost its usual majority in popular votes for the first time since its formation in 1955. This drop in the popularity of the conservatives reached its nadir in the 1972 House of Representatives elections at which time only 46.8 percent of the voters supported the LDP. (See Table 1.) If this electoral trend continues, there could be a substantial reduction in the Diet strength of the LDP in the future. As I have pointed out elsewhere, the TATOKA pattern of party support will, for various reasons, emerge even more clearly in the years to come.[22]

If this is the case, what sort of power configuration would emerge in the future? For the foreseeable future, I have basically three scenarios in mind, each of which will have a significant impact on Japan's foreign policy options. The first scenario is that the conservative LDP will be electorally ousted, and an opposition coalition will take over the reins of government. This is theoretically possible if the four opposition parties unite, since their combined popular votes already exceed the LDP's. Should this happen, the result will be a coalition of the left and center, with serious consequences for Japan's external relations, particularly with respect to U.S.-Japan relations.

22. For details, see Kan Ori, "Patterns of Electoral Behavior in Postwar Japan: An Analysis," a paper presented to the Faculty-Staff Seminar, University of Malaya, September 1974.

The second scenario is one where a center-based coalition is established. This may well come about should the LDP split, with the splinter "left-wing" of the conservative party joining a center-party coalition composed of the Komeito, the Democratic Socialist Party, and the "right-wing" of the Japan Socialist Party. Again, this scenario cannot be entirely ruled out, since the LDP, formed in 1955 as a union of two conservative parties, is presently a coalition of about ten semi-autonomous factions, and since the Japan Socialist Party can, as it has in the past, split. The probable consequences of this center-based coalition government on Japan's external relations are difficult to predict since the stand of the two center parties (that is, the Democratic Socialist Party and the Komeito) on foreign policy have been rather ambivalent. But one thing seems clear in the context of future U.S.-Japan relations: the center-coalition government is likely to insist on a more definite policy of disengagement from the United States than the present LDP, and would probably carry out foreign policy more independently of the United States.

The third scenario is that the present Liberal Democratic Party, or a similar conservative-dominated coalition group, however fragile, will continue to hold power. In my opinion, the third scenario is most probable for the immediate future. This is due to several reasons. First, the virtually insurmountable divisions in the opposition will make a coalition government of all four opposition parties most unlikely. The Japan Socialist Party is as faction-ridden as the conservative Liberal Democratic Party, and the ideological differences in the party ranging from left (Maoist) to right (social democrats) wings are so great that any attempt to merge with an existing left or right party will be practically impossible. The right wing of the Socialist Party does not approve of a union with the Communists, while the left factions are not prepared to associate with the Democratic Socialist Party which they consider to be a neo-conservative party. Even though the Komeito and the Japan Communist party appear on the surface to be able to work together, comprehensive and long-term cooperation between them is also extremely unlikely because of the long-standing and bitter confrontation that exists between them electorally and otherwise. Likewise, the Japan Socialist Party and the Democratic Socialist Party, which broke away from the Socialist Party in 1960, are not on the best of terms. Furthermore, the two parties have different support bases. The Socialists are supported by the leftist *Sohyo* labor federation (the General Council of Trade Unions of Japan), while the Democratic Socialists are backed by the politically moderate *Domei* federation (the Japanese Confederation of Labor). In other words, the long-existing rivalries among the opposition parties stemming from ideological, personal, and electoral-base conflicts will make any future union very improbable.[23]

Second, a split within the LDP is most unlikely to happen. There was an attempt in the past to split the party, but this failed mainly because big business was against the idea of supporting two conservative parties, particularly when there existed a fairly strong Socialist Party. The business community can, of course, change its mind in a crisis situation, but as long as the present LDP can hold on to the reins of government, it is unlikely that it would encourage any splinter movement. Furthermore, even if an LDP splinter group and some elements of the opposition could form a coalition, it would probably be short-lived since such an alliance would be nothing more than a marriage of convenience.

Third, the strength of the present LDP should not be underestimated. Comparatively speaking, it is one of the most secure conservative parties in the world judging by its ability to maintain a comfortable majority in the Diet and electorally dwarfing the next largest party.[24] Other empirical evidence suggesting the LDP's resilient strength is provided in a recent study by Professor Roger Benjamin and myself.[25] Our concern in this study was with first, the level of party-system stability over the last twenty post-Occupation years from the 1952 elections for the House of Representatives to the ones in 1972, and second, the support pattern of the LDP within the framework of political party system institutionalization as measured by the party system entropy. Our major findings were that the Japanese political system achieved a high degree of system stability early, that it has continued to maintain that stability, and that the conservative parties (the LDP since 1955) were major contributors to that system stability.[26] In another study, Professor Benjamin also found that the strength of the LDP should not be underestimated even in the face of rather rapid socio-economic changes. In this case, the popular support of the conservative party

23. Cf. my "Japanese Political Parties and their Socio-electoral Bases," a paper delivered at Lecture Series, the Institute of International Relations, Sophia University, 1969, Tokyo, Japan.

24. Shigeki Nishihira, *Senkyo no kokusaihikaku* (Tokyo: Nihon Hyoronsha, 1969), p. 224.

25. Roger W. Benjamin and Kan Ori, "Process Analysis and Change and Stability in Japanese Electoral Politics," a paper presented to the International Sociological Association meetings, Toronto, Canada, August 19–24, 1974. Here "political party system institutionalization" is understood as "the degree of stability of competitive patterns" over time (*ibid.*, p. 9). Party system "entropy" is essentially a measure of such competitive patterns among various parties.

26. *Ibid.*

declined sharply only in those prefectures which achieved an extremely high level of urbanization.[27]

Consequently, the present LDP or some equivalent conservative-dominated coalition group can be expected to govern Japan in the immediate future with its style of factional politics intact. However, the foreign policy of the conservatives will be constrained considerably by the TATOKA development. For as the LDP continues to lose seats in the Diet, it will need the political help of the Democratic Socialist Party and the Komeito within and outside of the Cabinet. This will mean that the conservatives increasingly would be compelled to accommodate the foreign policy demands of these two parties, both of which advocate a more independent foreign policy that is less subservient to the United States. Even if the Liberal Democrats can form the government alone, they will, because of their precarious electoral base in the Diet, be more vulnerable to domestic pressures in the foreign policy field. At any rate, the increased strength of the opposition parties in the Diet (particularly the advances of the Japan Communist Party and the Komeito), will make the future political milieu in Japan more fluid, and this itself will essentially have a negative impact on foreign policy decisions of the governing conservative party.[28] It is to be recalled that past conserva-

27. Roger W. Benjamin *et. al.*, *Patterns of Political Development* (New York: David McKay Co., Inc., 1972), pp. 152–162.

28. Professor James Morley, at the Tokyo Conference, suggested that it has usually been contended that as the political balances at home begin to break down, that effect is fed back into the country's foreign policy decisions, bringing forth diplomatic immobility, and that though this seems to be the case under the Tanaka government recently, Japan was able to alter its foreign policy fundamentally. Examples of these are the Sino-Japanese relations and Japan's foreign policy toward the USSR. He further queried whether Japan would develop a more energetic foreign policy since the position of the conservative party (the Liberal Democratic Party) is delicately maintained in the Diet, so as to draw the attention of the public to external affairs and to split the opposition, thereby establishing a base for political reorganization. My reply was, and still is, that even though this is a matter of further empirical studies, I do not think so in the case of Japan. Regarding the effect of political structure (in this particular case, the degree of interparty competition) on a given country's pursuance of energetic or non-energetic foreign policy, the standard view was negated at least by one study. (Frank B. Weinstein, "The Uses of Foreign Policy in Indonesia: An Approach to the Analysis of Foreign Policy in the Less Developed Countries," *World Politics*, Vol. XXIV, No. 3, April 1972, pp. 356–381). After rather thorough reviewing of the literature on this very question raised by Professor Morley, P. J. McGowan and H. B. Shapiro concluded that [even in terms of international scale pursuit for the empirical data] "the most conspicuous gaps in the literature on political variables [on foreign policy behavior] concern pressure groups and the political party system." (McGowan and Shapiro, *op. cit.*, p. 90). Also consult their inventory of empirical propositions on this topic (*Ibid.*, pp. 75–91). Even here, the findings are far from definitive to answer the question raised by Professor Morley. However, as to a promising systematic empirical study in this field, see Barbara G. Salmore and Stephen A. Salmore, "Structure and Change in Regimes: Their Effect on Foreign Policy," a paper presented to the annual meetings of the American Political Science Association, Washington, D.C., U.S.A., September 5–9, 1972.

tive governments were able to carry out their basic foreign policy of close alliance with the United States despite opposition in the Diet throughout the post-Occupation era simply because they have always maintained a comfortable two-thirds majority in the Diet.

More significantly, the increased strength of the opposition parties in the Diet would lead to new pressures being placed on the conservative government in the foreign policy field by elements from within the ruling Liberal Democratic Party. The situation will certainly activate more intraparty factional activities in the conservative party over basic foreign policy decisions. It will most likely work as follows. Up to now, anti-American themes and calls for a more independent "nationalistic" stand in foreign policy have been the monopoloy of the leftist opposition parties, but they have been practically ineffective from the policy perspective because the LDP has had such secure control of the Diet. Now, as evidenced in the recent normalization of Sino-Japanese relations, the conservatives, owing to their precarious holdings in the Diet and because of their electoral unpopularity, will be forced to preempt with anti-American measures, and to adopt a "nationalistic" course of action. Furthermore, many of the attempts to achieve balance and compromise among the various foreign policy views will, by necessity, take place in the inner circle of LDP faction leaders, as the party leadership would prefer to have a show of unity in the Diet where they may have only a bare majority in the future.

At this point it should be noted that the ruling Liberal Democratic Party throughout the post-Occupation era has disagreed on almost all foreign policy issues with all other opposition parties. In fact, this political cleavage based on ideology is what characterized postwar Japan's domestic and international politics. Basically, LDP's foreign policy rests on close U.S.-Japan relations, especially on the security arrangement, while the opposition parties prefer other alternatives. Ideologically, the LDP is clearly capitalistic, while the opposition parties are leftist. Perhaps the "unarmed neutrality," and more recently the "peaceful neutrality" position of the Japan Socialist Party are good examples of the rigid ideological bent of socialist foreign policy. Furthermore, even though all the opposition parties are opposed to the conservative LDP and are all leftist-oriented (particularly in the foreign policy area), there are distinct differences among them. The Japan Communist Party constitutes the extreme left (although the left factions of the Japan Socialist Party are Maoists, and the Communists are presently anti-Maoists), the Japan Socialist Party is located in the middle; and the Democratic Socialist Party is at the other end of the spectrum. The Koeito, on the other hand, is the political arm of the religious organization, *Sokagakkai*, the Nichiren-shoshu sect of Buddhism; and is to that extent conservative. However, the supporters of the party (basically *Sokagakkai* members) are social-welfare inclined as they generally come from the low-income group. In fact, one research finding indicates that in general attitudes supporters of the Komeito can be grouped with the Communist supporters, both of whom are change-oriented.[29] Another study also reveals that it is the Komeito rather than the Japan Communist party that has performed best in those districts characterized by low income and low levels of education.[30]

Under these circumstances, it is extremely difficult, if not impossible, to have domestic politics ending at the water's edge as has been often the case in the United States. In fact, the exact opposite occurs more frequently in postwar Japan since many issues in foreign policy have domestic implications. Also, it has been difficult to arrive at a broad, public consensus on foreign policy issues in Japan because there are sharp differences between the LDP and the leftist opposition in their view of the world and of immediate political goals. This clearly contrasts with the situation in the United States where consensus on foreign policy is much easier to achieve, and where bi-partisan foreign policy is more or less a general rule. In this respect, it is interesting to observe that even when the Japan Socialist Party agreed in principle on foreign policy with the conservatives, the Socialists refused to accept a bi-partisan role in the Russo-Japanese peace negotiations of 1955–1956. This lack of a non-partisan foreign policy handicaps the decision-makers in postwar Japan. It would have been much easier had there been a tradition of non-partisan foreign policy. Instead, this very lack of consensus among various parties on foreign policy positions is in fact a well established and institutionalized aspect of postwar Japan's political party system.

While the lack of consensus in foreign policy will constrain Japan, particularly with the advent of the TATOKA era, future U.S.-Japan relations will be complicated further by recent developments in the United States. It appears that the "traditional" American posture of non-partisanship in foreign policy is replaced by a more partisan and domestic-politicized kind of behavior. This will create a situation in which domestic interests are to be reflected more frequently in external affairs, as exemplified by the recent textile controversy between the United States and Japan. Consequently, the American Congress will "interfere" more regularly in Presidential foreign policy as witnessed

29. Hajime Shinohara, *Nihon no seijifudo* (Tokyo: Iwanami Shoten, 1968), pp. 124–133.

30. Moriyoshi Nara, *Analysis of Voting Behavior in Tokyo Areas* (Tokyo: Minshushugi Kenkyukai, 1966).

in the recent failure of trade negotiations with the U.S.S.R. (Congressional restraints in this case, I presume, were basically caused by domestic political needs, *viz.*, the Jewish votes).[31] Hitherto, the decentralized character of American domestic politics had little bearing on the country's external relations as the President was more or less given a free hand in the formulation and execution of American foreign policy, thanks to the postwar "tradition" of bi-partisan foreign policy.[32] The situation, however, is rapidly changing. As many of the potential areas of conflict between the United States and Japan, be they economic or security, have domestic repercussions, the domestic politicization of foreign policy together with the emerging "neo-isolationism" in the United States will have grave consequences on future U.S.-Japan relations.[33]

Another factor which in the long run cannot be overlooked in the context of "party system" variables is the possible establishment of a socialist or some equivalent form of leftist government in Japan in response to *catastrophic* political and economic-social developments. If and when such leftist forces take over the reins of government, says Professor Hiroharu Seki, the impact of this "Nippon shock" on U.S.-Japan relations will be greater than those provided by the Nixon shock. As discussed earlier, I personally do not think this will occur in the next decade or so. But with dramatic and drastic changes in the politico-economic-social milieu of Japan such as a Great Depression this possibility may not, by the end of the 1980s, be entirely ruled out. Of course, should this happen it will have serious consequences on U.S.-Japan relations, partly because many seem to take it for granted that Japan and the United States will continue their close alliance system.[34]

31. See my pieces in Uchida *et al.* (eds.), *op. cit.*

32. For a more detailed discussion on this topic, see Kan Ori, "Daitoryo o kosoku surumono," *Chuo Koron*, April, 1968. Cf. also Kessler and Ori, *op. cit.* (1971), for a case of domestic-politicization of external relations in the United States.

33. For various views on this development by Japanese specialists on American politics and diplomacy, including my own observations, consult *Nihon bunka* forum (ed.), *Nihon wa dokoe yuku* (Tokyo: Jiyusha, 1974).

34. These are Professor Hiroharu Seki's suggestions in the Tokyo conference on the United States-Japan Relations, April 6, 1974. (Seki is a Professor of International Relations at the University of Tokyo). For the reasons given in this section we should in particular look into two variables which relate the Japanese party system to foreign policy decisions. One is the degree of interparty competition, with special reference to whether the Liberal Democratic Party is able to dominate the party system. The other research task is to identify the extent to which consensus-cleavage occurs among various parties, and relate that variable to future foreign policy decisions. On the Japanese political party system in general, consult, in terms of the books available in English, Robert A. Scalapino and Junnosuke Masumi, *Parties and Politics in Contemporary Japan* (Berkeley: University of California Press, 1962).

Big Business and Other Groups. The third possible determinant of Japan's foreign policy decisions is big business. Curiously enough, big business does not appear to have played any decisive role in postwar external affairs as far as the case studies examined here are concerned. In fact, the lack of its involvement in foreign affairs has been most marked. Of the three major relations (U.S.-Japan, Sino-Japanese, and Russo-Japanese), only in one case, the normalization of relations with mainland China, was big business more or less involved. Here, big business seems inclined toward Taiwan. Yet we are not entirely sure of the extent to which this attitude affected the decision of Tanaka to restore diplomatic relations with Peking. Furthermore, the attitudes of big business toward both mainland China and Taiwan have been ambivalent since the 1972 normalization with Peking. On the other hand, Professor Hellmann concludes in his study of the 1956 Russo-Japanese peace agreement that "most difficult to reconcile with the standard interpretations of postwar Japanese politics is the failure of the major business organizations to influence party decision-making to any great extent."[35] Likewise, Professor Gerald Curtis warns against overestimating the role of big business in *general* postwar Japanese politics.[36]

And yet, I am rather hesitant to dismiss big business as having little influence in Japan's foreign policy formulation. (This does not mean, however, that I believe that big business controls Japanese politics). My guess is that big business has been significantly involved in the foreign policy of postwar Japan, and that it will continue to be so, particularly in those areas related to international economic relations and national defense. This is because the financial community in Japan is an exceptionally powerful group and as such its leadership is potentially a crucial element in Japan's foreign policy-making.

It is well to remember that none of the case studies I have used here deal primarily with economic matters. Nonetheless, we might indeed find rather close involvements of big business in the economic sphere of foreign affairs. For example, big business would have exerted, and is likely to wield, considerable influence upon the government in Japan's dealings with the United States on business, financial, and economic matters. And, as seen in the textile controversy between the United States and Japan, there may develop a conflict between big business

35. Hellman, *op. cit.*, p. 151.

36. Gerald L. Curtis, "Big Business and Political Influence in Japan," a paper presented to the research Conference on Japanese Organization and Decision-Making, Maui, Hawaii, January, 1973.

and the LDP political leaders to the extent of even involving factional elements of the party.[37]

Another important factor which should not be overlooked in assessing the role of big business in Japan's foreign policy is the fact that there has been a congruence of interests between big business and the governing LDP. This has developed in the three important areas of primacy of economics, anti-leftism, and close ties with the United States. Under these circumstances, it is not necessary for big business to articulate its specific demands on foreign policy issues. Such overt lobbying activities are rendered superfluous by the fact that their needs are taken care of by LDP leaders and the government. In fact, one Japanese observer said that big business had been a dominant influence in postwar Japan's foreign policy, and that one of the consequences of big business' involvement in Japan's "economic diplomacy" has been the lack of a distinct political orientation in its postwar foreign policy.[38]

However, if a clear division develops between the ruling party and the business community in the future, this will certainly complicate the foreign policy process in Japan. In such a situation, the position of the LDP is likely to be increasingly weakened as big business will then become an active factor in Japan's foreign policy. This problem will be further compounded by various networks of influence which business has with intraparty factions of the LDP. An indication of such a possibility has already appeared in the recent textile controversy with the United States.[39]

The third factor to be noted is the difference in the structure of interest articulation between the United States and Japan. Although American interest groups deal directly with a decentralized Congress through individual Congressmen who serve as "pressure politicians," big business in Japan works either through the LDP leadership, the Ministry of International Trade and Industry, or other related government agencies. Furthermore, big business, the governing party, and the higher bureaucracy have both formal and informal channels of communication with each other for this purpose. Most effective of these, I think, are the informal channels of interest representation. It is further to be noted that this kind of special relationship between various in-

37. Royama's comments at the Tokyo conference on the U.S.-Japan Relations, April 1974.

38. Professor Hitoshi Hanai (Kyoto Sangyo University) in *Nihon bunka* forum (ed.), *op. cit.*, pp. 117–118.

39. Royama, *op. cit.*

terests and the parties is not uncommon in Japan since all other parties are more or less a single pressure-group party as well. (As examples, the Japan Socialist Party with *Sohyo*, the Democratic Socialist Party with *Domei*, and the Komeito with *Sokagakkai*.) It is this tightly-knit triple alliance of big business, the Liberal Democratic Party, and the higher civil service that has maintained the conservative dominance in postwar Japan.[40] The relationship between big business and the governing LDP has taken on a more permanent and institutionalized feature, and therefore the influence of big business on foreign policy is made quietly through the leaders of the conservative political party. In the United States, the impact of interest groups on foreign policy is more *ad hoc*, despite the character of "interest politics" in the country, and their demands are usually channelled through Congress and its committees. Thus, the effects of these factors on foreign policy are manifested in the President-Congress relationship.

It is also interesting, in the context of United States-Japan relations, to observe that business interests in both countries are developing routinized channels of contact and consultation. Some of these are international in character as with the Pacific Basin Economic Cooperation council, while others, such as the Japan-California Association and the Japan-Midwest Economic Conference, are regional. Moreover, business organizations such as the Federation of Economic Organizations (*Keidanren*), the Japan Chamber of Commerce and Industry (*Nissho*), and the Committee for Economic Development (*Keizaidoyukai*) in Japan have mutual contacts with their U.S. counterparts, and joint conferences of businessmen are also frequently held. Important business leaders such as the presidents of the *Keidanren*, *Nissho*, and *Keizaidoyukai* often travel to the United States to consult formally or informally with the American business and political elite, including Congressional leaders. It is difficult to evaluate the importance of this interaction of business interests in both nations on foreign policy decisions of the respective countries, but these regularized channels may prove to be effective mechanisms of pressure on their respective governments in the future.[41]

As far as the case studies examined in this chapter are concerned, the most noteworthy phenomenon is the mushrooming of *ad hoc* political interest groups associated with specific foreign policy issues. This has been particularly evident in the case of the reversion of Okinawa and

40. For a fuller discussion of this topic, see Kan Ori, "The Japanese Higher Bureaucracy," a paper presented to the International Management Development Seminars, Tokyo, Japan, 1969. Cf. also, Japanese Political Science Association (ed.), *Gendai-nihon no seito to kanryo* (Tokyo: Iwanami Shoten, 1967).

41. Cf. Professor Sadako Ogata in *Nihon bunka* forum (ed.), *op. cit.*, pp. 118–120.

the normalization of relations with the People's Republic of China. In both cases, mass media, particularly major newspapers, seemed to have played a significant intermediary role.[42] In the case of the Russo-Japanese peace agreement negotiations, established, though specialized, interest groups such as the fishery association were even more significant than big business in influencing a specific foreign policy outcome.[43] These *ad hoc* and special interest groups are usually associated with political leaders, political parties, or intraparty factions, and thus are partisan in nature. In fact, it may be argued that they were effective because they were partisan and served as agencies of these political actors.[44]

As to future U.S.-Japan relations, the most critical factor, in my opinion, would most likely be the degree of congruence (or discongruence) of interests between big business and leaders of the ruling LDP. This is because as the United States looks inward, and the role of the President in foreign policy decisions is constrained by domestic political factors through increased Congressional "interventions" in foreign affairs, conflicts of economic interests between the United States and Japan may emerge more readily.[45]

42. See Binnendijk, *op. cit.* and Ogata, *op. cit.* Cf. also Kessler and Ori, *op. cit.* (1971); J. B. Kessler and Kan Ori, "Nichibei-kankei no imeji to beikoku-renposeido" in Japanese Association of International Relations (ed.), *Nichibei-kankei no imeji* (Tokyo: Yuhikaku, 1967) for the prewar cases.

43. Mrs. Sadako Ogata notes three levels of business "interest articulation": (1) financial community, (2) trade organizations, and (3) individual companies. She contends that the financial community represented by *Keidanren*, for example, [big business in this paper] tends to go along with the government and LDP foreign policy from a broader perspective of Japan's national interests. The second group is more specific in its "foreign policy" demands, while the third is most profit-minded and least likely to go along with the government and the LDP leadership should their interests conflict with the government's foreign policy. (Mrs. Sadako Ogata's comments at the Tokyo conference.)

44. In some cases, these groups were quasi-government organizations, serving as a front for various government agencies or for the prime minister directly. For a more detailed account of this phenomenon, see Binnendijk, *op. cit.*

45. Regarding the role of big business in Japan's foreign policy decision-making, several research questions may be raised. For instance, in which area(s) of foreign policy decisions does big business have most involvement? Under what conditions are business interests activated? What are the channels of influence that big business normally uses, and what is the relationship between big business and the Liberal Democratic Party in particular? If the party configuration of power in the Diet changes in the future, how will this affect relations between big business and the government decision-makers? To what extent does the structural difference between the American and Japanese systems (e.g., the developmental level of the interest-group system) affect the style and channels of business influence on external affairs? For general literature on big business in Japanese politics available in English, see Marshall E. Dimock, *The Japanese Technocracy: Management and Government in Japan* (New York: Walker, 1968) and Chitoshi Yanaga, *Big Business in Japanese Politics* (New Haven, Conn.: Yale University Press, 1968).

Bureaucratic Involvement. The principal bureaucratic component involved in Japan's foreign policy decisions is, of course, the Ministry of Foreign Affairs. The Ministry of International Trade and Industry and the National Defense Agency are also closely associated with issues of external relations. On occasions, other government agencies are also drawn in. For example, in the case of the Okinawa reversion, the Office of the Prime Minister and the ministries of both Justice and Education were directly involved.

The critical question is whether these formal government agencies have played any decisive role in determining Japan's postwar foreign policies. To the extent that the relevant case studies provide evidence, it seems clear that the major decisions in foreign policy in postwar Japan were made by the prime ministers and other political leaders, and that career bureaucrats in the Foreign Office and other ministries played only a secondary role. It was even suggested in a case study covering foreign policy developments of the mid-fifties that "the formal governmental institutions dealing with international affairs found themselves unable to exercise their defined roles" in the foreign policy-making process.[46] Other case studies referred to here also corroborate this pattern of passive bureaucratic involvement in major decisions of foreign policy, although a somewhat more active participation of the government agencies is observed in the case of the Okinawa reversion.

To be sure, in any modern nation-state the day-to-day operational decisions are made by the bureaucrats. This, coupled with their monopoly of information, would make them a formidable force in decision-making. Perhaps this is more so in Japan as Japanese higher civil servants not only possess expertise in policy-making but are also an extremely capable group. Also, bureaucratic involvement in politics has been one of Japan's long-established legacies. Indeed, the higher bureaucracy could be said to have played a central role in the prewar political process, and perhaps it still does in certain fields such as finance and economic planning.[47] Even in foreign policy decisions, it may be that the role of the bureaucracy is more decisive in certain issue areas and in certain kinds of decisions (e.g., the Ministry of International Trade and Industry in foreign economic policy decisions). And yet, I would essentially subscribe to the view that "foreign policy"

46. Hellmann, *op. cit.*, p. 149.

47. Akira Kubota, *Higher Civil Servants in Postwar Japan* (Princeton, New Jersey: Princeton University Press, 1969), p. 173. Cf. also, T. J. Pempel, "The Bureaucratization of Policymaking in Postwar Japan," *American Journal of Political Science* Vol. XVIII, No. 4 (November, 1974).

bureaucrats did not have a determining role, but that they yielded, willingly or unwillingly, to the political leadership in major decisions of foreign policy in the postwar era. This is primarily because many decisions in foreign policy of the postwar era were as mentioned earlier domestic political decisions and thus the major political actors (namely, LDP leaders) were also actively associated with the decision-making process of foreign policy.

In any case, this declining role of the bureaucratic elements in postwar foreign policy decisions contrasts sharply with the prewar situation. Professor Chihiro Hosoya who has made a thorough study of major foreign policy decisions of the prewar era found that it was the "middle echelon" of the higher bureaucrats[48] in the military and civilian agencies of government, and not so much the political or military leaders at the top, who played a primary and critical role in the formulation of foreign policy. He further argues that these "middle echelon" groups of the higher civil servants were more influential than were their counterparts in the United States in the prewar years, and that top-level leaders, whether formal or informal, were "more vulnerable to initiatives and pressures from below" than in the case of the United States.[49] Among the various data used in Professor Hosoya's study are those of the Russo-Japanese War of 1904, the Siberian Intervention of 1918, the Manchurian Incident of 1931, and the Pacific War of 1941.

On the other hand, the fact that the Japanese bureaucracy has not been one of the primary determinants of Japan's postwar foreign policy does not mean that it will not be so in the future. In fact, there are reasons to believe that it will reassert its influence in the field of foreign policy since the senior civil service as a group has been part and parcel of the postwar Japanese "establishment." In this connection, two salient characteristics of the Japanese higher bureaucracy may be noted. One is the migration of ex-bureaucrats into politics. It is to be noted that approximately one-fourth of all the Liberal Democrats in the House of Representatives today are ex-civil servants in the national government (*viz.*, 1967, 26 percent; 1969, 25 percent; 1972, 23 percent). Not only do these former officials make up a large segment of the Liberal Democrat membership of the Diet, but they also hold positions of

48. Note that when Professor Hosoya refers to the "middle echelon" bureaucrats, these are higher civil servants [as used in this paper] who have passed the prewar senior civil service examinations (*Kobun*) or/and the higher civil service (*Jokyushoku*) examinations for those in the postwar era. For details, see Ori, *op. cit.* (1969).

49. Chihiro Hosoya, "Characteristics of the Foreign Policy Decision-making System in Japan," a paper presented to the 1972 Annual meetings of the International Studies Association, Dallas, Texas, March 1972.

power both in the government and in the party. This is the result of their expertise in policy matters as well as other factors. As a matter of fact, few Japanese prime ministers in the postwar era have not had a bureaucratic background. Significantly, some of the early postwar prime ministers and foreign ministers were from the Ministry of Foreign Affairs proper (e.g., Ashida, Yoshida, Shidehara, and Shigemitsu).[50] Some scholars suggest that these bureaucrats-turned-politicians often acted as spokesmen for the various administrative departments in the Diet and in the policy bodies of the party.

Certainly, the politicized character of the Japanese higher civil service must be taken into consideration as we assess bureaucratic involvement in external affairs. The critical question is, of course, the extent to which civil servants represent the interests of government agencies with which they are associated, and the extent to which they serve the interests produced by the political process. Are they amenable to postwar political changes or do they resist, overtly or covertly, these democratic tendencies? We have no clear answer to these questions, but one very recent study[51] indicates that in the future the Japanese bureaucrats may be willing to accept a secondary position to that of the men in the Diet. Its major findings are that even though the higher civil service is still held in relatively high regard by the Japanese general public, Diet membership is viewed to be more important to the future of Japan and more suitable for exceptionally talented people. Moreover, although the higher bureaucrats regarded themselves as the most important and most talented single major occupational group in Japan (out of twelve occupations), even they clearly recognize the Diet as being the second most important influence on Japan's future. A career in the Diet was held to be the third most suitable position for highly talented people (the second being university professors).[52] If this is the case, the bureaucratic components in foreign policy decision-making might continue to be weak in the years to come.

Another characteristic in the Japanese bureaucracy which may have considerable bearing on foreign policy decisions is its ministerial sectionalism. The Japanese bureaucracy is well noted for its compartmen-

50. Most of these ex-Foreign Office officials served as prime ministers during the American Occupation (1945–1952), and others who followed them were more often than not "economic" bureaucrats. This may be due to the fact that the diplomats and Foreign Ministry officials were more suited for the liaison function with the Occupation authorities.

51. John A. Cicco, Jr. and Kan Ori, "A New Perspective on the Japanese Higher Civil Service: An Empirical Study of Its 'Prestige'," Institute of International Relations, Sophia University, 1974.

52. *Ibid.*

talization, and the government agencies related to foreign affairs prove to be no exception.[53] In his case study of the Okinawa reversion, Professor Akio Watanabe observed that there existed sharp conflict between the Foreign Office and the "domestic" ministries such as the Office of the Prime Minister. The Foreign Office, being more sensitive to the American reaction, was rather passive concerning the question of a prompt return of Okinawa, whereas the Office of the Prime Minister sought the reversion more actively.[54] Likewise, there was a dichotomy on the China issue. The Ministry of International Trade and Industry took a more pro-Peking line, while the Ministry of Foreign Affairs was basically pro-Taipei. More recently, it was reported that the Foreign Office was more inclined to accommodate American demands on the textile issue than the Ministry of International Trade and Industry, which was more responsive to the interests of the textile makers in Japan. It is to be noted further in this particular case that the conflict between the Ministry of Foreign Affairs and the Ministry of International Trade and Industry was closely linked to the factional alignments within the LDP. In some instances the Foreign Ministry itself is factionalized and this often parallels the factional divisions in the ruling conservative party. Certainly we cannot overlook possible influences of this kind of ministerial sectionalism on Japan's foreign policy decisions, particularly if it is to be expected that "foreign policy" bureaucrats will be more actively involved in major decisions in the future.

Despite ministerial sectionalism, the Japanese higher bureaucracy is a homogeneous group with a high degree of *esprit de corps,* and this is so mainly because inter-ministerial transfers are infrequent and bureaucratic careers are usually permanent within a particular ministry. This contrasts sharply with the American civil service system. Bureaucratic involvements in policy decisions in the United States are essentially a component of the Presidential institution, while in Japan the higher civil service itself is an important and independent base of power. Furthermore, the American "bureaucratic" involvement is *ad hoc*, functionally specific and dependent on situations and the President's personality, whereas in the case of Japan the involvement of the bureaucracy is more permanent. It is also to be remembered that when American scholars talk of the bureaucratic politics model,[55] they

53. See, for example, Kiyoaki Tsuji, *Nihon kanryosei no kenkyu* (Tokyo: University of Tokyo Press, 1969).

54. Watanabe, *op. cit.*

55. For a criticism of the literature of the bureaucratic politics model for the analysis of foreign policy, see Kan Ori, "Seisaku ketteiron ni kansuru ichikosatsu," a paper presented to the annual meetings of the Japanese Association of International Relations, Kyoto, Japan, October 15–16, 1973.

include among their major players not only career bureaucrats but also political appointees such as the Presidential advisors on foreign policy and under-secretaries of the State Department. Although the President is, in the final analysis, the chief foreign policy-maker in the United States, in Japan other factors are just as important, as previously discussed. For these reasons, higher bureaucrats associated with foreign policy decisions in Japan are perhaps a more potent force *latently* than their American counterparts, *if* they were to exert leadership and authority in the foreign policy field.

In speculating on the probable role of the Japanese bureaucracy in future foreign policy decisions in the context of U.S.-Japan relations, two sets of pertinent questions may be asked. The first relates to the behavior of the "foreign policy" higher civil servants under a nonconservative government. Would they be able to arrive at a congruence of interests with the ruling party or governing coalition as well as with big business as they presently do? What kind of power can they wield under a leftist government? The second touches on the rather intimate relations that exist between the Japanese bureaucracy and their American counterpart as a result of the special U.S.-Japan relations during the entire postwar era. Would this feature have any bearing on future U.S.-Japan relations, particularly under a leftist government, if it is ever formed in Japan?[56]

56. Cf. Seki's comments in the Tokyo Conference on the U.S.-Japan Relations (April, 1974). This is a very difficult area to do research in, but we urgently need systematic, over time, empirical studies on the subject of bureaucratic involvements in postwar Japan's foreign policy decisions. We should ascertain the areas and the kind of foreign policy decisions in which political leaders have in fact been more important, and the areas and types of foreign policy decisions in which higher bureaucrats have been most decisive. It may also be that, as Professor Hosoya suggested in the Tokyo conference, with the future political fluidity (*i.e.*, the control of the Liberal Democratic Party becoming more uncertain) in the Japanese political arena, higher bureaucrats, even in the foreign policy field, may have more leverage thereby becoming a major determining factor in Japan's foreign policy decisions. My observations in this section are based on (1) case studies presently available but which are far from being systematic, (2) my conversations with Liberal Democratic political leaders and social critics (publicists), both of whom may be biased, and (3) my informal discussions with journalists in the political desk who are knowledgeable but at times impressionistic. In this conjunction, it should be noted that a high-ranking Japanese diplomat, Minister Toshio Yamazaki, then Minister for Political Affairs, the Embassy of Japan in Washington, D.C. (now Director-General, American Affairs Bureau, Japanese Ministry of Foreign Affairs), who attended the Chicago conference thought that higher civil servants did in fact play a much more important role in Japan's foreign policy decisions than I described here. Again, that may be the case, but this assertion must be corroborated or falsified by empirical data. Although there is no dearth of impressionistic descriptions of the Japanese higher bureaucracy, we have very few systematic studies even concerning in general the Japanese higher civil service. Of the few systematic works on this subject in English, consult Akira Kubota, *op. cit.*, and Benjamin and Ori, *op. cit.*, chapters 8 and 9, and Pempel, *op. cit.*

III.

Four major components have been isolated here as being important in the political context of major foreign policy decisions in postwar Japan. They are: (1) the Liberal Democratic Party and its factions, (2) the Japanese political party system as a whole, (3) big business, and (4) "foreign policy"-related government agencies. Of the four, the first element, that of the LDP and its factions, has been seen as most important as far as the case studies I have examined here are concerned.[57] The ruling conservative party and its top leaders have dominated much of the postwar foreign policy-making process, and they in turn have been very much influenced by the factional nature of Japanese politics. It is therefore not difficult to speculate that as long as the LDP stays in power, the present pattern of decision-making in foreign policy will remain fundamentally unchanged. This means that Japan is likely to continue with this peculiar party-dominated pattern of foreign policy decision-making, and there will be powerful intraparty factional constraints on the chief foreign policy-makers.

However, as we look into the 1970s and 80s, two other components, the political party system and big business, will increasingly become important. This is because the LDP is steadily losing popular support, and because future international relations increasingly will revolve around economic issues as far as Japan is concerned. In other words, political parties other than the LDP, together with their foreign policies, will become increasingly relevant in the future. At the same time, big business will most likely have a greater say over Japan's foreign policy. These developments in particular will complicate future U.S.-Japan relations. As to the probable role of the bureaucratic component in foreign policy-making, it is difficult to work this out. My

57. Although each case study examined here has competently dealt with the problems it set out to do originally (in fact, three of them were part of Ph.D. theses), I am fully aware that they are inadequate for the kind of task I am attempting in this paper. But we must start somewhere, and I chose to examine existing case studies involving Japan's postwar foreign policy decisions as a preliminary step to identify major determinants of Japanese foreign policy in the postwar era. More systematic use of case studies is needed, and I understand the Brookings Institution is now undertaking such a study. As to the extreme lack of systematic, behaviorally-oriented, empirical studies in the areas covered in this chapter, with the exception of electoral voting behavior and public opinion surveys, see Kan Ori, "The State of Political Science Discipline in Postwar Japan," a paper presented to a Colloquium on Political Science, Miami University, Oxford, Ohio, May 1971. Cf. also James W. White, "Tradition and Politics in Studies of Contemporary Japan," *World Politics*, Vol. XXVI, No. 3 (April 1974), pp. 400–427. I did, however, try my best to bring those empirical findings we have at present on Japanese politics which are relevant to domestic political factors I covered in this chapter. For some promising studies, see four articles on political socialization, institutionalization, political culture, and electoral behavior in Japanese Political Science Association (ed.), *op. cit.*, (1971).

guess is that it will continue to play a secondary role to that of the political leaders in *major* foreign policy decisions. Certainly the role will be much less than the one it previously played in the pre-1945 era.

At any rate, political factors at home will continue to be crucial in Japan's future foreign policy. The effects of domestic political fluidity in Japan will be especially felt in future U.S.-Japan relations. As has been discussed throughout this chapter, recent political developments are such that we can no longer take the special U.S.-Japan relations for granted.[58]

58. As to a modeling effort for the analysis of Japan's (U.S.) foreign policy determinants in the context of the U.S.-Japan relations, see Roger W. Benjamin and Kan Ori, "The Impact of Inter-Nation Communication Patterns on Foreign Policy Decision-making between Japan and the United States," a research proposal presented to the conference on Peace and Communication in the Pacific, East-West Center, University of Hawaii, August 1973. Cf. also Richard I. Hofferbert, "Elite Influence in State Policy Formation: A Model for Comparative Inquiry," in *Polity* (March 1970), pp. 316–344, particularly Figure 1, "A Model for Comparative Study of Policy Formation," p. 327, a model which I consider to be one of the best in the field.

III.
Economic Issues

The Prospects for Japan's Role in the World Economy

Koichi Hamada

Introduction

When Japan started her recovery from the destruction of World War II, she could be regarded as a point with location but without mass or measure in the world economy. Now, after her remarkable growth in the last decade, Japan presents herself as an entity with substantial mass. Ten years ago it was said that if the United States sneezes, Japan catches pneumonia. At present, the economic activities of Japan have substantial impact on many national economies the world over. Not only trade relations but also monetary relations in the world are strongly affected by the behavior of the Japanese economy and the attitude of the Japanese government.

Therefore, it is natural that Japan encounters various kinds of economic frictions and conflicts as she expands rapidly in the world economy. Japan is a "nouveau riche" country in the world. Such phrases as "Japan Incorporated" and "the ugly Japanese" are, unfortunately, not uncommon. The higher the relative importance of the Japanese economy, the more it is likely that Japan will be involved in

I would like to thank Professor Victor D. Lippit of University of California, Riverside, for his constructive criticisms and suggestions.

economic, social, and political frictions and conflicts with other countries.[1]

Trends and Forecasts

Table 1 shows the growing magnitude and relative importance of the Japanese economy. The figures in the last row are the forecasted values of a group headed by Hisao Kanamori at the Japan Economic Research

Table 1

Growth of the Japanese Economy
(in billions of dollars)

Years	GNP (Nominal)	Trade		Accumulated Direct Investments	International Reserves	IMF Quota
		Import	Export			
1950	—	0.8(1.5)	1.0(1.7)	—	0.6(1.2)	—
1960	43.1	4.1(3.6)	4.5(3.8)	0.3(—)	1.9(3.2)	0.5(3.2)
1970	197.2	19.3(6.9)	18.9(6.4)	3.6(2.8[2])	8.5(9.2)	1.2(4.1)
1980	1,052.7	90.7(10.8)	93.0(—)	27.5(—)	—	—

Numbers in parentheses represent percentages.
1. Percentages are with respect to the total world values.
2. As percentages to the total investment by DAC member countries.
Source: Actual figures, *International Financial Statistics*, MITI *Foreign Trade of Japan*, 1972. Estimated figures, JERC, *A Long-Term Outlook of Japanese and U.S. Economies, 1980*, 1973.

1. The change in attitude among Japanologists in the United States reflects the change of the relative position of Japan in the world. It seems that most Japanologists, especially specialists in the Japanese economy, were motivated largely by pure academic and exotic interests in Japan. But recently, they are motivated by a more pragmatic purpose, that is, by the purpose of obtaining information from the United States's economic rival as fast as possible. Reflecting these pragmatic interests, for example, they are eager to know the Japanese managerial system in order to find out the secret of the fast expansion of the Japanese economy, and eager to reevaluate the relative advantages and disadvantages of a different system.

Center.[2] We have to note that these figures tend to represent some overestimate of Japan's growth potential because they were estimated before the oil crisis.

In 1950, the Japanese share in world trade was only 1.5 percent. During the last decade it has grown nearly fourfold in the case of imports, and more than fourfold in the case of exports. Moreover, it is predicted that in 1980 the share of Japanese exports in total world imports will reach 10.8 percent. Japan started her foreign investment around 1951. In spite of its spurt in recent years, the relative importance of Japanese direct investments in the share of direct investments by the DAC[3] members is still small. During the first three quarters of fiscal 1972,[4] the government authorized more than $1.7 billion, so that the total accumulated balance of the Japanese direct investments reached $6.2 billion at the end of 1972. Thus it is predicted that the total balance of accumulated direct investments by Japan will reach $27.5 billion in 1980.

In accordance with its growing importance in foreign trade and investment, the Japanese economy occupies a significant position in the monetary relations of the world economy. Partly due to the obstinate policy of resisting the revaluation of the yen adopted by the Japanese government during 1971, the share of liquidity held by Japan in the total world reserve reached 12.4 percent (13.8 billion) at the end of 1971. Japan's IMF quota, which indicates voting power as well as capital subscription, also has shown a gradual increase.

On the other hand, we have to notice that the openness or the relative reliance of the Japanese economy on trade is, at least quantitatively, not so strong as is often thought. Table 2 compares the import/GNP ratios of several advanced countries. It shows that the import/GNP ratio of Japan is much greater than that of the United States, but except for the ratio for raw materials and fuels, ratios are relatively smaller than those of most European countries. This tendency is not expected to change drastically, and the import-GNP ratio is predicted to be around 10 percent in 1980.[5]

Thus the growing importance of the Japanese economy is not so much due to its increased openness as to the rapid expansion of its scale. Needless to say, if the Japanese economy continues to grow at such a high rate as it did in the last decade, the cost may become

2. Japan Economic Research Center (JERC), *A Long-Term Outlook of Japanese and U.S. Economies, 1980*, March 1973.

3. Development Assistance Committee at OECD.

4. The fiscal year of Japan starts in April and ends in March.

5. Japan Economic Research Center, *The Long-Term Outlook, op. cit.*

Table 2

Comparison of Import/GNP Ratios in 1960 and in 1970

	Year	Japan	Germany	U.K.	France	Italy	U.S.
Total Imports/	1960	9.9	15.1	20.0	10.2	13.5	2.9
GNP	1970	9.6	16.2	21.1	12.7	16.3	4.1
Foodstuffs/	1960	3.0	6.6	9.5	3.8	3.6	1.1
consumption	1970	3.1	5.3	6.7	3.0	4.6	1.0
Raw Materials	1960	5.7	4.0	5.8	3.5	5.4	0.7
& Fuels/GNP	1970	4.4	2.8	4.3	2.6	4.4	0.5
Produced Material/	1960	1.5	4.6	4.9	2.5	3.5	0.9
GNP	1970	1.8	5.3	6.7	3.9	4.7	1.2
Capital Goods/	1960	0.9	1.3	1.4	1.4	1.7	0.2
GNP	1970	0.9	2.6	3.4	3.0	2.9	0.7

Source: MITI *Foreign Trade of Japan*, 1972.

prohibitive. Congestion and pollution that are already serious problems may become aggravated unless adequate city planning and antipollution regulations are promptly implemented. However, in spite of the possible slowdown necessitated by the consideration of external diseconomies, the general tendency of the increasing importance of the Japanese economy will still continue. And it will create lots of adjustment problems on the part of Japan as well as on the part of other countries.[6]

6. Here we must warn the reader against the naive belief that most economic predictions actually come true. Economists are, we believe, not yet in a position to replace the spiritualistic medium at Delphi to foretell the future. Accordingly, the figures we cite will come true, if at all, only approximately. They were forecasted before the oil crisis, so they do not take account of its impact. Moreover, the forecast of trade depends on the future course of the exchange rate and, accordingly, on the future course of the exchange rate policy of the government. (For example, the estimate by the Japan Economic Research Center, which we shall refer to as JERC estimate, assumes that the exchange rate is 280 yen per dollar in 1980.) Therefore, we need to refer to the forecasted figures with reservation. In making this note of caution, however, we by no means intend to neglect our great debt to these forecasting activities, especially those of the Japan Economic Research Center, that give concrete grounds for our discussion and enrich it throughout this paper.

Prospects of Trade, Investments, and Monetary Relations

Let us consider in more detail issues associated with international trade and direct investments by Japan, and international monetary relations involving Japan.

International Trade.[7] Most Japanese exports (more than 97 percent in 1970) consist of manufactured goods. During the course of recovery from the war, such labor-intensive industries as textiles and sundry goods were important export industries. With the advancement of Japanese technology, however, more sophisticated goods such as industrial machinery, transportation equipment, electrical machinery, and chemical products have become more important items, leaving labor-intensive goods to competitors in developing countries. This tendency is expected to continue, and more sophisticated products such as chemicals and capital goods with high technology will become some of the major export items. Table 3 contrasts the industrial structure of Japanese exports in the past and in the future.

Regionally, as Table 4 indicates, the United States has been the most important customer. But it is expected that because of the effect of revaluation the relative weight of the United States as the major export market will decline, and that the relative importance of Europe will increase. Since it is also expected that the export to communist bloc countries will increase to some extent, the Japanese export structure will become more regionally diversified.

Because of trade liberalization and the revaluation of the yen, the structure of Japanese imports has been changing. Imports of agricultural, forestry, and fishery products are increasing, but their relative weight is decreasing. On the other hand, the relative and absolute importance of the imports of mineral resources and of light industrial goods will increase considerably. In particular, Japanese imports of mineral fuels will take the share of 22 percent of the total world imports in 1980 according to the forecast by JERC.

Regionally, the relative importance of the United States is large, and it is expected to be large in the future. Since Japan will have to rely almost exclusively on the Middle East for the supply of mineral fuels, the imports from this area are expected to occupy 17 percent of the total imports of Japan in 1980. (See Table 5.)

So much for the general tendency of Japanese foreign trade. Now let us focus our attention on the United States-Japan economic relationship. In spite of the present economic tension between the two countries

7. We owe much to JERC, *A Long-Term Outlook, op. cit.*, for prediction and the description of the current trend.

Table 3

Industrial Distribution of Japanese Exports
(nominal, FOB, millions of dollars)

	1960	1970	1980
Agriculture, forestry, fisheries	184(4.5)	311(1.6)	402(0.4)
Mining	2(0.0)	15(0.1)	36(0.0)
Manufacturing	3,854(95.1)	18,836(97.5)	88,743(98.0)
Foods	251(6.2)	422(2.2)	1,164(1.3)
Textiles	924(22.8)	1,744(9.0)	3.325(3.7)
Pulp, paper	54(1.3)	182(0.9)	346(0.4)
Chemicals	213(5.3)	1,715(8.9)	9,927(10.9)
Petroleum, coal products	16(0.4)	42(0.2)	257(0.3)
Ceramics, stone, clay products	145(3.6)	331(1.7)	883(1.0)
Primary metals	414(10.2)	3,101(16.1)	13,195(14.6)
Metal products	148(3.7)	714(3.7)	2,639(2.9)
Industrial machinery	222(5.5)	2,006(10.4)	14,139(15.6)
Electrical machinery	276(6.8)	2,864(14.8)	12,159(13.4)
Transportation equipment	433(10.7)	3,443(17.8)	20,143(22.2)
Precision machinery	101(2.5)	676(3.5)	4,600(5.1)
Other	657(16.2)	1,596(8.3)	5,966(6.6)
Re-export, classification unknown	16(0.4)	155(0.8)	1,502(1.7)
Total	**4,054(100.0)**	**19,318(100.0)**	**90,683(100.0)**

Numbers in parentheses represent percentage proportion.
Source: JERC, *A Long-Term Outlook of Japanese and U.S. Economies, 1980*, 1973.

Table 4

Regional Distribution of Japanese Exports

(nominal, FOB, millions of dollars)

	1960	1970	1980
United States	1,102(27.2)	5,940(30.7)	21,455(23.7)
Canada	119(2.9)	563(2.9)	3,782(4.2)
OECD, Europe	467(11.5)	2,853(14.8)	14,481(16.0)
Australia, New Zealand	225(5.5)	1,032(5.3)	6,521(7.2)
Southeast Asia	1,307(32.2)	4,902(25.4)	21,809(24.0)
Middle East	137(3.4)	545(2.8)	4.430(4.9)
Latin America	304(7.5)	1,187(6.1)	5,899(6.5)
Africa	294(7.3)	1,094(5.7)	5,576(6.1)
Communist Bloc Countries	73(1.8)	1,045(5.4)	5,758(6.3)
Other	27(0.7)	157(0.8)	972(1.1)
World total	**4,055(100.0)**	**19,318(100.0)**	**90,683(100.0)**

Numbers in parentheses represent percentage proportion.
Source: JERC, *ibid.*

Table 5

Regional Distribution of Japanese Imports

(nominal, CIF, millions of dollars)

	1960	1970	1980
United States	1,554(34.6)	5,560(29.4)	22,271(24.0)
Canada	204(4.5)	929(4.9)	4,743(5.1)
OECD, Europe	392(8.7)	1,959(10.3)	9,868(10.6)
Australia, New Zealand	432(9.6)	1,979(10.5)	10,589(11.4)
Southeast Asia	915(20.5)	3,013(16.0)	14,000(15.1)
Middle East	420(9.4)	2,245(11.9)	15,520(16.7)
Latin America	311(6.9)	1,373(7.3)	6,250(6.7)
Africa	107(2.4)	784(4.2)	4,288(4.6)
Communist bloc countries	125(2.8)	887(4.7)	5,031(5.4)
Other	33(0.7)	153(0.8)	428(0.5)
World total	**4,491(100.0)**	**18,881(100.0)**	**92,987(100.0)**

Numbers in parentheses represent percentage proportion.
Source: JERC, *ibid.*

symbolized by the Burke-Hartke Bill, the American economy and the Japanese economy have mutually complementary structures. As Kanamori points out,[8] the United States abounds with natural resources, particularly land, and with very advanced technology, while Japan has plenty of well-educated labor and intermediate technology. Therefore, Japan imports from the United States such products of advanced technology as large-scale computers and aircraft; agricultural products like wheat, beans, and lumber; and minerals like coal. On the other hand, the United States imports from Japan such products of intermediate technology and ample well-trained labor as steel, automobiles, transistors, and television sets. In 1970, about 29 percent of Japanese imports were from the United States, and about 31 percent of Japanese exports went to the United States.

Since each economy has an industrial structure that complements the other, the economic relations between the United States and Japan can be harmonious in the long run if efforts are made to deal with specific conflicts concerning specific trade items or specific industries. Because of the magnitude of trade flows, however, conflicts in a specific industry could become very serious. The amendments to the Antidumping Act, the initiation of the survey in preparation for applying countervailing duties on Japanese electronics products, the introduction of a safeguard clause into the trade bill, and submission of the Burke-Hartke Bill are signs of conflict related to Japanese exports. On the other hand, the movements to place export restrictions on soybeans, lumber, and scrap iron are signs of conflict related to Japanese imports.

When we consider conflicts associated with trade relations, it is not sufficient to consider them only in terms of national interests. Through the imposition of import duties or quotas, the import-competing industry will gain, but the consumers of the imported product will usually lose. Usually, the conflict is between producers of the exporting country and producers of the importing country, and between consumers of the exporting country and consumers of the importing country. On the other hand, there is a complementary relationship of interests between producers of the exporting country and consumers of the importing country. Also we have to note the complementary relationship between the producer of an intermediate product and the user of the product, and the competing relationship among users of the same product or of the same resource. Unfortunately there is an asymmetry in the political system of most countries so that the interests of producers are reflected

8. Hisao Kanamori, *Nihon Keizai no Shinjigen* (New Dimensions of the Japanese Economy) Nihonkeizai Shimbun-sha, Tokyo 1972; see also JERC, *A Long-Term Outlook*, *op. cit.*

in policy-making more than those of consumers. We shall investigate by commodity classification what kind of conflict structures exist in the United States-Japan economic relations.

In the case of foodstuffs, the complementarity of interests between American farmers and Japanese consumers are strong. For such items as dairy products, oranges, and grapefruits, conflict of interests exists between American farmers and import competing Japanese farmers. The recent prohibition of exports of soybeans by the United States government is an indication that the conflict between Japanese consumers and American consumers could become serious under some situations. However, complementarity rather than competition seems to be dominant as far as foodstuffs are concerned.

In the case of lumber and coal, again the complementarity between American producers and Japanese consumers and resource users are dominant, even though possible conflict exists between resource users in both countries. One of the most important items is petroleum. Since the United States herself is an importer of petroleum, there is no complementarity between the two countries. Competition between consumers as well as between resource users could become serious. Since Japan relies almost completely on imports the strategic position of Japan vis-à-vis Middle Eastern oil producing countries is very vulnerable.

As for industrial products, conflict exists between American producers and Japanese producers. As the industrial structure of Japan has been changing, and will be changing, from labor-intensive light industry to more sophisticated products requiring advanced technology and capital equipments, the nature of industrial conflict will also change. The conflict between decaying industries in the United States and labor-intensive industries in Japan, for example, textiles and sundries, has been shifting to the conflict between the producers of both sides in industries with intermediate technology, such as electrical machinery and automobiles. From now on it is quite possible that industries with more advanced technology will compete severely in the future. We should not forget that there are complementary relations of interests between American producers and Japanese consumers, and between Japanese producers and American consumers. In order to prevent unnecessary movements toward protection, which overrepresent the interests of the producers of the importing country, consumer coalitions should be formed to represent the interest of consumers.

This analysis of conflict structures raise the following questions that are not only practically important but also interesting to economists in general.

The first problem is how to confront the predicted food shortage.

Given the present international productivity differences, the Japanese economy should move toward more imports of agricultural products following the principle of comparative advantage. The production cost of rice, for example, is more than twice its international price. If a world food shortage is right ahead, however, should Japan not keep protecting her agriculture with the walls of tariffs and quotas? The answer depends, of course, on how likely the shortage is to materialize, and how immediate it is apt to be; at the same time, it depends on the extent to which it is possible to rebuild agriculture after allowing it to decline. At present Japan has a comparative disadvantage in producing foodstuffs. If Japan can resume agricultural production without much difficulty and adjustment costs, it will be more economical at present to rely on the principle of comparative advantage and to import cheaper food rather than coproduce at home. If the process is close to irreversible and the adjustment cost is enormous, Japan should prepare for the possible world food shortage by protecting her agriculture. The current cost of producing expensive food would be regarded as an insurance premium if such were the case.

The next problem is the energy conservation problem. In the future, Japan will have to depend strongly on the supply of oil from the Middle East. As compared with the strategic position of the United States, which still has a domestic source of supply and which controls most of the international petroleum companies (Majors), Japan may be in a quite difficult position.

Recently, the Organization of Petroleum Exporting Countries (OPEC) is demanding higher prices for oil and the participation in the management of oil producing firms. These countries are trying to build monopolistic positions. According to neoclassical price theory, the tastes of the future generations are assumed to be reflected in the preference ordering of present households. But is the demand of future generations who will be living a hundred years from now reflected in the current prices and/or in the current expectation of future prices? But, if they are not reflected completely, there is a case for restricting the supply of energy resources by raising the opportunity cost of using resources to a higher level than the level that the competitive market solution commands. However, it is hard to imagine that the present price set by OPEC can be justified from this ground.

As the analysis of conflict structures has indicated, there is little room for the harmony of interests as far as energy resources are concerned. There is little room, either, for complementarity of interests in the case of the marketing competition between American firms and

Japanese firms in the rest of the world. Thus, we can expect the confrontation of American and Japanese interests seeking to secure stable energy sources in the Middle East and competing for commodity markets in various places in the world. This possible confrontation gives incentives for expansion to both economies in the form of direct investments, to which we shall now turn.

Direct Investments. On 1 May 1973, foreign investments in Japan were liberalized to a substantial degree. Most industries are now open to foreign investments and permit up to one hundred percent control by foreigners. Five industries—agriculture and fishery, leather, mining, petroleum, and retails—are still on the negative list; that is, foreign investments in these industries are subject to permission by the government. Seventeen industries, including computer production, sales, rentals, and real estate will be completely liberalized after certain intervals. The scale of foreign investments in Japan is still small and a large proportion of it is by the United States.[9] Because of this liberalization and other factors, the accumulated value of direct foreign investments is expected to reach $5.6 billion ($3.9 billion by U.S. firms), as compared to the actual value of $.5 billion ($.3 billion by U.S. firms) at the end of 1969.

However, much more remarkable will be the outward investments by Japan in the next ten years.[10] In order to defend and promote marketing, Japanese firms will be motivated to engage in market-oriented foreign investment. In order to secure a stable energy supply, they will also engage in resource oriented investments. Since wages will rise considerably in Japan, they will be induced to engage in labor-oriented investments. Finally, and unfortunately, there will be incentives to engage in environment-oriented investments—namely, the export of pollutions.[11]

How can we characterize the behaviors of Japanese firms abroad? Kiyoshi Kojima develops an interesting contrast of the dominating pat-

9. For a lucid exposition of direct investments in Japan, see Ryutaro Komiya, "Direct Foreign Investment in Postwar Japan" in Peter Drysdale, ed., *Direct Foreign Investment in Asia and the Pacific*, Australian National University Press, Canberra, 1972.

10. For an analysis of Japanese investments abroad, see Yasumi Sakamoto et al., *Nihon Kigyo no Kaigai Shinshutsu* (Oversea Activities of Japanese Firms), Toyokeizai, Tokyo, 1973. See also my "Japanese Investment Abroad," in Peter Drysdale, ed., *op. cit.*

11. To prevent the unfortunate results of this, we should require foreign subsidiaries of Japanese firms to observe the same environmental standards effective in Japan, as well as the standards set by host countries. Also, all the relevant information should be transmitted to the host countries, with respect to the possible polluting effect of the firms' activities.

terns of American and Japanese foreign investments.[12] Following Hymer and Vernon,[13] Kojima points out the following features of typical American direct investments. They are mostly made by large-scale firms having bases in many countries, that is, by multinational companies, that face oligopolistic rather than competitive market conditions. The majority of American direct investments are made in the industries that require the most sophisticated technology. Because of this, they tend to undermine rather than promote the comparative advantage of the United States. The motives of these multinational companies are to maximize profit possibilities, regardless of the national interest of host or parent countries.

On the other hand, Kojima points out the following features of typical Japanese direct investments. The majority of Japanese direct investments are made by small-scale firms. At the end of 1969, the average scale of Japanese investments was $.83 million. And more than half of Japanese investments are directed to developing countries, as compared to 40 percent of American investments. Profit rates are generally low in Japanese investments, indicating the fact that Japanese investments are accommodating trade and representing national, rather than private, business interests per se. Thus, Japanese investments are promoting rather than undermining the comparative advantage of Japan in foreign trade.

There are, of course, reservations to be made before accepting this characterization. For example, as Kojima himself recognizes, the Japanese pattern thus defined may be just a reflection of the fact that Japanese investments are still in an early stage. After the Japanese industrial structure becomes more advanced, and after the lag in human factors, that is, the lag in international communications, which we discuss later, is filled, Japanese investors may resemble the American type of multinational corporations. However, the comparison of the present distribution of Japanese investments in Table 6 and the forecasted distribution in Table 7 show that resource-oriented investment will dominate in the future so that the relative importance of the highly developed industries will not be too important as early as 1980. Thus, Kojima's characterization serves as a good framework even in the long run in this respect.

Another reservation I would like to make is on the validity of the

12. Kiyoshi Kojima, *Sekai Boeki to Takokuseki Kigyo* (The World Trade and Multinational Corporations), Sobunsha, Tokyo, 1973, especially Chapter 5.

13. For example, see Stephen Hymer, "United States Investment Abroad," in Peter Drysdale, ed., *op. cit.;* Raymond Vernon. "International Investment and International Trade in the Product Cycle," *Quarterly Journal of Economics*, May 1966.

Table 6

Japan's Direct Investments Abroad
Cumulative Authorized Amount—Actuals in Fiscal 1970
(in millions of dollars)

	All areas	North America	Latin America	South-east Asia	Europe	Middle & Near East	Africa	Oceania
Resource-	1,424	378	103	333	7	328	60	215
oriented	(39.6)	(10.5)	(2.9)	(9.3)	(0.2)	(9.1)	(1.7)	(6.0)
Labor- or	750	45	274	321	37	4	25	45
market-oriented	(20.9)	(1.3)	(7.6)	(8.9)	(1.0)	(0.1)	(0.7)	(1.3)
Financial service	1,422	489	182	125	595	2	8	22
and others	(39.5)	(13.6)	(5.1)	(3.5)	(16.5)	(0.1)	(0.2)	(0.6)
Total	**3,596**	**912**	**559**	**779**	**639**	**334**	**93**	**282**
	(100.0)	**(25 4)**	**(15.5)**	**(21.7)**	**(17.8)**	**(9.3)**	**(2.6)**	**(7.8)**

Numbers in parentheses represent percentages.
Source: JERC, *ibid*.

Table 7

Japan's Direct Investments Abroad
Projected for Fiscal 1980
(in millions of dollars)

	All areas	North America	Latin America	Southeast Asia	Europe	Middle & Near East	Africa	Oceania	Planned economy bloc
Resource-oriented	13,910 (50.6)	1,661 (6.0)	1,491 (5.4)	2,293 (8.4)	— —	3,719 (13.6)	1,292 (4.7)	2,494 (9.1)	960 (3.5)
Labor- or market-oriented	7,181 (26.2)	396 (1.4)	2,611 (9.5)	2,715 (9.9)	112 (0.4)	53 (0.2)	205 (0.7)	609 (2.2)	480 (1.7)
Financial service and others	6,367 (23.2)	2,510 (9.2)	835 (3.0)	534 (2.0)	2,157 (7.9)	3 (0.1)	1 (0.1)	287 (1.0)	40 (0.1)
Total	**27,458 (100.0)**	**4,567 (16.6)**	**4,937 (18.0)**	**5,542 (20.2)**	**2,269 (8.3)**	**3,775 (13.8)**	**1,498 (5.5)**	**3,390 (12.4)**	**1,490 (5.4)**

Numbers in parentheses represent percentages.
Source: JERC, *ibid.*

statement that Japanese investments are more nationally oriented than profit oriented. The observation of low profit rates for Japanese investments reflects the shortness of the history of Japanese foreign investments, as well as the tendency of Japanese firms to make decisions on the basis of combined profit of trade and investment activities. It is true that the Japanese government and private firms are associated by way of implicit guidance and solicitation. But it is not that Japanese firms are nationally oriented by themselves. Rather, the government creates regulations and guidelines in such a way that private profit seeking in the long-run perspective will be in the national interest. Firms going abroad do not try consciously to serve anything more than their self-interest, but they actually serve the "national interest," as conceived, for example, by MITI.

One interesting feature of Japanese investments is their heavy reliance on the organizing activities of trading companies (shosha). Besides investing by themselves, trading companies, which often have "zaibatsu" origin, organize direct investments of manufacturing firms of the group to which they belong. They also serve the investors by providing necessary information and know-how. As compared to the typical multinational corporations that invest in many places, Japanese trading companies coordinate the business activities of various kinds of direct investments of their own groups. As Yoshihiro Tsurumi points out, however, this phenomenon is partly a reflection of the fact that many Japanese investors do not have enough entrepreneurial ability to engage in oversea activities by themselves.[14] Therefore, even though we should recognize the efficiency of trading companies, they need to be evaluated in the light of their future development.

In any event, neither the fact that Japanese investments are relatively trade-promoting and trade-accommodating, nor the fact that they represent relatively macro- instead of micro-interests means that frictions with nationalism in the host countries are less severe. The fact that Japanese investments are small-scale and more competitive does not by itself help to mitigate possible frictions. For, as I shall explain below, the conflict with nationalism stems not only from the monopolistic behavior of the firms involved, but also from the nature of direct investment itself.[15]

14. Successful Japanese investors in advanced countries relied very little on the activities of trading companies. Yoshihiro Tsurumi, "Nihon Kigyo no Takokuseki ka no Joken (Conditions for the multinationalization of Japanese firms)," *Toyokeizai* Special Series, July 11, 1973, pp. 100ff.

15. I admit that I have changed my opinion from my "Japanese Investment Abroad," *op. cit.*, p. 181.

Let us ask the following question: Why should a Japanese firm invest abroad in an extracting industry, say, in petroleum, instead of having a long-term contract for imports? It is attracted to the form of direct investment since the contract pattern of direct investment is more favorable to the firm than the contract pattern of long-term imports. Ronald Coase developed a theory of the firm stating that the scale of a firm is determined by the consideration of the relative convenience and the relative economy of transaction costs among various forms of contracts.[16] Applying this theory to direct investments,[17] we can say firms invest abroad because the form of direct investments is more favorable than other forms of economic contract. If a long-term contract for imports is not carried out, the importer can at most sue the exporter for the default of obligations. But in the case of direct investments, the firm can organize production by gathering and supervising workers. Therefore, personnel and hierarchic relations are of necessity more involved in direct investments than in trade. The emergence of economic nationalism against direct investments can be explained from this standpoint. The fact that Japanese firms are more likely to engage in resource-oriented investments and labor-oriented investments rather than to engage in the multinational business activities of the American-type, using highly sophisticated technology and entrepreneurial ability, does not mean, therefore, that the conflict with the nationalism of host countries will be less severe.

Human Factors

We have seen that the position of Japan in the world economy is expanding very rapidly, so that she will encounter various kinds of economic, social, and political conflicts and difficulties in the near future. Since the speed of expansion leaves little room for gradual adjustments on the part of Japan and of other countries, it is quite possible that economic frictions can become serious.

There are two approaches to the analysis of those problems. One is to seek to overcome, or at least to minimize, the economic frictions, given the rapid expansion of the Japanese economy. The other is, more basically, to slow down the speed of economic expansion.

Let us start with the first approach. How can Japan minimize economic frictions in the near future if the speed of expansion is as fast as before? Here human factors are most important. What is needed is

16. Ronald H. Coase, "The Nature of the Firm," *Economica*, Vol. 4, November 1937.

17. See, A. E. Safarian, "Problems of Host Countries," in Drysdale, ed., *op. cit.*, though the emphasis and conclusions are quite different.

the acquisition of abilities to engage in international activities in an effective fashion; that is, to acquire the ability to express intentions clearly and to be understood by people with different economic and cultural backgrounds. I may call this ability an "ability for international communication."[18]

By an ability for international communication, we do not mean an ability associated only with business activities. We shall use the word in a more comprehensive sense; namely, as the ability to communicate effectively with different nationals in business, diplomatic, and cultural relations. This is the ability to express one's intentions clearly in an understandable form to people with different cultural backgrounds and to deal with various problems with sufficient understanding of the intentions of other nationals. If the development of this ability lags behind the growing importance of the Japanese economy, the frictions and difficulties resulting from the rapid expansion of the Japanese economy can be quite serious.

Three elements of the ability for international communication are worth mentioning. First, language ability is certainly an important element. The Japanese educational system has emphasized a reading ability sufficient for the absorption of Western culture and technology. Lacking in the system is a speaking and writing ability sufficient to express one's opinions and ideas clearly and smoothly. Of course, to speak a foreign language fluently or to behave sociably at a cocktail party is a necessary element, but it is by no means the most important element.

More important is the second element of the ability for international communication. This is the ability to express oneself clearly and distinctly and, at the same time, in a form that is understandable to people with different cultural backgrounds. When Japanese people engage in economic, diplomatic, and cultural relations with nationals of advanced as well as developing countries, there occurs a contact between Japanese and other cultural patterns. In such a case, Japanese people should have the ability to express their ideas in a form that is understandable to nationals with different experiences and different value systems.

Unfortunately, the Japanese educational system has emphasized uni-

18. For a different approach to the internationalization of Japanese entrepreneurial ability from the standpoint of system analysis, see Naoto Sasaki, "Nihon no Keiei Kokusaika no Tsuikyu (On the Internationalization of the Japanese Management)" *Chuo Koron* Special Issue on Management Problems, Tokyo, Spring 1973. See also Chie Nakane, *Tekio no Joken (Conditions for Adaptation)*, Kodansha Gendai Shinsho, Tokyo, 1972; and Yoshihiro Tsurumi, *op. cit.*

formity of ideas and conformity to a group. In many cases, school children are dressed in uniforms designed by the school, and a uniform curriculum is given to all children. To be competent in the entrance examination to colleges, they are not encouraged so much to develop individual aptitudes and viewpoints.[19] In expressing their opinions, they are trained to talk in a way that minimizes the impression of difference and maximizes the impression of conformity to the group.

Therefore, most Japanese lack the training to signal their opinions distinctly as well as smoothly. The smiling Japanese gentlemen at international meetings, keeping silent and never committing themselves to any potentially disadvantageous action, may look mysterious to many Westerners. For the Japanese government, as well as for the Japanese people, it has been difficult to behave in a multilateral rather than bilateral relationship. For the Japanese attitude pattern has been first to decide whether to belong to a particular group or coalition and then to follow blindly whatever that group or coalition commands. Thus, other parties are classified as either belonging to one's group or alien to it.

According to Kinhide Mushakoji,[20] the communication pattern of Japanese and other Orientals follows "the logic of adaptation" rather than "the logic of choice." If the Western pattern of communication or negotiation is to specify the possible alternatives for choice, and discretely to choose one strategy, the Japanese pattern of communication or negotiation is to adapt its attitude depending on the attitude of other parties. As Mushakoji indicated, the adaptive pattern may be effective in some situations. But at least Japanese people engaging in economic or diplomatic negotiations should realize this difference in the patterns of communication.

The third element of ability for international communication is to recognize, to understand, and to be tolerant toward value systems and frames of references different from one's own. Japan experienced a long period of isolation (Sakoku) in the pre-restoration period. During the Second World War, she experienced a *de facto* cultural isolation. Japan is an island country and is composed of a racially homogeneous people. Therefore, Japanese people are apt to project their way of thinking on other societies without admitting or recognizing different ways of

19. This might have been a successful tool for educating highly standardized, well-trained laborers, technicians, and bureaucrats required for economic growth with borrowed technology. From now on Japan needs technological development for herself, and this educational policy may become inadequate even for the purpose of domestic growth.

20. Kinhide Mushakoji, *Kokusai Seiji to Nippon* (International Politics and Japan), Todaishuppan, Tokyo, 1967, Chaper II.

thinking. Especially in contact with developing countries, Japanese people should learn to be tolerant of other cultures and behavioral patterns.

Incidentally, though gifted with the second element of the ability for international communication—to express oneself distinctly as well as smoothly—Americans often seem to lack the third element: understanding of other value systems. If Japanese are nouveau riche, then Americans are spoiled children, spoiled by the long dominance of American power in world politics and economics. The fact that American aid and economic cooperation are often involved with corrupt groups in developing countries stems partly from, in our opinion, their naive tendency to believe in the group that speaks softly to them, and also from their insufficient ability to understand foreign value systems. We are afraid, unfortunately, that Japanese may follow the American path in this respect.

Until recently, there has not been sufficient attention in Japan to fostering the ability for international communication. The shortcoming of the Japanese educational system was already mentioned. Other examples abound. Students returning from abroad have not been treated too well and sometimes have been misused as substitute interpreters. It is still the policy of some banks and companies that their trainees are not allowed to take their families abroad even though they can afford to do so.

It is difficult to foster the ability for international communication without changing the social and hierarchical structure in Japan. It is difficult to persuade Japanese employees abroad to enjoy leisure if in Japan everybody works six days a week with some additional overtime hours. It is hard to let them practice the equal treatment of both sexes abroad if male chauvinistic practices are prevalent in Japan. Japan may have difficulty in creating a sufficient number of people who have an ability for international communication. The long tradition of "wakon yosai"—Japanese spirit combined with Western talent—will not be good enough any more.

Concluding Remarks

So far I have discussed the adjustment of human factors under the assumption of a given speed of expansion of the Japanese economy. But, is the objective of growth itself, and the resulting international expansion, always inevitable as well as of positive value?

According to the JERC estimates before the oil crisis, the nominal per capita GNP of Japan was expected to be around $9,000 in 1980. More precisely, it was forecasted to exceed, though very slightly, that of the United States ($9,077 for Japan vs. $8,864 in 1980).[21] This forecast should be amended because the U.S. has a much more favorable position concerning the energy problem than Japan. Setting aside the problem of accuracy of the order of the two magnitudes in that year, is growth to such a magnitude truly desirable for Japan? Even if the nominal per-capital income were equalized, the scarcity of space in Japan should result in much higher rent for the same housing services. Food in Japan will be much more expensive than in the United States; and there is little doubt about the fact that Japan's air and water in 1980 will continue to be much more polluted than in the United States.

Then, considering the serious frictions to be expected in the process of the rapid expansion of the Japanese economy in the international scene, should Japan continue to expand at such a rate as the past trend indicates? I have mentioned in the last section that frictions between the nationalisms of developing countries and of the United States or Japan stem *partly* from the difficulty of adjustment and communication. One could argue more basically, however, that the liaison of corrupt groups with the U.S. or Japanese business is rooted in the coincidence of mutual interests. Development of human capital for international communication surely helps the mitigation of economic, social, and political frictions, but it does not solve completely the basic conflict of interests between citizens of developing countries and those in advanced countries. The basic remedy in the case of Japan may lie in the modification or the denial of the postulate of the incessant expansion of Japanese overseas activities. Of course, the denial or modification of the postulate requires fundamental changes in one's attitude toward society and nature.

When we look at even a small provincial town in the United States from the highway in the evening, it shines beautifully. It shines as if it were the manifestation of the triumph of Western civilization. Japanese cities and highways seem to follow the American paradigm. However, can the human race survive by following the kind of energy-consuming lives that underlie such scenes? In twenty years, two leviathans, the United States and Japan, may be competing with each other in looking for more stable energy resources.

Western civilization, perhaps rooted in Judaism and Christianity, is the civilization of conquering nature. To conquer nature it commands more energy resources. Even to fight pollution it needs more energy.[22]

21. JERC, *A Long-Term Outlook, op. cit.*
22. It is well known, for example, that anti-polluting automobile engines in cars require more gas.

On the other hand, in some Oriental philosophies, for example, in Buddhism, the adaptation of human beings to nature is emphasized. If the summer is hot, Western civilization suggests air conditioning, which requires lots of energy. Buddhism teaches adapting one's clothing, way of life, and body to nature. In the long run, given the limited space and natural endowments on earth, adaptive attitudes toward nature may become the more realistic way or even the only way for the human race to survive.[23] Is not the passive attitude of hippies in both countries a sign of the yearning of human beings for this kind of life?

23. There are ironic possibilities, however, in the adaptive attitude of Orientals. In some cases, people may adapt to pollution instead of claiming their environmental rights.

Japan's Role in the World

Garrett Scalera and Herman Kahn

Is Japan an Emerging Superstate?

After World War II, Japan was reduced to the status of a small power. At that time many agreed with General MacArthur's statement that Japan should be a "Switzerland" of the Orient (but most likely a poor and ascetic Switzerland) which would (and should) never again play a major role in world affairs. In the last twenty years Japan's rapid growth has made it the world's third largest economy; today it is anything but "poor and ascetic." Japan's influence is already decidedly disproportionate to its role in world affairs—which is in many ways surprisingly close to what one might think of as a "big Switzerland."

Thus, despite Japan's spectacular economic success, the atmosphere and many of the attitudes of the early postwar period still characterize the Japanese self-image and policies. Japan continues, quite successfully, to maintain its "low posture" policy, remaining as neutral and uninvolved as possible, while, paradoxically, also accepting a position as a U.S. protectorate at very little cost in terms of independence or burden-sharing. Under this policy Japan has focused on trade relationships, getting along with "everyone" (e.g., with both Koreas, both Chinas, both Vietnams, the U.S. and USSR, etc.), and avoiding controversial issues; the major exceptions have arisen as a result of various pressures to follow some U.S. or Chinese leads. Since "low posture" has proven very successful for Japan, there is no indication that the Japanese intend to deviate seriously from it in the immediate future, despite considerable discussion over the need for new policies, for example, "resources diplomacy." This policy has also been appropriate for Japan as a small- or medium-rank power which suffered defeat in World War II. But Japan is now very much the largest of the world's "major" economies (but still properly comparable to France or West Germany, rather than the U.S. or the USSR). But, if Japan's economy continues to grow even at rates considerably less than those of the 1960s, it will still clearly emerge in the next decade as the world's third "super-economy" (along with the U.S. and the USSR). Indeed, Japan's total GNP may well surpass that of Russia by 1985. Under these circumstances, Japan's low posture policy will become even more anachronistic than it is today. Japan will almost certainly want to assume the privileges and burdens of being a major force in world affairs which she will have little choice but to accept. The precise nature of Japan's future role is a key question of international relations today. The transition which we foresee for Japan is unique; no other nation could change from large to gigantic in the next ten to fifteen years.

Japan's potential has been widely overlooked or underestimated for a variety of reasons. Except for the short period between the Sino-Japanese War and the end of World War II, the West has almost always underestimated Japan. Since 1950 much more attention has been devoted to China. Outside observers have been chronically unwilling to believe that Japan's high growth rates reflected her long-term potential. At first, it was believed that Japan would never fully recover from the war. The remarkable growth rates of the early 1950s were typically attributed to reconstruction and the impetus provided by the Korean War (which was important, but not essential). The continuation of remarkably high growth rates after the Korean War was greeted by new theories designed to show that they could not continue for long. We were told that the "cream had been skimmed" from European and American technology, Japan's industries were under-capitalized, the work force was not increasing rapidly enough, infrastructure was lagging too much, and so forth. So far, these problems have not proven serious enough to curb rapid growth. Far from being a "fragile blossom," the Japanese economy has proven to be very strong and stable in weathering the major economic shocks of the last few years. It seems reasonable to assume at this point that Japan's growth rates simply reflect a more effective economic system, rather than some mysterious economic miracle.

It is ironic that, by 1973, the last twenty years of rapid growth of the

Japanese economy (not to mention the prewar experience) were seen almost universally to have been no mere temporary phenomenon. Most official and private estimates were forecasting that Japan would attain an average real economic growth rate of about 10 percent annually through 1985. Before 1973 came to an end, soaring prices of basic commodities, and especially the spectacular rise of oil prices following the Middle East War, made "pessimistic"[1] forecasts more pervasive than ever before.

The following arguments are central for people who take a pessimistic view, especially in Japan itself.

1. The era of "cheap raw material and energy," on which Japanese growth was based, is now over. Basic commodities will be increasingly scarce and will remain expensive (particularly food and oil) in the foreseeable future. This will require a dramatic shift from resource- and energy-intensive to knowledge- and infrastructure-related industries.
2. Continuing difficulties in resolving the international monetary situation will cause continued uncertainties and dangers to national economies and international trade.
3. Points 1 and 2 may produce continued world-wide inflation and possibly a severe recession or depression.
4. The labor supply is indeed drying up at last. The record wage increases of the last two years reflect long-term phonomena which will cause continued pressures on the system, cost-push inflation, and decreasing competitiveness of Japanese industries on world markets.
5. The obvious inadequacies of Japanese infrastructure and provisions for welfare will require a dramatic refocusing of the Japanese economy, which in turn will mean lower growth.
6. A mounting hostility to economic growth among Japanese intellectuals, the press, opposition parties, and the public at large may bring about a dramatic shift away from further development of industry toward a welfare society and improving the "quality of life."
7. These various pressures could prevent the implementation of many necessary programs which are currently planned, especially if combined with an increase in "localism"[2] (e.g., with regard to siting of

1. We put "optimism" and "pessimism" in quotes in recognition of an issue which is increasingly important in Japan. Someone who projects high growth rates in Japan today is widely assumed to be somehow rooting for rapid growth, which may or may not be the case but is definitely a separate issue. When a serious economist projects growth rates, he is only trying to identify what he thinks is likely to occur. He may or may not endorse the underlying policies and objectives.

2. Ability and desire of local groups to delay, modify, or block programs believed to be in the national interest.

nuclear plants, airports, new industrial zones, "polluting industries" in general, etc.).

8. Significant and widespread changes in values and attitudes especially among youth (reflected in Points 5-7), indicate declining loyalty to the firm, and decreasing willingness to work hard which could result in reduced efficiency for business and government as well as increasing problems with radical fringes (e.g., increasing terrorism and crime).

9. The continuing erosion of support for the Liberal Democratic Party, the declining popularity of the Tanaka administration (currently 18 percent, or 1 percent below that of former Prime Minister Sato at his lowest point, according to an October 1974 *Mainichi* newspaper poll), the resignations of Mr. Fukuda and Mr. Miki from the Cabinet, demands for reforms, scandals, etc., endanger future national political stability. This in turn would have adverse effects on the economy.

10. A deep-seated decline in fundamental morale reflected by a growing debate over Japanese goals (including an apparent consensus that "catching up with the West" is no longer an appropriate goal); the absence of a new consensus as to what Japan should do in the future is creating a sense of malaise contributing to all of the above problems.

11. Some fear of a hostile world context: e.g., the U.S. and/or Europe tries to keep Japan down; Europe tries to exclude Japan; hostility to Japan in Southeast Asia, China or USSR drags Japan into their quarrels or return to ideological and military hostility; the Arabs focus on Japan as a particularly "lucrative" and vulnerable hostage, etc.

Each of these eleven points represents, in our opinion, a potentially very real and serious impediment to future Japanese economic growth. Since it is beyond the scope of this paper to discuss all these points seriously, we will limit ourselves to a few brief comments, It should be stressed that, despite these widespread doubts, the official estimates released by the Economic Planning Agency and MITI in July 1974, still foresee the real growth rate at slightly over 7 percent for Japan through 1985. Although this represents a substantial reduction from earlier estimates, such a growth rate would still result in an expansion of the Japanese economy sufficient to make it at least the third "super-economy" in the world during the 1980s, and more probably the second "super-economy."[3]

3. Japan's GNP in 1973 and 113 trillion yen, about 375 billion dollars, at 300 yen to the dollar, or about 400 billion dollars at 280 yen to the dollar (the average exchange rate for the year). The official MITI estimates of GNP for 1974 are 131 trillion yen (as of October 1974) or about 438 billion dollars at 300 yen to the dollar. MITI estimates of the same period for average real growth rates from 1970 to 1980 are 7.3 percent, from 1980 to 1985, 7 percent. This would result in a GNP in 1980 of 331 trillion yen, and in 1985, of 578 trillion yen (in nominal prices) or about $1.1 trillion and $1.9 trillion, respectively, at 300 to the dollar.

We believe these estimates are likely to be low rather than high. First, it is significant that before 1971, official Japanese estimates have typically underestimated actual performance. Given the highly unfavorable economic climate of 1974 and the accompanying wide-spread opposition to growth, it is reasonable to assume that these current estimates represent an over-reaction. Second, it is worth noting that at least two prestigious organizations forecasting Japan's economic growth, the Boston Consulting Group and the Japan Economic Research Center, are still predicting higher growth rates for this period, 10 percent and 8.5 percent respectively. We expect growth to be closer to 10 percent than 7 percent.

These two groups expect, as do we, a substantial reduction in the price of oil in the next year or so and a successful program in Japan to deal with the domestic causes of inflation.[4] If the price of oil should remain high, however, Japan can still be expected to do relatively well. (Exports have increased by about 50 percent so far this year and, as a result, Japan achieved a positive balance of trade in September 1974 for the first time since December 1973.) The biggest impact would probably be on overseas investments, as capital available for these would be very much reduced. Also, some industries, such as petrochemical and related industries, would certainly face real problems. But Japan would probably still be able to achieve fairly high growth rates (along the lines of those officially projected now), and almost certainly should maintain a positive trade balance.

A continuation of very high oil prices would probably bring about a major worldwide depression, which would, of course, greatly affect Japan. But, even in a depression, Japan is likely to do better than many other countries. In a real depression, oil and other commodity prices would certainly decline drastically (presumably more than manufactured goods); Japan could do all right by exporting much less, while her large monetary reserves would be worth even more than they are now. Furthermore, Japan is already shifting the emphasis of its economy to infrastructure. Its current plans call for expenditures of over a trillion dollars by 1985 to provide much needed roads, railroads, dams, pipelines, pollution controls, etc. In a booming world economy, these projects would probably be stretched out to avoid overheating the economy (as occurred in 1973). But in a depression environment, pub-

4. The marginal spot price of oil in the Persian Gulf in real terms has already declined more than 20 percent in the first ten months of 1974 (if one takes inflation and gray market transactions into account); some other commodities have also declined dramatically. We concede that if Saudi Arabia and Iran get together and are willing to accept large cutbacks in production, the current price of oil could be maintained for four or five years. But neither country shows serious signs of taking this path.

lic works projects are extremely important; the Japanese could step up these projects to offset declining demand in other sectors. Yet almost none of these undertakings would be "make-work" projects.

Essentially, however, we are basing our projections on two assumptions: There will be no major depression, and the world will return to a period of prosperity within the next year or so. But regardless of whether the world is in a phase of prosperity or depression, we see no overwhelming reason why Japan cannot continue to achieve high growth rates for the 1976–1985 decade: their prosperity would be based more on internal demand than on the world market. Certainly the Japanese economy is facing new problems, but these are relatively manageable. Thus, Japan has less drastic problems with its labor force than any other developed country (with the possible exception of West Germany). The record wage increases in Japan during the last two years have been accompanied by average productivity increases of about 10 percent a year (20 percent in 1973). Demands for more and better social benefits are rising, but traditional social welfare benefits are currently lower in Japan than in any other developed country. However, company paternalism and lifetime employment may balance this. In short, Japan has faced problems in the past which seemed at least as difficult at the time. Since Japan has managed to surmount serious difficulties before, it seems a reasonable bet that it can do so again—*if it wants to.* This perhaps is the key issue; does Japan still want to grow? We will come back to this central issue.

Our basic argument is that, even when given growth rates for Japan have been accepted as realistic, their implications have often been overlooked. The current official projections for real growth would mean that Japan would become a huge force in the world economy in the 1980s. It would probably become the largest supplier of capital in the world, have the largest trade of any nation in the world, attain or soon reach the highest GNP per capita of any major nation, and would be rapidly approaching or surpass the USSR in total GNP. If Japan grows more rapidly than 7 percent annually, it only means that all this will occur sooner.

Why have these implications, which seem obvious to us, not received wider attention? We feel that the answer lies in a Japanese tendency to focus almost exclusively on their weaknesses and day-to-day problems. This phenomenon has been due in part to the speed of their recovery. For example, Japan was a deficit nation until the late 1960s, primarily concerned with exporting enough to pay for its imports and protecting its domestic industries from foreign competition. Success has come suddenly and the Japanese are still adjusting.

Furthermore, a traditional ingredient of Japanese behavior is an innate cautiousness. Even though virtually all Japanese economic projections predicted growth rates of about 10 percent through 1985, until late 1973 any discussion on the meaning of such growth rates in an international context for the 1980s was almost automatically taboo. To this day, there is no more certain way to make oneself unpopular in Japan than to predict that Japan will accomplish exactly what the Japanese themselves project. Statements that Japan will be one of the three "super-economies" of the world in the 1980s, with the productive capacity and technology to become a superpower in every sense of the word if it should so choose, are considered dangerous, overly provocative, and overly optimistic. The "polite," "constructive," and customary approach is to play down such potentials; accomplishments are "poor mouthed" for both superstitious and practical reasons.

There are, of course, practical reasons for not clearly explicating the implications of continued Japanese growth. Japanese business and government leaders, for example, are clearly concerned over the possibility of another record wage increase in the spring of 1975. By focusing on the difficulties the economy and business are now facing, it may be possible to persuade labor to reduce its demands. Similarly, emphasis on current problems can be seen as a means of trying to gain public support for reducing personal spending overseas (a virtual "orgy" of such spending between 1970 and 1973 has been greatly reduced), controlling inflation, reducing pressures for pollution control, curbing fears of foreigners, and so forth. But beyond these immediate reasons, it should be understood that a public debate in Japan about Japan's role as the world's next superstate would be unsettling and to some degree counterproductive. It would create real disunity at home (partly by being out of character and partly by polarizing very real disagreements), and increase apprehensions abroad. Real discussion of rearmament, for example, would undoubtedly be highly unsettling. On the other hand, it can be counter-productive in many ways not to debate such issues openly. We understand that one of the reasons the Japanese debate in the mid- and late 1960s about possible acquisition of nuclear weapons led to a unanimous rejection of this possibility was that most of those supporting acquisition shifted or changed their positions as the implications became clear. Similarly, avoiding debate about the implications of continued rapid economic growth risks overlooking major issues and problems. Much greater apprehension could result if silence leads to a belief that secret decisions have already been made.

As Japan's potential has become increasingly clear, the tendency to avoid discussing these issues in Japan has, if anything, increased. To a casual observer this attitude might appear to be deceitful or insincere. Actually, we believe that it reflects instead an increasing concern on the part of the Japanese regarding their future. Since the Meiji Restoration, just over 100 years ago, Japan's basic goal has been to "catch up with the West." Before World War II, this was interpreted to mean colonial power and expansion, the measure of great power status at that time. In the postwar era, this mission has been interpreted in terms of per capita income or achieving a standard of living comparable to the U.S. and Western Europe. The Japanese have now essentially accomplished this goal; the question of what they should do next has been a fundamental problem in Japan for the last few years. But discussion of this issue has been highly artificial. There are simply no widely acceptable proposals, let alone a consensus. The Japanese really don't know what goal or goals they should have, or what role they should play in the world in the future. In the absence of a new sense of direction or purpose, Japan is tenaciously clinging to the status quo for policy decisions, and deferring debate over options and issues which will be emerging.

The importance of the current concern in Japan over goals and national purpose can be overstated, but it is more likely to be underestimated. The Japanese are a purposeful people. Traditionally, they have seen themselves as a unique people with an identifiable national destiny. Although the prewar conceptualizations of this destiny, such as leader of the Asian nations or of an East Asian co-prosperity sphere, have been completely rejected, the concern itself suggests that these national characteristics are still very much a part of the Japanese personality. It therefore seems likely that Japan will again wish to play a major role in the world and that it will seek world recognition of its new status and influence.

We do not believe that emergence of Japan on the world state will be a smooth phenomenon under any circumstances. Already Japan's impact on other economies has created considerable problems. As Japan's economy doubles and doubles again, so may the problems and necessary adjustments. We do believe, however, that Japan's growth could be, on balance, a very positive force indeed for world peace and prosperity. But if major problems are to be avoided or minimized, they should be thought through well ahead of time. If the advantages to the world of Japan's growth are to be fully understood, they too should be explained well before the growth suddenly materializes. And if Japan is to avoid the danger of appearing to be a threatening new force, it must develop acceptable and credible goals and long-term policies and explain them to the world in good time.

The Importance of the International Context

A discussion of any nation's future role in world affairs always depends greatly on what one assumes the world situation will be like at the time; but this is especially true for Japan.

This results partly from the "low posture" which Japan has taken since World War II. Japan has largely avoided getting involved in controversial issues and still gets along quite well with both Koreas, both Vietnams, India and Pakistan, and so on. In the future Japan should therefore enjoy exceptional freedom to choose whatever course it deems best at the time. Increasingly, of course, Japan will find itself under great pressure to take sides and even to intervene in various conflicts. But in a sense it is starting from a clean slate.

More importantly, it is almost a basic characteristic of Japanese behavior to change their beliefs and attitudes to meet the situation in which they find themselves. This characteristic is often referred to by scholars as a "situational ethic." It essentially means that as individuals, or collectively as a nation, Japanese behavior is governed by what is considered appropriate in a specific environment; that it is immoral or self-indulgent to stick to certain principles when they are clearly inappropriate to the needs of the moment. For this reason, Japanese are often thought of as immoral by Western standards which tend to regard a principle as fixed regardless of the situation. For the record, we believe the Japanese to be, in their own terms, a highly moral and idealistic people. But their own morality permits more rapid change on basic "external" issues than could be achieved in the West. Until the very last days of World War II, for example, the Japanese seemed willing to fight to the last man, woman, and child for the sake of the fatherland. Immediately after surrender, they became completely pacifistic in philosophy and action. The point here is that if the world changes again, the Japanese are perfectly capable of dramatically changing their attitudes and behavior almost overnight, employing themselves and their resources effectively toward accomplishing whatever ends seem appropriate at the time.

Another important Japanese characteristic in this context is a recurring tendency to look outward for goals and a sense of direction—and then to reject this outside world. Thus, the Japanese have often had cyclical periods of looking outwards and turning inwards, while consistently maintaining their own distinct culture and sense of national identity. From the Meiji era to the Depression, and since World War II, the Japanese have been looking to the West for direction. Because of their absolute dependence on imported raw materials and foreign trade in general, it is extremely unlikely that the Japanese would attempt to cut themselves off from the world in the foreseeable future. But it is far from certain that they will continue to look to the West for a sense of direction or even see the West as the major focus of interest.

The question of "inward" or "outward" focus is complicated by the bipolar nature of the world. Since World War II, there has been a debate in Japan between the "progressives," who believe the future lies with the socialist camp, and the "conservatives," who support the U.S. and the capitalist nations as the basic model of the future. The conservatives have been in undisputed political control under the Liberal Democratic Party except for a brief period in 1948. Also, the progressives have lost considerable ground since China's cultural revolution and the split between China and Russia. Since the LDP has been steadily losing support, many political commentators are seriously considering the possibility that a new coalition may attain leadership in the coming years. Others have suggested that the LDP may retain power by shifting its position to either the left or the right. Opinion is virtually unanimous that the political situation is potentially volatile and that Japan is capable of taking a very different course in the future.

We believe that the nature of Japan's future course is very likely to be determined, or at least strongly influenced by the international environment in the next ten years, and that the key issue is likely to be the attitude toward economic growth. The debate over economic growth, which we discuss in the next section, has a special significance for Japan. The Japanese, after all, have very consciously pursued economic growth as a national goal. In recent years they have been told by intellectuals at home and abroad that such growth is not a worthy goal; that gross national product is really gross national pollution; the affluent society is really an unworthy effluent society; that their short-term national success is really a prelude in the relatively near future to national and international disaster.

During the next decade the world economy is likely to be evolving into what we refer to at the Hudson Institute as the "super-industrial economy." We are, for example, probably only entering the age of automobiles. There are only about 200 million automobiles in the world today and, except for a minority of affluent offspring of the "Atlantic Protestant culture," almost "everyone" appears to want one, regardless of his cultural milieu. It would be surprising if the demand for automobiles did not increase exponentially along with increasing disposable income. Similarly, we are probably only entering the age of computers, of steel production, of worldwide industrialization, and international trade. If so, the problems associated with industrialization and opposition to it, both real and otherwise, have most likely only begun. And for Japan, this searching for a new sense of direction and purpose, the international debate over the pros and cons of this process, are likely to have a profound influence. To an extraordinary degree, the domestic debate in Japan on this kind of issue mirrors and magnifies the international debate—sometimes deepening it, more often carrying it to an almost satirical extreme.

The Debate Over Economic Growth

From the perspective of history, the twentieth century is likely to be remembered principally as the century of worldwide economic growth (what we elsewhere refer to as the "great transition"). The debate that dominates the discussion of long-range issues today is whether this will be remembered as mankind's greatest disaster or its greatest triumph. In the press of day-to-day problems facing decision-makers, this question often seems purely academic. *It is not.* This confrontation is perhaps even more fundamental than that between communism and capitalism (both believe in economic growth). The viewpoint that comes to be widely accepted will have a profound influence on all nations in the years to come.

Since 1950, gross world product (GWP) has been increasing at about 5 percent or so per year, with an increasing number of countries doing considerably better. In 1974, the world's four billion people should produce about five trillion dollars worth of goods and services, or about $1,250 per person. If current population and economic growth rates continue, by 1985 world population should be about five billion people and GWP about eight-to-ten trillion dollars, or about $1,800 per capita; by the year 2000, about 6 billion people with a GWP of about 15-to-20 trillion dollars and a GWP capital of about $3,000.[5]

The question being raised today is whether or not this growth can be successfully achieved and, if so, how long can the world's resources sustain it. Our studies at Hudson Institute indicate that this growth can be successfully achieved and maintained, even at much higher levels of population with correspondingly greater levels of resource consumption. From our studies we expect that both world population and economic growth rates will peak and begin to decline sometime in the next few decades; they would decrease slowly during the next century when the world might have a population of perhaps 15 billion or so with a GWP of perhaps 300 trillion dollars and a per capita GWP of as much as $20,000 or more. Obviously, such a long-range projections cannot be, and are not intended to be, precise. Nor are they necessarily

5. All dollar figures are in fixed 1974 dollars.

intended as recommendations. Their main purpose is to provide a framework around which to speculate whether or not such population and consumption levels could be sustained.

Before going into this debate, it is worth pausing to consider what such a world might be like. The most important characteristic is that the overwhelming majority of people would have a material standard of living equivalent to or substantially better than that enjoyed by even the developed countries today. It might not be a very happy world (there appears to be no great correlation between wealth and happiness); it might not be a world of harmony but instead of disorders and unrest; it probably would contain major pockets of poverty; the gaps between rich and poor might be even greater than today.[6] But unless it were marred by major nuclear war or some comparable disaster, it would mean a new way of life for mankind. If this turns out to be a stable world, as we believe it could, it would mean a permanent end to poverty, famine, much disease, pestilence, illiteracy, and back-breaking toil, which has been man's lot throughout history. It would be post-industrial in the same sense that one can say the developed world is "post-agricultural" today; that is, more goods and services than ever would be produced but they would require fewer and fewer man-hours to produce. What the majority of people would do in this world is an open question. But the opportunities would clearly be enormous, and in the centuries to come, it might well be remembered as the time when mankind's true history began.

Despite the attractiveness of this scenario, an increasing number of intellectuals and highly educated people in the developed world would reject it on the grounds of both feasibility and desirability. Rather than an enthusiasm for the continued economic growth necessary to achieve such a world, we find mounting opposition to growth. Two basic arguments are most commonly made: first, it is claimed that

6. It is often remarked that the gap between rich and poor in actual terms is widening. The much more significant fact that actual wealth for the overwhelming majority of people in the world is dramatically increasing is often given less attention. If the per capita income of a developing country increases from $200 to $400 per year, while that of a developed country during the same period increases from $2,000 to $4,000 per year, for example, then the gap is said to have doubled from $1,800 to $3,600. But this does not mean that the "rich are getting richer and the poor are getting poorer." It means that the poor have also doubled their income and are getting richer also. The important point is that most people do not compare income with people in other classes or other countries. They compare their income this year with their income of last year and with that of their friends, neighbors, fellow-workers—and in general to others of their own socioeconomic status. Thus, rapid increases in real income, contrary to much popular wisdom, are far more likely to create satisfaction, as they have for the most part in the past, than revolution.

resources will not be sufficient to supply even a much smaller population than we have postulated above even at drastically lower levels of per capita income; second, it is asserted that even were it possible to deal successfully with the resource issue, the pollution associated with such a huge GWP would prove ultimately fatal to the world's environment.

In their extreme form, these arguments (which we refer to as neo-Malthusian) have recently been set forth most accessibly by the Club of Rome-sponsored study headed by Dr. Dennis Meadows and Dr. Jay Forrester. It predicts disaster, if our current growth rates continue, in the next thirty to fifty years. Numerous subsequent studies have revealed many flaws in their argument. Hudson Institute studies indicate that known resources, even if only *current* technology were used, are sufficient to meet even much greater levels of demand than we have projected; all clearly *perceived and understood* problems of pollution could be dealt with, assuming reasonable management of the world's economies. The key point here is that increasing wealth means ever increasing flexibility in dealing with these problems. A wealthy society can afford more costly processes, and more costly crops can be raised as people can afford to pay more. Certainly we expect new technology, new resources, and new ways of exploiting resources to simplify matters. But it is important to emphasize that, even without these, a wealthier world could cope with continued growth. It is only because we feel able to make such a strong statement that we feel safe in concluding that resources and pollution are not likely in themselves to constitute a crucial constraint to continued rapid economic growth.

The arguments against growth, however, are not limited to this simplistic neo-Malthusian thesis, although this is still the most common argument. Many who do not literally accept the neo-Malthusian arguments still oppose economic growth, either because they are concerned with dangerous mistakes or imbalances that may occur, or for personal or aesthetic reasons.

The concern that dangerous mistakes can result from rapid growth is definitely justified. As the economic scale and pace of growth have increased and various new technologies and products introduced, so has the likelihood of major dangers arising too suddenly to be dealt with in time to avoid disasters (e.g., thalidomide and minamoto disasters). This is also true for serious imbalances (e.g., worldwide food shortages in the next few years). Also, some kinds of industrial pollution are at such levels in some developed countries today that, if they are not dramatically reduced in the near future disaster will be certain. Fortunately, the necessity for dealing with these problems has been recognized, and programs to reduce pollution dramatically are now planned or already underway in most cases. The current concern over dangers that are perceived and correctible is mostly overdone. Indeed, in the years to come almost all of the highly industrialized nations are likely to have less pollution than they have now. But the danger of mistakes, imbalances, and major new problems arising which are as yet unperceived should not be dismissed—or overstated. We believe this danger to be serious enough to justify much greater efforts to establish safeguards and much more effective study, planning, and research. But we do not believe that these dangers can best be avoided, or even reduced much, by lowering the rate of economic growth.

What the most sensible opponents of growth are really calling for is caution. The more extreme are saying: "Why take a chance?" or "Why not stop growth, at least in the developed world, until we are more sure of the consequences?" At first glance this position seems reasonable enough, even though most of those who express it are often motivated by a conscious or unconscious personal distaste for an ever wealthier world. In the developed world the majority of even lower income people have sufficient income to satisfy at least all of their basic material needs, and the upper income people are virtually satiated with a vast variety of material goods and gadgets. Increasingly, even the middle classes are losing their motivation to continue to strive for economic ends. As a result, an emotional appeal is gaining favor among many affluent people for a simpler and less materialistic way of life. But few in the lower income group take this position and most of the relatively wealthy do not agree as yet.

It is also technically difficult to stop growth—or slow the drive significantly. If the developed countries were to achieve stable zero economic growth rates, it would mean, quite simply, a worldwide recession or depression, increasing unemployment, and fewer goods. Much less new capital would be available to invest for reducing pollution and solving other current problems, such as urban decay. Only by creating new wealth and continuing to grow can we deal effectively with these problems. The developed world could eventually adjust to zero growth, but it would be a hard and slow process.

For most of the less developed world, however, zero economic growth in the developed world would be a disaster. Almost all of the less-developed countries are dependent on the developed world for trade and investment. For them, zero growth would cause stagnant or contracting markets for their primary goods, and drastic reductions in the availability of outside capital, management, and technology which has played a key role in their development in recent decades. Certainly one could expect that widespread starvation would indeed occur in many countries, especially those with high population growth.

For a long-term perspective, the question of population growth is one important reason for continuing economic growth. It now appears that world population growth rates will top out in the next decade or so. Various ways of controlling birth rates are proving increasingly effective, but they may be insufficient to deal with all the problems of population growth in the near future. Our experience has been that, regardless of culture, virtually every country that has industrialized has also reduced its population growth. Thus one can expect—even with some confidence—that the faster the world develops economically, the faster population growth rates are likely to decline.

We believe that the real issue of the growth debate is not whether the world will stop growing. It would be very difficult, though certainly not impossible, to stop this process for a long time. However, it seems reasonable that the more it is believed that growth is pernicious, the greater the likelihood that major mistakes will be made, that motivations to create and accept innovations will be reduced, and that flexibility will be diminished. Talented people who should be working to facilitate growth will instead be expending energy to stop it—they may simply drop out. Those responsible for growth will spend much of their time combating opposition to growth and fending off criticism, public, private, and perhaps even personal. Their morale is likely to be correspondingly low or at least lower. Increasingly these drags are likely to affect developing nations as well. Even now, developing nations which have achieved exceptional growth rates get little credit for this achievement, unless they are led by a government of the left. Thus, the world's (or rather the intellectual elite's) judgment of a government's legitimacy or effectiveness seldom considers its economic record. This myopia reflects both a double standard and an increasing hostility toward and boredom with economic growth. Similarly, the great multinational corporations (which are playing a key role in making worldwide economic development possible) are often portrayed as villains and exploiters; their extraordinary contributions to economic well-being are largely ignored. We are not arguing that businessmen are pursuing anything other than the best interests of their firms, that economic growth justifies any measures, or that severe problems and inequities don't require attention. The burden of our argument is that these things can best be done in a world which takes a balanced view recognizing the vital and central importance of economic growth.

Let us consider what would really happen if the belief that the world is about to run out of resources came to be generally accepted. Some zero growth advocates would have us believe that, under these circumstances, nations would work out ways to share resources fairly. We are less sanguine. If history is any guide, the powerful would simply seize resources from the weak, refusing to accept the drastic sacrifices which would be required by equitable cooperation. Indeed, it is only because we believe that ample resources will be available for all, that we feel some limited degree of confidence in predicting a world of relative peace and prosperity for 1975–1985. Resources should not, of course, be wasted. On the contrary, more efficient resource use should be strongly encouraged; when temporary or emerging shortages arise, scarce resources should be shared. Our point is that sensible resource policies are most likely to be implemented if it is clearly understood that there will be plenty for all in the medium and even the very long run.

Despite what we think of as almost overwhelming arguments for continuing worldwide economic growth, this process is by no means inevitable, particularly from the viewpoint of any individual nation. Throughout the developed world, the opponents of growth are having an ever-greater impact; nowhere is this more evident than in Japan. In the last few years economic growth has changed from being considered—almost without argument—the national goal or objective, to being thought of as almost a "dirty word." Even those who advocate continued economic growth tend to refer to it, at least publicly, as a necessary evil rather than a good thing. While this change in attitude has so far had only a marginal impact on actual business and government policy, it is reasonable to expect that this could dramatically change. Therefore, a conscious Japanese decision to reduce their growth rate drastically cannot be ruled out. We do not expect such a decision, partly because it would be so difficult and counterproductive. Any such reversal would probably be temporary, followed by a pro-growth backlash.

This growth/no-growth debate could have more plausible effects in Japan. Let us assume, for example, that rapid economic growth continues, along with apparently mounting opposition. In such a situation, we doubt that the present political and business leadership could maintain its position by relying solely on an economic growth platform. But rather than trying to stop growth, this leadership might turn to growth plus something else, perhaps an effort to play a greater role in world affairs through acquiring great military power. In short, it could appeal to nationalism, the need for a "big Japan" to be number one. If this strategy failed, we could see a new coalition coming to power, almost certainly with a leftist and anti-business orientation.

One can imagine other alternatives: a turning inward in search for ideological renewal based on tradition, or a backlash in favor of rightist or leftist extremists trying to control or prevent what they considered to be irresponsible or dangerous tendencies. On the other hand, a renewed sense of the importance of economic growth in the world at large could well play a decisive role in preserving the status quo in Japan (for better or worse) for years to come.

In the next section we explore some scenarios for the possible courses Japan may take. The fundamental world-wide debate over economic growth is a critical, if not central, underlying factor in these scenarios. Nevertheless, we also assume that the basic position of the neo-Malthusians is wrong, and that their influence will not increase precipitously. A reasonable degree of political stability is also taken for granted. These assumptions are made out of conviction. Furthermore, to construct additional scenarios involving contrary expectations would exceed the limitations of this paper.

Alternative Roles for Japan

On many occasions in history nations have had a self-conscious concept of themselves and the role they expected to play in the world. Similarly, in many cases roles have been imposed upon nations; in still others, a clearly conceptualized role either did not exist or became evident only in retrospect. Nations, like individuals, are highly complex. They may play a number of different and conflicting roles simultaneously, and often behave inconsistently. Nevertheless, it is very useful to isolate specific themes or concepts which characterize or personalize a nation even though they are invariably oversimplifications. In this section we develop three basic scenarios (or overall self-images) and three more limited themes which we think might characterize Japan for the next decade or so. All six could exist together, even where they conflict, and still not exhaust the nuances of likely Japanese behavior. Indeed, we rather suspect that all of these aspects of Japanese behavior are likely to emerge as points of emphasis at one time or another in the coming years, without necessarily involving as much deemphasis of the others as logical consistency might seem to require. For the sake of simplicity, however, we will treat both the basic and the limited images of the future as if they were independent and competing in both the real world and as self-images.

Our three basic scenarios are: A "Big Switzerland," where the Japanese essentially continue to think of themselves as much as possible as a relatively small, neutral nation even though they may achieve, or be achieving, a status more like that of an economic giant; a "Superstate," where the Japanese openly accept their status as a super economy, financial giant, and master of advanced technology, but reject any attempt to become a superpower in the military and political sense; and a "Superpower," where the Japanese acquire military and political power which corresponds to their superstate's economy, finance, and technology.

Our three minor themes are: The "first post-industrial economy, society, and culture,"[7] where the Japanese clearly and self-consciously make it their goal to achieve this advanced status; the "first neutral, disarmed (or at least truly defensive), pacifistic nation," where the Japanese might, for a number of reasons, try to become crusaders for world peace and disarmament; and a "Byzantine state," where the Japanese would consciously focus on manipulating the weaknesses and strengths of others to obtain their own ends, depending more on diplomatic skill, financial power, and persuasion (and "bribes") rather than armaments—which would be used, if at all, only to manipulate a diplomatic, psychological, and ideological context. Although this last theme would presumably not be implemented in such an open and official manner as to appear cynical, it is hardly reassuring to note that it is already characteristic of some current Japanese behavior and discussions.

We will cite one example of the inept use of this approach. About a year ago, a prominent Japanese businessman seriously proposed that the colony of Papua, New Guinea, be purchased from Australia as a means of insuring a reliable source of resources. This concept was taken seriously enough to be a major subject of discussion at the Japanese Defense College and among other Japanese military elites. All of these themes and images of the future are to some degree already in existence—sometimes competing, more often supporting each other (particularly if one thinks of them as waxing and waning in some ordered sequence and as key elements characterizing various elements in current and future Japanese policy). But let us continue our intentionally artificial attempt to look at them in isolation.

"A Big Switzerland." This scenario is normally (but not necessarily) associated with an economic growth lower than that officially predicted today. Some of its proponents argue that, by the early 1980s, growth might be reduced to a rate below 5 percent annually. The central characteristics of this scenario are an emphasis on comfort, and all

7. We distinguish here between economy, society, and culture as follows: economy: economic and technological activities; society: laws and institutions; and culture: style, values, national character, attitudes, and priorities.

short-run quality-of-life issues, the raising of welfare and social expenditures, and discourangement of "excessive," "disrupting," or "destructive" economic development. Such a focus might be accomplished by a marked turning inward, in the sense of an increasing tendency to reject outside opinions and unnecessary interactions with foreign influences. The Japanese would focus on making a better living environment for themselves and show much less concern over what the rest of the world thought and did.

This scenario assumes that the Japanese would continue a low posture role in world affairs. They would still be trading at very high levels, but would probably strongly discourage overseas investments and long-term commitments that were likely to entangle them in political problems. They would still export many of their industries and maintain large transnational corporations, even more than the Swiss, but not emphasize these activities to the same degree as would an outward-looking Japan. They would probably rely on very large stockpiles of raw materials, eventually perhaps a year's supply or more of some, and give much greater emphasis than currently to reducing overseas dependence (e.g., nuclear energy, geothermal energy, deep sea oil, other ocean resources). They would probably seek to reduce or end their dependence on the U.S. nuclear umbrella by re-arming carefully, focusing on defensive weapons and the ability to mobilize quickly. (It is important to remember that, compared to other small powers, Switzerland and Sweden are armed to the teeth.) But Japan would probably seek to assure the world, and China and the USSR in particular, that they mean no harm to anyone. This would be done by drawing attention to Japanese efforts to disengage themselves as much as possible from foreign entanglements, and by insisting that all they really want is to be left alone.

Japan as a Superstate. This scenario assumes that Japan continues its rapid economic growth under much the same leadership and policies that it has today. The economy would continue its current partial shift from heavy and chemical industries to infrastructure, high technology industries, and increased social welfare. Investment and other economic involvement overseas would increase; by the 1980s, capital export would be a major impetus for continued economic growth. Major investment would be directed toward improving the quality of life at home and other domestic infrastructure. Opposition to growth might increase or decrease, but no major changes are foreseen.

There are several possible variations of this scenario. This might, for example, be a high-morale Japan. Japanese might take pride in the role they are playing in being a pacesetter for the development of their fellow Asian nations and the Third World generally. This might occur either as a result of a new worldwide acceptance that economic growth is a positive process or from a conscious effort of the government. Or a relatively nationalist government might argue that Japan could become a leading world power only by economic and technological achievements. In any case, this scenario sees a renewed sense of the importance and value of economic growth, both in Japan and worldwide.

A widespread acceptance of the long-term benefits of economic growth might have very positive effects for Japan. Arguments against growth would be replaced by arguments explaining why growth has transformed Japan from a small and unimportant power to one of the great powers of the world. This would be an outward-looking Japan, increasingly "dependent"[8] on the world for trade and resources, and making large-scale investments as the largest supplier of capital in the world. It would probably be a high-morale Japan, anxious to play a major, but still basically neutral, role in world affairs. One logical possibility would be an emphasis on playing a leading role in the development of the Pacific Basin. Thus we might see a focus on the benefits that Japanese trade and investment had brought to Korea, Taiwan, Southeast Asia, Brazil, and other Latin American countries. Japan might be extremely generous in its foreign aid and investment agreements, greatly benefiting its trading partners—and Japan itself in terms of improved relations and more reliable agreements.

The danger of the scenario emerges from the tremendous impact which such a Japan would necessarily have upon the world. Consciously or unconsciously, Japan would clearly be moving toward a role as a world power. Great adjustments would have to be made by the existing world powers, which might not be made willingly. The U.S., USSR, and European nations might well overreact and try to "keep Japan down." The developing countries of Asia might fear Japanese domination, and retaliate by nationalizing Japanese investments or taking other countermeasures. The Japanese are not likely to follow the American example by docilely accepting the slights of nations they thought they were helping. The Japanese are more likely to feel themselves deserving of the deference due a great nation. The resultant conflicts could well turn Japan sour in one way or another. They might

8. We use quotes because the increased use of the world's resources would doubtless be accompanied by various measures to reduce Japanese vulnerability to disruption and pressure from abroad. In fact, these defensive reasons themselves might be a major pressure for growth, as a means to reduce much vulnerability by achieving an economic and technological surplus.

lead Japan to focus on acquiring military power corresponding to its economic power in an effort to gain the respect it feels entitled to, or to a xenophobic rejection of the outside world—perhaps both.

This scenario could produce a quite peaceful Japan with high morale based largely on an inward focus. Japanese would see their primary objective as the successful transformation of their country into the first post-industrial economy, society, and culture, perhaps regardless of how the world's intellectual elites judge the process. In this case, enhanced pride could emanate from Japan being the first "unarmed" great nation. On the other hand, it might be a low-morale Japan, plagued by domestic dissent but maintaining much of its current character. In this case, the establishment might become increasingly cynical, acting more and more like "economic animals," at home and abroad, representing a "Byzantian" state.

The main characteristic of this scenario is that Japan would continue to grow, but would choose not to acquire military power to match its economic power—or at least would not do so in the 1975–1985 period. This choice might spring from a variety of motives: a spirit of leadership and altruism; a judgment that this policy is a "good buy" since, in the modern world, security cannot be obtained by power; and, finally, a more or less cynical attempt to get a "free ride"—at least for a while. Probably this choice would promote a relatively safe world, at least as long as the Japanese were not—and did not feel—directly threatened. But this policy would not necessarily serve the ends of peace and stability. Indeed, it could create a dangerous power vacuum since a relatively weak Japan might be a tempting target; excessive backlash could follow if some bad experiences led the Japanese to believe that "pacifism doesn't work." The U.S.-Japan security treaty would probably be prolonged in some form, or be replaced by international guarantees or a collective security system.

Japan as a New "Superpower." This scenario postulates that Japan will continue rapid economic growth and choose to focus again on its old goal of "catching up with the West," interpreting this in terms of total overall status and power.

Even more than the superstate role, this scenario involves potentially positive and negative consequences—for Japan and others. Whether they are considered good or bad can vary dramatically, depending upon the observer's position and interests. In any case, a new Japanese "superpower" would have a difficult and potentially dangerous role to play.

Japan would be consciously emerging as a world power; perhaps the most critical issues would arise during this transitional stage. The danger of the scenario results precisely from the tremendous impact that such a Japan would exert on the world. The impact would necessarily be far greater than even in the most extreme form of the superstate scenario.

One version of this scenario assumes that extreme nationalistic reactions would be generated domestically, either initially as a part of a conscious policy of an authoritarian government (which could be either leftist or rightist), or later as a result of international rejection of Japanese avowals of good intentions. We must stress that these possibilities are not unreasonable. In the absence of other goals, the Japanese are very likely to turn to nationalism—or be forced into such a role. Our best guess is that, if the world rejects Japan, Japan will in turn reject the world by consciously setting out to prove that Japan is better and stronger than anyone else. We would be surprised if Japan opted for accepting a "big Switzerland" posture under those circumstances.

However, we must try to see things with some perspective. In 1985, World War II will have been over for forty years. Japan will be—or soon will become—the second largest economy in the world. As such, Japan will have the greatest stake of any great power in the smooth functioning of the international system. It should surprise no one that such a nation would want to end its almost complete dependence—from the strategic point of view—on the United States, and accept full responsibility for its own security and for the protection of its interests in the world at large. In the most desirable situation this could lead to Japan's also accepting—and executing with wisdom and judgment—its full share of obligations toward the world community. In this novel setting, Japan might act ineptly or aggressively—perhaps even touching off a sequence of events leading to disaster for all. But both possibilities would represent a highly plausible course of events.

We believe that if the ordinary Japanese were polled today on the three scenarios presented here, he would overwhelmingly choose the first—the big Switzerland—as both the most desirable and the most likely. And if Japan were successfully to follow this course, the majority of the world's nations would applaud. We believe that, perhaps unfortunately, there is very little likelihood that the Japanese will actually be able to follow such a course—or be willing to do so on the big issues they will have to face.

As we have suggested, it is not easy to reduce the rate of economic growth rapidly. In the usual version, this scenario calls for a dramatic shift from a focus on industrial growth to a focus on quality-of-life issues, as is being called for by leftists in Japan today. But without rapid economic growth, sufficient capital will not be available to meet these social demands, and without additional productive facilities in at least the construction-related industries, it would be impossible to meet the requirements for additional infrastructure. Furthermore, to accomplish such a rapid change would require extremely authoritarian measures—in part to satisfy the quality-of-life needs of the ordinary man. The LDP certainly could not accomplish this under the current system. Business would have to oppose it. It would produce widespread bankruptcies, a terrible business situation for those that survive, rising unemployment, frustrated careers, even more frustrated expectations in terms of rising standards of living, and many other problems. One can only imagine this scenario occurring as the result of a collapse of the current system in favor of an authoritarian government of the left or the right.

Alternatively, the only way to achieve these social ends is to continue economic growth. In essence, this means that if Japan is to meet these demands under its current democratic system, it will have to continue its rapid economic growth and increase its dependence on the outside world for at least the next ten to fifteen years. This process alone should almost make Japan at least a "superstate"—heavily involved in world affairs, and practically eliminate the option for Japan to maintain a low posture role.

If an authoritarian government were installed and chose a course of rapid growth, other nations would almost certainly be alarmed, the U.S. and non-socialist world if the new regime is of the left, and the U.S. and the socialist world if it is of the right. Eventually, both the left and right would fear it—and probably sooner rather than later. It is also hard to believe that an authoritarian government could come to power or survive exclusively on a social welfare platform. It seems much more likely that it would be based on national sentiments. A sense of nationalism is growing in Japan today, especially among young people, and it is conceivable that this feeling could be exploited to bring an authoritarian government to power.

Our second basic scenario also postulates a major world role for Japan, but one which has an essentially economic focus. The positive version assumes that our long-term scenario for economic growth becomes widely accepted, possibly with Japan playing a key role—or at least a constructive role—in bringing this about. In its most desirable version, this could lead to a special, extremely positive role, for Japan: Japan would in effect become a model for the rest of the world as the first post-industrial economy, society, and culture. By way of explaining this, one might start by rephrasing the fundamental debate on economic growth as a question, perhaps the basic question of our time: how can mankind live in harmony with nature at high standards of living? Most of the developed nations of the world are already working on solving the problems of industrialization. But, except for Japan, no clear image exists of how this could turn out. Only Japan has a blueprint, demonstrating how this can be done on a comprehensive, nationwide basis: the "Comprehensive National Development Plan." If Japan chooses to devote itself to carrying out this plan or, more likely, later versions of the original, it could well become the avant garde for the world of the future.

One should not be misled by the current unpopularity of the Comprehensive National Development Plan. Over half of the total Japanese government expenditures are devoted to fixed capital investment, and the great majority of this investment is currently going into implementing this plan. It is not now treated as a comprehensive plan, but instead as individual projects, many of which are being delayed for a year or so in order to curb the current inflation. The plan itself is now being revised with the intention of extending the completion date from 1985 to the year 2000—but at the same time increasing its scope and comprehensiveness. It seems unlikely that the major features of the plan will be substantially changed. The lack of any consensus supporting the plan as a national effort at this time does not really contradict this forecast. It is characteristic of the Japanese decision-making process that, until a consensus is reached, sharp alternatives are not clearly elucidated. We would expect that the next revision, or perhaps the revision after that, would emerge as a truly national plan which could engage the energies and imagination of the Japanese people during the coming decades.

The importance of this plan lies in its size and scope: taken as a whole, it is decidedly the largest peacetime project in history. In its original form, it anticipates the planned expenditure by 1985 of over one trillion dollars, a sum which is almost certain to increase as the plan is redesigned to extend over a longer period. But even a trillion dollars is roughly equivalent to the entire fixed capital investment of Japan today. The plan thus quite literally anticipates remodeling the entire nation. It includes proposals to redistribute large portions of the Japanese population and industry, to create new cities, to install the most advanced railroad system in the world on a nationwide basis, to dramatically reduce pollution, and to clean up the environment; in short, to transform Japan into a kind of superindustrial Japanese garden and "information society."

Since Japan now has the most severe environmental problems of any developed nation, the plan would require a dramatic transition. As the world's first example of a post-industrial society, Japan would be subjected to much study of how it was done; other nations would follow her lead, copying some techniques and modifying all kinds of details. If the rest of the world recognized that Japan was leading the way, the Japanese sense of purpose and motivation to accomplish their tasks would be enhanced. The sense of malaise in Japan would be dissipated, and nationalist and other "free-floating" sentiments would find a positive outlet. The fact that Japan would be the first great economic power not to have equivalent military power would take on new significance. As a model nation of the future, the Japanese would be acutely conscious of the example they were setting. Rearmament might eventually occur, but at a much slower pace and perhaps with less dramatic consequences.

This goal would also explain to the world what Japan is doing as a nation: setting an example, cleaning up its own house, and demonstrating how mankind can live in peace if each nation both participates in the world community and minds its own business. There is much concern today, particularly in Asia, about what Japan will do with its great economic power. Japanese assurances that they will never again pursue an aggressive military course are not very reassuring as long as Japan has no recognized national goal. Just as the debate in Japan is: what should we the Japanese people do?, so a major question in Asian and other foreign capitals is: what will the Japanese people do? A national goal which is essentially inner-directed—although clearly dependent upon world trade and international cooperation—and inherently peaceful would enable Japan to deal with its most pressing domestic problems, while playing a unique and important role in history.

U.S.–Japanese Economic Relationships: Economic Structure and Policy in the 1960s, 1970s, and 1980s

Robert Z. Aliber

Introduction

If it were possible to develop an index of economic incidents between various pairs of countries, then the value of this index for the United States and Japan in the last fifteen years would be substantially higher than for any other pair of major countries. These incidents involve product-specific actions, like dumping, import quotas, and voluntary export quotas; and macro-incidents, like the foreign exchange value of the yen, the Japanese trade surplus, and Japanese policies toward the inflow of foreign investment. Even though trade and investment between the United States and Canada are substantially higher than between the United States and Japan, the value of the index for the United States and Canada would be substantially lower. That the index value would be higher for the U.S.-Japan pair did not just "happen"; either there were substantially more disturbances in U.S.-Japanese economic relations, or the same level of disturbances escalated into more policy incidents.

The product-specific incidents began in the late 1950s; the macro-incidents became important in the late 1960s. In both types of incidents the U.S. government took the initiative and asked or demanded a change in policies affecting Japan's exports, its imports, its trade surplus, and the exchange rate. Most policy measures were adopted by the

Japanese. The initial motivation for the U.S. demands were the complaints of U.S. producers of import-competing goods. Then U.S. firms wanted easier access to the Japanese market, both as a market for U.S.-produced goods, and as a source of supply for U.S. goods. Finally, the U.S. government was concerned about the impact of Japanese macro-variables on U.S. macro-variables; a substantial part of the variations in the U.S. trade and payment balances was the mirror of the variations in the Japanese trade and payments balances.

The level of U.S.-Japanese economic incidents may reflect that the U.S. government was more willing to intervene in support of the incomes—and economic rents—when U.S. producers were affected by Japanese competition than by competition in Europe and elsewhere. This proposition merits testing. The assumption of this paper, however, is that the level of the incident index arose from the rapid growth and peculiar structural characteristics of the Japanese economy. Rapid growth necessitated proportional increases in Japanese imports and exports. The burden of the surge in Japanese exports was most directly felt in the U.S. market; since the U.S. economy was growing less rapidly, Japanese exporters increased their share of the U.S. market. The shift to macro-incidents stems from the growing economic weight of Japan among the industrial countries, also a result of the much more rapid growth in Japan than in other trading countries.

The micro-incident level in the late 1970s and the early 1980s will depend on whether the Japanese economic growth rate will remain substantially higher than its trading partners'. The projected macro-incident rate will depend on whether cyclical variations in the Japanese growth rate will continue to lead to sharp swings in its trade balance.[1]

The next section of this paper describes the product-specific incidents. Some tentative generalizations are developed. The third section discusses the characteristics and sources of the macro-incidents in U.S.-Japanese relations. The final section considers developments in the incident level under various assumptions about the future levels of growth in income in Japan.

Product-Specific Incidents in U.S.-Japanese Economic Relations

Product-specific incidents can be grouped in several categories. Much

1. At the policy levels there are special aspects to U.S.-Japanese relations. One is the Annual Cabinet Meeting, which has no counterpart in U.S. economic relations with other countries.

the largest category covers Japanese exports to the United States. The surge in these exports imposed considerable losses on U.S. producers of competitive goods.

The primary policy instrument used to deal with product-specific incidents has been the "voluntary" export quota—a quantity limit on sales of Japanese produced goods in the U.S. market. These quotas were first used in 1955 to limit the sales of cotton blouses.[2] By the end of 1961, these quotas affected 25 to 35 percent of Japanese exports to the United States; the sales of twenty-five products were subject to quotas. In 1962 a Long-Term Cotton Textile Arrangement was negotiated to formalize the quotas and place them in a multi-national framework.[3]

Ten years later, seventy-three products were subject to voluntary export controls. Nearly forty products were various cotton textile products subject to the Long-Term Cotton Textile Arrangement. Wall tiles and wool suits were a result of bilateral negotiations between the U.S. and Japanese governments. Nearly twenty steel mill products were subject to quotas as a result of talks between the U.S. government and Japanese industry, and fifteen products, including umbrellas, umbrella frames, baseball gloves and mitts, and bicycle parts, were subject to voluntary quotas to prevent possible unilateral U.S. actions.[4]

In contrast, U.S. quotas on exports to Japan have been applied to walnut logs and soybeans to limit increases in the domestic prices of these products. The motive for the quota on walnut log exports was to assist U.S. producers of walnut veneers by providing them with a favored position in the market for logs. The motive for the quota on soybean exports—which lasted only a few months—was to limit increases in U.S. prices at a time of sharp inflation.

The explanation for the much greater demand by U.S. producers for trade-restraining measures is that most U.S. imports from Japan are largely competitive with U.S. domestic production. In contrast, a smaller proportion of Japanese imports from the United States are competitive with Japanese production. Moreover, the Japanese demand for commodities was growing three times as rapidly as the U.S. demand, so Japanese imports of U.S. products would have had a smaller

2. One sharp difference between export quotas and import quotas is their generality. Importing countries are reluctant to apply quotas on a discriminatory basis. Exporting countries have much less reluctance to discriminate, since the country-specific problems differ.

3. Committee for Economic Development, *Japan in the Free World Economy*, New York, April 1963, pp. 42–43.

4. Release, United States-Japan Trade Council, Washington, D.C., May 1971. For a discussion of the various motives for these quotas, see Leon Hollerman, *Japan's Dependence on the World Economy*, Princeton University Press, 1967, pp. 204–217.

impact in reducing sales of domestic products than U.S. imports of Japanese products.[5] In some product-lines, U.S. imports grew so rapidly that U.S. firms abandoned production.

That government and business in Japan limited the exports to the U.S. markets may be considered a concession to U.S. power; there is no formal basis in the GATT for voluntary export quotas. The Japanese may have recognized that they received the larger part of the share of the gains from trade; the Japanese resources used to produce exports to the U.S. market would have been extremely inefficient in producing substitutes for imports within Japan. In contrast, the gains to the United States from a larger volume of imports from Japan have been small, because the resources displaced by imports have had minimal opportunity cost in the short run. Finally, the competitive response to imports within the United States and Japan differs—increased imports in the United States lead to unemployment at the given wage rate, whereas in Japan the threat of increased imports leads to a decline in money wages, so that domestic factors remain employed.[6]

Over the last decade the composition of U.S. imports from Japan has shifted; a larger share are from more capital-intensive industries—automobiles, steel, and electronics.

As U.S. imports from Japan consist increasingly of more capital-intensive products, the number of product-specific incidents may decline. U.S. firms in the more capital-intensive industries may be in a better position to cope with increased imports from Japan. Moreover, the demand is growing more rapidly in these capital-intensive industries, so that Japanese producers can increase their share of the U.S. market without reducing the rents of U.S. factors in these industries. Yet because the Japanese export base is now very much larger than in 1960, maintenance of the growth rate may mean a decline in sales of U.S. firms in the more advanced U.S. industries. Hence product-specific incidents might still increase.

Macro-Incidents in U.S.-Japanese Economic Relations

Two macro-incidents dominate U.S.-Japanese economic relations—one

5. In 1970, Japanese imports of manufactured goods were smaller than those of Italy, and of Belgium and the Netherlands. Japan does not import products which are competitive with domestically produced goods. See GATT, Studies in International Trade, No. 2, *Japanese Economic Expansion and Foreign Trade*, 1955 to 1970. Geneva, July 1971, p. 10.

6. This proposition is tentative. The underlying premise is that the pattern of wage-setting in the United States differs sharply from that in Japan. Within the United States, wages tend to be uniform across firms in the same industry. In Japan, there are no industry-wide patterns for wages.

is the package of the exchange rate and the trade and payments balances, and the second is the Japanese regulation of foreign investments in Japan—meaning U.S. investment. The U.S. government has leaned on Japan to liberalize its regulations affecting the inflow of direct foreign investment. U.S. firms wanted access to the Japanese labor skills on terms similar to those available to Japanese firms, they wanted direct access to the rapidly growing Japanese markets, and they wanted a direct means to demonstrate certain facets of interdependence to Japanese firms—they wanted to make defensive investments in Japan.

The major issue—identified as "Nixon shock"—is the exchange rate-trade balance nexus. The underlying question is the size of the trade surplus Japan should be allowed—how large a deflationary impulse it can export to its trading partners. In 1971, the United States, by its 10 percent tariff surcharge on dutiable imports, forced the revaluation of the yen from ¥360 to $1 to ¥308 to $1. In 1973, the yen was floated and appreciated to the range of ¥260 to $1. Within eighteen months, the yen appreciated by nearly 40 percent. This appreciation is one of the most rapid in recent history; by comparison the appreciation of the mark of nearly 50 percent took more than twelve years.[7] The rapid appreciation of the yen has now conditioned some investors to predict that further revaluations of the yen are only a matter of time, which is a reversal of the general expectation of six or eight years ago that Japan would be subject to persistent payments deficits.

Since most other major currencies were revalued relative to the U.S. dollar in late 1971 and again in early 1973, not all of the factors involved in the revaluation of the yen are Japan-specific. The French franc was revalued by 8 percent in 1971 and by 10 percent in 1973, while the mark appreciated by more than 20 percent over the same period. The revaluations of the European currencies and part of the revaluation of the yen are an adjustment to the U.S. inflation and are U.S.-specific; nevertheless, a revaluation of the yen by 20 percent probably would have been necessary even without the U.S. inflation.[8]

The tendencies toward secular revaluation must be explained; one question is which of several competing theories of the balance of payments best explains the disequilibrium that led to the large Japanese payments surplus. The second is why the disequilibrium in the Japanese international accounts was not adjusted through the operation of market forces—why were policy measures necessary?

7. These data are from International Finance Statistics, unless otherwise noted.

8. Elsewhere I have argued that the yen was revalued more or less continuously throughout the 1960s by the reduction in Japanese barriers to imports. See Robert Z. Aliber, "Japanese Growth and the Equilibrium Foreign Exchange Value of the Yen," *Southern Economic Journal*, November 1972.

Balance-of-Payments Theories and the Revaluation of the Yen

In the fifteen years prior to 1968, Japan had a sequence of balance-of-payments cycles. The phases of these cycles coincided with accelerations and decelerations of the growth of Japanese national income. During the acceleration phase, the rate of growth of imports increased while the rate of growth of exports fell; as a consequence, the payments deficit became more severe. As the ability to finance the deficit became exhausted, the Japanese authorities pursued a more contractive monetary policy. Then, as the rate of growth of income decelerated in both nominal and real terms, the rate of growth of imports diminished more rapidly (indeed imports sometimes fell in absolute value, even as income was rising), and the rate of growth of exports accelerated. The growth rate for exports was counter-cyclical to the growth rate for income and for imports.

One striking feature of this cycle was its periodicity; each cycle tended to last four years. Another was the rapidity with which exports responded to variations in the rate of growth of domestic income. A third was that rapid growth appears unassociated without any secular tendency toward a payments surplus. During this period, reported foreign exchange reserves showed greater stability than might be inferred from year-to-year variations in the trade balance; variations in the trade balance were financed by variations in short-term foreign borrowing.[9]

What needs to be explained is why the cyclical behavior of the trade balance after 1968 differs from that before 1968, and why since then exports have increased sharply relative to imports.[10] Several factors distinguish the balance-of-payments developments since 1968. One is that exports began to grow rapidly, even as income continued its rapid growth rate. Thus in 1968 exports grew at a rate of nearly 25 percent, while national income, during a year of credit restraint, grew at a rate of nearly 20 percent.[11] Monetary tightness in 1968, unlike that in previous

9. It is interesting to contemplate how the yen price of the dollar might have varied over the balance-of-payments cycle if the yen had been floating. Because of the very imperfect substitutability between Japanese and foreign goods, these cyclical variations in the exchange rate would have been extensive in the absence of stabilizing speculation.

10. Rapid growth and payments surpluses appear correlated in the postwar period; thus the rapidly growing countries include Japan, Germany, Italy, and France, which also tend to be at the top of the list of countries which have had payments surpluses.

11. 1967 appears as the boom year at the end of the balance-of-payments cycle; exports increased by 6 percent over 1966 while imports increased by nearly 25 percent. The current account surplus fell by more than $1 billion; reserves fell modestly. Thereafter the increase in domestic income appears not to be associated with decreases in the growth rate of exports.

periods, had a minimal impact in depressing the growth of money income. Similarly, credit restraint in 1970 also did not have a significant impact in dampening the growth of money income. Monetary ease in 1969 and 1971 appears not to have been associated with a spurt in national income.[12] The responsiveness of the economy to changes in monetary policy appears smaller than in the late 1950s and early 1960s.

At least five theories of the balance of payments might explain the post-1967 increase in the Japanese trade surplus. The theories include Purchasing Power Parity, a Keynesian theory of cyclical income disturbance, a theory based on the demand for international reserves, the monetary theory of the balance of payments, and a "theory" of structural change. The structural change theory differs from the others in that it is not systematic, but essentially an explanation of the residual—that component of the change in payments balance that cannot be explained by the changes in relative prices, incomes, and the supply and demand for money. Evaluation of these competing theories requires prior identification of the behavior of specified variables that might contradict the theory; otherwise the theory is a definition. Moreover, the theory should explain the apparent change in the behavior of Japanese international accounts that occurs in the late 1960s.

The easiest theory to test is the Purchasing Power Parity, which is that the rate of change in the equilibrium exchange rate conforms to the difference in the rates of change of relative national price levels. A disequilibrium in the international accounts occurs because the exchange rate peg is maintained while relative price levels and hence the equilibrium exchange rate change. A change in the exchange parity is necessary to reattain equilibrium—to bring the market exchange rate in line with the equilibrium rate. This theory "predicts" a revaluation of the yen as a result of a less rapid increase in Japanese prices than in world prices.

The procedural question in evaluating the applicability of this theory to the Japanese experience involves determining which price indexes should be used to compute the equilibrium exchange rate. The consumer price indexes have a smaller component of internationally traded goods than the wholesale price indexes, and therefore provide a better indication of relative inflation in Japan and in the rest of the world. The use of consumer price indexes to compute the equilibrium

12. These conclusions are based on casual empiricism. They conform to the idea that monetary linkages have increased. Data on sources of monetary growth in Japan are available in Warren D. McClam, "Credit Substitution and the Euro-Currency Market," *Banca Nazionale del Lavoro*, December 1972.

exchange rate suggests the yen should have depreciated relative to the dollar, since consumer prices in Japan rose much faster than consumer prices in the United States. The changes in relative wholesale price indexes predict that the yen should have been revalued; if 1968 is the base year, the U.S. wholesale price index has increased by about ten percentage points more than the Japanese wholesale price index. The change in the relative wholesale price indexes roughly captures the U.S.-specific change and leaves the need for a revaluation of the yen unexplained. It appears that a substantial revaluation of the yen would have been necessary even if the relative wholesale price indexes had not been changed.[13]

The Keynesian approach to the analysis of changes in the trade balance focuses on the difference between the domestic supply of resources and the domestic demand for resources. When domestic supply and domestic demand are in equilibrium, the trade balance is in equilibrium. Excess domestic demand leads to a trade deficit, while excess supply leads to a trade surplus. Thus, variations in the trade balance over time reflect variations in domestic income on the presumption that world demand and hence world income can be taken as given.

This theory would be proven wrong if the trade surplus increased as domestic income increased or if the variations in the trade balance represent a response to changes in exports rather than changes in imports. Within Japan, changes in income and changes in the trade balance have been negatively correlated, as the theory would suggest—at least prior to 1968. And over the 1967–71 period, gross national product grew at a rate of 19 percent, while imports grew at the rate of 15 percent. Exports, however, increased.

This theory can be examined in terms of deviations from trend values. In the late 1960s—as in the pre-1968 period—the increase in the trade surplus occurred as income and domestic demand were increasing at a rapid rate. The data does not support the theory, except for 1971—when income increased by 11 percent, imports increased by 3 percent, and exports by 20 percent; and even then the growth in exports was several times more rapid than the theory would predict.

One theory of the balance of payments, in vogue in the 1960s, is that an individual country develops a payments surplus to increase its

13. Implicit in this statement is the view that the price elasticity of the demand for imports in Japan is identical with that in the rest of the world. If, however, the price elasticity is higher in the rest of the world than in Japan, the procedure suggested is inappropriate. In that case, a theory would be desirable indicating why the price elasticities differ.

holdings of international reserves; the country might depress export prices, domestic income, or raise import barriers to achieve a payments surplus. This theory is more about trends than about levels. The difficulty with applying this "theory" to Japan is that in the years before 1967 Japan showed great skill in managing its international reserves by short-term foreign borrowing. Except for the increase in the interest rates on foreign loans, there is no explanation why Japanese policy toward the level of reserves, either in absolute level or in trend, should have changed in the late 1960s.

The monetary theory of the balance of payments rests on the assumption that the central bank within a country cannot control the domestic supply of money; rather the central bank can control only the domestic component of the reserve base. The demand for money is determined by the public; the supply of money adjusts to the demand, and the reserve base adjusts to ensure that the supply is appropriate to the demand. If the money supply demanded by the public differs from that available, given the domestic component of the reserve base, then the international component of the monetary base adjusts so that the desired money supply is attained. Changes in the international component of the monetary base induce changes in the payments balance. The theory is not explicit about whether the trade balance or the capital account adjusts to changes in the demand for money and about whether the adjustment involves changes in imports or in exports.

The demand for money is determined by the real income and the domestic price level; the country is assumed to be a price-taker in the world markets in that the domestic price level is the product of the world price level and the exchange rate. Real income is endogenous, and determined by the economy's supply capabilities; hence the theory is essentially a long-run theory. The labor market, like the money market, is always in equilibrium.

If the domestic component of the monetary base increases too rapidly, the supply of money exceeds the demand and a payments deficit results; the international component of the reserve base declines. As long, however, as the payments deficit can be financed, the domestic price level is unchanged, since the exchange rate is unchanged. Only when the exchange rate is changed does the domestic price level change.

The monetary theory of the balance of payments is more comprehensive than the other theories in that it includes prices, incomes, money demand, and money supply. Whereas Purchasing Power Parity assumes that the domestic price level may diverge from the world price level at the prevailing exchange rate, the monetary theory implicitly assumes that the exchange rate is always an equilibrium rate, since domestic prices cannot differ from world prices. While the Keynesian theory implicitly assumes that the income can depart from its equilibrium full-employment level, the monetary theory does not recognize such deviations; the only disequilibrium that can occur is between money supplied and money demanded.

One observation that might confound the monetary theory is an increase in the supply of money that occurs at the same time as an increase in the domestic price level.[14] The increase in domestic prices is the basis of the inference that the supply of money is increasing more rapidly than the demand. A second observation that might confound the theory is more rapid or less rapid increases in domestic prices than in international prices.

The monetary theory of the balance of payments is intuitively appealing for Japan prior to 1968. The years of rapid increases in the money supply are years of payments deficits; the years of slow growth in the money supply are years of payments surpluses. The Japanese authorities followed a restrictive monetary policy in 1968; total net credit fell as a percentage of GNP (as it had in previous years of credit restraint, 1964, 1961–62, 1957, and 1954). Before 1968, credit restraint was associated with a turnabout in the payments balance; international reserves, which had been declining in the year before the credit restraint, then began to increase. The monetary theory predicts reserves should have fallen in 1969, which was a year of credit expansion; instead they increased. The theory predicted that international reserves should have increased in 1970, since it was a year of credit restraint; and they did. The theory says that international reserves should have declined in 1971, which was a year of credit expansion; but they increased sharply. The year-by-year increases in reserves since 1967, regardless of the monetary policy, confound the theory.

If changes in relative prices, incomes, the demand for reserves, and the supply and demand for money provide inadequate explanations of the Japanese payments surplus, then an explanation in terms of structural change might. One such change in economic structure involves a shift in the demand—both foreign and domestic—for Japanese goods relative to non-Japanese goods at the same relative prices. Alternatively, the Japanese supply of exports and perhaps of import substitutes may increase at the same relative prices.

14. If domestic prices are effectively world prices, then there is no independent way to determine whether the money is growing less rapidly or more rapidly than money demand, other than by changes in international component of the reserve base. And in this case, the theory is a definition.

A descriptive explanation of the change in the trade balance in terms of structural changes should be distinguished from a "theory" of the structural change which might explain why exports have increased relative to imports. Japanese firms in a few industries have achieved economies of scale; as their costs have fallen they have been able to cut their prices in that they have supplied the same volume of goods at a relatively lower price. In most foreign product markets, Japan has been a "small country" so that it can increase its exports without affecting the price; from the Japanese point of view, the world demand is perfectly elastic. Consequently, Japanese export sales increased rapidly as Japanese costs fell. Since 1968, the growth in export sales may have reflected a partial diversion of goods originally intended for the domestic market, because domestic demand increased less rapidly than had been predicted.

This explanation in terms of changes in economic structure in a few industries is consistent with some anecdotal evidence. Japanese prices of a few industrial products, including steel, automobiles, and electronic products have fallen as Japanese producers have realized economies of scale. Japanese export prices have fallen relative to other Japanese price indexes, more so than in other countries, because large productivity gains have been limited to a few industries producing timetables. Other industries have had to raise wages in response to the pull of wages in the rapid growth industries; these wage increases have exceeded the productivity gains and so firms in these industries have raised prices.

The rapid shifts in output between home and foreign markets are consistent with discriminatory pricing or dumping practices; prices in the smaller, protected home market exceed those in the larger, more competitive world market. Firms prefer to sell in the more profitable domestic market. Recognition of mutual interdependence means that Japanese firms direct goods to the export market rather than seek a larger share of the domestic market. Moreover, because variable costs are low relative to total costs, selling at the lower world price may be preferable to reducing output. Since world demand for most Japanese goods is smaller than the Japanese demand, a relatively small decline in the domestic demand is consistent with a larger percentage increase in the exports (e.g., world demand) of these same goods. This "theory" might explain the rapid growth in exports and the cyclical surge in Japanese exports, but it does not explain why the tendency toward a larger surplus resulting from the export growth is not offset by an equally rapid growth in imports, so that a large payments surplus does not result.

Each of the theories about the disturbance has an answer to the question of why the disequilibrium was sustained—why it is not self-correcting. The implication of the monetary theory of the balance of payments is that the payments surplus continues until the domestic component of the monetary base increases at the rate appropriate for the desired rate of growth in the money supply.[15] The structural theory says that imbalance continues as long as the prices, incomes, money, exchange rate, structural variables, or policy variables do not adjust to the imbalance generated by structural forces.

One possible adjustment to the increase in foreign exchange earnings is an increase in imports; this adjustment occurs as wage increases in the rapid-growth, high productivity industries spill over to the slower-growth industries, raising their costs, and hence leading to an increase in the demand for imports. The increase in the demand for imports depends on the extent of the substitutability between labor in the export industries and in the import industries. The greater the substitutability, the more nearly the payments surplus would prove self-correcting. Disequilibrium might also be self-correcting if the payments surplus leads to a growth in the money supply; Japanese prices would increase and the demand for foreign goods would rise relative to the demand for domestic goods.

The disequilibrium which seemed large in the context of the international economy is small relative to the Japanese economy; then this adjustment might be weak. Until 1971, the trade balance—net exports—was at most about 3 or 4 percent of GNP; usually it was less than 1 percent of GNP. Year-to-year changes in the trade balance were small in terms of the growth and swings in national income so that the price-raising consequences of the trade surplus were minimal, especially in an economy with such a high savings rate and with substantial excess capacity. Consequently, the potential inflationary effects of the large increase in the payments surplus appear too small, in the short run at least, to lead to a sharp reduction in the payments surplus.[16]

Whether macro-incidents are likely to continue depends on the fu-

15. While there undoubtedly is a rate of growth of the domestic component of the reserve base so that Japan would be in payments surplus, this growth rate might involve substantially more rapid increases in Japanese prices than the authorities would accept. In the short run, the authorities might be able to control the price level but not the payments balance; alternatively, they might be able to control the payments balance but not the price level.

16. Over the last several years the newspapers have contained numerous accounts of Japanese acquisitions of French impressionists, Saratoga yearlings, Waikiki hotels, etc. These purchases are part of the adjustment process to the large payments surplus and the lack of adequate objects for the accumulation of wealth within Japan.

ture growth rate within Japan, and on changes in structure and policy. As long as rapid growth occurs, and there are cyclical variations in the growth rate, then large swings in the growth of exports appear inevitable. Whether these swings lead to comparable variations in the trade and payments balances—and hence a rise in the index for macro-incidents—depends on whether there are likely to be similar swings in the imports.

Unless the market forces operate to minimize the variations in the trade balance, the burden of reducing the incident level will fall on the authorities. They must decide whether they want to control the price level or the payments balance.

Japanese External Balance, 1975–1980 and Beyond

The thesis of the previous sections is that the source of both product and macro-incidents is the more rapid growth of Japan than of the United States. The increase in the foreign exchange value of the yen has resulted from sharp increases in export competitiveness in a relatively few Japanese industries, and a less than corresponding growth rate for imports. Predicting the future level of incidents involves extrapolating the growth rate—are rapid productivity gains likely to continue in autos, steel, and similar industries, and are they likely to develop in other industries? Is there a range of industries producing internationally traded goods in which domestic demand will grow at 20 or 30 percent a year, and in which rapid productivity gains are attainable because the characteristics of the product involve capital intensive techniques and require minimal labor skills? If so, product incidents are inevitable. It is not inherent that macro-incidents develop even if such growth occurs, either because the demand for imports will increase with the demand for exports, or because the Japanese authorities might adopt the monetary policies such that the yen does not become overvalued—they might prefer more rapid increases in domestic prices and a stable foreign exchange value for the yen than a less rapid increase in domestic prices and an increase in the foreign exchange value for the yen.

These issues can be put in the context of two questions—the first is what is the trend rate of growth of real income that would result in a trade balance (or a payment balance), assuming the achievement of certain price level targets; the second is whether this growth is likely. A shortfall in the growth rate below the level consistent with the equilibrium in the trade balance means that Japan would not achieve the productivity gains in certain industries, and there would be no sharp improvement in its export potential. In contrast, a short-term or cyclical shortfall in the growth rate below the secular growth rate, regardless of the trend growth rate, is likely to mean in the future, as it has in the past, a sharp increase in the trade surplus. Moreover, any change in the secular growth rate consistent with long-run trade balance equilibrium—for example, from a 10 percent growth rate to an 8 percent growth rate—might be expected to result in a substantial surge in the trade balance.

Conclusion

The basic question that must be answered to develop a view on the future level of economic incidents in U.S.-Japanese relations involves the growth rate in Japan.[17] Continued rapid growth in Japan will require a roughly equivalent rate of growth of exports. Given that the Japanese share of world markets is now much larger than a decade ago, the impact on foreign producers is likely to be considerably greater than it was. So the number of product-specific incidents would increase, and they will be more severe.

Three factors may have somewhat offsetting impacts on the incident level. The first is that the product mix of Japanese exports is somewhat larger, so the competitive impact is felt over a wider range of products. The second is that industries in which Japanese exports are likely to grow are likely to be subject to a higher rate of growth. The third is that the countries to which Japan exports are likely to be more numerous, so that the U.S. share of Japanese exports is likely to decline.

At the macro-level, the problem is whether Japan will be able to achieve stability in its trade and payments balances, given its growth rate. If not, then the structural characteristics suggest that Japan will run large payments surpluses whenever the growth rate in the domestic economy falters, as Japanese producers shift from selling in the domestic market to selling in the foreign market. Again, simply in terms of scale, this is more likely to be disruptive in the future because Japan is so much larger. One policy response would be to vary the rate of increase in the domestic price level to reduce the swings in the trade balance. A second would be to continue with a floating exchange rate—or to change the pegged rate much more frequently.

17. One view is that the Japanese growth rate until the end of the century will be an extrapolation of its growth rate since the mid-1950s. The adherents of this view do not explain why the Japanese growth rate should be so much higher in this period than in the 1880–1940 period. Nor do they recognize the inevitable growing severity of the external constraints if Japan continues to grow so much more rapidly than other countries.

Japan and Southeast Asia: The Geography of Interdependence

Norton S. Ginsburg and James Osborn

Japan and Southeast Asia have long been important to one another, but the nature of their interdependence has been changing, and Japan has become increasingly ambivalent about its political role in the region after the American military withdrawal from Vietnam. Even as Japan is coming to dominate the economies of the Southeast Asian countries and depends heavily on them for raw materials, paradoxically its relative dependence on the region both as a market and as a source of raw materials is lessening. On the other hand, the Southeast Asian countries, other than the Indochina bloc, depend ever more heavily on Japan for assistance, investment, trade, and technological transfer.

Although these facts are clear, what are not are the quantitative aspects of the economic flows in recent years, and particularly in the last several. Aspects of these are set out in tabular form below. Equally significant are the political-geographic implications of these changes. Insofar as Japan views Southeast Asia as a region, to what extent is that view more than the sum of bilateral economic relations between Japan and the individual countries in the area? Conversely, does increasing dependency on Japan on the part of the Southeast Asian countries contribute to their sense of regional identity, or might that dependency obstruct the rise of regionalism in the area? Let us begin with a discussion of Southeast Asia as a region.

Southeast Asia as a Region[1]

Until the Great Pacific War, Southeast Asia was less a region in its own right than a buffer zone between South Asia and East Asia. From the Indian (and European) point of view the area was regarded largely as an extension of the Indian subcontinent and frequently was referred to in the literature and in common parlance as "Farther India." From the Chinese and Japanese point of view, however, it was viewed as a southerly extension of the Sinitic world. The characters for "Nan-yang" (in Chinese) and "Nan Yō" (in Japanese) literally mean "Southern Seas," that is, the region associated with the South China Sea. It was only during the war that Southeast Asia as a general term came to be applied to the area that lies between India and China. Fragmented among a number of cultures, diversified as Europe, and populous as Africa south of the Sahara, the area came to have an identity of its own, partly in negative terms and partly as a result of Japan's occupation and control of almost all of it. Since then, it has come to be recognized as a region in its own right, not so much for any inherent homogeneity and in spite of its lack of regional integrity, but as a result of its distinction from the Indic and Sinitic worlds which lie to the west and north of it.

Following the war, the region passed swiftly and painfully in most cases from a general condition of colonial dependency (except for Thailand) to one of national independence. By 1958 the map of Southeast Asia had been transformed. Only a few territories remained under foreign domination. By the early 1960s no parts of Southeast Asia other than Portuguese Timor and Brunei could be regarded as politically dependent, if one excepts South Vietnam as a prospective client state of the United States.

On the basis of the two criteria by which regions commonly are defined, homogeneity and organization, Southeast Asia's identity is suspect. Not only is it divided among a number of states, but also these states are variable in size, culture, resources, and recent historical heritage. What they share, however, is also important. All are underdeveloped, that is, comparatively poor; all, except Singapore, are predominantly agricultural; all share some aspects of a colonial heritage, even Thailand which has a history of domination in economic affairs by foreign interests; all lie within the tropics and share environmental characteristics markedly different from those of the areas to the west and north; all experienced Japanese rule during the Pacific War; and all

1. For a more detailed discussion of Southeast Asia as a region, see N. S. Ginsburg, "The Political Dimension: Regionalism and Extra-regional Relations," in A. Taylor, ed., *Focus on Southeast Asia* (New York: Praeger, 1972), pp. 3–12.

(again with the exception of Thailand) since that war have followed a difficult path toward independence. Above all, they differ from their neighbors in that they are not part of either the Indic or Sinitic (other than Vietnam) worlds, and they are markedly conscious of the cultural imperialisms to which they have been exposed over the past millennium. On the mundane level, this self-consciousness is marked, except for Singapore, by an antipathy toward the Chinese minorities in their populations.

In terms of the organizational criterion for regional definition, the recent evidence suggests an incipient regionalism that marks a trend toward regional identity on functional and perceptual grounds, despite the great variation within the region. Over the years, there have been discussions of the possibility for Pan-Buddhist associations and later Pan-Malay and Pan-Indonesian federations which would have included the entire Malay-speaking part of the area. During Sukarno's regime in Indonesia, the idea of a subregional entity called Maphilindo was mooted, but it foundered on the shoals of rivalries between Indonesia and the Federation of Malaysia. In 1962 the Association for Southeast Asia (ASA) came into being, consisting only of The Philippines, Malaysia, and Thailand,[2] and it laid the groundwork for a more substantial but still weak organization, unsure of its purposes, the Association of Southeast Asian Nations (ASEAN), founded in 1966, consisting of the ASA states plus Indonesia and Singapore.

ASEAN clearly symbolizes a search for regional self-identity on the part of most of the Southeast Asian states. Additional evidence of that drive has been the pressure placed upon the Asian Development Bank to support major studies of the economy and transportation as related to development in Southeast Asia, projects which the bank was reluctant to undertake because many of its foreign officials were unwilling, at first at least, to recognize the strength of growing Southeast Asian regionalism.[3]

From the Japanese point of view, the idea of the region as it pertains to Southeast Asia is inconsistently applied. Still, it is worth noting that in the prewar and midwar literature about the region, there was little ambiguity and great consistency in references to the region as a territorial entity. No one then identified Korea and Taiwan as being South-

2. See Vincent K. Pollard, "ASA and ASEAN 1961–1967: Southeast Asian Regionalism," *Asian Survey*, X, No. 3 (March 1970), pp. 244–55.

3. *Southeast Asia's Economy in the 1970s* (Tokyo: Tokyo University Press, 1971) and *Southeast Asian Regional Transportation Survey* (Manila: Asian Development Bank, 1972).

east Asian—although Taiwan was recognized as the stepping-off point to that great region—perhaps because they were then parts of the Japanese Empire, but more likely because Southeast Asia's distinctiveness was more generally and better understood then than it now appears to be. The end of the war and Japan's severance of relations, for a time, with Southeast Asia brought about a kind of myopia toward the region which was associated with the general inward-facing view of the universe that characterized Japan during the immediate postwar period. However, when the first stirrings of interest in Southeast Asia appeared after the war, the perception of the region as an areal entity separable from the rest of Asia seemed strong enough.

One of the more recent problems of definition that have helped obscure and confuse the Japanese perspective relates to the postwar changes in East Asia (that is, China, Korea, and Japan). With China effectively removed from diplomatic and economic relations for most of the period 1949–72, Korea divided between north and south, Taiwan detached both from the mainland and from Japan, and the Ryūkyūs in a limbo between Japan and the United States, East Asia lost its regional identity and to most observers appeared more highly fragmented than at any time since the Tokugawa period. Thus, as South Korea and Taiwan once more became economically important to Japan in the postwar period, there was no convenient East Asian regional framework into which to set them; and they usually are now grouped simply with other Asian countries or with those in Southeast Asia proper. One even finds JETRO, for example, applying the term "Southeast Asia" to all Asian countries from Afghanistan east, except for China and Japan itself. Moreover, GATT uses the terms "South Asia" and "East Asia" to include all of what was termed long ago the "Asiatic Triangle," but excluding China and Japan, thereby eliminating reference to Southeast Asia as a region together.[4] Data aggregated in these ways must be laboriously disaggregated, if one is to deal with Southeast Asia as such.

In spite of these difficulties, the precedent for dealing with Southeast Asia as the region from Burma to The Philippines seems strong enough to justify its continued use, as it is in this paper. To most Japanese concerned with these matters the expression *Tōnan Ajia* conforms reasonably well to this definition. We shall see that Japan indeed appears to have "special interests" in the region and a distinctive foreign relations strategy devoted to it.

4. GATT, *Japan's Economic Expansion and Foreign Trade, 1955 to 1970,* GATT Studies in International Trade, No. 2 (Geneva: GATT, 1971).

The Diplomatic Dimension

Treaties and Agreements. During the Great Pacific War, in a way vastly distorted by the misuse of power, Japan came to have more experience in dealing with indigenous non-colonial governments in Southeast Asia than any other country; and its postwar reinvolvement with the region was inevitable. In fact, that involvement was guaranteed by the Peace Treaty signed at San Francisco in 1951, in which a clause was inserted at the request of certain Southeast Asian countries to mark Japan's responsibility for indemnities or reparations as a consequence of the war.

Moreover, in keeping with cautious policies directed toward reconstituting herself as an Asian country with neighborly intentions, in 1954 Japan joined the Colombo Plan, which had been drawn up in 1950 for "cooperative economic development in South and Southeast Asia" and which was joined by almost all the Asian nations.[5] In 1955, the U.N. Economic Commission for Asia and the Far East meeting was held in Tokyo; and that year Japan attended the Asian-African Conference at Bandung. Although she did not join ANZUS or SEATO, Japan went on to specialize in economic organizations. She was a founding member, *inter alia*, of the Development Assistance Committee of OECD in 1960 (and, it is said, used it as a wedge for entrance to OECD in 1964), took an active part in GATT, and was host to the Asian Productivity Council. Later, Japan became a member of the Asia and Pacific Council (ASPAC) whose purpose at its establishment in 1966 was to foster "greater cooperation and solidarity among the free Asian and Pacific countries."[6]

In 1957, Premier Kishi launched his "Asia-centered diplomacy."[7] This signaled two principles: (1) that, despite Japan's obvious and growing economic and diplomatic affinity with the United States, Asia—or a large part of it—was regarded as exceptionally important to Japan in ways supportable by diplomacy; and (2) that Asian attitudes toward Japan, mostly negative as a result of the war, might not preclude cooperation if only with a view toward economic development.

Therefore, when the Asian Development Bank was founded in 1966 with capital of $1,100 million, $200 million was Japanese, making Japan, with the United States, the Bank's largest contributor (and later the largest contributor to the Bank's Special Fund, providing $20 mil-

5. Keesing Publications, *Treaties and Alliances of the World*, (New York: Scribners, 1968), p. 136.
6. *Ibid.*, p. 197.
7. See Jo Yung-hwan, "Regional Cooperation in Southeast Asia and Japan's Role," *Journal of Politics*, XXX, No. 3 (1968), pp. 780–96.

lion of $23 million to the Fund for Agriculture, and $80 million of $125.8 million to the multipurpose fund).[8] But the time (1966) was premature for wide Asian public acceptance of Japanese economic leadership, and Manila, rather than Tokyo, was the compromise site chosen for the Bank's headquarters, although the Bank's first president was a Japanese.

Reparations. It was with reparations, however, that Japan first reentered the economic scene in Southeast Asia. The requirement for war reparations included in the Peace Treaty of September 1951 did not specify amounts, timing, or type, although Japan's capacity to pay was a noted condition, and across-the-board restitution of war losses was ruled out.[9]

The first discussions about reparations to Southeast Asian countries began at the end of 1951 with Indonesia and then the Philippines, countries which ultimately received the largest reparations packages after long, sometimes comical, sometimes rancorous bargaining. While the Indonesian and Philippines negotiations were going on, a second pair of countries, Burma and Thailand, settled. In 1955, Burma and Japan agreed to grants of $20 million each for ten years in the form of goods and services, and $50 million in private loans, to be individually negotiated later. In 1965 additional reparations of $11.7 million were agreed to.[10] These negotiations were not accompanied by the same kind of difficulties involving the Philippines and Indonesia, nor was there the same kind of rancor, understandably, in the case of Thailand which had been a nonbelligerent and in some senses an ally. The "Special Yen Problem" in Thailand, which arose from wartime yen issued by Japanese banks in Thailand, was solved on 9 July 1955 with an agreement for Japan to pay $15 million in five installments. In January 1963, a new agreement was signed whereby Japan agreed to supply an additional $26.7 million in eight annual installments, the last in 1969 of $7.2 million.[11]

In April 1956, a compromise agreement between Japan and the Philippines was reached. It provided, over twenty years, $500 million in goods grants and an additional $30 million in cash for war widows and orphans. Relatively low-interest commercial loans of up to $250

8. Japan is also the principal market for ADB bond issues, yielding $74.7 million in three issues. See *Japan Report*, XVIII, No. 11 (June 1, 1972), p. 2.

9. Lawrence Olson, *Japan in Postwar Asia* (New York: Praeger for the Council on Foreign Relations, 1970), pp. 16–17; and Keesing, *op. cit.*, p. 19.

10. Olson, *op. cit.*, pp. 19 and 22; and United Nations, *Treaties and International Agreements Series* (UNTIAS), Vol. 251 (New York: United Nations, continuous), p. 216.

11. UNTIAS, Vol. 230, pp. 14–16, and Vol. 450, pp. 422–24. *N.B.* Olson's figures (p. 210, *op. cit.*) are off by one decimal place.

million over twenty years were also agreed to.[12] In 1958 the Indonesian reparations issues also was settled. It provided $223 million over twelve years and cancellation of past trade debts of $177 million. In addition, there was to be a commercial loan of $400 million.[13]

The third set of reparations-like agreements was with the countries of Indo-China. In 1955, Cambodia renounced war reparations voluntarily in a Treaty of Amity with Japan. Laos having done likewise, these two countries, in 1959 and 1958 respectively, signed agreements with Japan for economic and technical cooperation. Cambodia was to receive $4.2 million over three years in the form of supplies of Japanese commodities and services from Japanese persons and corporations.[14] Laos, in two years, was to receive $2.8 million with an extension of two years from July 1962.[15] The Republic of Vietnam did not renounce reparations but received similar treatment in 1959, with an agreement for receipt of $39 million in five years. In addition, two Vietnamese loan agreements were signed, one for $7.5 million for acquisition of Japanese products and services, and a long-term commercial loan of $9.1 million, both to run over five years.[16]

Lastly, Malaysia and Singapore, following their split, came to agreements in lieu of reparations with Japan in 1967. A "blood debt" was to be paid to Malaysia in the amount of $8.3 million, particularly in ships and other capital goods; and Singapore agreed to the receipt of $17 million in grants and loans.[17]

One consequence of these reparations discussions was the increased diplomatic involvement of the Southeast Asian countries with Japan. In addition, the reparations payments meant growing intrusion of Japanese consumer and capital goods, financial institutions, and styles, which helped provide a basis for increased future dependence on Japan. All this was achieved at remarkably little cost to Japan. In 1962–65, when reparations payments reached their height they averaged only 2 percent of the annual Japanese government budget. In 1956 they were only 0.6 percent, in 1958, 1.1 percent, in 1959, 2.1 percent.[18] In fact, the total value of reparations provided came to only a little more than $1 billion.[19] The reparations allocations are shown in Table 1.

12. Olson, *op. cit.,* p. 25.
13. Olson, *op. cit.,* p. 26; and UNTIAS, Vol. 324, p. 235, and Vol. 325, p. 14.
14. UNTIAS, Vol. 341, pp. 165–75.
15. UNTIAS, Vol. 341, pp. 27–29.
16. UNTIAS, Vol. 373, pp. 129–35, 145, 161, 167, 175.
17. Olson, *op. cit.,* pp. 202 and 197.
18. Olson, *op. cit.,* p. 26.
19. S. Okita, "Japanese Economic Cooperation in Asia in the 1970's," in G. L. Curtis, ed., *Japanese-American Relations in the 1970s* (Washington: Columbia Books, 1970), p. 95.

Table 1

Japanese Reparations to Southeast Asia[1]
(in millions of U.S. dollars)

	Total Grants			Loans	
	From	To	Total Amount	Amount	Period
Burma	1955	1977	351.1	50	10 yrs.
Thailand	1955	1969	41.8	—	—
Malaysia	1967	—	8.3	—	—
Brunei	—	—	—	—	—
Singapore	1967	—	—	—	—
			17.0		
Indonesia	1958	1969	400[2]	400	20 yrs.
Philippines	1956	1975	550	250	20 yrs.
Laos	1959	1960	2.8	—	—
Cambodia	1959	1961	4.2	—	—
South Vietnam	1960	1964	39	16.6	5 yrs.
Southeast Asia	—	—	1,405.2	725.6	—
Hong Kong	—	—	—	—	—
Taiwan	—	—	—	—	—
South Korea	1966	1975	300	—	—

1. Years indicated are not consistent calendar periods among countries. Source: U.S. Department of State, private communication.
2. Includes $176.91 million trade debt cancelled in 1958.

Aid. Japanese bilateral aid in Southeast Asia, as it followed and overlapped reparations, has had four characteristics seemingly unattractive to the Southeast Asians: (1) there was too little government—as opposed to private—aid, a corollary of which is difficulty in separating what is properly "aid" from government-backed private investment; (2) terms were relatively unfavorable (an average to 1969 of 19.5 years to pay loans at 3.7 percent, with a 6.1 years grace period, as contrasted with the DAC average respectively of 27.8 years, 2.8 percent, and 6.7

years);[20] (3) the aid was tied to the purchase of Japanese products; and (4) low priority was given to technical assistance.

Lately, much of this seems to be changing. Although aid has not been demonstrably very useful to Southeast Asian countries for the solution of basic problems, and problematical as loan repayments may be, it is now apparently believed by Japan to be central to its Southeast Asian foreign policy. As Western aid in the region tapers off, Japan has been promising more. At the 14 April 1972 UNCTAD meeting, Japan pledged to raise its Official Development Assistance to 0.7 percent of GNP.[21] Some Japanese sources have described the rate even in 1971 as 0.96 percent of GNP, but that figure included all transfers, of which government funds were only a small part.[22] In 1969, Foreign Minister Aichi stated his government's desire to double the flow of aid to Asia in the coming five years,[23] and giving clear regional priority to East and Southeast Asia. Masao Sawaki, Consul-General in New York, allowed in 1972 that, east of West Malaysia and excluding Indochina, Japan was "quite prepared to take on the heaviest burdens."[24]

The overall pattern of Japanese aid, as related to aid from all sources, can be seen in Table 2. As with reparations, most aid has gone to Indonesia and the Philippines in Southeast Asia, and to Korea and Taiwan in East Asia. South Asia also has received a large amount not shown in the table. Southeast Asia received only 28.5 percent of total Japanese aid from 1959 to 1968 (not counting reparations). However, if 1969 can be taken as a year exemplifying the new trend, we see that although the same countries predominate, Southeast Asia got 47.3 percent of Japanese Official Development Assistance; and the region received more than twice the ODA figure in export credits in the same year. Thus, aid from Japan has been becoming more important to Southeast Asia and relatively more significant in Japan's overall program in Asia.

However, Japanese aid has been distributed unequally among the various Southeast Asian countries. In examining the proportions of cumulated government-based aid from 1959 through 1968 as part of total DAC (including multilateral) grants from 1960 to 1970, we note the following percentages: for Burma, 63 percent; Thailand, 6 percent; Malaysia and Singapore, negligible; Indonesia, 39.3 percent; the

20. See Kei Wakaizumi, "Japan and Southeast Asia in the 1970's," *Current History*, LX, No. 356 (April 1971), pp. 200–206.
21. *Japan Report*, XVIII, No. 10 (16 May 1972), p. 1.
22. *Japan Report*, XVIII, No. 11 (1 June 1972), p. 2.
23. Saburo Okita, *op. cit.*, p. 96.
24. *Japan Report*, XVIII, No. 11 (1 June 1972), p. 3.

Table 2

Aid to Southeast Asia

(in millions of U.S. dollars)

Countries	All Grants-in-aid (inc. Japanese) (1960–70)[1]	Japanese Aid (1959–1968)[2] Total	Japanese Aid (1959–1968)[2] Gov't. Based	Japanese Aid (1969)[3] Official Development Assistance (calendar 1969)	Japanese Aid (1969)[3] Export Credits (FY 1969–1970)	Development Assistance Committee Aid (1969–91) (average year)[1]
Burma	255.5	180	161	14.8	4.5	28
Thailand	448.4	160	27	14.9	95.8	89.7
Malaysia	208.6	—	—	12.4	31.8	45.5
Brunei	1.5	—	—	—	—	.01
Singapore	40.0	—	—	0.5	42.2	38.5
Indonesia	854.6	451	388	65.8	30.4	457.5
Philippines	558.0	470	256	49.2	164.8	78.9
Laos	595.4	—	—	—	—	69.2
Cambodia	172.4	—	—	3.0	—	23.1
South Vietnam	3,615.1	44	44	0.3	4.6	452
Southeast Asia	6,749.3	1,305	876	160.9	374.1	1,282.4
World Total	42,138.6	4,573	—	339.7	—	7,551.17
Hong Kong	32.2	—	—	—	—	1.1
Taiwan	514.8	183	64	13.5	107.9	13.4
South Korea	2,037.6	442	180	103.5	93.3	330.5

1. Edwin M. Martin, *Development Co-Operation, 1972 Review* (Paris: OECD, 1972), pp. 80–81, 238–41.
2. Saburo Okita, "Japanese Economic Cooperation in Asia in the 1970's," in Gerald L. Curtis, ed., *Japanese American Relations in the 1970's* (Washington: Columbia Books, 1970), p. 97. "Government Based" aid may be assumed to be equivalent to Official Development Assistance, the OECD definition of which is: "All contributions which are administered with the promotion of economic development and welfare of developing countries as the main objective and whose financial terms are intended to be concessional in character."
3. Atsushi Murakami, "Economic Policies of Japan toward Developing Asian Countries: The Role of Japan in Economic Cooperation," *Kobe University Economic Review*, XVII (1971), p. 42.

Philippines, 45.8 percent; South Vietnam, 1.2 percent. For 1969 alone, the same figures approximately were: Burma, 52.8 percent; Thailand, 16.6 percent; Malaysia, 27.2 percent; Singapore, 1.2 percent; Indonesia, 14.3 percent; the Philippines, 62.3 percent; Cambodia, 12.9 percent; South Vietnam, negligible. Except for the special cases of Vietnam (because of the war) and Indonesia (because of heavy American and multilateral commitment and Japanese preference for other forms of assistance than grants there, e.g., joint resources exploitation ventures), Japanese aid of late has been of increasing relative importance to the countries concerned, and absolutely much higher in keeping with Japan's stated goals. Yet, in 1969 Japan expended only 12.5 percent of all DAC aid in Southeast Asia, as compared with 14.4 percent in the average year of the decade before. The huge U.S. aid volume to Vietnam, of course, is largely the reason, but Japan nevertheless cannot be thought of as a super aid-giver to Southeast Asia, even though the terms of aid are being loosened.

Among all the countries of Southeast Asia, Indonesia is becoming the most important in the Japanese aid program. In the 1958–1969 period, Indonesia received $451 million, 34.3 percent of Japanese government-based aid to Southeast Asia. For 1969, the Japanese ODA figure was 40.8 percent, not counting multilateral transfers. Of this aid, government grants and loans, as contrasted with export credits and other private transfers, were far more important, although as time goes on the latter have taken on increased importance. In general, closer economic ties, in aid as well as other terms, have been developing over the past several years. In May 1972, Japan agreed to a government loan of $200 million, over a period of years, plus $100 million of private capital for oil exploration and the Asahan Valley Dam project. In exchange, Indonesia agreed to the supply of 58 million kiloliters of low-sulphur oil to Japan over a ten-year period. Japan thus replaced the United States as Indonesia's largest aid donor.[25]

However, the Philippines throughout the 1960s had been the largest recipient of aid from Japan, $470 million from 1959 to 1968, of which $256 million was government-based aid, that is, 36 percent and 44 percent respectively of Japan's total aid to Southeast Asia. In 1969 Japanese export credits to the Philippines were far more important than ODA (3.35 times as great), and far more important than credits from elsewhere.

25. See Allan A. Samson, "Indonesia 1972," *Asian Survey*, XIII No. 2 (January 1973), p. 136; and *The New York Times*, 28 August 1972, p. 14.

Investment and Trade

Investment. At the end of March 1973, Japanese capital approved for investment abroad totaled $6,773 million, 86 percent of which had been approved since 1965.[26] The Japan External Trade Organization (JETRO) predicted in 1972 that by 1980 Japan would be the second largest international investor after the United States, providing a total of $25 to $30 billion. JETRO cites the following factors as causal in its forecast: (1) Japan's mounting demand for raw-material resources; (2) domestic problems of industrial location and tightness of the labor market; and (3) increasing foreign interest in encouraging Japanese investment (including import-substitution policies).[27]

To the present, Japan's investment in the world manufacturing sector has been low (27 percent in value of all Japanese investment) in comparison with that of other developed countries, and most of it has gone to Asian and Latin American countries (63 percent altogether). Japanese investment overall in developing countries, however, is comparatively high (50 percent), most of it concentrated in primary and tertiary activities.[28] However, the investment pattern in manufacturing is rising and diversifying, and moving from light industry toward the heavy and chemical industry sector.[29]

Through 1969–70, southern and eastern Asia's share of Japanese foreign investment was 22.5 percent (80 percent of which was in Southeast Asia proper), as compared with North America's 26.3 percent; Western Europe's 11.2 percent; and Latin America's 19.1 percent. In this period, 38.5 percent of Japanese foreign investment in southern and eastern Asia went into mining and 49.4 percent to all primary production. Manufacturing investment was concentrated in textiles (35 percent of manufacturing investment), metals (15.7 percent), and electrical machinery (5 percent). Tertiary sectors accounted for 39.5 percent, finance and insurance being most important.[30]

26. See U.S. Department of State News Release, "Japanese Overseas Private Investment—Growth and Change," 23 October 1973. Consult also the tabulated data in Table 3.

27. JETRO information derived from a U.S. State Department airgram (Ref: Tokyo A-599, 13 June 1972), which summarizes the Japanese-language, JETRO *White Paper on Japanese Investment in 1972.*

28. GATT, *Japan's Economic Expansion and Foreign Trade 1955 to 1970*, GATT Studies in International Trade, No. 2 (Geneva: GATT, 1971), pp. 44–45.

29. JETRO, *op. cit.*

30. GATT, *op. cit.* See also United Nations ECAFE, *Economic Survey of Asia and the Far East* (Bangkok: ECAFE, 1971), pp. 27–28. The proportion of direct investment in Southeast Asia is from A. Murakami, "The Economic Policies of Japan toward Developing Asian Countries: The Role of Japan in Economic Cooperation," *Kobe University Economic Review*, XVII (1971), p. 42.

Japan's investment in Southeast Asia has represented about 31 percent of world investment in the region, and the proportion is increasing. Thus, although only about 7 percent of all world foreign investment has been going to Southeast Asia, Japan accounts for nearly one-third of it. Southeast Asia, in short, is considerably more important as an investment target to Japan than to the world at large.

Of course, there are differences among the Southeast Asian countries (see Table 3). As a group, Burma and the Indo-Chinese countries have received little Japanese or even world private investment since World War II. Japanese investment in Thailand, while only 8 percent of Japanese investment in Southeast Asia in 1973, was relatively very important to the Thai economy. Japan also is emerging as a significant investor in Malaysia, accounting for about 10 percent of all foreign investment. Most recent investment there has been of the import-substitution type in light manufacturing and in primary-products processing. However, Japan's investment in Brunei (not part of the Federation of Malaysia) was nearly 100 percent of all foreign investment, 83.5 percent of which was in the form of loan capital, exclusively in the oil and gas industry. Singapore has in recent years actively sought investment from Japan and the world. Investment from Japan between 1951 and 1969 totaled only 13 percent of all foreign investment, but from 1969 to 1972 the total more than doubled and the percentage nearly so; and equity capital has come to almost triple loan capital. The bulk of these investments have gone into light industries and trade and services.[31]

Foreign investment of any kind is particularly important to Indonesia. The pre-*Gestapu* economic decline only accentuated the fact of Indonesia's low domestic investment capability, and because of debt servicing, its paucity of foreign exchange. Indonesia is preëminent in Japanese foreign investment in Southeast Asia, receiving 49.9 percent of that investment through 31 March 1973, with a 10-to-1 rate of loan-to-equity capital through 1969.[32] Japanese investment from 1965–6 through June 1970 (12.2 percent of the total foreign) was 51.1 percent in mining. By contrast, the United States devoted 78.6 percent of a total investment to mining, more than three times that of Japan. Japan invested an amount of the same order of magnitude, but nearly three times the American percentage (30.6 versus 11.5) of her total investments were manufacturing, especially textiles.

To an even greater extent and with a broader spread, the United

31. Asian Development Bank, *Southeast Asia's Economy in the 1970's*, (N.Y.: Praeger, 1971), pp. 402–4.

32. *Economic Survey of Asia and the Far East, 1970* (Bangkok, 1971), pp. 35–37.

Table 3

Investment in Southeast Asia

Countries	World Private Investment (to end of 1967)[1] (U.S. $ Mil.)	Japanese Investment Growth (1969–72) (percent)	Japanese Private Investment[2]		Japanese Private Investment (1951–69)[4] (U.S. $ Mil.)				
			No. of Cases (to April 1972)	Amount (to April 1973) (U.S. $ Mil.)	Equity	Loans	Total Gross	Total Net	Average Volume Per Project
Burma	9.7	—	—	.44	—	—	.44	—	.055
Thailand	210.7	128	273	129	52.51	25.52	78.03	68.91	.365
Malaysia	679.4	174	137	76	23.34	12.36	35.70	24.70	.418
Brunei	85.5	0	11	86	14.21	72.10	86.31	86.31	9.589
Singapore	182.8	203	152	90	17.37	6.25	23.62	14.80	.304
Indonesia	254.0	184	135	473	17.49	175.34	192.83	150.50	4.192
Philippines	722.7	175	90	88	10.92	33.73	44.65	18.12	.721
Laos	8.3	—	8	1[3]	—	—	4.25	—	.179
Cambodia	83.9	1,000	3	1[3]	—	—	0.1	—	.250
South Vietnam	152.1	3,000	11	3[3]	—	—	0.1	—	.136
Southeast Asia	2,389.1	158	820	947.44	135.84	325.3	462.85	363.34	av.=.913
World Total	34,232.4	—	4,922	6,773	—	—	—	—	.850
Hong Kong	285.1	361	336	100	18.11	1.28	19.39	16.62	.093
Taiwan	147.5	161	441	108	52.93	7.27	60.20	57.89	.168
South Korea	78	407	710	207	11.75	3.27	15.02	12.13	.492

1. Edwin M. Martin, *Development Co-Operation, 1972 Review* (Paris: OECD, 1972), pp. 80–81.
2. Ministry of Finance, Japan.
3. April 1972.
4. United Nations ECAFE, *Economic Survey of Asia and the Far East, 1970* (Bangkok: ECAFE, 1971), pp. 23–26.

States dominates foreign investment in the Philippines. Most of the foreign investment is in timber, manufacturing, and mining; but domestic investment is far more important. It accounted for 82.5 percent of all investment through 1969, with the U.S. providing 12.5 percent of all investment; Spain, 0.8 percent; Taiwan, 0.5 percent; and Japan, a mere 0.3 percent.[33] Japanese business expansion has been severely hampered by the lack of a treaty of commerce between the two countries, as a result of which the establishment of branches of Japanese companies is illegal. The Philippines accordingly has a relatively small place in Japan's investment pattern in Southeast Asia (9.3 percent of total investment through fiscal 1972, a small decline from the 1951–1969 percentage). As with the other countries in which resources exploitation rather than the sale of manufactures is the objective, loan capital from Japan to the Philippines has far exceeded equity investment (a ratio of three-to-one through 1969).

It is important to note that equity capital has been far more important in the considerable Japanese investment in East Asia, in Hong Kong, Taiwan, and South Korea. In fact, the fastest growth rates in Japanese investments in Asia are found in South Korea and Hong Kong. The largest overall investment among the three is in Taiwan. All three of these areas are and can be expected to continue to be severe competitors of the Southeast Asian countries for Japanese manufacturing investments aimed at reexport.

Trade. The phenomenally rapid growth of Japan's trade is well known.[34] Imports rose from $2,340 million in 1936 to $3,230 million in 1956 to $23,395.3 million in 1972. Exports have grown in the same years from $2,262 million to $2,503 million to $28,419.3 million.[35] These changes have followed spectacular growth in the economy,

33. See Asian Development Bank, *Southeast Asia's Economy in the 1970s*, *op. cit.*, Table 4, Chapter Five. However, in 1965 31.8 percent of the stock of capital was foreign-owned, along with about 70 percent of the largest corporations, according to ECAFE, *op. cit.*, p. 43.

34. See Hla Myint, "The Inward and Outward Looking Countries of Southeast Asia and the Economic Future of the Region," in *Japan's Future in Southeast Asia* (Kyoto: Kyōdai Center for Southeast Asian Studies, 1966) for a discussion of Japanese trade motivations and the meaning of import substitution to Japan's trade policies in Southeast Asia.

35. 1936 figures in 1956 dollars. See Arthur W. Mercer, *A Comparison of the Pattern of Japanese Foreign Trade*, unpublished M.A. Thesis, Department of Geography, University of Chicago, 1960, pp. 31–32, 35–36; JETRO, *White Paper on International Trade 1973*, (Tokyo: JETRO, 1973), pp. 149–164. The data for the prewar period are only roughly comparable to the recent postwar data, of course. Table 4 summarizes the data in a somewhat different way, using 1934–36, 1938, 1958, 1963, 1970, and 1972 statistics.

Table 4

Japanese Trade with Southeast Asia
(in millions of U.S. dollars)

Countries	1934–36 Average[1] Im-ports	1934–36 Average[1] Ex-ports	1958[2] Im-ports	1958[2] Ex-ports	1963[2] Im-ports	1963[2] Ex-ports	1968[2] Im-ports	1968[2] Ex-ports	1970[2] Im-ports	1970[2] Ex-ports	1972[3] Im-ports	1972[3] Ex-ports	Percentage Growth of Trade with Japan (1958–72)
Burma	N.A.[4]	N.A.	12.3	41.4	20.1	76.3	12.4	39.3	13	39	23.8	44.0	126
Thailand	1.5	10.7	21.7	83.8	90.7	181	147	365.4	190	449	252.1	522.2	734
Malaysia	23.8	.5	159.3	14.3	269.9	56.2	343.4	104.5	419	167	395.5	263.9	380
Brunei	—	—	—	—	—	—	—	—	—	—	101.7	15.8	—
Singapore	0	16.5	12.7	77.2	22.4	111.9	61.8	209.2	87	423	120.9	701.5	802
Indonesia	24.6	41.6	37	49	104.8	49.1	251.8	146.6	637	316	1,197.5	615.5	2,108
Philippines	7.6	13.1	99.8	89.5	230.2	150.3	397.9	411.1	534	454	470.4	457.4	490
Laos	N.A.	1.1 (Laos, Cambodia, South Vietnam combined)			—	—	—	—	—	—	—	—	—
Cambodia	N.A.		1.4	8.4	3.9	14.5	6.6	20.3	6	11	1.9	11.2	134
South Vietnam	N.A.		1.3	39.5	6	33.3	2.7	198.9	5	146	13.9	104.7	291
Southeast Asia	57.5	83.5	345.5	403.1	748	672.6	1,220.9	1,495.3	1,891	2,005	2,577.7	2,536.2	683
World Total	955.4	932.6	3,033.0	2,877.0	5,710	5,452	10,870	12,970	18,883	19,319	23,375.3	28,419.3	877
Hong Kong	0.7	13.6	10.6	100.1	28.8	246.4	54	467.6	700	92	119.4	909.7	930
Taiwan	92	61.7	75.6	90	122.6	107.1	150.7	471.6	700	251	421.9	1,090.6	913
South Korea (1934–36)	136.4	159.1	11	56.7	26.9	159.7	101.6	602.7	229	818	426	979.8	2,077
U.S.A.	234.5	147.7	980	690	1,840	1,520	2,930	4,130	—	—	5,848.8	8,838.4	879

1. Warren Hunsberger, *Japan and the United States in World Trade* (New York: Harper and Row for the Council on Foreign Relations, 1964), pp. 184–85. All table figures in dollars of the years indicated.
2. Saburo Okita, "Japanese Economic Cooperation in Asia in the 1970's," in Gerald L. Curtis, ed., *Japanese-American Relations in the 1970s* (Washington: Columbia Books, 1970), p. 101; and *Ibid.*, pp. 410–11.
3. JETRO, *White Paper on International Trade 1973* (Tokyo: JETRO. 1973), pp. 149–64.
4. N.A.: Not available.

whose primary base in the postwar period was the domestic market.[36] Thus, the percentage of the GNP at market prices contributed by imports and exports were 10.5 percent and 11.3 percent respectively in 1959, and 9.4 percent and 11 percent respectively in 1969, while at 1965 market prices growth in GNP in those ten years was at the rate of 29 percent per year.[37]

The commodity composition of Japan's world foreign trade has changed significantly as well. Of imports, food imports declined from 23 percent of the total in 1936, to 22 percent in 1956, and to only 15.2 percent in 1972 by value; and the mix had changed as paddy imports ceased and other grains, partly for animal feed, and meat products replaced it. Raw materials rose from 50 to 54 to 55 percent of imports, with fossil fuels taking the lead; and manufactures rose from 23 to 25 to 29 percent. Exports showed even greater change in composition over the years: food exports declined from 9.2 percent in 1936, to 7.2 percent in 1956, to 2.3 percent in 1972. Raw materials similarly plummeted from 18 to 4 to 0.9 percent of total exports. Textiles slumped from 28 to 25 to 10.2 percent, but machines and transportation equipment exports jumped from 7 to 19 to 53.9 percent from 1936 to 1956 to 1972. Similarly, metals went from 5 to 11 to 17 percent of exports in the respective years.[38]

In the 1962 to 1969 period, food imports from developing countries increased their share of Japan's total food imports from 30 to 34 percent; but southern and eastern Asia's share dropped from 19 to 17 percent of the total. Similarly, the developing countries in the sixties increased their share of the growing fuel import market from 66 to 74 percent; but southern and eastern Asia's share remained the same, at 10 percent, although it rose gradually thereafter as Indonesian, Malaysian, and Brunei production increased (see Table 6).

Among exports, the only categories in which the proportion going to developing nations increased were textiles and primary products. For all commodity exports, the proportion going from Japan to developing countries declined from 45 to 39 percent (and to southern and eastern Asia from 31 to 27 percent) between 1962 and 1969.[39]

In other words, in the sixties Japanese imports from the Third World

36. See Leon Hollerman, *Japan's Dependence on the World Economy* (Princeton: Princeton University Press, 1967), p. 61.

37. United Nations, *Statistical Yearbook for Asia and the Far East* (ECAFE: Bangkok, 1971), p. 161.

38. Mercer, *loc. cit.*; JETRO, *Trade White Paper, loc. cit.* Table 5 summarizes the data according to the years 1934–36, 1966, and 1972.

39. Table 6 examines Japan's total and Southeast Asian trade by commodity categories for the years 1934–36, 1966, and 1972.

Table 5

Japanese Trade with Southeast Asia by Commodity
(in percentages of the trade with each country)

Countries	Foodstuffs				Raw Materials (excl. mineral fuels)			Mineral Fuels	
	Imports		Exports		Imports		Exports	Imports	
	1966[1]	1972[2]	1966[1]	1972[2]	1966[2]	1972[2]	1972[2,5]	1966[1]	1972[2]
Burma	77.0	20.4	0.6	1.3	18.9	37.6	neg.	neg.	4.9
Thailand	49.7	44.9	0.3	neg.	48.2	33.5	1.7	neg.	neg.
Malaysia	3.8	6.3	10.7	2.1	78.8	65.6	1.0	1.8	1.3
Brunei	neg.[4]	neg.	neg.	0.2	neg.	neg.	1.1	N.A.	99.5
Singapore	neg.	3.4	2.8	1.8	30.2	8.7	1.0	63.2	71.6
Indonesia	3.6	5.1	0.9	2.9	38.5	27.0	0.9	56.5	65.3
Philippines	6.0	15.1	4.7	3.6	93.2	80.6	2.0	neg.	N.A.
Laos	N.A.[3]	N.A.	N.A.	N.A.	N.A.	N.A.	N.A.	N.A.	N.A.
Cambodia	neg.	neg.	2.7	3.8	N.A.	91.1	neg.	neg.	neg.
South Vietnam	N.A.	39.3	0.7	6.4	N.A.	56.6	0.6	N.A.	neg.
Hong Kong	18.7	17.2	3.1	3.1	35.0	9.9	1.6	neg.	neg.
Taiwan	88.0	46.5	1.2	1.9	9.6	13.8	2.0	neg.	2.2
South Korea	36.1	21.6	neg.	neg.	44.5	24.6	3.7	6.4	4.0

1. Japan, *Japan Statistical Yearbook* 1966 (Tokyo: Government of Japan), 1967, pp. 302–5.
2. JETRO, *White Paper on International Trade 1973* (Tokyo: JETRO, 1973), *loc. cit.*
3. Datum not available at place of writing.
4. Negligible.
5. Comparable data for 1966 not readily available.

Table 5 *(continued)*

Countries	Chemicals				Machinery				Other Manufactures		
	Imports		Exports		Imports		Exports		Imports	Exports	
	1966[1]	1972[2]	1966[1]	1972[2]	1966[1]	1972[2]	1966[1]	1972[2]	1972[2]	1966[1]	1972[2]
Burma	neg.	neg.	5.2	5.2	N.A.	neg.	25.4	55.8	neg.	56.4	22.9
Thailand	1.1	neg.	8.6	15.8	neg.	neg.	38.0	48.9	16.0	43.5	33.0
Malaysia	0.6	neg.	5.6	7.9	0.6	neg.	35.0	56.8	26.8	41.4	26.5
Brunei	N.A.	neg.	N.A.	3.1	N.A.	neg.	N.A.	50.8	neg.	N.A.	2.6
Singapore	0.4	neg.	5.0	5.0	neg.	8.9	21.5	47.3	1.8	54.8	44.1
Indonesia	0.7	neg.	7.9	12.4	neg.	neg.	37.8	43.9	1.1	38.8	38.9
Philippines	0.6	neg.	8.5	12.9	neg.	neg.	33.9	39.8	N.A.	45.1	40.0
Laos	N.A.	N.A.	N.A.	N.A.	N.A.	N.A.	N.A.	N.A.	N.A.	N.A.	N.A.
Cambodia	neg.	neg.	9.2	6.0	N.A.	neg.	43.6	63.0	neg.	26.9	26.7
South Vietnam	neg.	neg.	5.1	5.0	N.A.	neg.	17.3	30.8	neg.	64.6	58.1
Hong Kong	2.1	4.2	8.5	9.0	2.1	4.1	18.5	34.0	50.5	53.0	51.6
Taiwan	1.2	neg.	15.0	19.2	neg.	14.7	40.9	45.5	36.0	35.3	35.9
South Korea	neg.	2.7	28.0	19.1	neg.	5.8	23.9	39.3	31.5	20.8	39.2

Table 6

Japanese Southeast Asia and World Trade by Commodity
(in U.S. $ millions and percentages)

Trade Categories	Food-stuffs	Raw Materials	Mineral Fuels	Chemicals	Machinery	Other
			1966			
Imports						
From S.E. Asia	107.0	565.0	106.7	5.8	0.5	N.A.[2]
From World	1,958.0	3,194.3	1,612.6	404.8	705.4	3,540.4
% S. E. Asian	5.5	17.7	6.6	1.2	Neg.	N.A.
Exports						
To S. E. Asia	26.0	Neg.[1]	Neg.	72.3	319.8	448.3
To World	341.0	Neg.	Neg.	542.4	2,620.9	3,585.6
% S. E. Asian	7.6	Neg.	Neg.	13.3	12.2	12.5
			1972			
Imports						
From S. E. Asia	284.3	1,089.9	975.0	Neg.	17.6	148.5
From World	3,556.1	7,182.4	5,685.1	1,146.4	2,596.9	1,941.8
% S. E. Asian	8.0	15.2	17.2	Neg.	0.7	7.6
Exports						
To S. E. Asia	62.1	31.4	Neg.	281.7	1,260.0	1,059.3
To World	653.6	255.8	Neg.	1,762.0	15,318.0	10,174.1
% S. E. Asian	9.5	12.2	Neg.	16.0	8.2	10.4

1. Negligible.
2. Datum not available.

increased 31 percent in share of total imports; but imports from southern and eastern Asia kept about the same share of Japan's total imports. The trend in Japanese exports has been away from the developing countries (which dropped 6 percentage points) and away, but not so drastically, from southern and eastern Asian countries (a drop in 2 percentage points). Thus, even as Japan is becoming decreasingly trade-dependent on Asia, she has now become the world's largest market for raw materials and fuels, and has increased her share in world exports of manufactures from 3.8 percent in 1955 to 9 percent in 1969.[40]

Although Southeast Asia's share of Japan's imports increased from 6 percent in the mid-thirties to 11 percent in 1972, recent trends have been downward or stable from the peak of 13 percent in 1963. Similarly, Southeast Asia took 8.9 percent of Japan's exports in the mid-thirties and 8.9 percent in 1972, but the latter figure represents a decline from 14 percent in 1958. Thus, the Southeast Asia trade, after peaking in the early sixties, appears to be declining in significance to Japan as time goes on.

On the other hand, the Japan trade appears to be of even increasing significance to Southeast Asia. In the late 1930s, Japan's imports from Southeast Asia were only about 7.5 percent of that region's total exports. In 1958, this percentage had increased to 9 percent, in 1963 to 16 percent, in 1968 to 23.6 percent, and in 1971 to about 28 percent. Meanwhile, Southeast Asia's imports from Japan were 14.5 percent of its imports from the world in the late thirties, decreasing slightly to 14 percent in 1958, rising to 18.5 percent in 1963, to 22 percent in 1968, and to about 25 percent in 1971. Trade between Southeast Asia and Japan in the late sixties and early seventies, moreover, has been weighted slightly in favor of Japan.

These aggregates, however, cover significant variations in trade relations among the various Southeast Asian countries, which may be seen by interested students of the subject in Tables 4 through 6. In 1972, Japan's exports to Southeast Asia were chiefly to Singapore, Indonesia, Thailand, and the Philippines (between 1.5 and 2.5 percent each of all exports), as compared with 1.2 percent to Taiwan, 3.4 to Korea, 3.2 to Hong Kong, 2.1 to China, and 31.1 to the U.S.A. Imports came chiefly from Indonesia (5.1 percent of world imports), the Philippines (2.0), and Thailand (1.1), as contrasted with 2.1 percent from China and 35.1 percent from the U.S.A.[41] In general, there is a trend toward increasing imports by Southeast Asian countries of heavier machinery and relatively lesser emphasis on light industrial and consumer products. In its turn, Japan imports increasing quantities of raw materials from Indonesia and Thailand, but decreasing amounts from Malaysia and the Philippines.

40. GATT, *Japan's Economic Expansion, op. cit.*, pp. 38–41.
41. JETRO, *Trade White Paper, loc. cit.*

Perspectives on the Future

The foregoing discussion illuminates a basic contradiction in Japan-Southeast Asian relations, the increasing importance of Japan to Southeast Asia on the one hand, and on the other, the relative decline in economic importance to Japan of Southeast Asia, as Japan's trade moves toward geographical and commodity diversification. How might this contradiction be resolved?

One possibility is simply that these economic trends will continue and that Japan will increase her trade and other economic relationships with developing countries other than those in Asia, but particularly with the developed countries, including, of course, the United States. It is significant in this connection not only that Japan is almost uniquely dependent upon foreign trade for most of her raw materials, but also that some 60 percent of those raw materials already come from the already developed countries.[42]

That this percentage will increase seems almost certain,[43] and it is in keeping with at least one plausible scenario at the world scale, in which the several great "developed" nodes in the world order (North America, Western Europe, the Soviet bloc, and Japan) will continue to become increasingly dependent upon one another and proportionally less dependent upon the poorer countries. The result of such a trend would be even more marked division of one world into two, that is, a First World of the developed countries intimately related in terms of trade and capital flows, and a Second World of the poorer countries which will be left increasingly to their own devices. That there are obvious flaws in this portrait is apparent, especially when one takes into account the distribution of the world's known petroleum resources, but the argument still has merit. The comparative self-sufficiency of the developed countries in terms of major natural resources is almost universally underestimated, especially since petroleum clouds the thinking of even the most objective student of the problem. One must consider not only the still vast resource endowment (including agricultural) of the United States, but also those of Canada, even Western Europe, and certainly European Russia and Eastern Europe, and perhaps most significant for Japan itself, Soviet Siberia and Australia. Although certain important raw materials other than petroleum are more readily accessible (technologically) in the developing countries, there are remarkably few such resources that, at lower grades of ores for example, are not found in abundance in the de-

42. Okita, *op. cit.*, p. 105.

43. Although the rate of increase will slow as a result of the transformation of petroleum prices shortly after this was written.

veloped countries—and this does not take into account the as yet undetermined wealth of the continental shelves, the continental slopes, and the floor of the great ocean, which is accessible only to those countries with the technological capability of tapping it.

However, in assessing the prospects for the further evolution of Japan-Southeast Asian commercial relations, it is necessary to take into account both Japan's position among the developed regions of the world as being uniquely dependent on foreign raw materials, *and* the comparative resource wealth and proximity of Southeast Asia, especially since, as the GATT study observes, distance is a key factor in determining trade patterns, although by no means the dominant one.[44] Southeast Asia presents unusual opportunities for providing many of the raw materials Japan requires—certain kinds of timber, petroleum, animal feed, and a variety of minerals. Equally important is Japan's specialization in a limited array of exported manufactured producers' goods which lend themselves, albeit in part through protectionist measures adopted by the importing countries, to an ever more rapid transfer of technology and economic modernization as measured by the increasing importance of the manufactural sector in several Asian countries. Evidence of these latter trends is greatest, to be sure, in the former Japanese dependencies of South Korea and Taiwan, but it appears also in the cases of certain Southeast Asian countries such as Thailand and Singapore, and even the Philippines, as well as Hong Kong, the political future of which, of course, is darkly clouded.

These circumstances must be associated also with the growing labor shortages in Japan and the concomitant increases in labor costs, which drive certain kinds of industry to areas outside of Japan where labor costs are lower and presumptive skills high. Such areas are not as likely to be found in Africa and Latin America as they are in Asia. Of course, these factors have been at work most conspicuously in the neighboring areas best known to the Japanese where, *inter alia*, the Japanese language can still be employed—again Korea and Taiwan,[45] but the case of the "Third China," Singapore, is illustrative of the probably more limited, but still substantial, possibilities farther south.

This reasoning suggests intensified relationships between Japan and the Southeast Asian countries, *ceteris paribus*, on reasonably objective

44. GATT, *op. cit.*, p. 29.

45. The importance of familiarity and longevity in commerical relations is suggested by Chie Nakane when she writes: "The widely observed Japanese ethic is that, once firmly established, a relationship should be maintained even (sic) despite economic loss. Such a loss, however, may be offset in the long run, since the . . . relationship develops a high credit relationship benefiting mutual interests." *Japanese Society* (Berkeley: University of California Press, 1970), pp. 98–99.

economic grounds alone, admittedly leading to the greater dependency of Southeast Asia on Japan, but not necessarily the reverse. However, there also are non-economic factors at work, which relate to the perception held by the Japanese (to the extent that over 100 million people can be said to share a perception at all) of their role as an Asian power.

Japan is not just another developed country or even a remarkable one; it is an *Asian* developed country, and it sees itself as such in spite of its acceptance by the West as almost one of its own. Moreover, the Japanese seem inordinately preoccupied with their neighbors and therefore with their relations, actual and potential, with them. The frequency with which references appear in the literature to Japan's special role in Asia is remarkable. Okita, for example, says: "It is inevitable that the future course of the Japanese economy will influence the economies of these (Asian) nations. In turn, this makes it necessary that Japanese domestic policies be considered in the wider perspective of their impact upon the economies of the region."[46] If economic self-interest alone predominates, need a *keizai taikoku* have to worry about such things? Wakaizumi also writes: "Japan must make a positive contribution to the building of the foundations for peace and security in Asia through cooperation with the developing nations of the continent."[47]

These quotations illustrate the feelings of special responsibility that Japanese seem to feel toward the rest of Asia, and particularly those parts of it about which they know the most and with which they have had the most experience, namely East Asia and Southeast Asia.[48] South Asia appears considerably removed in degree, at least if not in kind, from these nearer regions, and indeed to many Japanese, India and Pakistan appear not to be properly Asian at all but something else, Middle Eastern perhaps. In any event, such feelings appear to be a consequence of a mixture of guilt and sentiment on the one hand, and on the other, the perception of a Japan-centered world view in which

46. Okita, *op. cit.*

47. K. Wakaizumi, "Japan and Southeast Asia in the 1970s," *Current History* Vol. LX (April 1971), p. 201.

48. To the extent that most of the Asia with which the Japanese are preoccupied is south of Japan, the unfortunate phrase "the North-South problem" rings true in Japanese ears; but obviously, Indonesia is north of Australia and North Dakota of Texas. Reference to the middle-latitudes as contrasted with the inter-tropical regions has somewhat greater merit, but even that simplistic dichotomy is gainsaid by China, the greatest of the underdeveloped countries, less than 10 percent of which lies south of the Tropic of Cancer and only a fourth of which lies south of Japan itself. Clearly, these Japanese who use the phrase must regard China as falling into some category other than the "South," and they are right. Japan's traditional view of her role in Asia has been to regard China as requiring special arrangements, and the Nan Yō as the region in which the expansion of Japanese interests is "natural."

the distance-decay gradient, as weighted by cultural variables, is remarkably steep over-all, trade patterns (as vis-à-vis the U.S.) to the contrary.

In that view, Southeast Asia would appear to be of considerably greater "value," though not necessarily on readily demonstrable economic grounds than, say, South Asia, let alone Africa and Latin America, just as Korea and Taiwan would take precedence in turn over Southeast Asia itself. That this perception may lead to biases toward Southeast Asia in Japan's economic policies seems apparent, and that these would draw Southeast Asia into further dependency upon Japan as market and source of technology and capital seems indeed inevitable.

This discussion could not be complete without reference to the future relationships between China and Japan. The recent détente and rapprochement between the two countries point to a rapid expansion of trade between the two countries. The naive view of China simply as 800 million customers is held by very few Japanese, but the notion of a "special relationship" between the two countries is held by many. As a comparatively disciplined, rapidly developing, but very poor country of highly accomplished and motivated people, China is not likely to be satisfied with the role of supplier of raw materials (e.g., petroleum, tin, precious metals, and soybeans) and importer of consumers' goods as is Indonesia, for example, also a huge country, but hardly beyond puberty in the life-cycle of nation-states. And China's terms are likely to be far harder than any other of Japan's Asian trading partners, whatever their rhetoric. The probability of joint enterprises in which the contributions from both parties are large seems much greater in the case of China and Japan than between Japan and any other countries. Indeed, it is likely that the perceived and real interests of the two countries will converge over time.

This convergence should have some effect on Southeast Asia, the markets of which already are being penetrated, albeit modestly, by Chinese manufactured goods, both consumers' and producers', in reasonably successful competition with Japanese products, though not on the same scale. From the standpoint of China, Southeast Asia also means "special interests," and China's perspective has far longer historical precedent than that of Japan. It is probable that the two countries will continue to compete for both markets and influence in that great region, with China increasing her strength in the mainland Southeast Asian countries and Japan doing better in insular Southeast Asia, in short, the two sub-areas forming recognized or implied "sub-spheres of influence."

An increasingly effective rapprochement between the two countries over the next decade or two, however, could mean a reconciliation of their competitive positions in Southeast Asia and their cooperation in joint ventures of comprehensive resources development and industrial management. Such a prospect would scarcely be comforting to the political elites in Southeast Asia, especially if the region remains as fragmented as it now is, but it might in turn lend support to the as yet weak attempts at regional integration and development, as expressed by ASEAN. In that case, a partnership working toward development might evolve, whereby Japan, China, and ASEAN would become increasingly involved in a broad tripartite regional system that would be unique in the world and increasingly independent of the rest of it.

In any event, the thrust of Japan's current policies is toward the evolution, not necessarily deliberate, of some sort of regional economic system incorporating most of Southeast Asia, South Korea, Taiwan, and Japan,[49] in which Japan would be the dominant partner and metropole and China would become increasingly involved.

All this is, of course, futurological speculation, but it ought not to be discussed as *mere* speculation. Regional futures are as much a part of the study of international relations as regional pasts; and they evolve from those pasts in ways that may only seem comprehensible after they have come to be. Effective national policies depend on attempting to achieve such comprehension earlier rather than later. And in the process, "retrospective futurology" has its role to play.

49. No doubt embedded in some yet broader regional framework in which Australia would have to be included.

Economic Relations in Southeast Asia and the Position of Japan

Tadashi Kawata

Change in the Development Policies of Southeast Asian Countries

Japan, the sole industrialized country in Asia, is heavily enmeshed in interdependent economic relations with the Southeast Asian countries. The economic development problems of this region are problems of Japan's *neighbors*, and it is in this particular perspective that Japan's economic relations with Southeast Asian countries should be viewed. The Sino-American rapprochement, China's reinstatement on the world stage, normalization of diplomatic relations between Japan and China, and the end of the Vietnam conflict increasingly have intensified the military and political fluidity in Southeast Asia. And although the growth potential of Southeast Asian countries is generally estimated to be greater than that of other developing countries, such problems as the conspicuous shortage of foreign currencies and the dilemmas of economic development are still enormous. These factors make it difficult for us to prognosticate the political and economic situation of the area in the 1970s.

The industrialization strategy pursued by the Southeast Asian countries in the 1960s generally sought to foster import-substitution industries, but by the beginning of the 1970s circumstances compelled a reassessment of this policy throughout the region. Almost all of the

Southeast Asian countries, except Hong Kong and Singapore, still remain in a state of "Asian poverty." Their comparatively high rate of economic growth in the last ten years has been offset or even overtaken by explosive population increases. Population control and family planning ended as virtual failures. The succession of hostilities, internal conflicts, and the like compelled even essentially agricultural countries (with only one or two exceptions) to spend precious foreign currencies for importing foods. The Philippines had introduced the new grains and technical improvements of the so-called "Green Revolution" hoping to attain self-sufficiency in foods. But she, too, is facing serious food problems as the result of the unexpected weather of 1972. Moreover, the "Green Revolution" and other new techniques require farmers to invest a large sum of working capital. And since it is only a limited group of wealthy farmers who can provide such capital, the gulf in income between wealthy farmers and poor peasants is becoming even greater. Land reform could be one effective measure to do away with this gulf, but land reform bills tend to be mutilated by the wealthy farmers and land-owners who control politics. Hence, no appreciable improvements have taken place.

In addition, the import-substitution policy, pursued by introducing enormous funds from abroad, only resulted in a bigger trade deficit and the accumulation of foreign liabilities, thus making the development dilemma of Southeast Asian countries even more serious. On top of the great import demand caused by what was intended to be an import-substitution policy, the decline in prices for primary products, which are the major export commodity, was an added headache. And contrary to first expectations, the promotion of import-substitution industries proved unsuccessful in increasing labor utilization, bringing extremely limited relief to the unemployment problem.

Because of the ineffectiveness of the industrial policy of import-substitution, the Southeast Asian countries in the 1970s began seeking to shift from an import-substitution policy to an export-intensive policy, with the primary emphasis placed upon the promotion of exports in order to gain foreign currencies. At the same time, such a policy should lay stress on the promotion of agriculture, increase of employment, and correction of regional differences, rather than merely pushing for industrialization.[1]

1. It is worthy to note here that *Southeast Asia's Economy in the 1970s* (Asian Development Bank, 1971), edited by Professor Hla Myint, is regarded as the book which exerted a great influence upon this change in policy. The so-called "Myint Report" is based on the recognition of the failure of the import substitution policy of the 1960s, and it finds the driving force for the new economic development in obtaining foreign curren-

This change in policy has already been reflected in the various social and economic development projects recently adopted by the Southeast Asian countries. For example, the points generally stressed throughout the countries involved are, first, to raise the gross national product; second, to promote agriculture and the associated agricultural processing industries; third, to expand employment projects in the fields related to infrastructure; fourth, to encourage labor-intensive industries; and fifth, to reduce differences between cities and villages. At present, no significant effects of these policy changes have yet become evident. The Southeast Asian countries are struggling just as before; but it is quite clear that their policies have changed from import-substitution industrialization to export promotion. This shift might intensify export competition among the Southeast Asian countries themselves in the future, but it is believed that the tendency toward economic independence will no doubt be fostered in their economic relations with industrialized nations, and that they will also make efforts to improve presently unbalanced trade relations. Furthermore, the unlimited dependence on foreign capital evident in the 1960s are bound to be modified toward a course of controlling foreign capital within the framework of domestic economic development.

Western Capital Invested in Southeast Asia

Britain was the leading foreign capital investor in the Asian and Pacific area from the end of the Second World War until the middle of the 1950s when the United States took over that position. The United States continued to increase and accumulate foreign capital investments thereafter. In the 1960s, Japanese capital, chiefly for manufacturing enterprises, made a remarkable advance in the region. Yet, 1971 data show that the investment balance by U.S. enterprises in the ECAFE developing region including Korea and Formosa amounts approximately to $3 billion, or $7 billion when Australasia is added.[2] It is indeed a colossal sum, we must say, especially when we compare the

---

cies by means of increasing exports of agricultural products and primary resources or full- and half-processed resources, as well as in creating reproduction cycles for agricultural and light industries.

2. According to *Survey of Current Business*, the cumulative balance of U.S. investments for Asia in 1971 reached $4,866 million by the end of the year, $3,048 million when Japan is excluded, and $6,960 million in the Asian and Pacific region when U.S. investment in Australasia (which is $3,912 million) is added. This is approximately 8 percent of the total balance ($86 billion) of overseas investments in 1971, which seems to be a small percentage. However, within the Asian and Pacific region, the cumulative balance of U.S. investments is conspicuously bigger than that of other countries.

amount with the investment balance of Japanese enterprises for the same period (March 1972) which amounts to $1,030 million, or $1,420 million if Australasia is included.[3]

American economic aid will be continuously extended to the entire Southeast Asian region in the future. Along with the aid, direct investment by big U.S. enterprises will continue to increase, especially in the form of multinational enterprises. Priority will be given to the exploitation of mining resources, like oil fields, and to labor-oriented investment. In consequence, the position which the U.S. multinational enterprises occupy will be increasingly important in the Southeast Asian economy, and the export of the related U.S. products, especially large-scale machinery, will also grow extensively. The export items from the United States to Southeast Asia at present are grains, fertilizers, medical supplies, agricultural machinery, mining and construction machinery, office machines, airplanes, and so on, most of which are the U.S. products that are highly competitive in the world market. Japan competes with the United States in fertilizers, medical supplies, mining materials, and so on. Machinery is divided into two parts; large-scale machinery is usually produced in the U.S., while small-scale machines are Japanese-made.

Because Southeast Asia, since the end of the war in Vietnam, has been attracting world-wide attention as an export market, a capital investment market, and a market for acquiring raw materials and resources, U.S. investors have by no means been the only group keenly interested in this region. Along with Japanese capital, British, West German, French, Dutch, and other European capital shows great interest in this region. The present reevaluation of the economic significance of Southeast Asia today stems largely from attention to the possibilities of resource exploitation of the region. Due to the accelerated international competition for resource exploitation, and the strategy of gigantic international capital to minimize risks by drawing from several mining sources, some Southeast Asian countries hope to gain a foothold for their own economic development by emphasizing a new policy of resource exploitation. Foreign capital in this region (including Australasia) has in fact since the late 1960s become even more active in the exploitation of natural resources, especially mining resources.[4]

In addition, Southeast Asia is full of many more factors spurring

3. This is approximately 32 percent of the cumulative balance of Japan's foreign direct investments which stood at $4,480 million in March 1972.

4. According to *Metal Statistics* in 1971, the proportion of the mineral resources of the Asian and Pacific region to total world production is not necessarily large: for example, nickel or makes up 32 percent of total world mineral production (Asia 2 percent, Australasia 30 percent); bauxite ore, 26 percent (Asia 7 percent, Australasia 19 percent); lead ore, 18 percent (Asia 3 percent, Australasia 15 percent); zinc ore, 12 percent (Asia 2

industrialized countries to invest in the region—there is abundant, inexpensive manpower; an inflow of large-scale aid funds is expected; the region has Japan as a big market already, and China as a potentially big market; Hong Kong and Singapore are anticipated to grow increasingly as *entrepôt* trade bases or financial centers; the Asian dollar market, which is said to exceed already $3 billion is showing rapid expansion since being born in Singapore in April 1969.[5]

In view of the points discussed so far, it seems likely that competition will increase in the fields of capital investment and marketing and procurement of raw materials and resources as the enterprise advancement of Western European and Japanese capital increases in Southeast Asia. Insofar as such rivalry exists, there is fear that a "struggle for markets" by major powers' capital, especially multinational enterprises, may become intense.[6]

China's Appearance on the Scene of the Southeast Asian Economy

The Southeast Asian economy today, as is clear from what has been said, stands at a vitally important turning point. But in addition to

---

percent, Australasia 10 percent); copper ore 8 percent (Asia 5 percent, Australasia 3 percent); etc. Despite the figures above, as a result of some of the Latin American and African countries which carried out nationalization policies in mining industries since the latter half of the 1960s, mining capital was compelled to make efforts in exploiting new mineral deposits in South Africa, North America, and Australasia where foreign capital can be invested comparatively more freely. It is in this particular context that the mining resources of the Southeast Asian countries have come to attract worldwide attention.

5. The birth of an Asian dollar market in Singapore came about in April 1969. Dollar holdings by overseas Chinese, which play an important economic role in Southeast Asia, are said to reach approximately $5 billion. The financial resources of these overseas Chinese have been flown to the European dollar market in London either via Hong Kong or directly, up to the present time. Then, the Bank of America (BOA) came to think of one scheme of absorbing this financial resource and utilizing it for the purpose of economic development in the Asian region. The Bank of America thus called out to the Singapore government to establish an Asian dollar market and succeeded in obtaining the agreement. BOA started its first activity in April 1969. With participation by the First National City Bank in this scheme, by the end of 1971 constituent banks of the Asian dollar market have increased to twenty-two in number, including Mitsui Bank of Japan and Bank of Tokyo. Although this market stands no comparison with the European dollar market in London, its growth rate is high and its scale today is comparable to that of the European dollar market ten years ago.

6. It is worthy of special attention in this particular context that at the ECAFE meeting recently held in Tokyo (April 1973), the Chinese delegate restressed China's fundamental principle that she would not seek hegemony in the Asian and Pacific region. At the same time, she criticized the Russian proposal of an "Asian Collective Security Plan" as a plan for invasion or intervention into this region. She also criticized the "imperialist powers" for depriving the Asian countries of their abundant natural resources and for trying to put the Asian countries under their control.

changes in the development policies of Southeast Asian countries which seek new economic independence, and to the increasing economic interest that industrialized countries recently began to take in this region, the impact of China's appearance on the international stage will be immensely significant to the economy of Southeast Asia. First, China may provide Southeast Asia with valuable precedents and new guidance stemming directly from its own experiences. Interest in this experience is already growing; the *Asian and Far East Economic Survey in 1972* (ESCAFE Annual), recently published by the ECAFE executive office, states that despite fundamental structural differences such as nationalized production means, China's economic and social development experiences will be profoundly suggestive to the ECAFE developing countries, providing even those countries having different socio-economic structures with many valuable guidelines.

Within China itself, as is generally known, sharply divided opinions exist; one line attempts independent economic development adapted to Chinese circumstances, the other line tries to follow the Russian precedents. In order to establish the former "self-reliance" policy, China took the extreme means of the Great Proletarian Cultural Revolution, even though this meant a temporary stagnation in her economic development. In this connection, however, the ECAFE Annual points out that after the Cultural Revolution the Chinese economy showed such a rapid growth in improved living conditions that even a labor shortage arose. The ECAFE report lists six major measures of China's effective socio-economic policy: self-reliant regional exploitation, decentralization, flexible planning adapted to actual circumstances, education, stress on villages, and well-balanced development. China's experience is, in short, that of self-reliance based on agriculture and guided by industry. It is of profound interest, then, that at precisely the moment when China made her giant figure appear once again on the Asian scene, the shift in the development policies of Southeast Asian countries began to take place. Because of this coincidence in time, China's experience in economic development will likely provide valuable lessons to Southeast Asia and suggest a feasible course for its future economic development.

At present, the most vital relations that China maintains with the Southeast Asian countries today are of course trade relations. Since these trade relations will form the foundation for future economic relations between China and Southeast Asia, let us discuss this subject briefly. Generally speaking, the structure of China's international trade consists of both the developing country-type with respect to trade with industrialized countries, and the developed country-type with respect to developing countries. That is, China exports agricultural products and raw materials to Japan and the industrialized countries of Europe, and imports machinery and equipment from them. At the same time, she exports food and industrial manufactures to many Asian and African countries, while importing raw materials from them. The trade balance of China shows an excess of imports from industrial countries, balanced with an excess of exports to Southeast Asia, her biggest market for the acquisition of foreign currency.

The great majority of China's trade with Southeast Asia up to the present time has been through Hong Kong and Singapore, earning foreign currency amounting to nearly $650 million (1966–1971 average). This is approximately equal to her unfavorable trade balance with the Western industrial countries, and at the same time, to her total imports from Japan. China's export commodities to Southeast Asia consist chiefly of textile manufactures, and vegetables and grains, while its major import is rubber, which has been growing quite slowly. China's trade with Southeast Asia has thus been functioning as an important factor for her economic development in the sense that her exports greatly exceeded imports, providing China with foreign currencies needed for importing capital goods from the Western industrial countries. China's excess in exports to the region is partly due to unnormalized political relations with the Southeast Asian countries, to the extremely limited number of commodities which these countries can export to China, and to the special unique consumers' market of Chinese products in such overseas Chinese societies as Hong Kong and Singapore. When China-Southeast Asia trade relations are put onto a more normal course after the restoration of diplomatic relations, what changes will emerge? Let us now turn to this question.

Prospect of China's Trade with Southeast Asia

International trade is generally based on economic demands necessitated by an internal economic build up, especially the function of acquiring foreign currencies. Nevertheless, China's export-import policy stresses that trading has to be in conformity with the economic needs of the partner countries. Judging from her actual trading attitude, China seems to act in accordance with this trade principle, particularly when the partner countries happen to be developing countries. Further, China firmly believes in the principle that bilateral trading in general should be in balance with each country for the sake of consistent and steady development of bilateral trading.

The principle of trade equilibrium stated here is clearly provided in

The Basic Knowledge of China's Foreign Trading compiled in 1958 by the Bureau of Foreign Trade of the People's Republic of China. Export and import policies of China provided in this material are as follows:

Import Policy. (1) To import mechanical equipments, materials, raw materials, and scientific machineries which are considered essential for socialistic industrialization, expansion of industrial and agricultural production and promotion of scientific researches, based on demands from the build-up of Socialism. (2) To import consumption goods of appropriate quantities necessary to increase the people's standard of living and stabilize domestic markets. (3) To import as many goods as possible from all "brother nations, " provided that they profit by exporting, for the purpose of promoting the total economic development of the Socialist countries. And taking into consideration the needs of the Asian and African countries, which obtained national independence and are making efforts toward their aim of overcoming economic difficulties and accomplishing economic independence, to strive to strengthen and develop the economic and trading relations already established with those countries, and to import systematically the goods which those countries wish to export.

Export Policy. (1) To promote industrial and agricultural development, and at the same time to promote progress in production and the raising of technical standards by organizing production and exports of various kinds of commodities. (2) To acquire foreign currencies necessary to pay for imported goods. (3) To provide Socialist countries, Asian and African countries and friendly nations of the West with commodities within her bounds of possibility, and to fulfill needs of production and consumption of the above countries to the extent that is possible.

Looking at the above policies of export and import, it is understood that both 1 and 2 are based on economic demands from China's economic build up, but 3 reflects clearly China's careful political consideration of foreign policies in which Asian countries are given an important position.

In consequence of China's trade principles, no matter how flexibly she operates on these principles in the future, it seems impossible for China to pursue sheer acquisition of foreign currencies and expansion of exports in the Southeast Asian region. Indeed once China's trade is carried on through normal channels, her trade, except that with Hong Kong and Singapore, will be expected to follow her principles more diligently.

Leaving the industrialized nations aside for the moment, China has so far concluded trade agreements with almost all the countries with which she has restored diplomatic relations. By the end of 1972 she had trade agreements with as many as thirty-four developing countries of the non-Communist bloc. In view of this, it is strongly anticipated that China will make trade agreements concomitant with normalization of diplomatic relations with the Southeast Asian countries. If previous trade agreements are any indication, China's trade relations with developing countries will aim at attaining mutual most-favored nation treatment, will reassert the principle of trade equilibrium, and will then decide, in the form of a protocol, the types and amounts of commodities to be traded each year. In principle, this is how China's trade is being conducted.[7] In addition, China has signed economic and technical agreements with many developing countries, offering assistance to them in the form of grants or long-term, interest-free loans, regardless of the amount of money involved. Interested in economic cooperation through trade and based on her trade equilibrium principle, China is making a noteworthy effort to purchase whichever commodities the partner countries wish to export to her, even if she is not in need of them.[8]

In this manner, considering that China's exports to many developing countries usually exceed her imports from them, we believe that with the exception of some countries who can offer commodities China wants to purchase, there even may be a decline in her trade rather than an expansion because of the principle of balanced trade. Hence, even if China-Southeast Asia trade relations are officially established in the near future, it is an open question whether or not expansion of trade will be realized immediately, since China will observe the above principle strictly.

7. In a trade agreement with Cambodia (26 April 1956), for example, the principle of trade equilibrium is very specifically and concretely prescribed. If the trade deficit of either side reaches £1 million, it can stop importing or the partner country can stop exporting. Also, China's settlement of foreign trade is generally operated by a "clearing account" established in the Central Bank of both China and the partner countries.

8. China used to import sugar from Indonesia in order to modify her trade balance with Indonesia. In 1958, China resold 41,000 tons of imported sugar from Indonesia at a lower price to the neighboring markets of Indonesia, which eventually disrupted Indonesia's sugar export markets. In consequence, she stopped exporting sugar to China from 1959 on. As for maize, rice and leaf tobacco, these items are basically China's export items. Therefore those items, once imported by China, are often re-exported. For instance, China exports imported rice from Burma to Sri Lanka according to their Rubber-Rice Agreement with the price lower than China paid Burma. Import and re-export issues like this are bound to raise troubles for China. The worst case is that of coffee from Guiana, for which there is no demand within China but which is imported into China simply to keep their trade in balance. Items like this have to be resold directly or through Hong Kong, which tends to cause problems resulting in disturbing export markets of the partner countries for their primary products, as seen in the case of Indonesia's sugar.

Looking at exports, we have noted that China's main export commodities to Southeast Asia are foods and light industrial products, especially cotton materials, textiles, and clothing. Sooner or later, however, it will be necessary for China to shift the present export pattern to other commodities such as iron and steel, machinery, chemicals, construction material, etc., in order to avoid possible frictions with developing industries in the Southeast Asian countries. In fact, signs of a shift in export commodities from cotton products to machinery is already evident. Such a tendency will be accelerated, especially since, to the extent of her capabilties, China would take into special consideration the economic needs of her trading partners.

But imports will be a major problem in this connection. As mentioned earlier, China's imports from Southeast Asia have been quite stagnant in the past. Imports include rubber, timber, plywood, palm oil, coconut oil, copra, maize, rice, sugar, spices, leaf tobacco, etc. These primary products, and processed goods made from them, are what the Southeast Asian countries wish to export, but there is little hope that China's demand for them will expand much in the future.

Yet, taking due consideration of the Chinese demand for imports, and granting that China will make efforts to expand her imports, an increase and expansion of imports from Southeast Asia need not be ruled out altogether. Potential needs may be found in non-ferrous metals, for example, high quality bauxite ore, copper, nickel, and also wood (lauan), jute, etc., which might show considerable growth; while rubber, plywood, palm oil, and rice may also increase somewhat. In all prospects, however, we see hardly any basis for rapid expansion of exports from Southeast Asia to China.

The expansion of China-Southeast Asian trade seems to be limited both with respect to exports and imports, especially the latter. Further, judging from the aspect of China's financial resources at present, it is unlikely that China will go far ahead to assist with large-scale projects which might have great influence on her trade balance with the Southeast Asian countries. Thus, even if normalized trade relations may bring some trade growth, still the rate will be hardly appreciable. Although China's trade with Southeast Asia, owing to the existence of the special markets of Hong Kong and Singapore, will continue to play an important function in terms of the acquisition of foreign currencies essential for importing manufacturing machinery from the Western industrial countries, still it will be directed toward balanced trade on the whole. In so doing, China will likely strive to expand her exports to the Western industrial countries more than ever in order to maintain balanced trade with Southeast Asia.

China as a Trade Rival

As is clear, the majority of China's trade with Southeast Asia has been that of *entrepôt* trade through Hong Kong and Singapore. Therefore, China's commodities are seen only in limited areas, apart from those two *entrepôt*-market countries and Malaysia.

In regard to the Southeast Asian market in 1970, Hong Kong's import share from China amounted to 16 percent, Singapore's 5 percent, and Malaysia's 5 percent. As a result, with the exception of Hong Kong, Japan-China trade rivalry in the Southeast Asian market is manifest only in Singapore and Malaysia, and is limited to a few light industrial products.

Along with the normalization of political relations between China and the Southeast Asian countries, it is easily prognosticated that China's exports will see regional expansion into respective Southeast Asian markets in the 1970s. Still it does not appear correct to overestimate the upcoming economic competition brought about by China's appearance on the international stage. It is not with China so much but with the Western industrial countries that Japan will most likely compete over the Southeast Asian market, as is already evident. As previously mentioned, it is expected that competition will emerge not only in the field of marketing but also in capital investment and resource exploitation.

China's new participation in the Southeast Asian economy will in the long run no doubt exert great impact upon various economic relations in the region, directly and indirectly. But, so far as trade rivalry is concerned, it will be not so much on the quantitative level as in the qualitative area of trading conditions and aid that China's impact will manifest itself more conspicuously. Judging from China's attitude toward foreign countries up to the present, China in promoting her economic relations in Southeast Asia will definitely give priority to maintaining and enhancing friendly relations. From this standpoint, too, China mostly likely will select a course of respecting the economic interests and economic needs of her trading partners.

As discussed previously, the Southeast Asian countries, seeking their economic independence, are now groping for such changes in their development policy as promoting agriculture, expanding employment, rectifying internal imbalances, strengthening selective foreign capital introduction, etc. Therefore, China's style of trade and aid, with its great concern for its partners' needs, will definitely attract the interest of the Southeast Asian countries. In addition, China's policy of self-reliant economic development will stimulate and encourage a change in the development policies of Southeast Asian nations. Japan and the Western industrial countries will have to cope with China's qualitative challenge. It is imperative for us to give priority to the economic independence of the region, and to set up concrete measures for an export-import policy, an investment policy, an aid policy, a resource exploitation policy, etc., in line with that principle of economic independence. Of course, it would be ideal if these countries, including China, cooperate in such a way as to complement each other's contribution toward the prosperous economic development of Southeast Asia in a spirit of international cooperation.

The Direction of Japan's Economic Cooperation

Finally, let us discuss the position Japan occupies in the Southeast Asian economy in order to find what course Japan's economic cooperation should take. First, Japan's trade with most Southeast Asian countries is conspicuously one-sided, showing an extreme excess in exports. Japan's trade structure is typical of vertical trade, with importing of raw materials and exporting of manufactured goods. It is quite obvious that a strong undercurrent of criticism against this trade imbalance with Japan is responsible for the recent increase in anti-Japanese sentiment throughout the region. Second, more than half of the flow of financial resources from Japan to developing countries goes to Southeast Asia. Private direct investment also has been growing increasingly year after year, putting Japan in second place after the United States as a major supplier of investment. A closer look at this private investment shows a high percentage of it is put into labor-intensive industries such as textiles, electronics, wooden products, machinery, etc. Most of the enterprises investing in the region are of small-scale; and they tend to operate on a "profit-first" principle, pursuing short-term, lucrative business. It is this trend that has been exposed to recent pervasive criticism. Third, the extent of Japan's dependence on Southeast Asia, including Australasia, for natural resources in 1970 was as high as 52 percent for timber and 38 percent for metal materials (bauxite 98 percent, copper ore 46 percent, iron ore 42 percent, etc.).[9] These data enable us to predict that Japanese investment in natural resources, especially mining and oil, will be increased in the future.

9. Indonesia's production of crude petroleum occupies merely 1.8 percent (880,000 barrels) of world production in 1971. However, Japan's import of crude petroleum from Indonesia has been rapidly increasing these days, amounting to almost 10 percent of total imports of crude petroleum of Japan. This means that in 1971 approximately 70 percent (481,100 barrels) of Indonesia's exports of crude petroleum (655,100 barrels) was exported to Japan.

Japanese trade with Southeast Asia developed very much in the 1960s. If the rate of growth of exports and imports on the part of Southeast Asia, and that of exports to and imports from Japan in Southeast Asia in the period of 1966–1970 continues in the future, Japan's share in Southeast Asian countries' imports in 1980 will be as high as 48 percent and exports will reach 23 percent. Japan's oversees investment is expected to reach $10 billion in 1975 and $25 to $30 billion in 1980; and approximately one-third of the increase will probably be concentrated in the Southeast Asian and Pacific region.[10] No matter how Japan's export may grow in Southeast Asia in the future, it is hardly possible for her to occupy half of the market. In any case, if the growth continues at its present rate, Japan's economic influence in Southeast Asia will be increasingly powerful through trade and investment. In consequence, some political and psychological frictions between Japan and the Southeast Asian countries will be bound to emerge to a much greater extent.

Japan's economic policy toward foreign countries in the past gave priority to promoting exports, and aid given to Southeast Asia was often aimed toward expansion of exports from Japan to aid-recipient countries. Furthermore, she tended to seek export markets for industrial products and import markets for raw materials from her trade with Southeast Asia. In regard to direct investment, the investments were made initially in conformity with the import-substitution policy of the partner countries while seeking to supplement her own exports. Then, as Japan's domestic problems of labor shortage, scarcity of resources, and environmental pollution began to emerge, her direct investment capital started looking for overseas plant sites. In this manner, there was a strong tendency for Japan to extend her internal problems directly into foreign economic relations. It is self-evident that if Japan goes on developing on an "export-first" principle or on a "Japanese economy-centered" policy, in the long-run her economic relations with Southeast Asia will be definitely jeopardized. It is now imperative that Japan should seriously and thoroughly examine and improve her

10. At the end of 1972, the cumulative balance of Japan's direct outward investments stood about $6.3 billion. In the latter half of the sixties, the average yearly rate of increase in Japan's outward investments was the highest (32 percent) among the advanced industrial nations, and the size of Japan's overseas investments, although extremely small compared with the old capital-exporting countries such as Britain and the United States, has been fast approaching the level of the other advanced countries. It is extremely difficult to make a quantitative forecast of direct investments; but on the basis of several projections, the average yearly rate of increase may be estimated at about 25 percent which will bring the cumulative balance of direct outward investments in 1980 to $25 to $30 billion.

economic cooperation policy from the standpoint of a long-range plan. This rethinking and revision of policy should be even more emphasized in the light of China's reappearance on the international stage and the strong commitment of Southeast Asian countries to economic independence through their change of internal economic development policy.

As discussed above, it is foreseeable that China-Southeast Asia economic relations in the future will become normalized, eventually providing an opportunity for China to expand her exports to the region in the 1970s; there will be an advance in her export structure, and progress in her economic cooperation such as the provision of aid, all of which help China exert greater economic influence on the region. The new participation of China in the Southeast Asian economy, however, will hardly come to threaten Japan's economic position in the region, for the reasons mentioned earlier. Contrary to such apprehension of competition between Japan and China over the Southeast Asian market, we are convinced that if Japan endeavors to make adjustments in her internal industrial structure for the future and to expand imports from developing countries while making improvements in her export structure, she can probably maintain harmonious relations with China in the field of Southeast Asian economic relations, and furthermore, both countries together can contribute to the economic independence and progress of Southeast Asia.

With the clear desire for economic independence observed in the Southeast Asian countries today, China's appearance on the scene, and the increasing interest in the region by Western European capital, there are several problems Japan must solve in order to keep developing her economic relations with Southeast Asia in a friendly atmosphere. First of all, she must immediately correct faults disclosed in her past assistance, exports, and direct investments in the region; in other words, she must revise the "export-first" policy or "Japanese economy-centered" policy, and then make efforts to establish new means of economic cooperation.

Now with the end of the war in Vietnam and the reassessment of the Southeast Asian market, the Western industrial countries and Japan are beginning once again to set out simultaneously in competition for Southeast Asia's resources, investment opportunities, and consumer markets. In this very critical situation, if Japan were to commit herself to a tendency toward "imperial expansion" and become deeply involved in it, her economic relations with Southeast Asia would become irreparably damaged.

Some External Constraints in the Development of Sino-Japanese Relations

Gene T. Hsiao

After twenty-two years of cold-war confrontation, the People's Republic of China and Japan finally established diplomatic relations under the impact of the Sino-American detente.[1] In bilateral terms, the rapprochement had the immediate effect of removing certain artificial political and financial barriers that had impeded the normalization of relations. It also promoted the normal interchange of visits and goods between the two countries. The two-way trade in 1974 reached $3.29

This article was based on my discussions at the following three meetings: "Japan's Emerging Role in the International System and Japanese-American Relations in the 1970s and 1980s" sponsored by the Faculty Arms Control Seminar of the Center for Policy Study and Norman Waith Harris Foundation of the University of Chicago in cooperation with the Institute of International Relations, Sophia University, in Chicago on October 4–6, 1973, and in Tokyo on April 25–27, 1974; "China and the Current Era of Detente"—the 13th working session of the Centre d'Etude du Sud-Est Asiatique et de l'Extreme-Orient, Universities of Brussels and Ghent, in Waterloo on December 13–14, 1973.

A shortened version of this article, entitled "Prospects for a New Sino-Japanese Relationship," was published in *The China Quarterly* No. 60 (October–December 1974), pp. 720–49. The present version has been revised and updated to 5 December 1975.

1. For a discussion of this matter, see Gene T. Hsiao, "The Sino-Japanese Rapprochement: A Relationship of Ambivalence," *China Quarterly* No. 57 (January–March 1974), pp. 101–123. A longer version of this article appears in Gene T. Hsiao, ed., *Sino-American Detente and Its Policy Implications* (New York and London: Praeger Publishers, 1974), pp. 160–188.

million, representing a triple increase over the volume for 1972.[2] In conformity with the provisions of the Sino-Japanese statement of 29 September 1972,[3] the two governments concluded an undersea cable accord, a memorandum for the increase of resident news correspondents in each country from five to eleven, a three-year official trade agreement (5 January 1974) granting each party most-favored-nation treatment with respect to tariffs, customs clearance, and other matters relating to bilateral trade, an air transport agreement (20 April 1974), a maritime transport agreement (13 November 1974), and a fishery agreement (15 August 1975).[4] Pending the conclusion of a treaty of peace and friendship, the two countries seem to have entered into a normal course of relationship that may eventually benefit both.

However, in international politics bilateral relations are often complicated by the interplay of the principal parties' domestic and foreign affairs on the one hand, and their individual relationships with third countries on the other. This is particularly the case in the Asia-Pacific region where a new international order based on a four-power relationship of China, Japan, the United States, and the Soviet Union is emerging. Since each of these nations is affected by the development of relationships among the other powers, the prospect of Sino-Japanese relationships will not be determined solely on the basis of their bilateral interests. Rather, it will be affected by their mutual relationship with other countries. In this connection, there are four important issues to be discussed. First, there is the perennial dispute between the People's Republic and Japan over the status of Taiwan despite Japan's severance of formal diplomatic ties with the Nationalists. This problem was most clearly demonstrated in Japan's negotiations for the air transport agreement with China in 1973–74. Second, the fate of Taiwan is intimately linked to Japan's relationship with the United States, and the United States relationship with Taiwan. An American decision on this question with have a tremendous impact on Japan's relationship with the People's Republic. Third, Japan is in the process of searching for a new role in world politics. The most critical aspect of Japan's foreign policy in general, and her relationship with China in particular, lies in her future defense posture and security alliance. Any Japanese decison to acquire nuclear armaments would inevitably upset the pres-

2. See *Japan Economic Review*, No. 2 (15 February 1975), p. 10.

3. The English text of the joint statement is in *Peking Review* no. 40 (6 October 1972), pp. 12–13; the Chinese text in *Jen-min jih-pao*, 30 September 1972, p. 1.

4. "Japan, China Ink Pact on Undersea Cable," *Japan Times*, 5 May 1973, p. 11; "Scribe Exchange Okayed," *ibid.*, 6 January 1974, p. 3. The official texts of the last four agreements were released by the Japanese Government.

ent power structure in the Asia-Pacific region and require new adjustments. Fourth, the triangular tug of war between China, Japan, and the Soviet Union since the beginning of the Sino-American detente in 1971 has created another potential danger in Sino-Japanese relations. The role of Japan in this contest will be important in determining the course of development in her future relationship with China.[5]

The Air Transport Agreement: A Dispute over the Status of Taiwan

The Sino-Japanese rapprochement was achieved by Japan's acknowledgement of three Chinese demands centering on the question of Taiwan: recognition of the People's Republic as the sole legal government of China, acceptance of Taiwan as an inalienable part of the territory of the People's Republic, and abrogation of Japan's peace treaty with the Nationalists. The Japanese government accepted the first Chinese demand without reservation, expressed its "understanding and respect" for the second, and complied with the third by a press statement.[6] Because this settlement did not clearly confirm the status of Taiwan, the Chinese government sought to clarify the ambiguity in its bilateral agreements with Japan.

The first such agreement that both countries agreed to negotiate was a civil aviation accord. In the opinion of many Chinese and Japanese officials, such an accord could lead to the conclusion of a treaty of peace and friendship—the final hallmark of a full rapprochement.[7] Accordingly, on his arrival in Peking in early January 1973, Minister Yuichi Hayashi of the Japanese Embassy presented a draft aviation agreement to the Chinese authorities.[8] The Chinese responded by submitting a counterproposal, and negotiations started in March.[9] After three rounds of preliminary discussion, however, the negotiations

5. Southeast Asia and Korea are also important issues in the development of Sino-Japanese relations. However, in comparative terms they are not so important as the other issues mentioned above. Besides, space limitation simply does not permit inclusion of Southeast Asia and Korea in this article.

6. The Sino-Japanese Joint Statement (29 September 1972), Articles 2 and 3; "Foreign Minister Masayoshi Ohira Holds Press Conference in Peking," *Jen-min jih-pao*, 30 September 1972, p. 2. The English text of Ohira's statement is in *Peking Review*, No. 40 (6 October 1972), p. 15.

7. See Editorial, "A New Chapter in the Annals of Sino-Japanese Relations," *Jen-min jih-pao*, 30 September 1972, p. 2; "Japanese House of Representatives Adopted Unanimous Resolution Supporting Sino-Japanese Joint Statement," *ibid.*, 11 November 1972, p. 5.

8. "China Asked to OK Air Link with Japan," *Japan Times*, 12 January 1973, p. 1.

9. "China Hands Draft Aviation Pact to Hayashi," *ibid.*, 21 February 1973, p. 10.

bogged down because of Chinese opposition to the continued flights of Taiwan's China Airlines (CAL) to Japan.[10]

The gist of the Chinese argument can be summarized in one sentence: Japan must stop treating Taiwan as a "state." Proceeding from this premise, the Chinese government demanded that the Japanese must cancel the Japan-Taiwan route operated by CAL and Japan Airlines (JAL) or at least reroute CAL flights to some other Japanese airports, such as Nagoya and Okinawa, remove the Nationalist flag from CAL planes, change CAL's official designation to something like "Taiwan Airlines," and transfer its branch office in Japan to a local agent. The rationale of the argument was that Taiwan is only a province of China and consequently the use of the name "China" and the "Chinese nationalist flag" by CAL is misleading. Moreover, the Chinese contended that to allow CAL—Taiwan's flag carrier—to use the same airport (Haneda) in Tokyo, side by side with the real Chinese flag carrier, the Civil Aviation Administration of China (CAAC), would inevitably create the "two-China" impression.[11] The pro-Taiwan Dietmen led by Takeo Fukuda, then Minister of Finance, countered the Chinese by saying that while representatives of the People's Republic and Taiwan "co-existed" in Washington it was "absurd" that their airplanes could not sit side by side at Haneda.[12]

Encouraged by the Fukuda faction's support, the Taiwan authorities on 14 July 1973 issued a stern warning that should Japan accept the Chinese conditions the Nationalist government would "stop allowing any Japanese airplanes to land in or fly over" Taiwan and "any flying object entering our Air Defense Identification Zone (ADIZ) without permission shall be regarded as an unidentified flying object and treated as such."[13] Although this threat was most likely a political maneuver to enhance Taipei's bargaining position, the potential financial losses and physical risks involved for the many JAL flights to Taipei and Southeast Asia could be very great.[14] Meanwhile in Tokyo,

10. "Aviation Talks in Peking Ended," *ibid.*, 16 March 1973, p. 1; "Japan, China Wind Up First Air Talks," *ibid.*, 18 March 1973, p. 10.

11. The Chinese demand was first made by Premier Chou En-lai in his conversation with Minister of International Trade and Industry Yasuhiro Nakasone in January 1973. See *Japan Times*, 20 January 1973, p. 1. Later it was formally conveyed to Japanese negotiators for the aviation agreement and revealed by the Japanese government in January 1974. Sources of this revelation will be cited below at appropriate places.

12. See Kazushige Hirasawa, "Sino-Japanese Relations," *Japan Times*, 25 May 1973, p. 1; "Japan-China Air Pact Opposed by LDP Dietmen," *ibid.*, 26 May 1973, p. 1.

13. "Japan Warned about Air Accord," *Free China Weekly* (Taipei) No. 28 (22 July 1973), p. 1.

14. JAL's profit from the Taiwan route in 1973 amounted to $20 million. See "Japan, Taiwan Fail to Reach Air Accord," *Japan Times*, 6 March 1974, p. 4.

a Chinese economic delegation refused to initial the three-year intergovernmental trade agreement because of the controversy over the aviation accord.[15]

In order to break the deadlock and to reassure Taiwan of Japan's continued goodwill and cooperation, a seventy-one-member Japanese Dietmen's delegation led by former Education Minister Hirokichi Nadao visited Taipei at the end of September for the first time since Japan's severance of diplomatic ties with the Nationalists.[16] This was followed by another visit by former Prime Minister Nobusuke Kishi in October to celebrate Chiang Kai-shek's birthday.[17] After their return to Tokyo the Nadao mission submitted a statement to the Japanese government contending that "as shown clearly by the Japan-China joint statement last autumn, Japan only 'understood,' not recognized, China's insistence that Taiwan is a part of the Chinese territory. Therefore, Japan should maintain the present air and other transportation means which are the basis for economic, cultural, and other exchanges with Taiwan."[18] This protest notwithstanding, Foreign Minister Ohira was able to announce—after Kishi's visit to Taipei—his plan to meet with the Chinese leaders in Peking at the end of November to complete the negotiations for an aviation agreement.[19]

Ohira's trip was delayed by the oil crisis until January 1974. During his four-day stay in Peking he successfully signed the trade agreement along with the memorandum for the increase of resident correspondents in each country with the Chinese government on the basis of a mutual understanding about the basic principles of the proposed aviation accord and the maintenance of the Taiwan route. As later revealed in Tokyo, the understanding consisted of six points:

1. The Japanese government will promptly conclude a civil aviation agreement with China on the basis of the Japan-China joint statement of September 1972, but at the same time present Japan-Taiwan air services (including stopover flights) will be maintained under a nongovernmental arrangement.

2. The government will see to it that the Japanese flag carrier, JAL, will not serve the Japan-Taiwan route.

15. "Japan, China Officials Agree on Trade Rules," *Japan Times*, 31 August 1973, p. 1; Richard Halloran, "Chinese Return from Japan Talks," *The New York Times*, 3 September 1973, p. 23.

16. See Nadao's press statement at the Taipei airport, *Chung-yang jih-pao*, 1 October 1973, p. 1.

17. *Free China Weekly* No. 43 (4 November 1973), p. 1.

18. "Pro-Taiwan Dietmen against Air Pact Change," *Japan Times*, 5 October 1973, p. 1.

19. "Ohira May Wrap Up Japan-China Air Pact," *ibid.*, 4 November 1973, p. 4.

3. The government will not seek changes in the name and emblem of CAL against CAL's will, but will make clear its own view concerning the nature of CAL's name and emblem on another occasion. The Japanese authorities henceforth will refer to CAL as "China Airlines (Taiwan)."

4. The government will see to it that CAAC aircraft will use the new Tokyo International Airport in Narita and those of CAL will use the Tokyo International Airport at Haneda. Before the new international airport is opened, the government will temporarily permit both CAAC and CAL to use Haneda airport, by allotting them different operational hours.

5. The government will redesignate an alternative airport to CAL which will be agreed upon between Japan and Taiwan.

6. The government will see to it that ground services for CAL will be entrusted with its agents or a separate company. However, the government will give due consideration to ensure the operational safety of its flights and guarantee a stable living situation for CAL employees.[20]

Immediately following the announcement of the government plan, an ultranationalist group in the Diet, named Seirankai (Blue Storm Society or Young Storm Association), reacted violently to the proposed aviation agreement with China, shouted abuse to pro-Peking members, and even resorted to physical violence by toppling tables and grappling with the necks of their opponents in a party meeting. On 26 January 1974, it organized a mass rally of 25,000 people to oppose Japan's "abandonment" of Taiwan, arguing that continued cooperation with the Nationalists was "a matter of life and death" to Japan's security. The group was formed in July 1973 under a feudalistic "blood oath" by thirty-two junior Liberal Democratic Party (LDP) members affiliated with the various LDP factions led by Fukuda, Yasuhiro Nakasone, LDP Vice-President Etsusaburo Shiina, the then Deputy Prime Minister Takeo Miki, and others. It enjoyed the support of a right-wing organization formerly led by the late novelist Yukio Mishima, certain revived prewar secret societies, and some senior LDP members. Seven of its members were vice ministers of the Tanaka cabinet.[21] The organization's basic thinking is that "Japan should never be turned into a socialist or communist country; to realize this, it is

20. "Government Announces Policy to Keep Up Air Service between Japan, Taiwan," *ibid.*, 18 January 1974, pp. 1, 4.

21. Koji Nakamura, "Sierankai, Forming the Battle Line," *Far Eastern Economic Review* No. 8 (25 February 1974), p. 23; "Seirankai: the Young Turks Flex Their Muscles," Special Report on Japan in Asia 1974, in *Far Eastern Economic Review* No. 19 (13 May 1974), p. 21.

necessary to reform the conservative structure with bold methods; and to achieve this, the Constitution must be revised." It challenged the Japanese government's foreign policy under the direction of Prime Minister Kakuei Tanaka and Foreign Minister Masayoshi Ohira, particularly in respect to its China and Korea policy, opposed the ratification of the Nuclear Nonproliferation Treaty, and threatened to split the LDP into two.[22]

The presence of such a menacing political force in the Japanese government naturally aroused China's concern. In a series of articles, the Chinese official organ, *Jen-min jih-pao*, recalled Prime Minister Tanaka's visit to China which revived the hope of the Chinese and Japanese people for generations of peace and friendship, and charged the Seirankai as an inheritor of the concept of "the greater East Asia co-prosperity sphere" and a fascist-militarist force intending to recapture Taiwan and Korea. Finally, the organ warned that "the Chinese people are determined to liberate Taiwan!"[23]

Foreign Minister Ohira, however, threatened to resign should the China aviation deal fail. He also insisted that the Nationalist flag and emblem carried by CAL were "private identification marks" that had nothing to do with Taiwan as a "state."[24] Under pressure, the LDP Executive Council finally endorsed on 9 February the government's six-point plan on the condition that the Taiwan route would not be interrupted while negotiating for the aviation agreement with Peking.[25] Toward this end, the Japanese government sent Osamu Itagaki, president of the Japan-Taiwan Interchange Association, to Taipei at the end of February to negotiate for a settlement. The Nationalist authorities accepted all but the following: insertion of the word "Taiwan" in brackets after CAL's name in all markings, the denial that CAL is the flag-carrier of the Republic of China and the "sun-in-the-blue-sky" flag its national flag, and the transfer of CAL's agents and ground services

22. Minoru Shimizu, "Rivalry among Junior LDP Dietmen," *Japan Times*, 17 January 1974, p. 10; "Tanaka LDP Faction Gives Sierankai Return Blast," *ibid.*, 21 February 1974, p. 1; Kazushige Hirasawa, "LDP Factionalism," *ibid.*, 8 March 1974, p. 1; "Seirankai Nagoya Rally Blasts Ohira," *ibid.*, 11 March 1974, p. 1.

23. Lin Po, "A Noteworthy Tendency," *Jen-min jih-pao*, 2 February 1974, p. 5; "Seirankai Calling For Closer Cooperation With the Chiang Gang," *ibid.*; "Japan LDP Inaugurated a Committee to Normalize the Party against the Seirankai," *ibid.*, 10 February 1974, p. 6; "Japan: A Handful of Rightists Stage Anti-China Force," *Peking Review* No. 10 (10 March 1974), p. 22; "Japan: Seirankai Militarists Denounced," *ibid.* No. 12 (22 March 1974), p. 22.

24. "The Dirt Begins to Fly," *Far Eastern Economic Review* No. 8, p. 5; Kazushige Hirasawa, "LDP Factionalism," *Japan Times*, 8 March 1974, p. 1.

25. "LDP Gives OK to Basic Government China Air Policy," *ibid.*, 10 February 1974, p. 1.

in Japan to a non-Taiwan company.[26] At the same time, CAL had begun to prepare for the opening of a new route to the United States through Guam just in case the Japan route could not be maintained. For Japan, failure to conclude the aviation agreement would mean a devastating blow to its newly established relationship with China. Accordingly, the Japanese government resumed formal negotiations with China in March on the basis of Foreign Minister Ohira's earlier understanding with the Chinese authorities and successfully concluded the agreement in Peking on 20 April, despite the strong rightist protests at home and Taiwan's suspension of bilateral civil aviation relations with Japan.

Under this agreement, which consisted of nineteen articles and an annex, JAL will have landing rights at Peking and/or Shanghai, and CAAC at Tokyo and/or Osaka. From China, JAL will have the right to fly to London via New Delhi, or Bombay or Karachi; Tehran; Beirut or Cairo or Istanbul; Athens or another point in Europe; Rome or another point in Europe; and Paris. CAAC will have the right to serve the following points beyond Japan: Vancouver, Ottawa, or another point in Canada; one point in North America excluding Canada; and four points in Latin America, including Mexico. Detailed arrangements were to be made after the two countries had ratified the agreement, and the first commercial flights were expected to start before the second anniversary of the normalization of Sino-Japanese relations on 29 September 1974. The same agreement also provided for most-favored-nation treatment concerning charges for the use of airports and other facilities, and stipulated that the aircraft crew members of the designated aviation enterprises of one country flying over the territory of the other country should be nationals of their own country.[27]

The conclusion of the air transport agreement was immediately followed by negotiations for a maritime transport accord. Using Japan's acceptance of the Chinese terms with respect to CAL and JAL flights as a precedent, the Chinese negotiators insisted on the removal of the Nationalist flag from Taiwan's vessels calling on Japanese seaports as a precondition for the maritime accord. For Japan, compliance with the new Chinese demand would probably risk the break of its shipping

26. "Japan, Taiwan Fail to Reach Air Accord," *ibid.*, 6 March 1974, p. 4; "Osamu Itagaki Returns to Japan," *Chung-yang jih-pao*, 10 March 1974, p. 1.

27. "Japan, China Ink Civil Air Pact," *ibid.*, 21 April 1974, p. 1; "Outline of Japan-China Air Pact," *ibid.*, p. 2; "Taiwan Breaks Off All Civil Aviation Relations with Japan," *ibid.*, p. 1. The lower and upper houses of the Diet ratified the aviation agreement on May 7 and 15 respectively. See "Japan-China Air Accord Okayed by Upper House," *Japan Times*, 16 May 1974, p. 1. Taiwan's decision to suspend all CAL flights to Japan and halt all JAL flights to Taipei does not affect seven other foreign airlines' regular services between Taiwan and Japan.

lines with Taiwan which in some respects are far more important than the air route in the maintenance of bilateral trade; conversely, refusal to follow the precedent established in the air agreement would inevitably impede the normalization of trade and political relations with China. However, before this dilemma developed into a deadlock, the Chinese government consented to concluding the maritime agreement in Tokyo on 13 November 1974 without further insisting on the Taiwan problem.

There were at least two reasons for the Chinese concession. One was the Chinese hope for the early conclusion of a treaty of peace and friendship with Japan which would finalize the territorial status of Taiwan and Tiaoyüt'ai or Senkaku Islands. In fact, following the ratification of the air transport agreement by the Japanese Diet in May 1974, the Chinese government issued a statement approving of Japan's limited non-governmental "regional intercourse" with Taiwan as a "transitional measure," thus allowing the continuation of trade between Tokyo and Taipei.[28] The other was Japan's pivotal position in the Chinese attempt to frustrate the Soviet policy of encirclement of the People's Republic, including a possible Taipei-Moscow collusion if and when the Nationalist government could no longer count on U.S. support for its survival. In other words, Chinese insistence on Japan's breaking away from Taiwan under present circumstances could only cause harm rather than do any good to the overall Chinese foreign policy objective, of which the problem of Taiwan is only a collateral issue. Accordingly, when CAL and Japan Asia Airways (a subsidy to JAL) finally resumed their flights between Tokyo and Taipei in the summer of 1975 on the basis of a newly signed non-governmental agreement, China only registered an unofficial complaint through the China-Japan Friendship Association without reviving the issue of CAL's Nationalist flag.[29]

The Taiwan syndrome in Sino-Japanese relations is deeply rooted in two causes: Japan's highly lucrative trade with Taiwan and the latter's strategic position in the United States-Japan security alliance. For this reason, a discussion of the Taipei-Tokyo-Washington axis is in order.

The Taipei-Tokyo-Washington Axis: Money and Security

Japan has been trading simultaneously with both China and Taiwan

28. *Jen-min jih-pao* Commentator, "Greeting the Signing of China-Japan Air Transport Agreement," *Peking Review*, no. 21 (24 May 1974), p. 18.

29. See "Agreement Signed to Restore Japan-Taiwan Airline Flights," *Japan Times*, July 10, 1975, p. 1; "Japanese Airliner Leaves for Taiwan to Restore Link," *ibid.*, September 16, 1975, p. 1.

since 1950. In the case of China, Japan was unable to achieve a favorable balance until 1965, when she replaced the Soviet Union as China's leading trading partner.[30] Japan's favorable balance of trade with China in the last ten years (1965–1974) amounted to $1,731 million out of a total trade volume of $10,963 million; but in the same period Japan had a favorable balance of approximately $4,232 million from her trade with Taiwan which totaled about $11,284 million. (See Table 1). Furthermore, by the end of 1974, Japan had a total investment of $193 million in 572 factories in Taiwan, in addition to approximately $330 million in both government and private loans. The number of large Japanese trading companies in Taiwan totaled forty-eight, including such old *zaibatsu* establishments as Mitsui and Mitsubishi. Many of them have acted as overseas agents for Taiwan's exporters and importers, sharing about 17 percent of Taiwan's total foreign trade—$12,620 million in 1974. In addition, Japan had over 300 technical cooperation projects with numerous local enterprises.[31]

Although these figures represented only a small fraction of Japan's overall foreign trade and overseas investments, Taiwan was nevertheless Japan's third largest purchaser 1973 and fourth in 1974. It also ranked fourth among all Asian countries and areas which received private Japanese investments. By contrast, China ranked ninth and sixth among Japan's top purchasers in the respective years and received no direct Japanese investments except for short-term credits. (See Tables 2 and 3). To a Japan whose postwar policy was almost solely for economic prosperity, the importance of Taiwan became self-evident.

Commercial intercourse required institutional support. For this purpose, the Japanese established in March 1973, among other organizations, a Dietmen's committee comprising ninety-nine LDP members of the lower house and fifty-three LDP members of the upper house to promote political ties with Taiwan.[32] In accordance with a semi-government agreement, Japan accepted the Taiwan-sponsored Association of East Asia Relations as a substitute for the Nationalist embassy in Tokyo, with a total staff of ninety-eight persons as compared with a thirty-member staff maintained by the Chinese embassy. In return,

30. In the fifteen years from 1950 to 1964, Japan's total trade with China amounted to $1,307 million with an import deficit of $257 million. See Robert F. Dernberger, "Prospects for Trade Between China and the United States," in Alexander Eckstein, ed., *China Trade Prospects and U.S. Policy* (New York: Praeger Publishers, 1971), Table A3, p. 288.

31. *Free China Review*, no. 4 (1975), p. 34; *ibid.*, no. 3 (1975), p. 35; Ching-sung, "The Development of Sino-Japanese Economic Relations," in *Chung-yang jih-pao*, 30 January 1974, p. 1.

32. See *Chung-yang jih-pao*, 14 March 1973, p. 1; 15 March 1973, p. 1.

Table 1

Japan's Trade with China and Taiwan, 1965–74
(in millions of dollars)

	Japan's Trade with China				Japan's Trade with Taiwan			
Year	Export	Import	Total	Balance	Export	Import	Total	Balance
1965	245	224	469	+ 21	206	152	358	+ 54
1966	315	306	621	+ 9	230	142	372	+ 88
1967	288	269	557	+ 19	315	135	450	+ 180
1968	325	244	569	+ 81	424	152	576	+ 272
1969	391	234	625	+ 157	489	179	668	+ 310
1970	569	254	823	+ 315	582	236	818	+ 346
1971	578	322	900	+ 256	767	267	1,034	+ 500
1972	609	490	1,099	+ 119	1,091	420	1,511	+ 671
1973	1,041	969	2,010	+ 72	1,643	891	2,534	+ 752
1974	1,986	1,304	3,290	+ 682	2,011	952	2,963	+1,059
Total	**6,347**	**4,616**	**10,963**	**+1,731**	**7,758**	**3,526**	**11,284**	**+4,232**

Sources: Respective issues of *Far Eastern Economic Review*, *China Trade Report*, *Japan Economic Review*, *Foreign Trade of Japan*, and *Foreign Trade Quarterly* (Taipei). The trade figures for 1973 and 1974 were reported by the *Japan Economic Review* no. 3 (March 15, 1974), p. 12; *ibid.*, no. 2 (Feb. 15, 1975), p. 10. All figures are approximate, not absolute.

Table 2

Japan's Ten Top Purchasers in 1973–74
(in millions of dollars)

Country or Area	1973 Exports	1973 Imports	Rank	1974 Exports	1974 Imports	Rank
United States	9,459	9,257	1	12,807	12,680	1
South Korea	1,790	1,214	2	2,656	1,570	2
Taiwan	1,643	891	3	2,011	952	4
Liberia	1,552	45	4	2,344	36	3
Britain	1,358	760	5	1,530	876	9
West Germany	1,272	1,112	6	1,500	1,459	10
Australia	1,195	3,496	7	2,000	4,027	5
Hong Kong	1,118	278	8	—	—	—
China	1,041	969	9	1,986	1,304	6
Canada	999	2,021	10	1,586	2,675	7
Singapore				1,568	618	8
Others	15,478	18,260		25,590	35,879	
Total	**36,914**	**38,303**		**55,578**	**62,076**	

Source: *Japan Economic Review*, no. 3 (March 15, 1974), p. 12; *ibid.*, no. 2 (Feb. 15, 1975), p. 10.

Taiwan accepted Tokyo's representation in the name of a Japan Interchange Association staffed by officials of the Japanese Ministry of Foreign Affairs "temporarily on leave."[33]

In the twenty-two years prior to the normalization of Sino-Japanese diplomatic relations, China never seriously objected to the Japan-Taiwan trade in purely economic terms. As a matter of fact, it was Japan who, sometimes acting under the pressure from Taiwan and the United States, discriminated against China by enforcing Western embargo regulations (some of these are still in force), refusing to conclude a governmental trade agreement involving the mutual grant of certain privileges, and denying Japanese exporters the privilege of using government credit facilities in transactions with their Chinese

33. See Agreement Between the Association of East Asia Relations and the Japan Interchange Association (26 December 1972), *Chung-yang jih-pao*, 27 December 1972, p. 1; Leonard Pratt, "The Strange Partnership," *Japan Times*, 6 January 1974, p. 8.

Table 3

Japan's Private Investments in Nine Top Asian Countries as of March 31, 1973
(in millions of dollars)

Country or Area	Acquisition of Securities	Private Loans	Real Estate and Direct Investments	Overseas Branches	Total
Indonesia	121	351	1	1	474
South Korea	195	5	1	7	208
Thailand	86	40	1	3	130
Taiwan[1]	89	16	—	3	108
Hong Kong	72	24	0	3	99
Singapore	67	16	3	3	89
Philippines	29	58	—	1	88
Brunei	14	72	—	—	86
Malaysia	50	24	1	1	76
Others	24	6	0	1	31
Total	**747**	**612**	**7**	**23**	**1,389**

1. According to Taiwan sources, in the calendar years 1973 and 1974 Japan made an additional investment of $85 million, including "pledges," bringing Japan's total investment in Taiwan to about $193 million. See *Free China Review*, no. 4 (1975), p. 34.

Source: "Japan's Overseas Private Investment-Growth and Change," in Department of State News Release, October 23, 1973, attachment IV. All figures are based on the Japanese Ministry of Finance.

counterparts.[34] Thus, much of China's criticism about Japan's trade with Taiwan and the alleged Japanese intent to reduce Taiwan to an "economic colony" was basically a reaction to Japan's political hostility rather than a deliberate attempt to disrupt the Taipei-Tokyo trade. Indeed, the famous "four conditions" laid down by Premier Chou En-lai in April 1970 to govern China's trade relations with Japan were clearly politically motivated—a response to the Sato-Nixon communi-

34. For a discussion of these matters, see Gene T. Hsiao, "The Role of Trade in China's Diplomacy With Japan," in Jerome A. Cohen, ed., *The Dynamics of China's Foreign Relations* (Cambridge, Mass: Harvard University Press, 1970), p. 41.

que of 21 November 1969 that enlarged Japan's security role in East Asia.[35] But even in this case China did not strictly enforce the rules, and as a result large Japanese companies were still able to trade with China through their "dummy" firms—a fact well known to the Chinese.

After establishing diplomatic relations with Japan, China virtually dropped all public criticism of Japan's economic ties with Taiwan. In a series of interviews with overseas Chinese from Japan and the United States, Premier Chou En-lai repeatedly said that after Taiwan was reunified with the mainland the government would do nothing to lower the Taiwan people's living standards. He pointed out that Shanghai, for example, used to have a higher living standard than all other cities in China before 1949 and this remained so at the present time. One reason for this policy is obviously that Taiwan's assets eventually can be used to help build the mainland economy.[36]

Then in November 1973, the official Chinese news agency, Hsin Hua, released a long dispatch about the Taiwan economy. Without naming any individual countries, but clearly directed against the two top trading partners and investors of Taiwan (the United States and Japan), the report stated that in order to maintain their external contact and internal stability the Nationalist authorities created a "fictitious economic prosperity" by selling out Chinese national interests for large-sum foreign investments. Quoting Nationalist statistics that by May 1973 there were already 737 foreign factories in Taiwan, most of them being processing industries, Hsin Hua charged that Taiwan thus became nothing but a source of cheap labor power for foreign monopoly capital, and the wealth created by the vast working people's "sweat and blood" only filled foreign capitalists' pockets. In consequence, the report continued, the Taiwan economy became further "colonialized."[37]

China's criticism of Japan's economic expansion in general and its role in the Taiwan economy in particular was nothing new. For a decade or so before the rapprochement, the Chinese news media had

35. These four conditions were: China would not trade with (1) those Japanese firms that help Taiwan to invade the mainland and South Korea to invade North Korea, (2) those that have large investments in Taiwan and South Korea, (3) those that supply arms and munitions to United States "imperialism" to wage aggression against Vietnam, Laos, and Cambodia, and (4) the joint American-Japanese enterprises and American subsidiaries in Japan. See Ta-kung-pao (Hong Kong), 3 May 1970, p. 2. The text of the communique is in *The New York Times*, 22 November 1969, p. 14.

36. For an interesting discussion of this possibility, see Robert W. Barnett, "A Future for Taiwan," in Gene T. Hsiao, ed., *Sino-American Detente*, p. 262.

37. "The Chiang Kai-shek Gang Continues to Sell Out National Interests for Large-Sum Foreign Capital," *Kuang-min jih-pao* (Peking), 7 November 1973, p. 3. For reference to Taiwan's recent economic situation, see William Glenn, "Taiwan's New Status," *Far Eastern Economic Review* No. 6 (11 February 1974), p. 40; "Taiwan's Fragile Prosperity," *ibid.* No. 8 (25 February 1974), p. 36. For Peking's comment on Taiwan's agriculture and its relationship with foreign investment, see *Jen-min jih-pao*, 3 February 1974, p. 4.

frequently referred to Japan's rapid economic growth as a precursor to the revival of militarism. The criticism reached its climax when Premier Chou En-lai in April 1970 in Pyongyang openly accused Japan of plotting to restore South Korea and Taiwan as Japanese colonies through economic expansionism.[38] And interestingly enough, about a year later the former native Taiwanese mayor of Taipei and now the Nationalist Minister of Communications, Kao Yu-shu, seemed to echo Premier Chou when he said in an interview with a United Press International correspondent: "First, the Japanese will dominate Taiwan economically. Already, Japanese investments and industry are considerable and are expanding. Second, they will control the island politically, and third, the military will arrive. Japan will try to annex Taiwan. Wait and see!"[39] Thus, the revived Chinese criticism in 1973 may be seen as an expression of Peking's growing concern about the question of reunification with Taiwan and the related political implications of Japan's economic role in Asia.

Chinese leaders know perfectly well that the key to a final settlement of the Taiwan question lies in the United States, not in Japan.[40] But Japan's growing economic cooperation with the Nationalists has made the settlement more difficult. It is a fact that together with the United States, which in 1974 had a two-way trade of $3,712 million with Taiwan and a private investment of nearly $500 million, Japan has enhanced Taiwan's economic potential, technological know-how, and defense capabilities. As their economy continues to improve, the Taiwan people may become less receptive to China's call for reunification.[41]

Then, too, the presence of a semi-official Nationalist diplomatic mission in Tokyo and the emergence of the Seirankai, whose membership is in some ways overlapping with the powerful pro-Taiwan lobby in the Diet supported by Deputy Prime Minister Take Fukuda, former Prime Minister Nobusuke Kishi and others, have combined to give the appearance, if not the substance, that Japan is still pursuing a "two China" policy.

Moreover, Taiwan is militarily tied up with Japan's defense in its

38. "Speech by Premier Chou En-lai at Pyongyang Mass Rally," *Peking Review* No. 15 (10 April 1970), p. 18.

39. In Albert Axelbank, *Black Star Over Japan: Rising Forces of Militarism* (New York: Hill and Wang, 1972), p. 154.

40. For example, in an interview with Japanese Socialists in April 1957, Chairman Mao Tse-tung frankly admitted that settlement of the Taiwan issue would take a long time because it involved the United States. See Shao-chuan Leng, *Japan and Communist China* (Kyoto: Doshisha University Press, 1958), p. 98.

41. China's call for peaceful reunification with Taiwan was issued by the National Committee of the Chinese People's Consultative Conference on 28 February 1973. See *Jen-min jih-pao*, 1 March 1973, p. 1.

treaty with the United States and the latter's security alliance with Japan.[42] It is well known that the "Far East clause" of the Japan-United States treaty included the defense of not only Taiwan and Penghu (the Pescadores) but also that of Quemoy and Matsu—the two groups of islands off the China mainland coast which are still under Nationalist control.[43] Mr. C. L. Sulzberger of *The New York Times* reported that there in fact existed "a secret but binding commitment" between the Nationalists and the United States tying the fate of Taiwan to that of Okinawa and therefore of Japan.[44] Then the 1969 Sato-Nixon communique virtually established a "sphere of influence" for Japan by specifying that "the security of the Republic of Korea was essential to Japan's own security" and that "the maintenance of peace and security in the Taiwan area was also a most important factor for the security of Japan."

The Sino-American detente raised some grave doubts in the Japanese minds about the usefulness and necessity of both the "Far East clause" and the "Taiwan clause" (in the Sato-Nixon communique), and even about the security treaty itself.[45] There were suggestions that President Nixon's pledge in the Shanghai communique not to "challenge" the Chinese claim to the title of Taiwan has in effect cancelled the Taiwan part of the Japan-United States security alliance.[46] However, the fact is that Nixon's pledge is a qualified promise: it rests on the assumption that the Chinese on both sides of the Taiwan Strait will remain in agreement that "there is but one China and that Taiwan is a part of

42. The purpose of Taiwan's treaty with the United States was "to strengthen the fabric of peace in the West Pacific Area. . . . Pending the development of a more comprehensive system of regional security" in the Area, which was defined to mean, "in respect of the Republic of China, Taiwan and the Pescadores; and in respect of the United States, the island territories in the West Pacific under its jurisdiction"; as well as "such other territories as may be determined by mutual agreement." These territories were generally understood to mean at least Quemoy and Matsu. See Mutual Defense Treaty Between the Republic of China and the United States of America (2 December 1954), Preamble and Articles V and VI, in Ministry of Foreign Affairs, *Treaties Between the Republic of China and Foreign States (1927–1961)* (Taipei, 1958), pp. 824–6.

43. See Treaty of Mutual Cooperation and Security Between the United States of America and Japan (19 January 1960), Articles IV and VI, in Department of State, *U.S. Treaties and Other International Agreements*, vol. 11, TIAS 4509, pp. 1632, 1634. For a discussion of the definition of the "Far East clause," see F. C. Langdon, *Japan's Foreign Policy* (Vancouver: University of British Columbia Press, 1973), pp. 39–41.

44. C. L. Sulzberger, "An Okinawa-Taiwan Deal?", *The New York Times*, 18 November 1970, p. 43.

45. Fuji Kamiya, "Japanese-U.S. Relations and the Security Treaty: A Japanese Perspective," *Asian Survey* No. 9 (September 1972), p. 717.

46. See F. C. Langdon, *Japan's Foreign Policy*, pp. 199–200. In his analysis, however, the author pointed out that there was no clear agreement between Japan and the United States on this matter.

China."[47] Supposing one day the Taiwan Chinese choose to issue a "declaration of independence," then the United States can still support such a move without expressly violating Nixon's promise.[48] In fact, it is doubtful whether Nixon actually intended to fully normalize relations with China at Taiwan's expense. Before setting out to Peking, he reported to the Congress:

> In my address announcing my trip to Peking [on 15 July 1971], and since then, I have emphasized that our new dialogue with the PRC would not be at the expense of friends. Nevertheless, we recognize that this process cannot help but be painful for our old friend on Taiwan, the Republic of China. . . . We regret the decision of the General Assembly to deprive the Republic of China of its representation although we welcomed the admission of the People's Republic of China. With the Republic of China, we shall maintain our friendship, our diplomatic ties, and our defense commitment. The ultimate relationship between Taiwan and the mainland is not a matter for the United States to decide. A peaceful resolution of this problem by the parties would do much to reduce tension in the Far East. We are not, however, urging either party to follow any particular course.[49]

After his return from China, the United States terminated its military aid to Taiwan (in 1973) and reduced its military forces in Taiwan to slightly over 3,000. However, in other fields of activities American cooperation with the Nationalists appeared to have increased. Aside from the vast amount of trade and private investments mentioned above, the United States granted the Nationalist government large-sum loans and credits from the Export and Import Bank and other American sources for the purchase of military supplies, the manufacturing and assembly of combat aircraft, helicopters, and automobiles, as well as the building of nuclear power plants.[50] Under the Ford Administration,

47. See the Joint Communique, 28 February 1972, in *Peking Review* No. 9 (3 March 1972), pp. 4–5.

48. In theory, Taiwan still maintains the "one China" position. In practice, the present Taipei authorities clearly want to separate the island from the mainland for an indefinite period. See Tillman Durdin, "Taiwan's Premier Bars Peking Deal," *The New York Times*, 1 January 1974; "Chiang Ching-kuo's Taiwan," *Pacific Community*, No. 1 (October 1975), pp. 92–117.

49. Richard Nixon, *U.S. Foreign Policy for the 1970s: The Emerging Structure of Peace* (A Report to the Congress, 9 February 1972), (Washington, D.C.: U.S. Government Printing Office, 1972), p. 35.

50. "Continued US Loans for Purchase of Military Supplies," *Chung-yang jih-pao*, 6 February 1974, p. 1; "Aircraft Factory Planned," *Free China Weekly* No. 43 (4 November 1973), p. 2; "Chinese Air Force Starts Making Its Own Choppers," *ibid.* No 21 (28 May 1972), p. 4; "Ford and Lio Ho Partnership," *ibid.* No. 47 (26 November 1972), p. 1; "U.S. Steel to Help Build Mill," *ibid.* No. 32 (19 August 1973), p. 4; "5th, 6th Nuclear

$123 million worth of arms are sold to Taiwan in the current fiscal year (1975–1976) and another $100 million worth are proposed to be sold next year. In each case, it was reported that $80 million of the total is on credit.[51]

Meanwhile, on the eve of President Ford's visit to China (December 1–5, 1975), a Gallop poll financed by the Nationalist Embassy in Washington showed that 61 percent of the United States public favored diplomatic relations with Peking, but 70 percent opposed withdrawing recognition from Taiwan. Further, a Congressional resolution sponsored by Democratic Representative Dawson Mathis of Georgia against the improvement of relations with China at Taiwan's expense was signed by 214 House members (the number was increased to 218 or more than the total while Ford was meeting Chinese leaders in Peking).[52] Thus, it is not surprising that before and during the presidential visit both Ford and Secretary of State Kissinger publicly emphasized the international aspect of American-Chinese relationship, meaning the Soviet factor in global politics, and ignored the question of Taiwan.[53] The visit ended without a formal communique or an agreement on such minor collateral issues as bilateral trade and the blocked assets.

In these circumstances, it seems reasonably clear that the status quo of Taiwan will remain for some time to come, at least until after the 1976 election. At the same time, many of the Japanese who do not feel responsible for the prolonged separation of Taiwan from the mainland will continue to make economic inroads into the island, and the Japanese rightists, who almost invariably serve as lobbyists for the business circles, will continue to argue that Taiwan is an independent political entity in its own right. Indeed, the *Japan Times*, which sometimes reflects the views of the Japanese Ministry of Foreign Affairs, has always maintained this position.[54] In short, Taiwan will remain an obstacle in China's relationship with both Japan and the United States,

---

Generators Slated," *ibid.* No. 40 (14 October 1973), p. 4; William Glenn, "Isolation: A Spur to Taiwan," *Far Eastern Economic Review* No. 5 (4 February 1974), p. 44.

51. Richard Dudman, "Detente Hampers Ford on China Trip," *St. Louis Post Dispatch*, News Analysis, November 30, 1975, p. 1.

52. Robert Keatley, "Politesse In Peking," *The Wall Street Journal*, November 28, 1975, p. 18.

53. E.g., Secretary of State Henry A. Kissinger's interview with NBC-TV, October 12, 1975, Department of State release; Secretary Kissinger's speech before the Economic Club of Detroit, November 24, 1975, Department of State release; Richard Dudman, "Ford Ends Visit to China," *St. Louis Post Dispatch*, December 4, 1975, p. 1.

54. In an editorial on the aviation agreement, for example, the newspaper contended: "the fact is that Taiwan enjoys complete independence and is territory over which Peking has no control whatsoever. . . ." *Japan Times*, 26 March 1974, p. 10.

but its effect on China's overall relationship with these countries is not likely to be determined solely on the basis of its own merits but in connection with China's broader strategic interests in such other matters as Japan's future defense policy and the Soviet threat.

Japan's Defense Policy: The Question of a Joint Nuclear Force

The late English philosopher Bertrand Russell once wrote: "Economic power, unlike military power, is not primary, but derivative. Within one State, it depends on law; in international dealings it is only on minor issues that it depends on law, but when large issues are involved it depends on war or the threat of war."[55] The question that Japan has to face in the next decade or so is therefore one of its defense policy. Will an economic giant like Japan remain a "military pygmy," as Professor John M. Maki calls it, for an indefinite future?[56] Since any change in Japan's present defense and alliance policy will inevitably affect China's security interests, it is fitting that I review briefly the mutual perception of China and Japan as a potential military threat before the rapprochement, and then discuss their present attitudes toward each other and the possibility of establishing a Sino-Japanese nuclear force supported by the United States.

Before the Sino-American detente, China's perception of Japan as a security threat was based on a number of premises. Historically, Japan was the principal source of aggression suffered by China. The damages that Japan had done to China were practically beyond repair: they involved about 15 million human lives and $50,000 million property losses—measured in the dollar value of 1950.[57] Ideologically, from the Marxist point of view, Japan's more recent capitalistic economic expansion cannot help but lead to imperialism—meaning aggression and war.[58] Politically and militarily, the Japan-United States security treaty was originally directed against China and the Soviet Union, and the concurrent program for Japan's rearmament was almost for the same

55. Bertrand Russell, *Power: A New Social Analysis* (New York: Barnes and Noble, Inc., 1962), p. 82.

56. John M. Maki, "Japan and World Politics in the 1970s (article review)," *Pacific Affairs* No. 2 (Summer 1972), p. 290.

57. See Shen Chun-ju, "On the Prosecution and Punishment of War Criminals (6 September 1951)," in *Jih-pen wen-t'i wen-chien hui-pien* (Compilation of Documents on the Question of Japan) (Peking: Shih-chieh chih-shih ch'u-pan-she, 1955), Vol. 1 (1942–1954), p. 74.

58. See V. L. Lenin, "Imperialism, the Highest Stage of Capitalism," *Selected Works* (Moscow: Foreign Languages Publishing House, 1960), Vol. 1, pp. 781–2.

purpose.[59] A recent study on Japan's postwar rearmament revealed: "In October 1950, when the world thought occupied Japan had no naval forces, forty-six of its ships [manned by former Imperial naval officers] were ordered into combat in Korea."[60] Socially and psychologically, China saw traces of fanaticism in postwar Japan as symbolized by the dramatic suicide of the famous novelist Yukio Mishima in strict observance of the *Bushido* ritual.[61]

For these and other reasons, China regarded the revival of Japanese militarism armed with nuclear weapons almost as a foregone conclusion.[62] This was most clearly and authoritatively revealed in Premier Chou En-lai's August 1971 statement to Mr. James Reston:

- The Japan-United States security alliance has helped to promote Japan's militarism.
- With its economic power and technology, Japan is already capable of making all means of delivery; what is lacking is the nuclear warhead.
- Japan's output of nuclear power is increasing daily as more enriched uranium is imported from not only the United States but other countries as well, with the result that Japan can readily produce nuclear weapons.
- If the United States is to withdraw its forces in Japan, the Japanese can make use of the American nuclear bases left behind.
- Economic expansion is bound to bring about military expansion, and the United States security treaty with Japan cannot serve the purpose of stopping Japan from going nuclear.[63]

Japan, on the other hand, perceived that China was a security threat on the basis of the Sino-Soviet treaty of 14 February 1950 which specified "a revived imperialistic Japan" as the principal enemy of China's participation in the Korean conflict, and its support for the

59. For a discussion of the origins and development of the Japan-United States security alliance, see Martin E. Weinstein, *Japan's Postwar Defense Policy 1947–1968* (New York: Columbia University Press, 1971).

60. James E. Auer, *The Postwar Rearmament of Japanese Maritime Forces, 1945–1971* (New York: Praeger Publishers, 1973), p. 254.

61. For a discussion of this incident, see Albert Axelbank, *Black Star Over Japan*, p. 71.

62. For a non-Chinese Marxist view on the subject, see Jon Halliday and Gavan McCormack, *Japanese Imperialism Today* (New York: Monthly Review Press, 1973).

63. See "Transcript of Reston Interview With Chou," in Frank Ching, ed., *Report From Red China*, pp. 93–4. For a similar report see "Interview with Premier Chou En-lai by the Committee of Concerned Asian Scholars Friendship Delegation to China," in *China: Inside the People's Republic* (New York: Bantam Books, 1971), pp. 353–359.

Japan Communist Party.[64] By the 1960s, however, all three premises supporting the Japanese perception of a Chinese threat had lost their validity as a result of the cessation of the Korean conflict, the breakdown of the Sino-Soviet alliance, and the split between the Chinese Communist Party (CCP) and the Japan Communist Party. Meanwhile, the Chinese perception of a Japanese threat not only remained valid but was reinforced by Japan's continued nonrecognition policy and other hostile acts toward China, including her assistance to the United States in the Indochina war and her normalization treaty with South Korea.[65] At the same time, China's nuclear explosions aroused new apprehensions in Japan.[66] Through this process of interaction, Sino-Japanese relations were virtually in deadlock toward the end of 1970.

The impasse was broken by the Sino-American detente, with the result that China and Japan began to see each other in a new light. During a "casual talk" with the senior LDP Dietman and former Minister of Construction Takeo Kimura, three months after the normalization of Sino-Japanese diplomatic relations, Premier Chou En-lai made these significant remarks:

- The Japan-United States security treaty would become unnecessary in Sino-Japanese relations because it would be unbecoming of an independent nation like Japan.
- However, since Japan needed United States nuclear protection it would be "unavoidable" for Japan to keep the pact vis-à-vis the Soviet Union.
- China's nuclear arms were strictly for defense purposes and for this reason it would be no use for Japan to try to replace the United States with China for nuclear protection.
- While Japan as an independent nation would need defense power, its fourth defense buildup plan appeared to be a different matter. However, it would be up to the Japanese to decide whether the program should mark the beginning of Japanese militarism or whether it should remain within the limits of self-defense.

64. See Shigeru Yoshida, *Japan's Decisive Century, 1867–1967* (New York: Praeger Publishers, 1967), p. 83.

65. Young C. Kim, "Japan and the Vietnam War," in Gene T. Hsiao, ed., *The Role of External Powers in the Indochina Crisis* (Edwardsville, Ill: Southern Illinois University Publications, 1973), p. 152; Sung Yoon Cho, "South Korea's Relations with Japan as Seen in the Normalization Treaty-Making Process 1964–1965," in Young C. Kim, ed., *Japan in World Politics* (Washington, D.C.: Institute for Asian Studies, 1972), p. 99.

66. As late as June 1973 when China exploded her fifteenth nuclear device, the Japanese government filed a formal protest with the Chinese goverment. See "Government Files N-Blast Protest in Peking," *Japan Times*, 29 June 1973, p. 1.

- The ending of the Indochina war should ease tensions in Asia, but there has emerged a new problem over the Asian horizon—the shadow of the Soviet Union.[67]

Premier Chou thus cancelled out the China part of the Japan-United States security treaty—presumably on the basis of his understanding with President Nixon and Prime Minister Tanaka—and identified the Soviet nuclear threat as the only cause of justification for its continued operation. He also implied the possibility of a Sino-Japanese security alliance and confirmed Japan's right of self-defense. In fact, Japan's fourth defense plan went into effect soon after Prime Minister Tanaka's return from China, reportedly with Premier Chou's "understanding" of the plan's criterion. It focused on the modernization of equipment other than on the expansion of size. When completed, the plan would make Japan seventh among the world's leading military powers after the United States, the Soviet Union, China, Britain, France, and West Germany. If nuclear powers were excluded, Japan would become a leading non-nuclear power in the world with thirty times the fire-power it possessed during World War II.[68]

The rationale of the plan was based on an assessment of the current international situation. China was not singled out as a military threat. As the planners saw it, the potential threat to Japan exists in a possible conflict of the "intricately intertwined" interests among the three big powers (the United States, the Soviet Union, and China), in a possible breakdown of the detente, and in other factors in various other nations which make for tension. For these reasons, the Japanese government believed that while the possibility of a total war is further diminishing as a result of the detente among the big powers, the danger of limited local armed conflicts remains. In line with this reasoning, the keynote of Japan's defense concept under the fourth plan consisted of two pillars: in the case of indirect aggression or a small-scale direct aggression, Japan will counter it with her own forces; in the case of an attack beyond such a scale or nuclear threats, Japan relies on the existing security arrangements with the United States to cope with the situation.[69]

The plan provided for a total budget of Y4,630,000 million, or about

67. "Premier Says U.S. Will Accept PRG, Saigon, Hanoi," *Japan Times*, 19 January 1973, p. 1.

68. Koji Nakamura, "Introducing 'Positive' Defense," *Far Eastern Economic Review* No. 43 (21 October 1972), p. 15.

69. "4,630,000 Million Yen Outlay Nearly Double Last Plan," *Japan Times*, 10 October 1972, p. 1; "Improvement of Defense Capabilities the Object of Five-Year $15 Billion Defense Budget," *Japan Report* No. 12 (16 June 1973), pp. 1–3.

$15,400 million, for five years (1972–1976), doubling the total budget for the previous plan of 1967–1971 (Y2,340,000 million). The annual appropriations for the three years since the plan started have been as follows: $2,670 million for 1972, $3,120 million for 1973, and $3,640 million for 1974. The Japanese government emphasized that in each case the annual appropriation represented less than 7 percent of the total government budget, or less than 1 percent of the gross national product.[70] Accordingly, in terms of GNP ratios Japan ranked as only the twenty-first largest defense spender in the world, the first being Israel (23.9 percent), followed by Egypt (21.7 percent), the Soviet Union (15.7 percent), South Vietnam (12 percent), China (10.7 percent), Iran (8.5 percent), the United States (7.3 percent), etc.[71] This comparison is misleading not only in terms of Japan's enormous GNP size, but also in view of the very limited size of territories that Japan has to defend. But, on the whole, the buildup is hardly a threat to China. In long-range terms, the real question is whether this plan would lead to "militarism," as Premier Chou pointed out. And by militarism, he was probably referring to both Japan's acquisition of nuclear weapons and the socio-political circumstances under which these weapons are acquired.[72]

Japan is already a nuclear nation with six nuclear power plants capable of producing 2,283,000 kilowatts. Twenty-nine others with a total capacity of 24,216,000 kilowatts have been under construction and are expected to go into operation before 1981. It is estimated that Japan will be able to raise the combined total capacity of nuclear power to 60 million kilowatts or 25 percent of the nation's total power consumption by 1985, when Japan is expected to produce at least one third of the enriched uranium required for such purposes.[73] In addition, Japan is in possession of a nuclear-powered ship, the 8,350-ton *Matsu*, and can

70. The yen-dollar conversion rate has changed several times in the past three years. The dollar figures cited above and below are approximate, based on the rate of 300 yen to one dollar. The annual government budget was $38,222 million for 1972, $47,613 million for 1973, and $56,998 million for 1974. Japan's gross national product was $321,000 million in 1972 and over $400,000 million in 1973. See *Japan Report* No. 4 (16 February 1972), p. 5; "General Account Represents 24.6 % Increase Over 1972," *Japan Times*, 16 January 1973, pp. 1, 5; "Government Budget for Fiscal 1974," *ibid.*, 30 December 1973, pp. 1, 3. For reference to Japan's defense expenditures from 1954 to 1968, see Martin E. Weinstein, *Japan's Postwar Defense Policy*, Table 2, p. 123; for the period 1958 to 1972, see F. C. Langdon, *Japan's Foreign Policy*, Table 6.1, p. 118.

71. *Japan Report* No. 12 (16 June 1973), p. 2.

72. For a recent discussion of this matter, see Swadesh R. De Roy, "Prospects for Militarism in Japan," *Pacific Community* (Tokyo) No. 2 (January 1974), p. 289.

73. "Building of A-Power Plants Seen Rising," *Japan Economic Review* No. 5 (15 May 1974), p. 8; "MITI Energy Survey Reports," *Japan Times*, 26 September 1973, p. 10.

build nuclear-powered submarines without any difficulties.[74] As Japan's space program continues to advance, it is conceivable that a delivery system can be completed in a relatively short period of time.[75]

On the socio-political side of the scale, very few Japanese fifteen years ago were willing to discuss the question of nuclear armament. In a 1969 *Mainichi shimbun* poll, however, a combined total of 45 percent felt that Japan should acquire nuclear weapons, whereas those opposed to acquisition accounted for only 46 percent. In another poll three years later, those who favored acquisition dropped to 35 percent and those who were against rose to 58 percent.[76] In each case the "hawks" did not have a majority, but the percentages they represented remain impressive. Perhaps the most important evidence on the subject has been the government's deliberate delay in submitting the Nuclear Nonproliferation Treaty to the Diet for ratification despite Prime Minister Miki's avowed intention to do so.[77] There are many technical and partisan reasons for the delay. In essence, however, the question lies in whether or not Japan should keep the nuclear option open in order to protect its national interests.[78] This question has become all the more acute after India's nuclear explosion in May 1974 and the victory of the Communist forces in Indochina a year later.[79]

There is no doubt that internal opposition to Japan's military nuclearization is substantial. But if and when Japan's vital national interests call for nuclear armament, most of the Japanese, being a very patriotic people, are likely to go along with it. The real difficulties in materializing such a plan lie in external conditions. As an island country sandwiched between three giant continental nuclear powers, the

74. "Japan's Nuclear Ship is Stranded," *ibid.*, 7 May 1973, p. 2; "Japan's First N-Ship Begins Test July 29," *ibid.*, 27 July 1973, p. 3. The Japanese Socialists recently charged that Japanese heavy industries, such as Kawazaki, actually drafted plans for the building of nuclear-powered submarines as early as 1958. See "Government Trying to Build N-Subs," *ibid.*, 8 February 1974, p. 1.

75. Richard Halloran, "Japanese Launch Their 5th Satellite and Take a Major Step Forward in Space Program," *The New York Times*, 18 February 1974, p. 16. For reference to Japan's past and future space programs, see *Japan Report* No. 9 (1 May 1974), pp. 1–2.

76. In Kei Wakaizumi, "Japan's Role in a New World Order," *Foreign Affairs* No. 2 (January 1973), pp. 310, 314.

77. "Ratification of NPT Postponed," *Japan Times*, February 20, 1975, p. 1; "NPT Ratification Won't Be Sought," *ibid.*, November 7, 1975, p. 5.

78. Masaru Ogawa, "Dilemma Over NPT," *ibid.*, February 2, 1975, p. 1; also see F. C. Langdon, *Japan's Foreign Policy*, pp. 137–142.

79. Much argument has been made on the subject. Aside from the works already cited, for additional references, see Herman Kahn, *The Emerging Japanese Superstate: Challenge and Response* (Englewood Cliffs, N.J.: Prentice-Hall, Inc., 1971); John K. Emmerson, *Arms, Yen and Power: The Japanese Dilemma* (Tokyo: Charles E. Tuttle, Co., 1972).

options for Japan's defense arrangements are extremely limited: a decision to go nuclear will definitely require the support of at least one of these powers.

Under present circumstances, American support is absolutely indispensable not only because of the existing security and economic ties, which are vital to both nations, but also because of the fact that Japan will need United States protection against possible intervention by other countries during the acquisition period and the supply of enriched uranium and other materials essential to the successful manufacturing of nuclear weapons. Furthermore, given its compact geopolitical position, Japan is more likely to develop a second-strike force located in the Pacific Ocean than a land-based first-strike capability.[80] This will require American support; otherwise, the very presence of a nuclear-armed Japanese navy in the Pacific will constitute a direct threat to the United States other than to China or the Soviet Union.

Some observers believe that it may be in the interest of the United States to support Japan if the Soviet Union has begun to enjoy a nuclear edge. The rationale is that the United States probably will then need allies more than before and its support for the Japanese undertaking may serve the purpose of complicating Soviet strategic and political planning.[81] However, in doing so no strategic aim will be achieved if it does not have China's cooperation or support. A joint United States-Japan nuclear force can conceivably drive China back into the Soviet orbit. Or if this does not happen, it is certainly going to destroy the detente and entente with China that the United States and Japan have respectively so painstakingly built.

Chinese cooperation or support will be obtainable so long as the Soviet threat persists and provided that the Japanese nuclear force is not controlled by a reactionary political element like the Seirankai. In 1973 officials of the People's Republic openly charged that the situation along the Sino-Soviet border was so intense that only American diplomatic efforts prevented a Soviet nuclear strike.[82] The validity of this charge is not so important as the Chinese willingness to acknowl-

80. For an interesting analysis of this subject, see chapter 1 by Morton A. Kaplan, "Japan and the International System."

81. Zbigniew Brzezinski, "Japan's Global Engagement," *Foreign Affairs* No. 2 (January 1972), pp. 270, 278–9.

82. "USSR-China Rift Said to Be Quieter," *Japan Times,* 16 June 1973, p. 14. The Soviet Embassy in Washington denied this charge. See "Announcement to the Press by the USSR Embassy in the USA," *Pravda,* 2 June 1973, p. 4, in "Reported Soviet Threat to China Denied," *Current Digest of the Soviet Press* No. 22 (27 June 1973), p. 4.

edge with gratitude American nuclear protection.[83] Furthermore, it is well known that China has been enlisting Japan's support vis-à-vis the Soviet Union since September 1972. Consequently, in this hypothetical scenario of the joint United States-Japan-China nuclear project, the question boils down to whether Japan would like to enlist Chinese cooperation.

It has always been the Chinese contention that they are for complete nuclear disarmament by all nations and before that is done, for the establishment of nuclear-free zones, including one in Northeast Asia; and that the only reason they have built a nuclear force is to break the monopoly by the two superpowers.[84] This argument appears to have met with favorable response in Japan, which, in the process of developing its own nuclear weapons, may use the same argument to justify its position.[85] Moreover, China has repeatedly vowed not to become a nuclear superpower and never to be the first to use nuclear weapons. Given China's economic limitations, it is beyond doubt that the People's Republic will confine its nuclear capability to certain limits—a second-strike force for self-defense. Japan, on the other hand, is not constrained by money; but its geopolitical position, as already discussed above, will limit its options for alliance and its developing strategy to a second-strike force. Thus, Japan and China share a common strategic interest: while they are both protected by the American nuclear power against the Soviet Union, the establishment of a joint Sino-Japanese nuclear force could strengthen their own defense and also serve as a formidable counterweight and deterrent to the superpowers' first-strike forces and accordingly reduce the danger of a nuclear war—an idea that has already been under active consideration by the Common Market countries.[86]

For the United States, such a joint force could help to reduce its own defense burden and at the same time provide an otherwise unavailable opportunity to gain a certain degree of control over the Chinese and Japanese activities through cooperation and eventually bring both China and Japan to the conference table for the limitation, reduction,

83. Before the Chinese made the charge, columnist Jack Anderson reported that during his May 1972 visit to Moscow President Nixon told the Soviet leader Leonid Brezhnev that "a war between China and Russia would be against the national interests of the United States" and would "threaten world peace." See "China-Soviet Peace Kept by Nixon, Anderson Says," *Japan Times*, 28 May 1973, p. 4. Thus, the Chinese charge partly confirmed Anderson's account.

84. See "U.N. Debate on Disarmament: Chiao Kuan-hua Explains Chinese Government's Principled Stand," *Peking Review* No. 49 (3 December 1971), p. 14.

85. For a Japanese analysis of China's nuclear policy, see Hisashi Maeda, "Toward a Non-Nuclear Northeast Asia," *Japan Interpreter* No. 1 (Winter 1973), p. 16.

86. See *The Times* (London), 15 December 1973, pp. 1, 5.

and finally abolition of all nuclear weapons. In short, since China is already a nuclear power, and if Japan's nuclearization becomes unavoidable, the establishment of a Sino-Japanese self-defense project will be in the interest of the United States. Without specifically mentioning the possibility of supporting such a joint Sino-Japanese nuclear force, Secretary of Defense James R. Schlesinger testified on 28 February 1974 before the House Appropriations Committee that he expected Japan to increase her military spending and hoped that Japan would join with China in opposing the Soviet Union in Asia. "For both," he added, "the Soviets are the real threat."[87]

Soviet reaction to a Washington-Peking-Tokyo axis would be vehement. Since the late 1950s the basic issue in the Sino-Soviet dispute has been the question of China's nuclear development. Moscow obviously has seen no advantage in letting China become a nuclear power and "in the interest of a nuclear nonproliferation treaty" unilaterally breached its October 1957 defense agreement to supply China with a sample of an atomic bomb and the technological data for the making of such bombs.[88]

Soviet criticism of Japan's defense expenditures also has been frequent.[89] Realistically speaking, however, since Moscow has no control over China's nuclear development and since it will not have control over any Japanese project either, a Sino-Japanese alliance supported by the United States will not change the present strategic parity between the two superpowers—each already possessing sufficient nuclear power to destroy humanity as a whole.[90] American participation in the Sino-Japanese project can only benefit the Soviet Union by imposing certain restraints on China and Japan. Indeed, such an arrangement will facilitate the implementation of the American-Soviet agreement on the prevention of nuclear war which provides that each party will refrain from the threat or use of nuclear force against the other

87. Leslie H. Gelb, "No Cut Now Seen in U.S. Asian Units," *The New York Times*, 2 March 1974, p. 29.

88. Editorial Departments of *Jen-min jih-pao* and *Hung-ch'i*, "The Origin and Development of the Differences between the Leadership of the CPSU and Ourselves —Comment on the Open Letter of the Central Committee of the CPSU, July 14, 1963," *Jen-min jih-pao*, 6 September 1963, p. 1; English translation in *Peking Review* No. 37 (13 September 1963), p. 6. For Soviet responses, see a collection of documents in William E. Griffith, *The Sino-Soviet Rift* (Cambridge, Mass.: M.I.T. Press, 1964). Also see V. Rybakov, "The People's Republic of China and the Disarmament Problem," *International Affairs* (Moscow) No. 9 (September 1972), p. 26.

89. See *Pravda*'s editorial of 13 January 1973; Japanese comment in Minoru Shimizu, "Japanese-Soviet Relations," *Japan Times*, 8 February 1973, p. 14.

90. For a discussion of the matter, see Wolfgang K. H. Panofsky, "The Mutual-Hostage Relationship Between America and Russia," *Foreign Affairs* No. 1 (October 1973), p. 109.

party, against the allies of the other party and against other countries (Article II); that both parties undertake to develop their relations with each other and with other countries in a way consistent with the purposes of this agreement (Article III); and that both parties "shall immediately enter into urgent consultation with each other and make every effort to avert" the risk of a nuclear conflict if relations between the parties or between either party and other countries appear to involve such a risk or if relations between countries not parties to this agreement appear to involve such a risk (Article IV).[91]

The Moscow-Tokyo-Peking Triangle: A State of Uncertainty

Since the beginning of the Sino-American detente in 1971, Japan has become a center of contention between between China and the Soviet Union. Japan's role in the contest is therefore very important to her relationship with China. There are several complex issues involved in this three-way relationship: the Soviet offer to Japan for the development of Siberian resources in return for Japan's support of the proposed Soviet system of collective security in Asia; Japan's demand for the return of four northern islands as a condition for the conclusion of a peace treaty and economic cooperation; China's response to these problems; and Soviet intervention in the negotiations for a Sino-Japanese peace treaty.

Japan's postwar relationship with the Soviet Union has been basically economic. After the resumption of diplomatic ties in 1956 and the conclusion of a treaty of commerce in the following year, bilateral trade developed at a moderate pace.[92] By 1970, Japan had become the first capitalist trading partner of the Soviet Union with a total volume of $653 million. In the ensuing four years, the annual two-way trade rose to $873 million in 1971, $1,196 million in 1972, $1,564 million in 1973, and $2,515 million in 1974.[93]

In the field of economic cooperation, there are three major joint projects for timber production in the Soviet Far East on a Japanese credit of $130 million, the building of a seaport in the Bay of Wrangle with a Japanese loan of $80 million, and the supply of Soviet wood chips and

91. See Agreement on Prevention of Nuclear War, 22 June 1973, in Department of State Publication 8733 (August 1973), p. 30.

92. The text of the treaty (6 December 1957) is in *Japanese Annual of International Law* No. 2 (1958), p. 173.

93. See *Japan Economic Review* No. 3 (15 March 1972), p. 13; *ibid.* No. 3 (15 March 1973), p. 9; *ibid.* No. 3 (15 March 1974), p. 12.

pulpwood to the Japanese paper industry.[94] Negotiations for the establishment of five additional projects have been under way since the early 1970s for the development of natural gas in Yakutsk, oil in Tyumen, coking coal in southern Yakutsk, oil and natural gas on the continental shelf off Sakhalin, and the further development of forests in Siberia and the Soviet Far East. In order to operate these projects, the Soviet Union asked for a total Japanese loan of $4,500 million for five to twenty years.[95] Under the proposed plans, Japan would export machinery, equipment, and producer and consumer goods to the Soviet Union in exchange for the supply of Soviet raw materials not on an enterprise basis, as is the case today, but on an industry basis for a long period of time.[96]

Of these projects, the most significant one, in both economic and strategic terms, is the Tyumen oil project which, under the original proposal, called for the building of a pipeline and a parallel highway from Nakhodka to Irkutsk, linking the already built pipelines from the latter point to Tyumen. In some parts of the route both the proposed pipeline and highway would run very close to the Chinese border where a giant Soviet military complex is already located.[97] In addition, the project also called for the building of a refinery at Nakhodka. One half of the refined oil would be for the Soviet Union and the other half for Japan. According to the original Soviet proposal, Japan would receive an annual delivery of 40 million tons for a period of twenty years. Later the Soviet authorities reduced this amount to 25 million tons. Thus the annual production capacity of the Tyumen project was estimated at 50 million to 80 million tons. The Japanese figured that the present Soviet consumption of oil in the Far East was about 7,500,000 tons a year, but this might rise to 15 million tons in 1980 because of the arms buildup in the region.[98] Clearly, then, the project was not merely designed to meet the actual civilian needs of that region, but was a part of the Soviet military plan.

In purely economic terms, this project is beneficial to oil-thirsty

94. N. Shiryaev, "Soviet-Japanese Economic Relations," *International Affairs* No. 4 (April 1972), p. 76.

95. Another authoritative source estimated that by 1979 the total loan for the proposed five projects in Siberia would be about $4,800 million. See "Bank Estimates 1979 Loans Total for Siberia," *Japan Times*, 9 March 1974, p. 7.

96. Hiro Hiyama, "Materialization of Five Siberian Projects Will Enhance Japan-Soviet Relations," *ibid.*, New Year's Economic Supplement, January 24, 1974, p. 5.

97. See Koji Nakamura, "China: 'Political' Deal," *Far Eastern Economic Review* No. 4 (29 January 1973), p. 33; "Sino-U.S. Pincer," *ibid.* No. 10 (12 March 1973), p. 20; "Remember the Foe," *ibid.*, No. 14 (9 April 1973), p. 12.

98. "USSR Proposes Cut in Siberia Oil Supply," *Japan Times*, 7 September 1973, p. 12.

Japan, who consumed about 200 million tons of crude oil in 1973 and probably will need 300 million tons a year in the coming three years and about 600 million tons in 1980.[99] Since Japan has to import over 99 percent of its oil from abroad, the projected Tyumen supply would satisfy about 10 percent of its present demand. However, realization of the Soviet proposal was to some degree contingent upon Japan's willingness to support the Soviet collective security proposal, which was expounded by General Secretary Leonid I. Brezhnev in June 1969 as a very general idea.[100] Then about two months after Soviet Foreign Minister Andrei Gromyko's January 1972 visit to Japan, where he had conducted some preliminary discussions with Japanese officials about economic cooperation in Siberia and collective security in Asia,[101] and barely three weeks after President Nixon's return from China, in March 1972, the Soviet party chief declared that "complete normalization" of relations with Japan would be in the interest of both countries, and for this and other related reasons he enunciated a set of principles to guide the operation of an Asian collective security system. They were: (1) renunciation of the use of force, (2) respect for sovereignty and inviolability of frontiers, (3) nonintervention in internal affairs, (4) wide development of economic and other forms of cooperation on the basis of complete equality and mutual benefit, and (5) indivisibility of peace.[102]

At that time the Kremlin obviously hoped that, given Prime Minister Eisaku Sato's bitter disputes with Peking and Washington, the collective security proposal combined with the promised economic benefits might delay Japan's normalization of relations with China and exacerbate Tokyo's economic rivalry with the United States. Therefore,

99. See Editorial, "Oil-Thirsty Japan," *ibid.*, 15 February 1973, p. 14.

100. See Leonid I. Brezhnev, "For Strengthening the Solidarity of Communists, for a New Upswing in the Anti-Imperialist Struggle" (speech to the International Conference of Communist and Workers' Parties in Moscow on 7 June 1969), in *Pravda* and *Izvestia*, 8 June 1969, pp. 1–4, translated in *Current Digest of the Soviet Press* No. 23 (2 July 1969), p. 16.

101. For a discussion of Gromyko's visit to Japan and Soviet reaction to Nixon's visit to China, see George Ginsburgs, "Moscow's Reaction to Nixon's Jaunt to Peking," in Gene T. Hsiao, ed., *Sino-American Detente*, p. 137.

102. See Leonid I. Brezhnev, "The Decisions of the 24th Congress Are a Militant Program of Activity for the Soviet Trade Unions" (speech to the 15th Congress of the USSR Trade Unions), in *Pravda* and *Izvestia*, 21 March 1972, pp. 1–3; translated in *Current Digest of the Soviet Press* No. 12 (19 April 1972), p. 8. For a Soviet analysis of the Brezhnev principles, see V. Pavlovsky, "Collective Security: the Way to Peace in Asia," *International Affairs* No. 7 (July 1972), p. 23. The fifth principle regarding "indivisibility of peace" was not mentioned in Brezhnev's speech but was included in V. Pavlovsky's article as a component part of the Brezhnev principles. Soviet writers also contended that the idea of establishing a system of collective security in Asia was a traditional concept akin to V. I. Lenin's teaching.

Japan's subsequent rapprochement with Peking must have caught Moscow by surprise. Beginning in 1973, the Kremlin applied a dual tactic by simultaneously increasing economic temptation and political pressure on the Japanese. A couple of examples should suffice to illustrate the point. When Minister of International Trade and Industry Yasuhiro Nakasone was in Peking in January 1973 as the first Japanese cabinet-rank guest after the rapprochement, the Soviet Ambassador in Japan, Oleg A. Troyanovsky, officially sought Japanese economic cooperation with emphasis on the development of the Tyumen oil fields.[103] Then, in reply to Prime Minister Tanaka's earlier requests for a summit meeting, General Secretary Brezhnev chose to deliver his invitation to Tanaka through Ambassador Troyanovsky just a day after Chinese Ambassador Ch'en Chu arrived in Tokyo.[104] At the same time, the Soviet military suddenly increased its reconnaissance flights over Japanese territories and the Soviet press also mounted criticisms against Japanese defense expenditures and the possibility of Sino-Japanese collusion.[105]

It was against this background that the Tanaka-Brezhnev summit meeting took place in October 1973, which produced three administrative accords on scientific and technological cooperation, the protection of migratory birds, and cultural exchange. In addition, a joint communique provided for the resumption of negotiations in 1974 for a peace treaty to resolve "the yet unresolved problems remaining since World War II" and the joint development of Siberian resources with the possible participation of a third country (the United States).[106] The proposed Soviet system of collective security in Asia was not mentioned, nor was Japan's northern territorial issue. The omission of these two crucial items was clear indication of a diplomatic stalemate.

At the heart of the problem is Japan's demand for the return of four northern islands—Habomai, Shikotan, Kunashiri, and Etorofu—which the Soviet Union has occupied since the end of World War II. During

103. "Russian Envoy Seeks Japan's Cooperation," *Japan Times*, 18 January 1973, p. 1.

104. Tanaka's first request was made in September 1972 and his second in early March 1973. See "Premier Wants Talks on Treaty Resumed," 6 March 1973, p. 1; Editorial, "For Better Japan-Soviet Ties," *ibid.*, 9 March 1973, p. 14; "Peking's Envoy, Party Arrive Here," *ibid.*, 28 March 1973, p. 1; "Brezhnev Formally Invites Tanaka to Visit Soviet Union," *ibid.*, 29 March 1973, p. 1.

105. "Japan's Diplomatic Outlook," *ibid.*, 3 January 1973, p. 1; Minoru Shimizu, "Japanese-Soviet Relations," *ibid.*, 8 February 1973, p. 14; "Soviet Jets Highlight Japan Defense Fears," *ibid.*, 17 February 1973, p. 2.

106. For an unofficial English-language text of the Japan-Soviet joint communique (Moscow, 10 October 1973), see *Japan Times*, 12 October 1973, p. 12.

the 1955–56 London negotiations for the conclusion of a peace treaty, the Soviets agreed to return Habomai and Shikotan to Japan but rejected the latter's demand for the other two on the ground that the postwar territorial issues had been "settled." In fact, a decree of the Presidium of the Supreme Soviet on 20 February 1946 had already incorporated the islands into Soviet territory.

In order to break the deadlock, both governments finally reached a compromise whereby the state of war between the two countries would be ended and diplomatic relations resumed after the issuance of a joint declaration, but the transfer of Habomai and Shikotan would not be effected until after the conclusion of a peace treaty.[107] No mention was made in the joint declaration about Kunashiri and Etorofu, although from the Japanese point of view, the conclusion of a peace treaty should include the return of all four islands.[108] As a result, the issue was virtually shelved until Prime Minister Tanaka's visit to Moscow. There he emphasized to the Soviet party chief that recovery of the four islands was a Japanese "national aspiration" and relations between the two countries could not be improved without solving the territorial issue. General Secretary Brezhnev, on the other hand, repeated the importance of the proposed Siberian development projects and the broader aspects of a peace treaty, namely, the collective security system.[109] After heated exchanges, the Soviet leader was reported as blustering: "You only proposed the issue yesterday, and yet you want a solution today. No matter how dictatorial you are, Tanaka, that's impossible."[110]

However, it was obvious that neither side want to exacerbate the situation. In late March 1974, Prime Minister Tanaka again asked resumption of the negotiations for a peace treaty in a personal letter to General Secretary Brezhnev.[111] At the same time, Deputy Premier and Chairman of the State Planning Committee Nikolai Baibakov urged Kogoro Uemura, president of the Federation of Economic Organizations (Keidanren), to expedite negotiations for the conclusion of formal agreements on the Siberian development projects because his planning

107. See Joint Declaration by Japan and the Union of Soviet Socialist Republics (19 October 1956), Articles 1 and 9, in *Japanese Annual of International Law* No. 1 (1957), pp. 129, 131.

108. For a detailed analysis of the problem, see Shigeo Sugiyama, "Diplomatic Relations Between Japan and the Soviet Union With Particular Emphasis on Territorial Questions," in Young C. Kim, ed., *Japan in World Politics*, p. 21.

109. "Tanaka, Brezhnev Hold First Round of Summit Talks," *Japan Times*, 9 October 1973, p. 1; "Tanaka, Brezhnev Talks Deadlocked Over Islands Issue," *ibid.*, 10 October 1973, p. 1; "Territorial Issues Hangs on Amity, Premier Says," *ibid.*, 12 October 1973, p. 1.

110. See "Soviet Union: Four Fingers," *Newsweek*, 22 October 1973, p. 96.

111. "Siberia Development," *Japan Times*, 24 March 1974, p. 10.

committee wanted to incorporate these projects into a draft of the next five-year economic plan before the end of September. Uemura replied that no settlement could be expected unless the two countries exerted themselves toward making mutual concessions from a broad point of view—presumably referring to the northern territory issue and Chinese reaction to the Tyumen project.[112]

Instead of making a compromise, however, the Soviet authorities presented a new proposal for the building a new Siberian railway of 3,200 kilometers between Irkutsk and Sovietskaya Gavan as a substitute for the pipeline to deliver Tyumen oil to Japan.[113] This immediately aroused deep Japanese anxieties. *Tokyo Shimbun,* for example, editorialized that Japan should not decide on the proposal from a mere economic standpoint for the Soviet plan was apparently based on a world strategy, attempting to involve Japan in a military and political scheme against China.[114] Soviet Ambassador Troyanovsky disagreed that the proposed railroad would alter the power balance in the Pacific region and dismissed the Japanese worry as "a mentality characteristic of the early twentieth century." He pointed out that the construction work of the railroad was in effect already under way and would be completed in about five years, regardless of the attitude of Japan or any other country toward the project. To show Soviet goodwill to Japan, he also indicated that his country was not only willing to deliver Tyumen oil to Japan but enriched uranium as well.[115] Soviet party chief Leonid I. Brezhnev later backed up Troyanovsky's statement by ruling out any possible connection of the railway construction with military or political purposes, emphasizing that the project was originally formulated a decade ago but did not get party approval due to unfavorable economic conditions. According to Brezhnev, the new trans-Siberian railway will have an annual capacity to transport 80 million tons of materials to supplement the existing railroad.[116]

In the course of these developments, the Soviet government signed on April 22 a protocol with the Export and Import Bank of Japan for a sixteen-year loan of $1,050 million at a low annual interest rate of 6.375 percent for the exploration and development of coking coal in Southern Yakutsk ($450 million), natural gas in Yakutsk ($100 million), and the second phase of development of timber resources in the Soviet Far

112. "Japan Efforts to Reach Accord With Soviets on Siberia Projects Asked," *ibid.*, 24 March 1974, p. 1.

113. "Railway May Replace Japan-Soviet Oil Pipeline," *Japan Times*, 27 March 1974, p. 1; "Tyumen Plan Needs 3,000-Km. Railway," *ibid.*, 29 March 1974, p. 12.

114. In *ibid.*, 30 March 1974, p. 10.

115. "Soviet Envoy Expresses Regret Over Rail Reports," *ibid.*, 6 April 1974, p. 1.

116. Shinji Ikuta, "USSR Will Build Second Siberian Railway Alone," *Asaki Evening News*, 25 April 1974, p. 3.

East ($500 million). The arrangement obligates the Soviet Union to use four-fifths of the loan to purchase Japanese mining and lumbering equipment, and the protocol was signed on the assumption that Soviet-Japanese negotiations on the three projects will produce basic accord on technical details within six months.[117] Two preliminary agreements in the form of memoranda on the coal and natural gas projects have been concluded, and the United States is expected to take part in the natural gas project with a matching loan of $100 million. However, Washington has thus far refused to seriously consider cooperation with the Soviet Union in the development of Siberia, although American commercial banks have promised to provide the loans needed by the Soviet Union.[118]

With respect to the Tyumen oil project, the Soviet authorities indicated that they are prepared to resume negotiations at any time if Japan officially requests such talks. But Japanese business leaders are still suspicious of Soviet intentions. They fear that the Soviet Union eventually will want Japanese participation in the construction of the Siberian railway and will converge all the development projects under consideration (Southern Yakutsk coal, Yakutsk gas, Soviet Far East timber, Tyumen oil, Sakhalin oil and gas, and pulp industry) into one huge package deal involving a total Japanese investment of $62,500 million, despite many official Soviet statements to the contrary. Moreover, the Japanese government has considered the proposed Siberian railway to have military significance which could not only complicate Japan's relationship with China but also pose a potential security problem to both Japan and the United States.[119]

Nevertheless, Prime Minister Tanaka publicly declared that Japan would take a "positive initiative" to cooperate with the Soviet Union even if the United States' participation should become unavailable.[120] Japan's need for natural resources is, of course, one major reason for this attitude. Another important reason is undoubtedly Japan's determination to use its economic power as a lever in negotiations with the Soviets for the return of the northern islands. Indeed, for the Japanese

117. "$1 Billion Loan Accord Inked by Japan, USSR," *Japan Times*, 23 April 1974, p. 1; "Japanese Tied Loans for Siberian Project," *Mainichi Daily News*, 25 April 1974, p. 5; "A Loan In Siberia," *Time*, 6 May 1974, p. 54.

118. "Japan, USSR Sign Yakutia Gas Accord," *Mainichi Daily News*, 27 April 1974, p. 6; "Japan, Russia Sign Siberia Coal Accord," *Japan Times*, 1 May 1974, p. 8; "No US Participation in Siberia Projects Just Now: Kissinger," *Daily Yomiuri*, 25 April 1974, p. 1.

119. Editorial, "Re Siberian Projects," *Asahi Evening News*, 25 April 1974, p. 4; Koji Nakamura, "Economic Relations, Towards A Siberian Commitment," *Far Eastern Economic Review* No. 18 (6 May 1974), pp. 61–4.

120. "Premier Will Send Letters to USSR on Siberia Aid," *Japan Times*, 26 April 1974, p. 1.

the northern territories are not only a matter of national aspiration but they also have certain practical values. Economically, the whole area is a traditional Japanese fishing ground. As a result of the Soviet occupation, however, nearly 1,400 Japanese fishing vessels and 12,000 fisherman have been detained since 1946.[121] Strategically, all four islands are close to Japan's northern homeland Hokkaido.[122] Etorofu is of special importance in that it was the secret assembly base for Japan's task force of carriers, which attacked Pearl Harbor in 1941; and it is now a Soviet air base, as well as a fortified naval port and a listening-post for United States underground atomic tests in the Aleutians.[123] The late Prime Minister Sato once suggested that since Russia had sold Alaska to the United States, it might be possible to redeem the northern islands from the Soviet Union.[124] While the idea itself appears to be sincere, the matter of the fact is that all the major issues (Siberian development, Asian collective security, and northern territories) are intertwined and have implications far beyond pecuniary considerations.

One such implication has been the Chinese response to the Tyumen oil project. Officially China has remained silent on the ground that it is an internal matter for Japan and the Soviet Union to decide.[125] Privately, however, Chinese leaders have expressed serious concern about Japan's economic cooperation with the Soviet Union, especially the Tyumen oil project. In the Chinese opinion, implementation of this project would strengthen the Soviet military potential in the Far East and thus endanger China's national security. Accordingly, during his month-long tour in Japan in the spring of 1973, Liao Cheng-chih, president of the China-Japan Friendship Association, cautioned the Japanese to minimize the military significance of the project; otherwise, he said, China would be forced to take "appropriate measures."[126] Furthermore, the Chinese pointed out that given the strategic nature of the project it could be also used against Japanese interests when completed.[127] As a collateral action, the Chinese began to supply Japan with large quantities of crude oil (about one million

121. *Japan Times*, 12 October 1973, p. 1.

122. "Summitry, Tanaka's Life Buoy," *Times*, 22 October 1973, p. 57.

123. See Richard Hughes' report in *Far Eastern Economic Review* No. 43 (29 October 1973), p. 27.

124. "No Need For Japan to Go Nuclear: Sato," *Japan Times*, 1 May 1973, p. 1.

125. "China Mum on Soviet Oil Deal in Siberia, Keidanren Head Says," *Japan Times*, 11 September 1973, p. 10.

126. "From China, A Warning," *Far Eastern Economic Review* No. 18 (7 May 1973), p. 5.

127. Koji Nakamura, "China-Japan: the Wedge-Drivers," *ibid.* No. 16 (23 April 1973), p. 12.

tons in 1973, four million tons in 1974, and eight million tons in 1975), purchased drilling equipment from Japanese factories for the development of oil fields, and approved of Japan's invitation to the United States for participation in the Tyumen project in order to reduce its strategic implications.[128]

These Chinese countermoves seem to have appealed to quite a few Japanese, including the news media as well as some members of the ruling LDP and the Defense Agency, which has traditionally regarded the Soviet Union as the hypothetical enemy in its war games.[129] Moreover, many Japanese noticed the fact that China now ranks as the eleventh largest oil-producing nation in the world with an annual volume of 65 million tons in 1974, and probably will be able to supply Japan with more oil and than it can obtain from the Tyumen project (25 million tons a year), which is not expected to be completed until 1981 or beyond, when Japan's annual oil consumption will be well over 600 million tons.

Another Chinese response was directed against the Soviet collective security proposal. In Chinese eyes, the Soviet scheme actually grew out of the Brezhnev Doctrine, which was intended to justify the Soviet invasion of Czechoslovakia in August 1968 in the name of the collective security interests of the "socialist commonwealth" and the "stability and inviolability" of the postwar frontiers in East Europe.[130] The Czech affair was quickly followed by the outbreak of the Chenpao Island incident in March 1969, heightening the Chinese fear that the same doctrine, known in Chinese literature as the theory of "limited sovereignty," might also apply to the People's Republic.[131] Against this background, when Brezhnev first proposed the Asian collective security system in June of that year, China immediately denounced it as "Soviet revisionism's tattered flag for an anti-China military alliance."[132] Brezhnev, on the other hand, refuted the term "limited

128. Japan reached a general agreement with the United States to explore oil resources in third countries. See Japan-US Joint Communique, 1 August 1973, in Department of State Publication 8740 (September 1973), p. 7.

129. *Asahi Shimbun* editorial, "Japan-Soviet Projects," *Japan Times*, 24 August 1973, p. 14; "Soviet Jets Highlight Japan Defense Fears," *ibid.*, 19 February 1973, p. 2.

130. See Leonid I. Brezhnev's speech to the Fifth Congress of the Polish United Workers' Party, in *Pravda* and *Izvestia*, 13 November 1968, pp. 1–2; translated in *Current Digest of the Soviet Press* No. 46 (4 December 1968), pp. 3–4.

131. See "Theories of 'Limited Sovereignty' and 'International Dictatorship' Are Soviet Revisionist Social-Imperialist Gangster Theories," *Peking Review* No. 13 (28 March 1969), p. 23; Chi Hsiang-yang, "Smash the New Tsar's Theory of 'Limited Sovereignty,' " *ibid.*, No. 21 (23 May 1969), p. 20; Wang Chao-tsai, "Tear Off the Wrapping from the Soviet Revisionists' 'Definition of Aggression,' " *ibid.*, No. 22 (30 May 1969), p. 13.

132. In *Peking Review* No. 27 (4 July 1969), p. 22.

sovereignty" as a bourgeois concept used by the Chinese to insult the Soviets, arguing that he not only intended to include China in the proposed collective security system but also had offered a non-aggression treaty to the People's Republic, only to be rejected.[133]

The essence of the matter is that in making the proposal to Asian nations the Soviet party leader obviously intended to use it as a counter-measure against the Nixon Doctrine, and it goes without saying that under the plan the Soviet Union will dominate the system—a proposition which the People's Republic cannot possibly accept.[134] Specifically, four of the five principles set forth by Brezhnev to guide the system relate to the question of renunciation of force, respect for sovereignty and inviolability of frontiers, nonintervention in internal affairs, and indivisibility of peace. The Chinese are mindful of the postwar Soviet record in East Europe, especially the Brezhnev Doctrine which, in effect, insists that the standards of violation or nonviolation of these principles are to be determined on the basis of Soviet interests. As Premier Chou En-lai put it:

> If you [the Soviets] are so anxious to relax world tension, why don't you show your good faith by doing a thing or two—for instance, withdraw your armed forces from Czechoslovakia or the People's Republic of Mongolia and return the four northern islands to Japan? China has not occupied any foreign countries' territory. Must China give away all the territory north of the Great Wall to the Soviet revisionists in order to show that we favor relaxation of world tension and are willing to improve Sino-Soviet relations?[135]

Thus, China not only rejected the Soviet proposal as being a means to contain the People's Republic, but also supported Japan's claim to the four northern islands in the strongest terms. Japanese leaders shared the Chinese interpretation of the Soviet plan. Before setting out to the Tanaka-Brezhnev summit in Moscow, Foreign Minister Ohira stated that the Soviet plan was based on the Soviet belief that the postwar territorial status quo should remain unchanged. Japan, however, gave top priority to the question of recovering the northern territories and

133. Leonid I. Brezhnev, "For a Just, Democratic Peace, For the Security of Peoples and International Cooperation" (speech to the World Congress of Peace Forces), in *Pravda* and *Izvestia*, 27 October 1973, pp. 1–3; translated in *Current Digest of the Soviet Press* No. 43 (21 November 1973), pp. 1, 4–5.

134. For an analysis of the broad implications of the Soviet proposal, see Alexander O. Ghebhard, "The Soviet System of Collective Security in Asia," *Asian Survey* No. 12 (December 1973), p. 1075.

135. Chou En-lai, Report to the Tenth National Congress of the Communist Party of China, 24 August 1973, in *Peking Review* Nos. 35–36 (7 September 1973), pp. 17, 23.

before this matter was settled, he noted, the Japanese government would never discuss the collective security proposal with the Soviet Union.[136] Moreover, like the Chinese, the Japanese government was aware of the Soviet intention to use the Indo-Soviet treaty of peace, friendship, and cooperation (9 August 1971) as an example for other Asian countries to follow. Since this treaty (Article 9) does not rule out the possibility of a military alliance (by calling for mutual consultation in the event of an attack on either party by third countries),[137] the Soviet proposal naturally became less attractive to the Japanese. As Deputy Prime Minister in 1973, Takeo Miki stated:

> In the case of Japan, China and the United States, it is now possible to construct friendly triangular relations between the three countries as a result of the thaw in U.S.-China relations and the restoration of Japan-China relations. But in the case of Japan, China and the Soviet Union, we cannot expect the same happy outcome because of the problems existing in China-Soviet relations. Concrete details of the Soviet Union's concept of Asian security have not as yet been revealed; but if that concept envisages a state of confrontation with China, it will fail to win China's approval. If, on the other hand, China's concept of Asian security includes policies aimed at checking the Soviet Union, it will not be acceptable to the Soviet Union. Japan must take full cognizance of these realities of China-Soviet relations, and must seek a path of friendship that does not favor one over the other. . . . It could be that Japan might be able to play the role of a middleman in adjusting relations between the two countries.[138]

Japan's desire to play the role of a "middleman" or to conduct its diplomacy with China and the Soviet Union on the basis of "equidistance" so as to serve its national interests is not an easy task, however. One concrete example is seen in the controversy over the recent negotiations for a treaty of peace and friendship with China. The treaty is important in many respects, one of them being the fact that it will signify a final diplomatic rapprochement between the two countries. However, as soon as the formal negotiations started in the winter of 1974–1975, the Soviet Union intervened. At the heart of the problem is the "anti-hegemony" clause. Imitating a provision in the Shanghai

136. "Brezhnev's Security Plan Premature, Ohira Says," *Japan Times*, 4 July 1973, p. 1.

137. For reference to the text of the treaty, see *Current Digest of the Soviet Press* No. 32 (7 September 1971), p. 5.

138. See Takeo Miki, "Future Japanese Diplomacy," *Japan Quarterly* (Tokyo) No. 1 (January–March 1973), pp. 20, 22.

Communique between President Nixon and Premier Chou En-lai,[139] the 1972 Sino-Japanese Joint Statement, article 7, stipulates:

> The normalization of relations between China and Japan is not directed against third countries. Neither of the two countries should seek hegemony in the Asia-Pacific region and each country is opposed to efforts by any other country or group of countries to establish such hegemony.[140]

In accordance with this, the Chinese government insisted that a similar clause against hegemony by either contracting party or any other third party be included in the text of the treaty. While the Japanese government was deliberating the significance of the clause, in part as a bargaining level to gain a Chinese concession to exclude the territorial issue of Taiwan and Tiaoyüt'ai Islands from the treaty,[141] the Kremlin construed it to mean a Chinese scheme to involve Japan in an anti-Soviet crusade. Thus, in a formal statement to Japan on June 17, 1975, the Soviet government officially warned that "in developing its relations with third countries, the Government of Japan will not undertake anything that could be detrimental to the development of relations between the USSR and Japan."[142] In reply, the Japanese government, now under Prime Minister Miki, said that it had always maintained neutral attitudes toward third countries in its treaty negotiations with China, and then added that in order to stabilize its bilateral relations with the Soviet Union in a "real sense," "the Government [of Japan] is of the opinion that the two countries should conclude a peace treaty after settling problems pending between them since the end of World War II"—a reiteration of Japan's demand for the return of the four Soviet-held northern islands.[143]

As this three-way exchange unfolded, neither China nor the Soviet Union showed any willingness to compromise. Taking advantage of the annual United Nations meetings in September 1975, Japanese Foreign Minister Kiichi Miyazawa met with his Chinese and Soviet counterparts Chiao Kuan-hua and Andrei Gromyko separately in New

139. This provision states: "Neither [side] should seek hegemony in the Asia-Pacific region and each is opposed to efforts by any other country or group of countries to establish such hegemony." In Joint Communique, February 28, 1972, in *Peking Review* No. 9 (3 March 1972), p. 13.

140. In *Peking Review* No. 40 (6 October 1972), p. 13.

141. "Chinese Envoy Back After Pact Consultations," *Japan Times*, February 5, 1975, p. 5.

142. "Amity Treaty with China, USSR Gov't Asks Japan to Take Cautious Stand," *Japan Times*, June 19, 1975, p. 1.

143. "Russia Gets Peace Treaty Reply," *Japan Times*, June 20, 1975, p. 1.

York in an attempt to make a breakthrough in the treaty negotiations, but to no avail.[144] As things stand now, the Chinese might be willing to shelve the territorial issue of Taiwan and Tiaoyüt'ai Islands for the time being, but are not likely to accept any change in the form or content of the "anti-hegemony" clause in the proposed peace treaty. For from the Chinese point of view, Soviet expansionism is clearly far more a danger than the problem of Taiwan and Soviet intervention in the Sino-Japanese treaty negotiations constitutes part of the overall Soviet objective to bring Japan into the Kremlin-sponsored Asian collective security system. On the Soviet part, the intervention is clearly a retaliation against Chinese interference in Japanese economic cooperation with the Soviet Union and in the latter's Asian collective security scheme. Moreover, the Soviets obviously have a fear that the proposed treaty of peace and friendship between China and Japan may eventually lead to a Sino-Japanese alliance, although the Chinese have denied this possibility.[145] In regard to Japan, Gromyko warned that the Soviet Union would "strike back" at further Japanese demands for the recovery of the northern territories.[146]

Conclusion

The People's Republic and Japan differ in their official ideologies and socio-political structures. Since the rapprochement, however, these differences have appeared to be gradually compensated for by a conscious effort on both sides to reappraise their common cultural heritage, their mutual economic needs, and their respective strategic positions in world politics.

Before setting out to Peking in September 1972, Prime Minister Tanaka composed a Chinese poem as the prologue of his historical journey.

On concluding his visit, he received from Chairman Mao Tse-tung five volumes of classic Chinese literature, *Ch'u-tz'i chi-chu*, of which the principal contributor, Ch'u Yuan, is a well-remembered patriotic Chinese scholar-official in Japan. In fact, the annual festival symbolized by the display of *koinobori* or carp banners at virtually every Japanese household in the fifth month of the lunar year is a custom indirectly derived from the Chinese legend memorializing the venerable Ch'u Yuan's suicide in 278 B.C. in protest against social injustice and

144. "Japan, China Failed to Break Deadlocked Treaty Talks," *Japan Times*, September 26, 1975, p. 1.

145. "No Japan Alliance," *South China Morning Post*, March 19, 1975, p. 5.

146. "Soviets Take Harsh Stand on Isles," *Japan Times*, October 4, 1975, p. 1.

"imperialism."[147] However, since only few Japanese can read Chinese classics the actual meaning of the festival and its relevance to Ch'u Yuan's martyrdom have been lost in Japan. As language is an indispensable means in the conduct of international affairs, both governments have taken steps to improve their communications. In 1973 alone, more than 10,000 Japanese visited China and nearly 2,000 Chinese toured in Japan, surpassing all personnel exchanges that China thus far has had with other countries.

In the economic field, many Japanese realized that the pace of growth in their overseas sales could not continue to expand at the past rates as both the United States and Europe took up protectionist postures. The Japanese markets in Southeast Asia were rapidly growing but not large enough to provide alternatives. Consequently, more and more Japanese began to see the Chinese as their natural long-term partners. In his interview with Japan's "economic prime minister" Kogoro Uemura in September 1973, Premier Chou En-lai indicated that further expansions of bilateral trade on the basis of an exchange of Chinese raw materials for Japanese technology would benefit both countries.[148] The Japanese business circles agreed with Chou's assessment and predicted that the two-way trade would reach the $5,000 million mark in a couple of years, making China the second largest trading partner for Japan after the United States.

On the political plane, the dynamics of world affairs also seem to have pushed China and Japan into a closer relationship than ever before. In spite of Soviet intervention, the treaty of peace and friendship is likely to be concluded in the near future. Chinese leaders obviously attach great importance to Japan's economic cooperation and its strategic significance in their mutual relationship with both Moscow and Washington. Likewise, Japanese leaders apparently realize that Japan cannot solve many of its international problems without China's participation and cooperation. They also believe that the ultimate fate of Taiwan is not for Japan to decide but is a responsibility of the United States and the Chinese themselves.

As discussed above, the Sino-American detente was achieved not on the basis of any firm agreement concerning Taiwan's status but on the basis of a common strategic interest in establishing a relatively stable

147. For reference to Ch'u Yuan's biography, see Szu-Ma Ch'ien, *Shih chi* (Historical Records) vol. 8 (Peking: Chung-hau shu-chu, 1972), p. 2481. The traditional symbols in memory of that occasion are the rush-sword, the dragon boat race, and the taking of a "perfumed" bath and a medicated liquor drink. The Japanese have retained all but the dragon boat race, which was replaced by the carp banner.

148. "China-Japan Ties Will Be Improved: Chou," *Japan Times*, 7 September 1973, p. 12.

balance of power situation in the Asia-Pacific region. In this connection, the Sino-Soviet dispute, the Indochina war, and to some extent, Japan's changing relationship with the United States were the principal agents in bringing China and the United States together. Looking ahead, while the Taiwan problem will remain an obstacle in the development of Sino-Japanese and Sino-American relations, its significance in the overall context of international relations in the Asia-Pacific region will be minimized by the continued expansion of Soviet influence in that area. Indeed, the Soviet Union may well be the principal catalyst in pushing China, Japan, and the United States into a formal or informal security alliance should it fail to reach a limited settlement of the nuclear and border issues with China, continue to increase its naval activities in Asia, and refuse to return the four northern islands to Japan.

Japan's economic cooperation with the Soviet Union may exert certain adverse effects on the development of Sino-Japanese relations. However, the success of such cooperation largely depends on the Soviet political attitude toward Japan, including the northern territorial issue. Judging from the Soviet behavior in the postwar era, it is unlikely that the Soviet Union will yield to Japan's territorial demand without exacting a higher price in return, such as Japan's acceptance of the Soviet collective security system in Asia. But since this scheme has global strategic implications, Japan cannot participate in it without risking a total break of her relationship with China and the United States.

Finally, with respect to United States participation in the development of Siberia in order to minimize its impact on Sino-Japanese relations, it may not be a desirable idea at all. Aside from the question of detente which obviously is not a success, a fully-developed Siberia cannot avoid military significance to the other three powers concerned. The world will be happier and richer if the major powers can cooperate in economic development without political designs.

The Chinese Model of Economic Development: Its Impact on and Influence from Foreign Economic Systems

Katsuji Nakagane

Introduction

The Chinese economy and its development have aroused attention from at least three different perspectives. The People's Republic of China's big and promising market is attractive to business enterprises. For Marxists and radicals the PRC has been the stage on which an interesting experiment is being performed. Finally, some developing countries have been paying intermittent attention to the development pattern of the Chinese economy in the expectation that it may provide implications for economic planning.

Whether the Chinese economy is a market type of economy, an example of a socialist economic system, or a development model, nobody can deny that it is potentially influential, particularly with respect to China's neighboring countries. But in what aspects and to what extent? In turn, how the neighbors will be able to influence the Chinese economy is also a matter of concern.

This article aims to explore a possible future course of interrelationship among the economic systems of China and other Asian countries including Japan, while surveying its past trend. To this end, the main characteristics of the Chinese model are briefly summarized, and a simple conceptual framework is provided for the following analysis.

Main Characteristics of the Chinese Model of Economic Development

As is well known, the PRC started to employ a new development model in 1958, the year of the Great Leap Forward. In my view, this new model, often called the Chinese model, after many vagaries has crystallized since that time into a more consistent form.[1] The Chinese have created and developed a new type of economy over the last eighteen years; although it is variable when the environment changes,[2] it is radically different from that of the first five-year plan (1953–57), the so-called Soviet model.

It seems convenient to view the Chinese model in terms of three different systems of analysis—value/norm, institution/organization, and goods/technology.[3] The main characteristics of the model are summarized, corresponding to each of these systems, in Chart 1.

The characteristics of the Chinese model can be understood more clearly when contrasted with the Soviet model. First, regarding goods and technologies, the Chinese model stresses agriculture and local in-

Chart 1

Characteristics of the Chinese Model	System
Norm of egalitarianism, particularly within an economic unit Ideology of self-reliance	Value/Norm
Decentralization of decision-making Work incentive system of the Chinese type	Institution/Organization
Agriculture as the foundation of the national economy Formation of regionally self-sufficient areas (units)	Goods/Technology

1. Other authors argue that China has begun to walk on a basically different, but "normal" line—they call it a new "Liu Shao-chi" line—since the cessation of the Cultural Revolution (1966–68). See, for example, K. I. Chen, "The Outlook for China's Economy", *Current History*, September 1972. He argues that growth-oriented policies are going to be introduced in the PRC.

2. By environments I mean: (1) initial state of economic system, (2) resources, (3) present state of other social subsystems, and (4) foreign economic systems.

3. These three systems are described and the main characteristics of the Chinese model are examined more comprehensively in my previous paper. See Katsuji Nakagane, "Notes on the Chinese Model of Economic Development," *Developing Economies*, Vol. 12 (1) (March 1974).

dustry, while the Soviet model emphasizes industry, particularly the producer-goods industry, and management by central organizations. Second, regarding institutions and organizations, the Chinese model employs a decentralized system of decisionmaking, which gives more initiative and power to the organizations below the provincial (*sheng*) level than the Soviet type of centralized decisionmaking (in matters of planning, price making, budgetary control, etc.). The Chinese model is also characterized by its work-incentive system and gives higher priority to moral incentives than does the Soviet model, which is based on the principle that higher wages increase labor productivity. Third, regarding values and norms, the Chinese model stresses the value of egalitarianism, but among the members within an economic unit rather than between units, as the Chinese Communist Party (CCP) formally rejects the doctrine of "absolute egalitarianism" at the socialist stage. The Soviet model, on the other hand, lays more stress on economic rationality as a functional value or norm of the economic system. Finally, the Chinese model accentuates the role of an ideology of self-reliance, according to which not only must the national economy be self-reliant in its international trade, but so must the local sector be within the national economic system.

Definition of Economic Impact

We define economic impact as a change in one economic system (S_1) from its normal state caused by a change in another system (S_2). Thus, it can be said that system S_1 receives economic impact from system S_2, or, alternatively, system S_2 gives it to system S_1. This definition implies that when two economic systems are connected, for example, commodity trade, technological transfer, or informational flow, either an impact is occurring or the two are in a steady state.[4] An impact is called "effective" either when there are a great number of elements in system S_1 which receive the impact, or when an element in the system varies in great degree as a result of the impact. On the other hand, a system is called "impact absorptive" when the impact effect leads to the creation of a new equilibrium state with a lapse of time.

In analyzing how China's economic development was able to influence neighboring countries, Alexander Eckstein classified three types of effects: power effect, trade effect, and model effect.[5] Relying on

4. By steady state, I mean a state in which every element grows at the same rate.
5. Alexander Eckstein, *Communist China's Economic Growth and Foreign Trade*, McGraw-Hill, 1966, Chapter 1.

the definitions above, I can redefine Eckstein's trade and model effects as follows:

Trade effect—the impact effect which the goods/technology system of one country gives to that of another.
Model effect—the impact effect which the value/policy system of one country gives to that of another.[6]

Then, it must be clear what factors determine the economic impact in the above sense. Oskar Lange mathematically introduced the following two propositions concerning a system's reliability:[7] (a) Reliability decreases when the elements joined in a series increase. (b) Reliability increases when the number of elements selectively joined in parallel increases.

Analogous to these propositions I can suggest, first, the following two propositions on the impact effect: (i) The impact effect increases when the number of elements joined in series increases. (ii) The impact effect decreases when the number of elements selectively joined in parallel increases. (See Chart 2.)

I can add two more propositions, keeping in mind possible forms of connection between the system's elements. (iii) The impact effect decreases when the number of non-connected or independent elements increases. (iv) Even if joined in a series, the impact effect can decrease

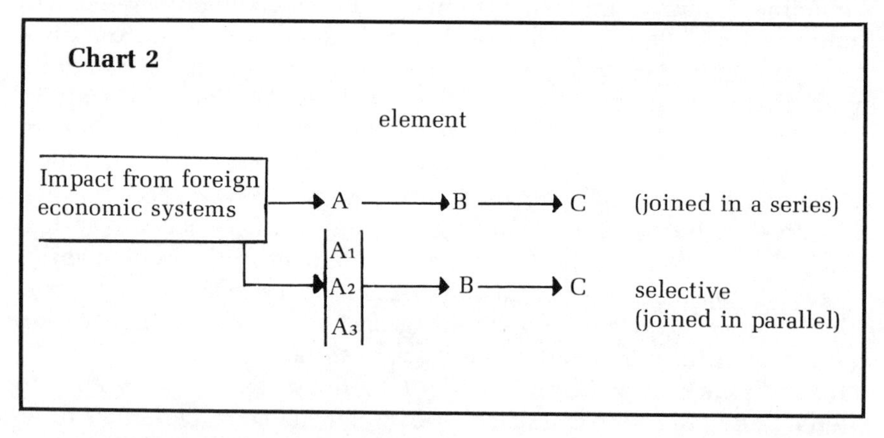

6. Value/policy system is the system consisting of three subsystems: values and norms, policies concerning institution/organization, and policies concerning goods/technology. See K. Nakagane, *op. cit.*

7. Oskar Lange, *Introduction to Economic Cybernetics*, PWN, Warsaw, 1965, Chapter 5.

when the connections between elements are weak, or when the element closer to the impact (e.g. element A in Chart 2) is more-impact absorptive.

The third proposition is self-evident. If elements B and C in Chart 2 are independent of element A, the impact effect from foreign economic systems cannot be transmitted to the elements B and C. The fourth proposition implies that even if element A receives relatively strong impact from foreign economic systems, it can be less influential over elements B and C according to its relationship with those elements.

The Chinese Model and Its Impact Absorptiveness

On the basis of the conceptual framework above, I can now analyze the impact which the PRC has received from foreign economic systems to date.

First, with respect to the trade effect, it was from the Soviet Union that the PRC received the most effective impact during the 1950s, when her economic relationships with the Soviet bloc were so intimate that trade with the socialist countries amounted to about 70 percent of the total of China's foreign trade. Furthermore, she depended heavily on the export of machinery and plant from the Soviet Union to support her industrial policy of developing producer-goods industries. In 1959, about 60 percent of the PRC's imports from the Soviet Union consisted of machinery and industrial equipment, about 40 percent of which was complete plant. As far as the economic impact of the Soviet Union on the PRC's goods/technology system in this period is concerned, the following statements are relevant. Eckstein says:

> The significance of the imports [from the Soviet Union] is heightened by the fact that China could not have obtained much in the way of machinery, equipment, and complete plant installations from any other source because of U.S. and allied trade embargoes. The same applies with possibly even greater force to Soviet technical assistance. Even without the embargoes and with a more favorable international climate, it is doubtful that China could have received, or indeed would have invited, technical assistance on such a scale and for such highly strategic capital projects as the development of electric power, atomic energy, and similar undertakings.[8]

On the basis of input-output analyses of the effect which the reduc-

8. A. Eckstein, *op. cit.* p. 168.

tion of the trade impact between Russia and China had on the PRC and the Soviet Union respectively, Niwa concludes:

> Although the changed trading patterns [between the PRC and the Soviet Union] between 1959 and 1965 had a total impact on China's gross national output of 2.8 percent, the influences on the sectors "petroleum and its products," "iron ore," "steel," "processed metal products," "machinery," and "other producer goods" are indicated [by his analysis] to be rather large, so that we can estimate that the Chinese economy had been dealt a fairly hard blow by the China-Soviet split. In particular, the rate of impact on "petroleum and its products" was 343 percent, proving that increased [domestic] production of petroleum was of vital importance [to the PRC] in this period. . . . [On the contrary] for the Soviet economy, it is clear that the impact of a marked decline in her trade with the PRC and of changes in its commodity composition between 1959 and 1965 were very slight."[9]

Niwa's conclusion seems to suggest the applicability of Proposition *iv* to China-Soviet trade relations, since such elements as petroleum could have had a far-reaching effect on China's entire goods/technology system.

Since 1960 the PRC has changed her trade partners from the Soviet bloc to the capitalist world, with advanced countries as her import market and developing countries, particularly South-East Asia, as her export market (see Table 1). At the same time her trade partners have been much more widespread than before. It was a policy of "risk-aversion," or one means of decreasing the impact effects that the PRC could potentially receive from foreign economic systems. Proposition *ii* is suggestive in this respect.

The second point regards the model effect. Since the PRC employed the Soviet model during the first five-year-plan period, a certain part of her value/policy system was apparently influenced by the Soviet Union's at that time. There had never been any doubt in the minds of Chinese economic planners, at least before 1956, that the Soviet model should be applied to the Chinese mainland. This is symbolized by such slogans as "lean to the Soviet Union," or "the Soviet Union is our elder brother."[10] After the PRC started to stand on her own feet, she came to

9. Haruki Niwa, *1956-nen Chugoku Sangyorenkanhyo Suikei-no Gaiyo* (outline of estimated input-output table of China 1956), Institute of Developing Economies, 1970, pp. 157, 159.

10. Schurmann said, "The details of the responsibility system as outlined by the directive are so similar to Soviet methods that there can be little doubt that the directive was drafted on the advice of Soviet experts." See Franz Schurmann: *Ideology and Organization in Communist China*, second edition, University of California Press, 1968, p. 252.

Table 1

China's Trade by Area and Country, 1965–70
(in millions of U.S. dollars)

Area and country	1965 Total	1965 Imports	1965 Exports	1970 Total	1970 Imports	1970 Exports
Total, all countries	3,880	1,845	2,035	4,220	2,170	2,050
Non-Communist countries	2,715	1,330	1,385	3,395	1,825	1,570
Developed countries	1,495	920	575	2,230	1,555	675
Japan	478	257	221	855	600	255
Western Europe	650	350	300	1,015	660	355
Less developed countries	860	405	455	790	265	525
Hong Kong and Macao	360	5	355	375	5	370
Communist countries	1,165	515	650	825	345	480

Source: Usack and Batsavage, "The International Trade of the People's Republic of China," in Joint Economic Committee, Congress of the United States, *People's Republic of China: An Economic Assessment*, 1972.

believe that China should provide a model of economic development to other developing countries. Thus, model effects from abroad disappeared after the Chinese model was employed.

What is more important is that China's goods/technology system has changed into one that substantially reduces any economic impact effect from abroad, thus indicating that the Chinese model has an inherent impact-absorbing capacity. Thus it may not be incorrect to conclude that the trade effect, too, has disappeared since the time when the Chinese model was initiated. The reason why the Chinese model is impact-absorptive can be inferred from its main features which have been summarized above.

Goods and technology. The main characteristic of the Chinese model in this area was to establish regionally self-sufficient areas (units) with agriculture as the basis. Since self-sufficient areas are "independent elements," they can decrease the impact effect from abroad (see Proposition *iii*). Furthermore, since agricultural production is a relatively closed system in China, the impact effect on the Chinese model is relatively slight compared to the Soviet type, which basically relies on complementary industrial production.[11]

Institutions and organizations. One of the characteristics of the Chinese model is decentralized decision making. In this system the joints in parallel are strengthened much more than in the purely centralized decision process. The reason is: whereas impact from abroad is at first joined to the "center" in both models—since foreign trade is monopolized by the central organization in any socialist system—even the units at lower levels can make decisions both on only orders (or impacts) from upper units (e.g., the center), and also on environmental conditions particular to their units. For instance, cadres at the people's commune or county level can decide to produce more, even though lower quality, fertilizers, utilizing local materials, even if imports of fertilizer from abroad have stopped. Thus Propositions *i* and *ii* seem to apply to the centralized and decentralized models respectively.

Values and norms. The Chinese model is impact absorptive in the sense that an ideology of self-reliance induces people to modify or reconstruct the elements that receive impacts from foreign systems. It should be kept in mind that the Chinese people were substantially able, although with difficulty, to absorb impact effects from the Soviet Union by designing their own industrial plants and machinery. My view is that these undertakings could not be accomplished unless they were indoctrinated by ideology.

The last statement, although it cannot be supported by any of the propositions with respect to impact effect, seems to be most important in understanding the impact-absorbing capacity inherent in the Chinese model, since values and norms are a subsystem underlying the entire economic system. In other words, insofar as an economic system involves the same value/norm system as in the Chinese model, it can be potentially impact absorptive in the sense above.

11. Compare agricultural and steel production, both of which rely, to some extent, on imports of materials, e.g., chemical fertilizer for agriculture and iron ore for steel, and assume that no inventory exists in both sectors and prices do not change. If the imports stop one day, steel cannot be produced at all the next day, whereas agricultural production can continue by utilizing, say, organic fertilizers or manure. In other words, elasticities of substitution are generally higher in agriculture than in modern, large-scale industry.

China's Economic Development and Its Relation to Asia

As pointed out in the previous section, China's economic development can have impact on Asian countries as long as she maintains economic relations with them. If she develops faster, her economic impact, *ceteris paribus*, can be more effective. Besides, I have suggested that there are two areas in Asia for the PRC to keep close but different kinds of contact with. One is Japan, which is the only major Asian producer of goods and modern technologies. Another is the vast area of the developing countries, including Hong Kong and Singapore, from which China can gain a considerable amount of foreign exchange.

What type of economic impact will the PRC be able to have on these two different areas? As Japan will not accept the Chinese model, either totally or in the near future, the problem is further confined to both trade and model effects from China on developing areas in Asia, and her trade effect on Japan. Two assumptions should be made here: (1) the Chinese model will not be substantially modified in the foreseeable future; (2) the bitter Sino-Soviet rivalry will continue in all areas, from political to ideological.[12]

First, my conclusions on China's trade effect on Asia's developing area can be summarized as follows:

(A) If, as is predicted by others, China's exports and imports will grow at a rate of from 5 to 8 percent annually, then the relative place of the PRC in Asian trade markets will not significantly change.[13] As a matter of fact, no scholar and no theoretical method of economics can provide us with exact information on how fast a country will be able to increase its foreign trade. However, if, as many economists believe, foreign trade is a function of GNP or other similar indicators, the above prediction of China's trade seems to be in keeping with assumption 1, because China's possible growth rate, given the Chinese model, will not be higher, at least in the shortrun, than the Soviet type.

Moreover, there is no country in this area, except for Hong Kong, which has been and is now heavily dependent on China's trade. We can hardly expect that this situation will drastically change in the near future, assuming that economic systems of those countries and their economic policies remain the same. It may be safe to say, therefore, that China's trade effect on the area concerned, as a whole, will not be great.[14]

12. These assumptions are vital in the sense that we cannot make predictions about the Chinese economy without them.

13. See Shigeru Ishikawa, "Impact of the Emergence of China on Asian-Pacific Trade," paper presented at the fifth conference on Pacific Trade and Development, January 1973.

14. Of course, how Asian trade markets expand, or how each country economically grows, remains to be seen.

(B) There has not been, nor will there be, any export commodity that can give the PRC effective impact on this area. More than half of her exports, including re-exports from Hong Kong, are in two categories: food and light industrial products. These are, as can be easily surmised, less influential over the entire goods/technology system of importing countries than, e.g., raw materials and producer goods. By taking into account progress in the industrialization of those countries and a shortage of excess supplies of food in the PRC, it can be concluded that she will hardly be able to have a significant trade effect on this area through the export of products designed to influence their economic systems.

(C) We should note, however, that a new situation centering around the PRC and Southeast Asia—Thailand, Malaysia, and the Philippines, in particular—has arisen in the 1970s. At the end of 1973 Thailand concluded an agreement with the PRC to import 50 thousand tons of diesel oil in return for timber, raw rubber, and hemp. In 1971 Sino-Philippine direct trade was opened, its total amount reaching $45 million in January–September 1973. Malaysia, too, opened a direct trade route with China in 1971, and their diplomatic relations were finally normalized in 1974. Thus, it may not be incorrect to predict—although in a sense that remains compatible with the prospect of China's trade effect on the developing area as a whole—that the impact of China's trade on some countries will increase.

(D) It is more difficult to predict what China's future aid to this area will be, since economic aid, whether grants or technical cooperation, is usually connected to the aid-donor's political considerations. For instance, if the Soviet Union decided to give $100 million in grants to India, the PRC might provide the same amount of aid to Pakistan to counterbalance Soviet influence on India. The total obligation amount of China's aid to developing countries was $2,791 million as of the end of 1972, 53.3 percent of which is for Africa. (See Table 2.) This shows that the PRC has attached strategic importance to political relations with developing countries in Africa. On the other hand, Asia has not been a region in which China's aid has had impact, except for Pakistan and Sri Lanka. Will she change the main direction of her aid from Africa to Asia? This is a political problem and there are numerous and complicated factors to be considered. But it seems reasonable to suppose that her aid to Asian developing countries will not be large in volume, nor will it increase at a higher rate of growth than her trade with the area. One of the grounds for this conjecture is that China's future trade balance will not be very favorable because of her need to import producer goods and modern technologies from advanced countries.

Table 2

Obligation Amount of China's Aid by Area
(in millions of U.S. dollars)

Area	1970	1971	1972	Total	Grants
Africa	444	294	281	1,486.1	49.6
Asia	212	90.8	88	901.8	253.3
Pakistan	200	—	—	322	122
Indonesia	—	—	—	137.4	—
Sri Lanka	12	31.5	44	128.5	26.3
Middle East	43	40	67	222.6	—
Latin America	—	40	91	135	—
Europe[1]	—	—	45	45	—
Total	**699**	**468.8**	**572**	**2,790.5**	**302.9**

1. Malta only.
Source: Masahiko Ebashi, "Chugoku-no Hatten-tojokoku Enjo-no Naiyo-to Mondaiten," in Y. Miyazaki and J. Nishikawa (eds.), *Tenkanki Azia-no Kokusai-kankei (International Relations in Transforming Asia)*, Nicchu-Keizai-Kyokai, 1974.

(E) China's potential for penetrating developing countries, either through trade or aid, will be checked to some extent by her foreign economic policy (or ideology). China has officially said many times:

> The reliable way to develop national industry and realize industrialization is to rely mainly on one's own efforts while taking international aid as an auxiliary on the principles of equality and mutual benefit. . . . We hold that countries giving truly internationalist aid must strictly respect the sovereignty and equality of the recipient countries, attach no conditions and ask for no provileges. If one thinks that by giving another something he is entitled to dictate everything to the recipient, or arbitrarily to tear up agreements, withdraw experts and sabotage the recipient's industrial effort when the latter refuses to be ordered about, this is out-and-out hegemonism and neo-colonialism.[15]

It is evident that the criticism of "out-and-out hegemonism and neo-colonialism" is directed toward among others, the Soviet Union. For

15. *Peking Review*, No. 15, 1973.

it was the Soviet Union, which the Chinese criticize bitterly, that tore up agreements and withdrew experts from China in 1960. More important, it is not unreasonable to expect that China's foreign economic policy or ideology will be maintained by the Chinese themselves so long as assumption *ii* concerning Sino-Soviet rivalry continues to hold, because China is likely to attempt to demonstrate its ideological superiority to the Soviet Union in this respect, also.

Second, in relation to China's model effect on the developing area, some authors have recently stressed the Chinese model's "exportability" to developing countries, and have pointed out the remark made in ECAFE's 1973 report:

> It should be emphasized that China's experience in the social and economic field is of extreme importance. The impressive effectiveness of certain pragmatic and logically simple steps provides an important lead for similar action in other countries.[16]

Ishikawa, too, concludes in a different context:

> The Chinese model of economic development will gradually disseminate among these developing countries. This dissemination will be facilitated by an extension of China's economic aid, which will play the role of missionaries of the Chinese model.[17]

My view is quite different. As far as ECAFE's remark on China's experience in economic development is concerned, it should be mentioned that it was given as a message greeting Chinese representatives participating for the first time in an ECAFE meeting. Moreover, as is easily inferred, a model created and developed in one country cannot be directly applied to another. It does not seem to work well with different institutions and organizations or values and norms.

I am inclined to think that the Chinese model's effect, if any, is related to its value/norm system alone, particularly the norms and ideologies for economic development.[18] In other words, this system might have more exportability because of its abstract nature than either

16. *Economic Survey of Asia and Far East 1972*, preliminary draft, p. 223.

17. S. Ishikawa, *op. cit.*

18. Michel Oksenberg concludes that "the situations are so different [between China and America] that only the spirit of the Chinese Revolution, in the broadest sense, seems applicable." He adds, "Beyond this, the problems of transferring specific Chinese programs, admirably suited to a different context, seem vast." See Michel Oksenberg, "On Learning from China" in his (ed.) *China's Developmental Experience*, Praeger Publishers, 1973, p. 5. If we insert "the Chinese Model" in place of "the Chinese Revolution," then his argument is relevant to the problem under consideration here.

policies concerning institutions/organizations or goods/technology. We cannot deny the possibility that China's ideology of self-reliance, for instance, might become influential among the young generation of this area, if they recognize that economic development pushed forward by foreign capital and technology usually produce corruption among political leaders and widened income inequality among the people of their own country.

Finally, several comments on China's trade effect on Japan are in order. Since the two countries normalized diplomatic relations in 1972, imports and exports have risen sharply, although the relative position of Japan's China trade is still low.[19] The total amount of imports and exports was approximately $2 billion in 1973.

Recent trends in Sino-Japanese trade may be characterized as follows: (a) A tendency to balance trade: although China's exports to Japan more than doubled between 1968 and 1972—from $224 million to $491 million—her imports increased at a slower pace from $325 million to $609 million. In 1973 their trade was almost balanced; China's exports amounted to $974 million while her imports rose to $1,039.

(b) Chinese petroleum exports: The PRC started to export petroleum to Japan in 1973, although the volume was limited to one million tons. In 1974 three million tons of petroleum is expected to be exported from the PRC. This indicates that significant changes are possible in the commodity composition of China's exports in the future.

(c) Plant exports to China: As China's industrialization geared up after the Cultural Revolution, she imported many complete plants from advanced capitalist counties, including Japan and the United States. It is reported that she has already completed contracts with Japan, the United States, West Germany, France, etc., to import plants amounting to $2,300 million. Particularly large quantities of chemical and steel-making plants have been imported, or are now under a contract to be imported from Japan.

On the basis of the above observations and assumptions, I can now project possible trends in future Sino-Japanese trade. First, China's exports of resources, for example, petroleum, iron ore, anthracite coal, and so on, will naturally grow much more. Japan, then, will have to make a careful decision between the two big exporters of mineral re-

19. Japan's China trade as a percentage of her total foreign trade is as follows:

	1968	1969	1970	1971	1972
Exports to China	2.5	2.4	2.9	2.4	2.1
Imports from China	1.7	1.6	1.3	1.6	2.1

sources, the PRC and the Soviet Union, as to not only economic but political benefits and costs.

Second, although the so-called development-export method, aimed at developing export goods with funds and techniques from the importing countries, has been rejected by Chinese officials, a similar method might be introduced excluding mineral resources. For example, the PRC might start to export to Japan, on contract, the goods whose comparative advantage Japan has lost or will have lost in the international market, particularly agricultural products and industrial consumer goods. The PRC admittedly can have an advantage over Japan in producing and exporting those products so long as the contemporary rate of inflation in Japan continues.

Third, an aspect of Japan's exports to China will be that plant export is accelerated for a while; but when the Chinese are almost self-sufficient in technology, further increases in this type of export cannot be expected. On the whole my conclusion is that Sino-Japanese trade cannot expand as much as is imagined from the 1973 and 1974 trend, so long as assumption 1 concerning the maintenance of the Chinese emphasis on self-reliance continues to hold.[20]

20. If, however, the prediction outlined in footnote 1 rather than that of my own assumption *i* is sustained, my conclusion would have to be revised.

IV. Technological and Environmental Issues

Environmental Factors and Japan in the 1970s

Michio Royama

This paper focuses its attention on the basic environmental factors that constrain Japan in relation to the international system and necessitate a reevaluation of Japan's external and domestic policies in the 1970s and beyond.

A widely accepted notion is that a discrepancy between the capabilities and power status of a state generally leads to a redefinition of the scope of its national interest,[1] and, therefore, necessitates readjustments of its external policies. In 1967, Richard Nixon pointed out in his widely read article:[2]

> Along with this dramatic economic surge, Japan will surely want to play a greater role both diplomatically and militarily in maintaining the balance in Asia. As the Prime Minister of one neighboring country put it: "The Japanese are great people, and no great people will accept as their destiny making better transistor radios and teaching the underdeveloped how to grow rice."
>
> . . . It simply is not realistic to expect a nation moving into the first rank of major powers to be totally dependent for its own security on another nation, however close the tie.

1. Joseph Frankel, *National Interest* (London: Macmillan, 1970), p. 70.
2. Richard Nixon, "Asia after Vietnam," *Foreign Affairs*, Vol. 46, No. 1, October 1967, pp. 122–123.

No doubt, there are many foreign observers who share Nixon's belief that a great economic power inevitably aspires to a great political role, and hence will acquire great military strength to support it. Herman Kahn, for one, asserted in 1970:[3]

> Indeed, if Japanese growth rates do continue to average around 10 percent, it is almost certain that Japan will be under many "external" pressures to take a "more active role" in world affairs. However, these external pressures are likely to be important only as a transition force or in supplying a rationalization, as the Japanese themselves are almost certain to insist on superpower status.

And, he went as far as to predict that "it is not unlikely that the Japanese in the early or mid-70s will take definite steps toward the acquisition of nuclear weapons or will actually acquire such weapons."[4] Or, putting it differently, as Donald Hellman has asked, can Japan's basic international role "remain essentially an echo of external developments" in spite of "the imperatives of *realpolitik*"?[5]

These arguments are very plausible in that there is hardly any historical precedent for a country with the level of Japan's economic capacity that was politically passive and militarily weak. (It must be noted, however, that there is also no historical precedent for a nation to acquire step by step, economic power, then political power, and finally military power.)

In order to prove or refute these opinions objectively, one needs a theory or hypothesis—and a body of empirical data to support it—concerning the correlations between the economic capacity of a nation and the level of its political aspiration, armament, and pattern of external behavior. Furthermore, perhaps, these must be adapted to the general external policies of a particular nation and to the variations of this pattern from one situation to another, and from one historical period to another.

Our knowledge of this is, so far, marginal at best. It is natural, therefore, that conventional views or conclusions drawn from "intuitive" observations prevail. This paper attempts to move beyond conventional arguments and intuition.

The most vital national problem that Japan is facing, and that it will

3. Herman Kahn, *The Emerging Japanese Superstate: Challenge and Response* (Englewood Cliffs, N.J.: Prentice-Hall, 1970), p. 153.

4. *Ibid.*, p. 167.

5. Donald C. Hellman, "The Confrontation with *Realpolitik*," in James W. Morley, ed., *Forecast for Japan: Security in the 1970s* (Princeton, N.J.: Princeton University Press, 1972), pp. 135–168.

have to cope with for many years to come, seems to be one that can not be solved unless Japan undergoes a "system transformation."[6] By system transformation we mean a restructuring of the entire national system, including political, social, and economic institutions, and the value systems that support existing institutions and policy orientations. That Japan today is in a crucial stage of national development in which a "system transformation" is needed is largely a result of two kinds of impact that are separate in origin, but that are interwoven in practice, and that produce a composite effect of high complexity:

1. An impact brought about by fundamental changes in international power configurations that are producing two distinct, yet interrelated problems: (a) Political (and to a lesser degree, military) multipolarization, that has made it extremely difficult for Japan to maintain a post-cold war pattern of external relationships; (b) A new tendency to use vital "natural resources" as a tool for influencing international power relations, as illustrated by the recent moves by some of the OPEC members.

2. An impact of a rapid and extremely high rate of Japanese economic growth: (a) A re-orientation of policies and a reconsideration of traditional value systems have been necessitated because of: (i) overall environmental destruction and pollution, and (ii) social structural (demographic) changes. (b) A re-examination of Japan's external policies has been necessitated in conjunction with: (i) increasing fears, suspicions, or expectations abroad of the future course of Japanese policies, as a result of rapid Japanese economic expansion abroad, and (ii) a question of effectively securing access to natural resources upon which Japan's economic growth has been dependent in an environment in which access is becoming progressively insecure as a result of reasons mentioned in 1-b, and of the greater competition for these resources because of the expansion of industrial activities in the developed nations in general.

Of these various problems that are produced by changes in the domestic and international environments, and that constrain Japan's course of action, three basic problems (only the second of which has

6. Cf. J. David Singer, ed., *Human Behavior and International Politics: Contributions from the Social-Psychological Science* (Chicago: Rand McNally, 1965). Especially, Part Four, "System Transformation," pp. 453–457.

More exactly speaking, it should be termed "subsystem transformation," because a transformation of the international system is not discussed in this paper. However, a system transformation at the subsystem level is not fully conceivable without reference to one at the international level. On the other hand, also, a system transformation at the subsystem level, especially in the case of such an important one as Japan, may affect the international system as a whole, as the latter is "subsystem dominant."

been studied extensively by students of international relations) are discernible that affect the options that are open (or closed) for Japan:

Type I problems: Those problems that arise from geographically and geologically determined factors that a national actor cannot change by its own efforts, that, hence, become effective political weapons for other states under some circumstances, and that it must adapt to or attempt to change by a policy of accommodation.

Type II problems: Those that are basically power-political in nature, and are mainly produced by interactions among national actors, and over which some degree of control is possible.

Type III problems: Those that are basically domestic in origin, and therefore are almost exclusively under the control of a national actor itself.

Although Japan may be more susceptible than most nations to the influence of these problems, they apply far more generally because: (1) economic questions that are deeply related to natural and food resource questions have become an overriding issue among developed as well as developing nations of the world; and (2) domestic issues have also become, through "linkage" phenomena, more and more difficult to separate from issues that have hitherto fallen exclusively within the sphere of external policies. Hence, the Type II problem needs to be assessed from a fresh angle, particularly in a world in which it is getting increasingly more difficult, even for a superpower, to translate military power directly into political influence.[7]

Under these circumstances, the basic problem of foreign policy for any nation is how to secure national survival against various perils of the international environment. This may seem almost like the classical notion of the goal of foreign policy: the maintenance of state sovereignty. However, it is different insofar as the traditional concept of "sovereignty"—meaning the absolute control by a nation of its fate—is essentially a legal concept that clashes with reality in a world in which the ever-increasing interdependence of "sovereign" nations is a salient feature. And this is occurring in a world in which patriotism, the identification of the self with the nation, and the willingness to sacrifice, or even to die, for the nation is on the decline, at least in the more developed countries. The concept of "national survival" suggested here literally means the survival of the nation as a collective entity of people who wish to maintain at least a reasonable and preferably increasing standard of living.[8] Of course, it must be recognized that

7. Henry Kissinger, "Central Issues of American Foreign Policy," in *Agenda for the Nation* (The Brookings Institution, Washington, D.C., 1968), p. 589.

8. Frankel, *op. cit.*, p. 46.

many nations are at or beneath the subsistence level, and are trying to achieve or maintain national independence in the hope that complete independence will bestow upon them economic independence and a better chance of development. (To their disappointment, however, it must be noted that economic development today implies some form or another of interdependence, and an insistence on pure independence is often tantamount to a rejection of development.)[9]

The arena of foreign policy today is formed by a limited space called the earth, where 140 or more sovereign nations are struggling to survive. There are also actors other than sovereign nations, such as international governmental organizations, international non-governmental organizations, multinational corporations, etc., that are playing increasingly important roles. Furthermore, individuals or groups of individuals, such as Palestinian guerrillas and terrorists, are acting in ways that cannot easily be brushed aside. However, essentially it is still the interactions—conflictful and cooperative—among states that constitute the important international political phenomenon—the struggle for survival.

This picture of world politics in some respects resembles a natural ecology in which a multitude of living organisms interact in the search for survival in the given limited environment. Of course, I am not suggesting an analogy to Social Darwinism in which the essence of international politics is "the survival of the fittest." That image of the world is as faulty in the world arena as it is in the domestic, where even the "unfittest" are provided a chance for survival through the advancement of science. Rather, the analogy between world politics and nature stems from the realization that the earth, which is an environment, has now become more and more a "restrictive condition" under which nation states—old and new, developed and underdeveloped —have to find a way to survive, and to maintain balance within the system.

Most of the notions and principles of international politics were developed in the eighteenth and nineteenth centuries. However, a radically different situation developed after the Second World War, when more than eighty new nations were born and practically the entire surface of the earth was transformed by the network of a developing world community. This resulted largely from a rapid development of communications which in turn facilitated nationalism in the newly-born nations. On the other hand, although the same technological de-

9. Kinhide Mushakoji, "Development and Control—Toward a Theory of Dependence, Independence, and Interdependence," *Peace Research in Japan-1972* (ed. and published by the Japan Peace Research Group, Tokyo, 1973), pp. 1–15.

velopment has brought about a phenomenal population explosion in the developing regions of the earth, simultaneously it has contributed to a rapid expansion of industrial activity among developed nations, thus giving rise to a scarcity of readily available resources, notably energy and food. Under such circumstances, Japan, if not the only country to suffer, is the one that suffers most because of its unprecedented rate of economic growth and its peculiar economic structure.

Nixon regarded Japan's economic capacity as a factor to be reckoned with in international politics six years ago. In the meantime, the Japanese economy has made a further leap forward. Herman Kahn made a great sensation in Japan when he remarked, "It would not be surprising if the twenty-first century was the Japanese century."[10] However, according to a recent assessment made by one of the more optimistic Japanese economists, Hisao Kanamori, it would not be necessary to wait until the twenty-first century.[11] He calculates (see Table 1) that by 1980 Japan's GNP will reach the one billion dollar level, while the American GNP would be two billion dollars, assuming that the exchange rate between Japanese yen and American dollar will remain at around ¥280 per $1.00. If this is the case, he

Table 1

Comparison of Gross National Product between Japan and the United States

	Japan			U.S.		
	1960	1970	1980	1960	1970	1980
GNP (in $100 million)	431	1,972	10,527	5,037	9,764	20,388
Avg. rate of increase of 10 yrs. (%)	12.4	16.4	18.2	4.8	6.8	7.6
Population (in millions)	93	104	116	181	205	230
GNP per capita (in $)	461	1,901	9,077	2,787	4,768	8,864

Source: Hisao Kanamori, "On Japanese-American Economic Relations," *Chuo Koron*, March 1973, p. 186. (Rate of exchange is assumed to be Y280 = $1.00 in 1980.)

10. Kahn, *op. cit.*, p. 2.

11. Hisao Kanamori, "Nichi-Bei Kankei o ikani kangaeru ka (On Japanese-American Economic Relations)," *Chuō Korōn*, March 1973, pp. 185–186.

argues, Japanese GNP per capita will be about $9,100, and American GNP per capita only about $8,900.

I do not believe in this kind of purely mathematical computation of economic factors, because it is very likely that various non-economic factors—political, sociological, and psychological—will increasingly serve to impede continued economic growth in Japan at such a high rate. However, it does not matter whether Japanese GNP per capita will surpass America's by 1980, or if it occurs after the year 2000. What really matters is the gravity of the problem which an overgrown Japanese economy will present to the Japanese people, as well as to other peoples of the world.

Since Japan opened its national doors to the world in the middle of the nineteenth century under the pressures of the big powers of the West, and started the effort for modernization after the Meiji Restoration in 1868, Japan has encountered many difficulties. However, on the whole, Japan's economic progress in the past one hundred years is a success story. Even the experience of defeat in the last World War did not detract from this pattern, for it paved the way for the spectacular economic development of the postwar years. In the entire process of modernization, despite its vicissitudes, one most important national goal for generations of Japanese can be singled out: to become a "wealthy nation." Until 1945 when Japan unconditionally surrendered to the Allied Powers, this national goal had been accompanied by another national goal; to make Japan a militarily strong nation. This latter goal was forsaken as the result of total defeat; but the former economic goal has been pursued by the Japanese even more vigorously ever since 1945. The postwar experience teaches that the attainment of a hundred-year-old national objective of economic growth, which has resulted in Japan's becoming the third great economic power in the world, was made possible by the fact that the objective of becoming a strong military power had been discarded.

However, when the economic objective had been achieved successfully, the Japanese people came to the realization that it was not entirely desirable; for spectacular economic development had produced an unwanted and unanticipated by-product; very grave environmental destruction and pollution. It is easy to explain why this occurred, but this does not diminish the effect of perhaps the most serious problem Japan has ever encountered. Unfortunately, Japan cannot turn to the experience of other nations to learn how to cope with this problem because Japan is by far more advanced in environmental pollution than any other nation.

The Japanese Economic Planning Agency produced in August 1973 an interim report on "the Megalopolis Problems and their Countermeasures"[12] as part of its work for the overall reassessment of the so-called "New National General Development Plan" (*Shin Zenkokuku Kaihatsu Keikaku*) which was initiated in May 1969, and which soon proved to be bankrupt because of rapid changes in the domestic and international economic environments. The report warned, with a sober tone of introspection, that the living conditions of such giant cities as Tokyo, Osaka, and Nagoya, will deteriorate intolerably by 1985 unless the government takes vigorous measures against shortages of water, electricity, housing, garbage disposal; traffic congestion; and atmospheric pollution. Furthermore, it said these will be worsened by the continued influx of population into these cities.

Such is the price of Japan's rapid and high rate of economic development. Ironically enough, such an economic development was possible because of the fact that Japan's large population of more than 100 million live in a small area (see Table 2), that is, a large population provided a sufficient domestic market for industrial products, while a high population density offered a densely-meshed communication network that worked to heighten the efficiency of economic activities.

These correlary characteristics of Japanese society worked together either as accelerative or impedimental factors in economic development depending on circumstances; and many economic optimists failed to recognize their future impact during the 1960s when the Japanese economy was believed to have a great future. Under such optimistic circumstances, many people believed erroneously that the greater the size of the economic pie, the easier the solution of the problems. Japan is still attempting to find solutions for the problems resulting from that miscalculation.

Japanese society is undergoing a qualitative change that calls for a system transformation. Even if the political leadership failed to take the initiative in carrying out such a transformation, mounting dissatisfaction among the public at large will force politics to change. The Japan of the 1970s is different, for better or worse, from the Japan of the 1960s and from the Japan that was projected for the 1970s.

It is very difficult to make a forecast for Japanese domestic politics, although that factor will be one of the decisive factors for the future posture and course of Japan vis-a-vis the world. The conditions that exist today indicate that the Japanese people are becoming more inner-oriented, that they do not aspire to great power status; but they

12. The Economic Planning Agency, *Kyodai Toshi Mondai to sono Taisaku-Chukan Hokoku* (The Megalopolis Problems and their Countermeasures—an Interim Report), commented in *Ashi Jaanaru*, Vol. 15, No. 36, 14 September 1973, pp. 104–106.

Table 2

Basic Statistics of Great Powers in 1971

	Area (million km²)	Population (million)	Density (per km²)	GNP ($ US)	GNP/cap ($ US)	Rate of Growth (%)
USSR	22.4	243	10.84			
United States	9.3	207.5	22.3	1,068.8	5,150	(2.8)
EEC	1.52	253	166	692.8	2,740	(3)
Japan	0.37	103.5	280	219.8	2,123	(6.3)
CPR[1]	9.60	787.2	82			

1. CPR figures are from U.N. *Statistical Yearbook*, 1972.
Source: *Bulletin EC*, No. 12, (1972), p. 32.

may also produce political confusion and instability as a result of accumulating popular dissatisfactions. In the latter case, there are two opposite but possible outcomes: (1) a re-emergence of a nationalistic Japan with an irrational posture toward the outside world; and (2) a Japan so confused and divided internally that the scope of its political or economic influence on the course of international events would be smaller, if not negligable.

In which direction is Japan more likely to turn? An answer to this question depends on many factors. But one thing seems fairly certain: because the scope and degree of Japanese influence in the international system depends so much on the scope of its economic capacity, whether Japan becomes an economic "superstate," or at least remains an economic giant, will be decisive.

Contrary to a widely assumed notion that Japan's economy vitally depends on its foreign trade, the fact is that Japan is not very dependent on foreign trade. The degree of dependency expressed in terms of the percentage of GNP is 9 percent for imports and 10.9 percent for exports in 1971. As compared to these Japanese figures, those of the Western European nations are much higher (see Table 3). However, one outstanding difference in the pattern of trade between Japan and most of the other Western nations is that Japan depends more on exports than on imports, whereas the latter depend more on imports.[13]

The drive for more exports and fewer imports has been regarded by the Japanese themselves as a sign of economic backwardness that contributed to such Japanese national traits as working hard and a high propensity to save. However, these traits did not simply disappear after Japan became a modern nation economically, for they were institutionalized by many historical and social factors. In spite of, or perhaps because of, the fact that Japan was deficient in many important mineral resources, the Japanese economy was structured to produce everything else, provided that the needed resources were somehow secured abroad. Japanese behavior after 1931 in large part can be explained in this context. The desire to become a great power that could produce everything from cannons to butter was keenly held by the military, especially after World War I, when they became aware of the importance of securing natural resources, particularly petroleum, in

13. This is one of the reasons why Japan accumulated foreign currency reserves to such a degree as to come into conflict with the economic interests of the United States. This originally economic issue soon turned into a hot political conflict between the two countries. It has begun to subside since the beginning of 1973, however, after a $4,100 million deficit was recorded in American trade vis-a-vis Japan. As the principal cause of trade imbalance was the undervaluation of the Japanese yen, the situation was rectified as a result of revaluation and the floating of yen.

Table 3

Ratio of Dependency on Foreign Trade in 1970

	Import %	Export %
Enlarged EC	18.6	18.4
Australia[1]	12.5	14.0
Japan	9.0	10.9
United States	4.3	4.1

1. Australian figures are from MITI, *Tsusho Hakuho: 1972* (White Paper on International Trade).
Source: *Bulletin of the European Communities* (*Bulletin EC*).

time of war. Hence, the strong notion in Japan of a gap between "haves" and "have-nots." However, the trait may have been more deeply rooted in the historical past, especially that of the Tokugawa period, whose economy remained effectively autarkic for nearly 300 years. Encouragement for rapid industrialization and modernization after the Meiji Restoration in 1868 was very much based on political leaders' realization of the superiority of the Western Powers, and a great national campaign for "catching up, and then surpassing" the Europeans started. In order to achieve this, the Japanese tried to import and borrow—as much and as quickly as possible—European know-how and the methods that could produce such know-how so that they would rely less on importing finished industrial goods.

Encouragement of purchasing domestically produced goods, and condemnation of those "un-Japanese" who admired Western products and commodities, were accepted by the majority of people during the 1930s and 1940s as a healthy national policy, as was the rejection of foreign capital investments. The historical experience of self-imposed isolation for 250 years, which was made possible by the fact of insularity and geographical isolation from the power center of Europe, and the resultant Japanese inferiority complex toward Europeans and Americans in later days, probably contributed strongly to sustaining a Japanese mentality that inclines toward a self-contained protectionist economy.

If the protectionist mentality—so ingrained in the minds of the Japanese that it was not easily eradicable even after Japan became a ranking economic power in the world—has been drawing criticism from the United States and members of EEC because of Japan's delay in liberalizing its market, the policy of importing raw materials for refining and manufacturing has been responsible for building up a peculiar structure of the economy that produces more harmful industrial wastes than any other industrialized nation.

The peculiar pattern of postwar Japanese economic development that has certainly contributed to the rapid spread of environmental pollution has yet another characteristic: an average annual rate of increase in the consumption of mineral resources in the 1965–70 period of 17.4 percent which was substantially higher than the 12.2 percent average annual growth rate of GNP in the same period. The consumption of nickel, aluminium, and petroleum is especially noticeable, the respective figures being 26.3 percent, 24.2 percent, and 18.8 percent (see Table 4).

The status of Japan as the second largest economy in the free world is illustrated in Table 5, which shows Japan's share in terms of a percentage of the world total consumption of seven important mineral resources: the Japanese share in 1969 was 13.2 percent on average, and ranked second after that of the United States in all but one item, lead. How highly "resources-consumption-oriented" the structure of Japanese economy is can be well understood when its performance is compared with other major industrial powers. The amount of money that six such countries spent in 1969 for the consumption of principle raw materials per $1,000 of GNP is as follows:[14]

(1) Japan $75.90
(2) West Germany $60.10
(3) Britain $58.50
(4) Italy $56.00
(5) U.S.A. $40.00
(6) France $37.50

As the first White Paper on the resources problem, published in 1971 by the Ministry of International Trade and Industry, somewhat embarrassingly confessed, Japanese experts on the question had hitherto held an optimistic idea about the relationship between the Japanese economy and natural resources.[15] It was generally believed and expected that the "weight of resources in economic activities will gradually decrease, and so will the relative importance of resources questions as a whole, as the development of the industrial organizations and types of technology that consume resources more economically

14. Mines and Coal Bureau, the Ministry of International Trade and Industry, *Shigen Mondai no Tembo 1971* (Prospects for Natural Resources Problem: 1970), p. 12.
15. *Ibid.*, pp. 133–134.

Table 4

Average Annual Rate of Increase Consumption of Mineral Resources and GNP Among Six Major Powers (1964–69)

	Oil	Copper	Lead	Zinc	Nickel	Alum.	Steel	GNP
United States	5.1	3.0	5.0	2.5	—	7.5	3.3	4.6
France	11.1	2.5	2.9	3.3	9.2	8.5	5.3	5.5
Italy	9.7	3.7	11.8	6.4	13.8	13.8	11.6	5.4
Germany	11.6	3.4	5.0	—	7.4	10.8	3.9	4.7
Britain	7.6	—	—	—	—	2.0	0.8	2.3
Japan	17.4	12.0	3.2	9.5	17.5	22.5	14.5	10.9

Source: *Prospects for Resources Problem—1971* (White Paper on Resources), published by Bureau on Mines and Coal, Ministry of International Trade and Industry, p. 3 (Table I-1-2).

Table 5

Japan's Share in the World Consumption of Mineral Resources, 1971

	Oil	Copper	Lead	Zinc	Nickel	Alum.	Steel
Share (%)	9.1	14.3	7.4	15.8	11.0	19.0	15.8[1]
Rank	2	2	4	2	2	2	2

1. 1968.
Source: *Prospects for Resources Problem—1971*, p. 5 (Graph I-1-2).

will arise as the economy develops." That is not what has actually happened, however. The white paper frankly admitted that prospects for the 1970s "have suddenly become very dark" and "it is highly likely that natural resources may become a significant factor to check economic development."

The extent of the natural resources that the Japanese economy will have to consume in the future depends on three factors: (1) the rate of economic development; (2) the direction and speed of change of the economic structure; and (3) the state of development of technologies for economization of resources, and for the use of alternative resources. However, it is projected, if the Japanese economy continues to develop at the present rate, that an average dependency on overseas supply of ten basic mineral resources, which was 90 percent in 1970, will increase to 93 percent by 1975 (see Table 6). In 1970 Japan already relied 100 percent on overseas sources for bauxite, nickel, and uranium, and 99.7 percent for oil, which will certainly reach almost 100 percent by 1975.

An increase of a mere 3 percent may not seem important, but it indeed matters, because of the absolute enormity of volume consumed. For instance, the import total of oil in 1972 was 270 million kilolitres, about 85 percent of which came from the Persian Gulf.[16] Prime Minister Tanaka recently told an American oil company executive that the estimated consumption of oil in Japan would reach the 750 million kilolitres level. Thus, although it will be extremely difficult, it is necessary to limit Japanese consumption to some 600 million kilolitres in order to avoid a serious world-wide shortage of oil.[17]

Equally, if not more significantly important in checking an unrestricted growth in the Japanese economy, is the fact that Japan's share of imported resources will jump from 12 percent in 1969 to 31 percent of the world total in 1980 (see Table 7). In addition to the anticipated effect on economic development and on the environment, the impact of such a sharp rise in Japan's consumption of minerals and other raw materials must be considered. Would other nations allow the Japanese, who constitute only one-thirty-sixth of the world's population, to consume nearly one-third of the world's natural resources?

Judging from the fact that Japan has already caused friction in various parts of the world at a time when its share in the consumption of

16. Assuming that the oil was carried by tanks in a 25,000 ton loading capacity, each of which sailed at an average speed of 12 knots along the 12,600 kilometer sealane between Japan and the Persian Gulf, it would have required 573 of them forming a chain of ships sailing 22 kilometers apart constantly for 365 days. If one flew a jet airliner over and along the sealane, he could have spotted below such tankers every two minutes or so.

17. *The Japan Times*, 13 June 1973, p. 10.

Table 6

Anticipated Trend of Increasing Dependency on Overseas Supply

		1970			1975			
	Unit	Demand	Domestic Supply	Dependency (%)	Demand	Domestic Supply	Dependency (%)	Average Demand Incorporated (1970–75)
Copper	1000t	880	215	(76)	1,420	225	(82)	10.0
Lead	1000t	216	98	(55)	303	163	(46)	7.0
Zinc	1000t	681	310	(55)	1,149	494	(57)	11.0
Aluminum	1000t	855	0	(100)	2,000	0	(100)	17.7
Iron	mil.t	111	13.2	(88)	200	18	(91)	12.5
Coal	mil.t	59.2	12.8	(79)	106	18	(83)	12.4
Oil	mil.kl	204.1	0.7	(99.7)	323	0.8	(100)	9.4
Natural Gas	mil.m³	3,662	2,387	(35)	9,500	2,599	(74)	21.0
Uranium	1000st	0.7	0	(100)	3.5	0	(100)	63.6
Average				**90**			**93**	**11.1**

Source: *Prospects for Resources Problem—1971*, pp. 134–35 (Table II-1-1).

Table 7

Japan's Import Share in World Resources Trade
(in 100 millions of dollars)

	1966			1969			1980		
	World	Japan	Japan's Share (%)	World	Japan	Japan's Share (%)	World	Japan	Japan's Share (%)
Raw Materials (SITC 2, 4)	260	31	(12)	300	41	(14)	445	173	(39)
Mineral Fuel (SITC 3)	189	15	(8)	249	25	(10)	523	126	(24)
Total	**449**	**46**	**(10)**	**549**	**67**	**(12)**	**968**	**299**	**(31)**

Source: *Prospects for Resources Problem—1971*, p. 138 (Table II-1-3).
SITC: Standard International Trade Classification.

resources is about 13–14 percent (its share in the total world trade is currently about 7 percent), it seems certain that frictions will increase if Japan must sell more in order to import more. One of the most crucial problems in this respect for the Japanese, as well as for the world, is how Japan will react to a hypothetical situation in which the rest of the world gangs up, possibly by means of a United Nations resolution, to sanction her? *Rationally* speaking, the answer is very clear: Japan must undertake a course of system transformation at its own volition and expense.

Even such a sketchy review of Japan's fundamental economic problems indicates that Japan, as the third greatest economic power in the world—and threatening to become the second soon—is even more "fragile" than Brzezinsky has brilliantly demonstrated it to be.[18] In spite of the fact that the advent of the nuclear age and the expansion of capitalist economic activities have made the traditional concept of the "territorial state" somewhat obsolete by making the meaning of "national border" less significant—albeit in varying degrees from one country to another—the value of a territory which produces raw materials in variety and in abundance is nonetheless undiminished. In some cases, on the contrary, the value has indeed increased.

This does not mean that the temptation to control others' territory by force for the purpose of acquiring raw materials has increased. Such a proposition is not open to Japan in today's world. And yet, the possession of raw material counts heavily, particularly in times of international crisis, for a nation that possesses them can influence the course of events by using them as a powerful diplomatic weapon. A corollary to this is the traditional notion that the fewer materials a nation controls, the more vulnerable it becomes, as the Japanese military is well aware.

As has been already indicated (cf. footnote 16), it has become an unrealistic proposition for Japan to try to defend the sealanes between Japan and the Persion Gulf, however vital they may become for its survival. The greatest irony of Japan's triumphant economic growth is the utter vulnerability of an economically powerful Japan. On the other hand, there are compensations if Japan properly realizes that a peaceful and stable international environment has become a *sine qua non* for the survival of Japan. Japan does not possess the basic conditions which make a nation "great" in the traditional sense in a world of nuclear technology and new nationalism (see Tables 7 and 8); nor does it have the capacity to change the situation by resorting to force.

18. Cf. Zbigniev K. Brezezinski, *The Fragile Blossom: Crisis and Change in Japan*, Harper and Row, 1972.

Table 8

Super Powers and Mineral Resources Production in 1969
(percentage of world total production)

	U.S.	USSR	CPR	Japan	Other No. 1 Producer
Crude Oil	(1) 22.1	(2) 15.7			
Natural Gas	(1) 60.9	(2) 18.7			
Coal	(2) 18.0	(1) 21.1	(3) 11.5		
Uranium	(1) 52.6	?			
Iron	(2) 12.5	(1) 25.7			
Copper	(1) 23.4	(2) 15.0			
Lead	(1) 14.4	(3) 13.7		(9) 2.0	
Zinc	(4) 9.4	(2) 11.5		(6) 5.1	Canada 22.5
Bauxite	(10) 3.6	(4) 9.9			Australia 15.1
Nickel	(5) 2.9	(2) 21.6			Canada 39.5
Gold	(4) 3.7	(2) 13.5		(10) 0.5	S. Africa 67.4
Silver	(3) 14.5	(4) 12.8			Mexico 14.9
Tin	—	(3) 12.1	(5) 8.9		Malaysia 32.3
Manganese	—	(1) 38.3	(6) 5.4		
Tungsten	(3) 13.2	(2) 20.0	(1) 24.6		
Molybdenum	(1) 62.0	(3) 10.0	(5) 2.0	(9) 0.3	
Chromium	—	(1) 32.3			
Antimony	(9–10) 1.3–0.9	(3) 10.1			S. Africa 27.9
Mercury	(4) 10.2	(1) 16.5	(7) 7.0	(9) 5.0	
Fluorite	(9) 4.4	(2) 10.6	(7) 6.6		Mexico 26.1

Source: *Prospects for Resources Problem—1971*, pp. 108–11 (Table I-4-4).
Note: Numbers in parentheses indicate world ranking.

Although a military approach to altering the political map of the world, or to protecting economic interests abroad is not feasible for Japan, some may still ask: Why should Japan be precluded from employing a "show of force" to influence the outcome of international political events? These critics should be asked: Would such a show of force remain credible if the ultimate use of force was incredible, or if direct action could not be expected to produce a desired outcome, or if it would undermine, rather than insure, Japan's security? In short, there are not many options open for Japan. The principle of diplomacy under such circumstances is quite different from the Clausewitzian concept, because military means cannot effectively take over if and when diplomacy fails in achieving its objectives. Any discussion of "Japan's emerging role in the international system and Japanese-American relations in the 1970s," to be fruitful, must begin from the sober recognition of this fact of Japan's vulnerability.

United States–Japanese Relationship in the 1970s: The Global System—Technology and Environment

Ryukichi Imai

I.

When discussing "technology" in terms of future U.S.-Japanese relationships, one immediately thinks of the important contribution of U.S.-based technology in the past quarter century toward advancement of Japan's capabilities as a modern industrial state. Whether the same trend will continue in the seventies, and what transformation may be expected in the process of interchange of further technology is a very important subject. One has to examine carefully the industrial structures of the countries, as well as research and development capabilities within the respective social systems. As is often mentioned, the different priorities accorded to military technology in the two countries seems an important consideration in this regard. It is also true that military capabilities, and thus the balance of Asian security are, in turn, governed by accumulation of their past research and development efforts. At the same time, these problems obviously are not determined only by U.S.-Japanese relationships. They would inevitably involve economic and political considerations of the other power centers as well as many developing countries of the world.

II.

I shall, however, try to focus my attention here on a subject of more global nature, that is the role of science and technology for the entire world in the coming decade, to see how this may influence the future of U.S.-Japanese relations. In this exercise I shall try to define problem categories, omitting detailed examinations.

One might describe the problem of global implications of technology and ask "what can the two countries do together, and what conflicts of interests may be foreseen in the process?" When considering such phases of the problem, it is useful to recall if there is any notable difference in the basic philosophies of Japan and the U.S. toward science and technology in general. I had an opportunity to discuss the Japanese approach to science and technology rather extensively in *Science Policy in Japan.* An important observation made therein was that the Japanese seem to have a somewhat different perspective concerning the intrinsic value of science and technology, a matter that is now under serious question on a world-wide scale.

III.

The fundamental issue of global science and technology in our time may be presented as follows: for a very long time, people did not question the pattern in which science and technology were employed to serve national objectives. In fact, science and technology have grown in size so much so that their development and full-scale utilization could be supported only by the financial and organizational capabilities of national governments. Implications of science and technology in the international sense would arise as different national objectives were encountered. The most notable example of this situation has been the case of nuclear weapons and their delivery systems.

It did not take very long before people realized that the tremendous power modern technology has provided to mankind may be having effects beyond the confines of national boundaries. Instead of a situation in which politics employs technology to suit its purposes, technology is shaping the course of international relations according to its own independent logic. It is interesting to reflect on the history of the world's nuclear and related disarmament and arms control negotiations up to SALT and MBFR, and try to identify different shades of technology's leadership in the process. Needless to say, technology was never the only ingredient in these negotiations, although there is little doubt that it has always been the most important and dominating factor. This indicates that science and technology have grown so large in their stature that their effects have expanded beyond human control capabilities. Unless we are very careful, men may end up waging wars which nobody really wants as a consequence of the cumulative effects of MIRVs, ULMSs, FOBSs and what-nots.

IV.

One need not necessarily make monsters out of science and technology as long as one is aware of the vast extent of their possible influences. If we continue to dwell further on nuclear technology, the counterpart to its military use is its peaceful use. Foremost among the peaceful uses is the fast growing nuclear power industry.

There is a big technological problem of distinguishing between the two modes of the same technology: the politics of the nuclear non-proliferation treaty is an example of how this problem is dealt with in the realm of international politics. The most recent developments of this problem as seen from Japan was discussed in my paper *Nuclear Non-Proliferation Treaty—Japanese Attitude Three Years after Signature* presented at the SIPRI symposium, June 1973, in Talberg, Sweden. Apart from the differences in interests between nuclear weapon states and non-nuclear weapon states, and notwithstanding the original intents of the treaty drafters, the point I tried to stress was that NPT could also be regarded as an instrument which symbolizes the transition from the military emphasis of nuclear technology to the era of predominantly civilian applications by moving toward appropriate political and technical control over the transition. One of the most complicated and difficult technical realities in this respect is the application of underground nuclear explosions for very large-scale civil engineering works and for recovery of vast amounts of relatively low-grade natural resources. The technology of Plowshare embodies both military and peaceful aspects.

V.

Although still far from being satisfactory, there is an internationally accepted technical means to carry out international control of nuclear technology for the purpose of distinguishing between the two modes of uses. Again, I have written rather extensively on the technical and political implications of nuclear safeguards (Adelphi Paper No. 86, The International Institute of Strategic Studies). In my view, nuclear safeguards have only a limited usefulness in preventing military diversion of nuclear material from the peaceful fuel cycle. More importantly, they symbolize the emergence of a systems analysis which tries to establish a certain degree of feasible international control over one of the most advanced modern technologies and the fastest growing modern industry.

It is interesting to realize that a number of people are saying today that the same systems-analysis approach that is employed in nuclear safeguards may be applicable for global control of atmospheric and ocean contamination by industrial pollution. One example often mentioned is the radiological contamination of the atmosphere as a result of the expanding nuclear power industry, or contamination of ocean surface by the increasing volume of oil transportation. Another example is to calculate and then monitor selected parameters of global climatic changes, some of which may be produced by increases in the world energy consumption.

VI.

There are very many cases of environmental concern as set against the expanding application of large-scale technological innovations on the global scale. Atmospheric pollution discharged from energy-producing facilities, increases in the carbon dioxide content of the stratosphere by SSTs, and thermal pollution of waterways are a few of the examples. It is, however, useful to recognize that there is at least one case in which concerted international action, through international organization, is being executed through development of an acceptable control technology.

There is no need to repeat here all of the environmental concerns of today. DDT, mercury in fish, changes in free oxygen level, changes in solar energy reflection pattern, more efficient utilization of mineral and other resources—these are all related to the rapid growth of modern technology. The world naturally would like to enjoy the technological advantages in full, yet reduce their undesirable environmental impacts to the minimum.

VII.

Mankind has only very recently become acutely aware of this type of problem, and this means that there are yet many things that need to be worked out. As one is talking about global effects and their control, any meaningful steps will require international agreement with provisions for appropriate monitoring systems, control authorities with rights for verification of compliance, authorities for technical interpretations, and sanctions in case of non-compliance. Technically, there is a great need for cooperative research and development in order to determine biological and other effects of various pollutants, and thus to set meaningful control limits. Establishing necessary systems for monitoring and determining cases of violation is a still more difficult technical and political issue.

At the same time, the world has very different levels of interest in the problem. For instance, optimum balance between the expanding use of technology and its limitations because of environmental concern will be very different between advanced industrial states on the one hand and developing countries on the other. The pattern of interactions between different interests is a fairly complicated one depending on the subject matter involved. For example, unanimous worldwide agreement over the law of the sea seems to be one of the most difficult things to achieve. Prolonged debates over territorial jurisdiction and resource jurisdiction of coastal states reflect differing maritime interests, economic prospects for use of continental shelf resources, or national security considerations in terms of rights of passage through international water. It is noteworthy that in this case also, major dividing lines seems to run between advanced countries and the developing countries.

VIII.

Nuclear technology, DDT, mercury, natural resources such as oil and whales, and contamination of the biosphere are only a few of the better-known examples which involve the global impact of modern technology and the need for concerted action by the international community. These include treaty writing, the creation of international control organizations, cooperative R & D, monitoring systems and verification techniques, and possibly execution of effective sanctions against violations. Many of these are familiar terminologies when applied in regard to collective security, or arms-control arrangements either on a global or regional basis. When one realizes the increasing importance of science and technology, and recognizes the imminent need to protect ourselves against adverse effects of runaway technology on a global scale, one may possibly reemphasize the importance of such new control concepts.

In doing this, one is not talking about a simple extension of the past into the future. For what is involved here is to provide new recognition of the role of big science and big technology on the international scene. Not only different national interests of different countries, but differences in their basic approaches to and their basic philosophies of science and technology seem to matter very much. Relations between Japan and the United States in the seventies will be strongly influenced by the extent of possible cooperation and conflict in this very area, exactly to the extent science and technology will affect their respective national security, economic prosperity, and their relations with their friends and foes, including the developing countries of the world. Much more attention is necessary and justified on this aspect of future U.S.-Japanese relationships.

Biographical Data

Robert Z. Aliber is professor of international economics and finance and director of the Program of International Studies in Business in the Graduate School of Business at The University of Chicago.

I. M. Destler is a research associate at the Brookings Institution, working on studies of United States-Japanese relations and U.S. foreign economic policymaking.

Norton S. Ginsburg is professor of geography at The University of Chicago and, at the time this paper was written, senior fellow and dean of the Academic Program at the Center for the Study of Democratic Institutions.

Koichi Hamada is associate professor of economics at the University of Tokyo.

Neil Harris is professor of history at The University of Chicago.

Chihiro Hosoya is professor of international relations at Hitotsubashi University, Tokyo, vice-president of the Japan Association of International Relations, and vice-president of the International Studies Association (United States).

Gene T. Hsiao is professor of government and director of Asian studies at Southern Illinois University, Edwardsville campus.

Ryukichi Imai is deputy general manager of engineering at the Japan Atomic Power Company, special assistant to the Minister of Foreign Affairs, and a member of the Advisory Committee on Disarmament (Foreign Ministry).

Akira Iriye is professor of American diplomatic history in the Department of History and in the College and chairman of the History Program in the College at The University of Chicago.

Herman Kahn is director and trustee of the Hudson Institute, one of its principal founders, and a member of the professional staff of the Institute.

Morton A. Kaplan is director of the Arms Control and Foreign Policy Seminar, chairman of the Committee on International Relations, and professor of political science at The University of Chicago.

Tadashi Kawata is professor at the Institute of International Relations, Sophia University, Tokyo.

Kinhide Mushakoji is professor of international relations and director of the Institute of International Relations at Sophia University, Tokyo.

Tetsuo Najita is professor in the Departments of History and Far Eastern Languages and Civilizations and director of the Center for Far Eastern Studies at The University of Chicago.

Katsuji Nakagane is a lecturer at Hitotsubashi University, Tokyo.

Kan Ori is a professor at Sophia University, Tokyo, and a full member of the Institute of International Relations at Sophia University.

James Osborn, formerly on the research staff of the Center for the Study of Democratic Institutions, is an international development consultant in Washington, D.C.

Hideo Otake is assistant professor of political science at Senshu University in Tokyo.

Michio Royama is professor of international politics and a member of the Institute of International Relations at Sophia University, Tokyo.

Garrett N. Scalera, an operations analyst, is director of Hudson Institute's East Asian Office in Tokyo.

Tang Tsou is a professor in the Departments of Political Science and Far Eastern Languages and Civilizations at The University of Chicago.

Joji Watanuki is professor of sociology at Sophia University, Tokyo.

Conference Participants

Robert Z. Aliber, The University of Chicago
Lyle O. Armel, United States Navy
D. J. R. Bruckner, Vice-President for Public Affairs and Director of the Center for Policy Study, The University of Chicago
Basil Condos, Staff Member, Senator Adlai Stevenson
Emmett Dedmon, Chicago *Sun-Times*
I. M. Destler, The Brookings Institution
Norton S. Ginsburg, The University of Chicago
Koichi Hamada, Tokyo University
Neil Harris, The University of Chicago
Chihiro Hosoya, Hitotsubashi University
Gene T. Hsiao, Southern Illinois University, Edwardsville Campus
Ryukichi Imai, The Japan Atomic Power Company
James Ingersoll, Borg Warner Corporation
Akira Iriye, The University of Chicago
Herman Kahn, Hudson Institute
Morton A. Kaplan, The University of Chicago
Tadashi Kawata, Sophia University
Morris Leibman, Attorney, Sidney and Austin
Al Lerner, Staff Member, Congressman Samuel H. Young
Herbert Levin, Department of State

Ralph Metcalfe, Congressman, United States House of Representatives
Kinhide Mushakoji, Sophia University
Tetsuo Najita, Director of the Far Eastern Language and Area Center, The University of Chicago
Katsuji Nakagane, Hitotsubashi University
Kan Ori, Sophia University
James Osborn, International Development Consultant
Hideo Otake, Senshu University, Tokyo
David Passage, Department of State
John Rielly, Chicago Council on Foreign Relations
Michio Royama, Sophia University
Garrett N. Scalera, Hudson Institute
Tang Tsou, The University of Chicago
Joji Watanuki, Sophia University
Toshio Yamazaki, Minister, Embassy of Japan

Observers

Joyce Carter, Staff Member, Congressman Ralph Metcalfe
Hellmut Fritzsche, The University of Chicago
N. M. Gelfand, The University of Chicago
Harry Harootunian, The University of Chicago
Chauncy D. Harris, The University of Chicago
Philip A. Kuhn, The University of Chicago
Richard Li, University of Wisconsin
Elmer Rich, Chicago, Illinois
David Rosso, Attorney and Partner, Ischam, Lincoln and Beale
Samuel Sarkesian, Loyola University, Chicago
Masahige Tsutsumi, The University of Chicago